FOOD
CITY

FOOD CITY

FOUR CENTURIES OF
FOOD-MAKING
IN NEW YORK

JOY SANTLOFER

FOREWORD BY MARION NESTLE

W. W. NORTON & COMPANY

INDEPENDENT PUBLISHERS SINCE 1923

NEW YORK · LONDON

For information about permission to reproduce selections from this book,
write to Permissions, W. W. Norton & Company, Inc.,
500 Fifth Avenue, New York, NY 10110

For information about special discounts for bulk purchases, please contact
W. W. Norton Special Sales at specialsales@wwnorton.com or 800-233-4830

Manufacturing by Berryville Graphics
Book design by Chris Welch
Production manager: Julia Druskin

Library of Congress Cataloging-in-Publication Data

Names: Santlofer, Joy, author.
Title: Food city : four centuries of food-making in New York / Joy Santlofer
; foreword by Marion Nestle.
Description: First edition. | New York, NY : W.W. Norton & Company, Inc.,
[2017] | Includes bibliographical references and index.
Identifiers: LCCN 2016024817 | ISBN 9780393076394 (hardcover)
Subjects: LCSH: Food industry and trade—New York (State)—New York—History.
| Food—New York (State)—New York—History. | New York (N.Y.)—History.
Classification: LCC TX360.U63 N48 2017 | DDC 338.4/766409747—dc23 LC record
available at https://lccn.loc.gov/2016024817

W. W. Norton & Company, Inc.
500 Fifth Avenue, New York, N.Y. 10110
www.wwnorton.com

W. W. Norton & Company Ltd.
15 Carlisle Street, London W1D 3BS

1 2 3 4 5 6 7 8 9 0

CONTENTS

V

III. SUGAR

IV. DRINK

V. MEAT

CONCLUSION: NEW FOOD CITY

FOREWORD

When Jonathan Santlofer asked me to write a few words of introduction to *Food City*, written by his late wife, Joy, I felt sad but honored. Joy, my friend and colleague at New York University, died
unexpectedly in 2013, leaving this book—her life's work—to be
completed posthumously by grieving family and friends.

Food City is a tribute to the memory of a wonderful person, but
it is also a very good book, standing easily on its own as a welcome
contribution to food history and to the field of food studies. In her
work at NYU, first as a master's student and later on our faculty, Joy
discovered evidence of New York City's food manufacturing past
and began writing about this largely unexplored topic. She published her discoveries as short pieces that formed the basis of this
book and also of her work as editor of the journal of the Culinary
Historians of New York.

For those of us who explore the most pressing social, environmental, and political issues through the lens of food—how we at

NYU define food studies—*Food City* is exemplary. In recounting the stories of the rise and fall of New York City's bakeries, breweries, dairies, and meat-packing plants, and of its makers and sellers of flour, sugar, pasta, ice cream, chewing gum, and soda water, Joy Santlofer necessarily wrote about slavery, immigration, unions, child labor, wars, ethnic and racial discrimination and segregation, and the migration of populations to the suburbs and their eventual return. How odd, she said, to think that factories spewing filth once occupied the sites of today's luxury apartments.

Food City's theme is the historical arc from artisanal food manufacture to the emergence and eventual disappearance of industrial manufacture to today's newly artisanal production of beer, chocolate, and coffee.

Joy put her scholarly curiosity to good use. She had a knack for finding just the right detail to bring history to life. I had no idea that New York City housed 2,000 bakeries by 1900, or that one of them employed 700 horses to deliver bread door to door, nor did I know that through the 1930s, $14 a week was the standard wage for factory workers, a synagogue on Rivington Street was located over a still, and cattle had to be driven across the entire length of 44th Street to be slaughtered. Such tidbits are so vivid that you even get a sense of what the city must have smelled like until well into the last century.

For several years, Joy had the office next to mine, and I was able to check with her often on the book's progress. I couldn't wait for it to appear and at last we have it. It's heartbreaking that she did not live to see its publication, but Joy Santlofer leaves *Food City* as a generous gift to us all.

—Marion Nestle, May 2016

ACKNOWLEDGMENTS

There are many people to thank in regards to this book, and I wish Joy were here to thank them all. I will do my best but I apologize in advance to any of her many friends and colleagues whom I may forget. It is a simply an oversight. Joy knows you helped her and so do you.

First and foremost, the true light of Joy's life, our daughter, Doria, who wanted to help and found a practical way to do so by creating an amazing and successful Kickstarter campaign that helped see this book through to completion.

And to the people who helped Doria with the Kickstarter—Drew Reilly, Alison Matheny, Anna Dunn, Teddie Davies, Nino Cirabisi, Colu Henry—her thanks and mine.

A heartfelt thanks to the artists who created works that honored Joy and were sold to help finish this book: Jane Kent, David Storey, James Sienna, Susan Crile, Kira Nam Greene, Brenda Goodman, Ben Edmiston.

Special thanks to Joy's colleagues and friends, Renee Marton,

Cathy Kaufman, Jonathan Deutsch, Ellen J. Fried, and Meryl Roshofsky, who, when asked to read segments of Joy's manuscript and make suggestions, all said they would be honored to do so and did a wonderful job. And again, Cathy Kaufman along with Ari Ariel at *Culinary Historians of New York*, where Joy once served as editor and helped create their beautiful newsletter journal, *NY Food Story*.

I know Joy would particularly want to thank Jay Barkdale, formerly of the New York Public Library, for his tremendous support of her research for this book, as well as everyone at the New-York Historical Society, where Joy researched so much of this book, and for whom she had the utmost respect.

To Joy's NYU colleagues and friends, Jennifer Berg, Krishnendu Ray, Laura Shapiro, Amy Bentley, and many others, Joy always said she was honored to be among you.

Joy's first mentor in the Food History world, Betty Fussell, and *Les Dames d'Escoffier*, who I believe awarded Joy her first food writing grant.

Thank you to Marion Nestle for her incredible generosity and beautiful words.

An enormous debt is owed to the brilliant and unflappable Jack Beatty, who did what almost no one else could do—edit and reorder Joy's epic manuscript, and did so with intelligence, calm, sensitivity, and grace. If anyone out there is in need of a great editor, Jack is your man.

With an additional debt of thanks to Emily Fairey for her research and hard work, and to Jessica Gordon, for excellent photo research.

Special thanks to Dan Conaway, Joy's agent, and a good friend, who not only stuck by this book, but stuck by me throughout.

And to Alane Mason, the editor who believed in this book from the beginning and made sure it was published—and to her very able assistant, Marie Pantojan.

I don't think I could have completed this project without my sister-in-law Kathy Rolland, who helped in every conceivable way by reading, editing, and contributing, who offered her shoulder to lean on, and is simply one of the best people in the world. Joy was smart to choose her as her sister.

With thanks to the following people, companies, and magazines who contributed generously to Doria's Kickstarter campaign for this book, and some who simply donated generously on their own: Jack & Jane Rivkin, Jane O'Keefe, Floyd Lattin & Ward Mintz, Lauren O'Keefe, Lewis & Ali Sanders, Susan Crile, Catherine Murphy & Harry Roseman, Caren & David Cross, Michael Lodish, Diane Keaton, Margo Alexander, Colu Henry, Bruce & Micheline Etkin, Michelle Leblond, Richard & Rhona Ross, Elaina Richardson, Patricia Towers, Noreen Tomassi, Janet Froelich & Richard Stepler, Karyn & Bruce Greenwald, Kathy Epstein, Pamela Sanders, Carol Browne, Sydie Lansing, Roberta Denning, Louise & Gerry Puschel, Joan Katsky, Caroline Hyman, Meryl Rosofsky, Max Nilsson, Jim Fusilli, Max Berlinger, Gail Gregg, Susan Yager, Janice Deaner, Thomas A. Servos, Peter R. Freeman, McKenna Jordan, Amy Bentley, Elizabeth Buonomo, Arik Nagel, Scott Bornkessel, Jane Friedman, Jordan Cross, Edie and Peter Kulla, Linda Kulla, Jeanne Vass, Gemma Sands, Anna Dunn, Jonas Paterno, Harriet Mays Powell, Lauren Peden, Felipe Saint-Martin, Glenn & Mia Brill, Jimmy Bradley, Kerry Diamond & Claudia Wu, Anna Hoberman, Dee Owen, Alison Matheny, Megan Abbott, Martha Bunch, Kristina Ho, Jilann Sneider, Edward Feuerstein, Janice Lee, Peggy Dervitz, Monica Carpentieri, Judd Tully, Barbara Toll, David Falk,

Susan Unterberg, Curt Brill, Nino Cirabisi, Dr. Joe Luciani, Sean Chercover, Douglas Lyle Thompson, Cecile Garfinkel Biltekoff, Joshua Jones, Barney Kulok, Jill Snyder, Kate Kuchler, Jana Nesbitt Gale, Jane Kent, Eva Orner, Jill Fisher, Heather Myers, Michael Casarella, Charles & Mariann Casarella, Jennifer Berg, Swanna & Alan Saltiel, Patrick Taurel, Archit Budhraja, Ivy Baer Sherman, Alexis Wisniowski, Catherine Davis, Pavel Zoubok, Rachel Tepper Paley, Todd Sinett, Jim Kempner, Bob & Didi Scott, Tess Baldwin, Christie Verola, Wendy Feinberg, Margo Viscusi, Warren & Eva Brill, Candace King Weir, Susan Verde, Doris White, Elisa & Guy Owen, Cheryl Tan, Nicole Bari Wyman, Drew Reilly, Annie Powers, Cassie Marketos, Maris Kreizman, Renee Park, SJ Rozan, Sierra Tishgart, Joe Campanele, Cyndi Ramirez, Sam Talbot, Angie Mar-Jane Kent & David Storey, Bonnie Vee, Peden + Munk, *Stay Best*, *Cherry Bombe*, *Gather Journal*, *Bon Appetit*, *Diner Journal*, Mast Brothers, Brooklyn Brine, Red Cat, Milk Bar, The Beatrice Inn, Food Book Fair, Concrete + Water, Prinkshop.

Thanks to all the companies, artisans, and people Joy interviewed for this book, who supplied her with invaluable information.

AN INVITATION TO
FOOD CITY

They were safety inspectors, not archeologists. All the same, during a routine 2006 inspection beneath the Brooklyn Bridge, they unearthed traces of a lost city: airtight receptacles, buried during a nuclear scare in the late 1950s, containing 352,000 "survival crackers." The survival of the crackers was less surprising than their provenance. They were made by the National Biscuit Company of New York, whose complex of factories, linked by pedestrian bridges, sprawled across 7 Manhattan acres. The crackers were unexpected products of a city that manufactured more food than anyplace else on earth, a city explored for the first time in this book.

Food City lies buried beneath New York's bridges, streets, and sidewalks.

Suppose you were standing at John and William Streets, a Wall Street canyon, and a passerby told you that three hundred years ago the area was called Golden Hill. You'd probably reply, "That figures. What better name for an early incarnation of the financial district?" You'd be wrong on the nomenclature; Golden Hill was so known from the color of the wheat grown there. But right on the production of wealth: sixteen years after the founding of New Amsterdam, the few dozen farmers and millers among the five hundred inhabitants were piling up guilders by exporting to Europe flour ground from Golden Hill wheat.

By the mid-nineteenth century, New York rivaled Chicago as a portal of the American grain trade. From 1825 golden hills of western wheat were barged down the Erie Canal and the Hudson River; after 1850 Cornelius Vanderbilt's New York Central Railroad maintained a constant flow of wheat to the twenty-two grain elevators on the Manhattan waterfront. The largest of these silos, at the foot of 65th Street, held 2.3 million bushels and could load 60,000 of them an hour into a ship. The place where Riverside Drive is now looked like Kansas-on-Hudson then.

Today a pedestrian mall occupies blocks of 42nd Street. But well into the nineteenth century, East 42nd Street was Manhattan's Chisholm Trail. The tourists snapping selfies would have been in the path of thousands of head of cattle—whipped by country drovers, nipped by city dogs—driven to the East River slaughterhouses every Sunday afternoon for the Monday market.

Until late in the nineteenth century, if you stood where Tiffany's is on Fifth Avenue, an "overpowering stench" announced the propinquity of "pig town," a district extending to the Hudson with piggeries in backyards and "bone boilers" on every block. You couldn't miss these smoking metal tubes, moated by heaps of bones "collected from the retail butchers whenever it best suited their convenience," no matter how long they had been rotting in the alleys behind their shops. In a manner typical of Food City ecology, the char yielded by burning animal bones was used by the city's sugar industry: the black bone dust whitened the yellow stain left on the crystals by the refining process.

From today's FDR Drive an eighteenth-century New Yorker could have seen the sugar works near City Hall on which the Roosevelt fortune was built. It was among the first of twelve factories producing the 190 million pounds a year that by the 1850s had made New York "foremost among sugar markets in the world." Yet sugar was never a clean or safe industry; throughout the city plaques could mark factories where sugar workers roasted alive in sweet infernos.

Tours could be given to the New York addresses where Twizzlers, Hellmann's mayonnaise, Thomas's English Muffins, Oreo cookies, and the chocolate-covered matzoh first saw life. Today manufacturers of products like Melba Toast in the Bronx are islands of endurance in New York's faded manufacturing economy.

Food City not only presents a fresh view of New York history but dishes out American history in new servings. The age of settlement, the Revolution, the Civil War, mass immigration and mass production, the Progressive Era of sanitary codes and factory inspections: the big turnings are seen as episodes in the history of American hungers. Food City both responded to changing tastes and changed them itself. There was no demand for Chiclets before American Chicle created it, or a market for the wildly popular American hot dog before it eclipsed the German frankfurter.

Dutch desires structured the enduring pyramid of food-making in New York—bread, meat, sugar, and especially beer. The settlers poured lager over their porridge. In New Amsterdam as in Old, people got their food from shops, which linked it with pleasure and commerce—unlike New England, where households made their own food, linking it with duty and labor. New Amsterdam's shop economy laid the foundation of Food City.

The beginnings were humble enough. Bachelor fur traders were the sole customers of the first Manhattan-made crackers, which could turn the leftovers of Thursday's soup into Friday's meal. But in 1647 the Dutch East India Company required its sailors to be supplied with 3½ pounds of crackers a week. Soon Manhattan bakeries were provisioning the ships of the Dutch seaborne empire. Over the centuries, crackers filled the bellies of George Washington's troops, Union soldiers, doughboys, and GIs, and if the city *had* been nuked, those "survival crackers" might have kept the few survivors alive.

Food City begins and ends with artisan production. In the seventeenth century residents of New Amsterdam consumed beer, candy, and bread made by hand; in the twenty-first century trendy New Yorkers do as well. In between came over two centuries of industrial production, which at its height in the 1920s, employed a million food workers. Decline began in the 1930s and accelerated in the postwar era, when companies followed customers to suburbia. National Biscuit moved in 1958, Sunshine Biscuits in 1963, Bond Bread and Rheingold and Schaefer breweries in 1976, American Chicle in 1982, Hebrew National in 1986. But starting with beer in the late 1980s, the artisan tradition revived. Craft beer and hand-dipped chocolates are niche products, but a New York niche.

After a first section on Food City's Dutch roots, the book charts the big four in New York food production—bread, sugar, drink, meat—in separate sections. A concluding chapter traces Food City's continuing legacy.

I discovered Food City in 2002 in a dusty government publication, *The Food Manufacturing Industries in New York and Its Environs 1924*. The yellowed pages of text and statistical tables described an enduring city filled with factories making every imaginable type of foodstuff. Virtually nothing, however, had been written about this epic of industry. So I decided to tell the story myself.

Having spent twenty years as a researcher in the food industry, distilling disparate pieces of information to create big-picture explanations for industry executives for companies like PepsiCo, McDonald's, Nabisco, and Sara Lee, followed by earning a graduate degree in food history, I was adept at nosing out sources. This proved invaluable as I dug through archives to extract the fragments of a fascinating history. For 380 years New Yorkers have been making foods for tables from Canarsie to Calcutta, but their story has never been told—until now.

I

APPETITE

DUTCH TASTES

The dauntless souls who ventured to the New World expected hardships, but hunger was not one of them. Domine Jonas Michaelius, the dour first minister of New Amsterdam, didn't like the mud or the ramshackle structures that passed for houses in the four-year-old settlement, but mostly he was appalled by the food. There were barely enough "beans and gray peas . . . barley and stockfish" to feed the widower and his three little girls. These "hard rations" were sparingly doled out to the 270 inhabitants while they waited for replenishment from Holland 3,000 miles away.

The Dutch had come to the Americas to make money trading fur, tobacco, and lumber. They hadn't come to farm. Nor was feeding them a priority of the Dutch West India Company, which was bankrolling the enterprise. In 1624, when the first eight settlers in New Amsterdam landed at the mouth of the Hudson River and set up a base on Noten (Governors) Island, then moved to Manhattan,

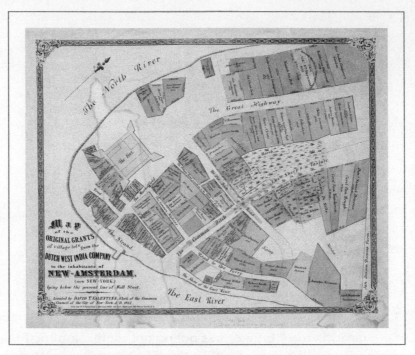

Map of the original grants of village lots from the Dutch West India Company to the inhabitants of New-Amsterdam (now New York) lying below the present line of Wall Street, circa 1650.

most didn't expect to outstay their six-year contract with the company. Although they were promised free land if they stuck it out, America for them was a short-term commitment. Their barely habitable "hovels and holes," as Michaelius called them, were lean-tos or huts dug into the ground, lined with logs and bark and covered with thatched roofs. The company encouraged settlers to operate fisheries, plant crops, and cultivate vineyards, but these directives were ignored in the pursuit of fur pelts. The settlers mainly dined on stores of preserved foods from home.

That was a risky way to live. The company directors thought feeding their employees was costing them too much, and their record of sending supplies was spotty at best. The settlers didn't starve, but one early inhabitant spoke for all when he wrote home, "We live here very plainly a hard and sober existence."

Alternatives were available. The waters surrounding Manhattan teemed with oysters and fish, the forests with herds of deer, wild turkeys, and ducks; grapes and other fruits grew in profusion, and nuts were plentiful. The local Lenape tribe traded corn, which, along with pumpkins and beans, was easy to grow. While some of the foods were similar to those in Europe—turkeys from the New World were common in Holland; partridges, geese, rabbits, oysters, and many fish were similar, as were strawberries and grapes "of very fine flavor"—much was unfamiliar. So even though their stomachs were often empty, the settlers spurned the bounty around them as too "unfit and wild to be gathered." While some native ingredients slowly found their way onto New Amsterdam's tables, the settlement staked its survival on reproducing the food of memory.

Michaelius was anguished at the prospect of "pass[ing] through the winter without butter," which he singled out from the "other necessities" he craved. The bread to slather it on was even more sorely missed. Bread sustained most Western Europeans. The Dutch ate over 2 pounds each a day.

Few of the early settlers were experienced farmers, and extra manpower to work the land was lacking. Dairy products, the heart of the Dutch diet, were scarce, and what little milk or cheese was produced sold "at very high price," Michaelius sadly reported. Farmers were allowed to keep their profits (the farms and the animals were owned by the company), but herds weren't large enough to meet the demand. Michaelius reckoned that "ten or twelve farmers with horses, cows and laborers" were needed to supply "bread, milk products and suitable fruits." A settler could order goods from Holland, at "great expense and with much risk and trouble," but with voyages taking from seven weeks to four months, it was a long wait between ships.

Wheat was in short supply, so the settlers had to rely on hardbread, "hard stale food, such as men are used to on board ship." Sailors ate these twice-baked, rocklike crackers during lengthy ocean voyages. Made without shortening, which could spoil, they would keep almost indefinitely. They were, however, short on taste and, earning their name, had to be soaked to be edible. Michaelius found them a trial to his teeth.

The harvest in the summer of 1628 was "larger than ever before," Michaelius wrote. On the first ship returning to Holland with piles of fur pelts were also small samples of the locally grown summer grains, to show that the settlement was worth the company's continued funding. Grain was used to make beer, the daily beverage of the settlers, and bread.

During Michaelius's second year, the population expanded as families from Fort Orange (today's Albany) moved to New Amsterdam for safety. Shortly afterward a group of immigrants arrived with 103 head of cattle, horses, hogs, and sheep, plus seeds, plows, and additional prepared food. It took several years, but once the new farmers adapted their husbandry to the climate, grain grew well, if still erratically.

In a milestone in Food City history, the company opened a brewery with a red-tiled roof near today's Stone Street. Beer was essential, because everyone—men, women, and children—drank it at meals and through the workday. Beer was considered safer than water, which was not reliably potable. It was "small" beer, with low alcohol content, which stayed fresh longer than regular beer and mitigated the buzz. Made from hops and fermented barley, it tasted like modern ale. Stronger varieties were served only on special occasions.

Soon a bakery opened on Pearl Street, and as people walked New Amsterdam's dirt roads to get their daily bread, they were following the rhythms of life in Holland, where city dwellers bought their bread and beer rather than making them at home. The Dutch settlers in New Amsterdam were not austere New Englanders. Their culture privileged the pleasures of the table. Their gustatory ideal was ample fare shared by all.

In 1639 the town's third director general, Willem Kieft, arrived along with a well-educated thirty-eight-year-old officer named Oloff Stevense Van Cortlandt. By then the village of four hundred consisted of eighty wooden structures plus a few stone buildings. Still, the food situation remained uncertain, as the company's five farms, Kieft noted, were "vacant and fallen into decay" and had "not a living animal on hand."

After years of letting its trading post languish, in 1640 the Dutch West India Company gave up its monopoly of the fur business and turned the town into a free trade zone. This encouraged the halting beginnings of a wheat trade, which by 1643 was sending flour to Curaçao and subsequently to Dutch colonies in Brazil.

Director General Kieft gave special permission to Willem Hendricksen to open a distillery on Staten Island, thought to be the first of its kind in America, which made brandy and jenever, a blend of spirits flavored with juniper berries. At least three private brewers began selling beer that, according to a Dutch merchant, was as good as that "in the Fatherland." He noted that all the ingredients—grain, malt, and hops—grew in the vicinity. The brewers were so successful that the company closed its own brewery.

Seeing beer in his future, Oloff Stevense Van Cortlandt left the military, married a wealthy widow, and bought a property near the former company brewery. The site had a well with abundant clean water, a necessity for producing good beer. Fortuitously, the brewery was on De Brouwer (Brewer) Straat, one of the first roads running from the fort to the waterfront, where regular ferry service was now bringing wheat, corn, and cows from farms in Brooklyn.

By 1647 life was still precarious, and during a series of brutal wars with the local Lenape tribes the town's population swelled, as those living in outlying areas gathered around the fort for safety, leaving their harvest-ready crops "standing and rotting" in the fields. This clash ended with the town gaining the upper hand over the Lenape, but left New Amsterdam with perilously low stores of grain. The next director general, Peter Stuyvesant, arrived not long afterward and promptly set about restoring order to the unruly town. He laid down rules for fencing livestock, promulgated fire-prevention laws, and cracked down on smuggling. With disgust, he observed that "one full fourth" of the buildings had been turned into taverns selling brandy, tobacco, and beer. The Heere Gracht (now Broad Street), a reeking ditch that gave the illusion of a Dutch canal at high tide, was lined with taverns where the brewers made a good living off drinking, the main source of entertainment.

There had been sporadic complaints about bread over the years, but in 1649 the outcry crescendoed. The supply of wheat was capricious; one bountiful harvest could turn into a disastrous shortage if the next year's crop failed. Rye and other grains grew more vigorously and were also used in making bread and beer, but what was most coveted and least available was white bread made from refined wheat flour.

The townspeople expected the bakers to make good bread, and would not abide loaves of questionable weight or quality. In the Netherlands bakers served long apprenticeships and had a powerful guild that regulated competition and adjusted prices in relation to wheat costs. New Amsterdam's bakers had no guilds— anyone could set up as a baker—and bakers were at the mercy of farmers, who often demanded valuable beaver skins in exchange for wheat.

Compounding the bread problem was the wampum problem. Most bread purchases were made in the wildly fluctuating shell currency. Much of New Amsterdam's population had very little of it, but the local Native Americans had an ample supply of shells, plus fur pelts and deer carcasses to trade. Having grown fond of white bread, they were buying up a large part of the supply and leaving very little for the colonists. The Common Council stepped in, denouncing the bakers for their "greed and desire for greater profits," which "cause[d] the savage[s] . . . to be accommodated with the best before [those in] the Christian nation." A law was passed that forbade bakers from selling the Indians loaves of "any fine bolted or white bread" or "cakes for presents" until the townspeople had had their fill. Fine white bread was not for the "barbarous natives."

Peter Stuyvesant used the occasion to render the supply of bread more reliable and the taste more similar to what was familiar at home. He ordered bakers to use only clean, unadulterated wheat or rye (rather than adding bran or other fillers to increase profits) and demanded that they make loaves of 2, 4, or 8 pounds at a fixed price, called an assize, so that the "inhabitants and natives [who were still good customers] might not be inconvenienced." Stuyvesant also ruled that the bakers could not make "cakes and cracknels" (a hard biscuit, possibly even a pretzel) unless their white bread met his quotas.

In 1650, in the midst of a food shortage and financial difficulties, Stuyvesant recklessly sent a shipload of provisions to Curaçao, creating even greater hardship in New Amsterdam. An advisory council appointed by Stuyvesant to represent the colonists complained to the government in Holland and took the opportunity to grumble about trade practices, high taxes, and their lack of autonomy. They continued to protest with some regularity, and three years later Holland granted the company town the right to incorporate as an autonomous municipal government: the City of New Amsterdam.

It took on a more permanent appearance with a number of impressive two-story Dutch-style houses. Prospering, its 1,500 residents began importing more food from Holland; pepper, sugar, cinnamon, and currants were often included on the ships, the latter three ingredients featured in all sorts of breads and sweets. Vinegar was in demand, although by the time it crossed the Atlantic it had become very expensive. The people of New Amsterdam could have made vinegar themselves—their vineyards were producing well enough to make wine, and there was abundant beer to make vinegar as people did in Holland—but some products just tasted better when they came from home, no matter the cost.

With New Amsterdam feeding itself, Stuyvesant saw a way to benefit the municipal coffers. Food began to be more widely taxed, with beer from the ten breweries the most heavily and consistently targeted. His large brewery made Van Cortlandt, still an appointed government official, one of the wealthier men in the colony. While he was looking after other interests, his teenage daughter Maria began to oversee the beer-making operation. Only her youth made this arrangement unusual. Many women worked alongside their husbands, and some, often widows, ran businesses themselves.

Over the next few years three new breweries opened on Brewer Street. Isaac de Forest built a brew house on the lot adjoining Van Cortlandt's property, and Jacob Wolfertsen Van Couwenhoven erected a "great stone brew-house" on a large corner property (today's 27 and 29 Stone Street). De Forest partnered with the brewer Johannes Verveelen, and their Red Lion Brewery produced what was probably the first name-brand beer in America. Brewing (followed by distilling spirits, milling, and brick-making) became the town's largest industry.

The unpopular excise tax on beer continued to dominate debate in the Common Council. Evading it was a local sport. Four brewers, including Van Cortlandt and Van Couwenhoven (ironically, both Council members at various times), were charged with such offenses in 1656. Van Cortlandt had refused "to pay the beer excise" or allow "his brewery to be inspected" and was fined a hefty sum. But being a member of the Council had its perks. Though found guilty, he was spared the fine. The other brewers were given smaller penalties.

Food production, distribution, and related activities were under the Council's control. As in the markets in Holland, farmers from Long Island and Brooklyn had to pay for the right to sell their produce and gain official approval from the measurer of grain or apples. There were stalls for selling cows, goats, sheep, and pigs, and twelve officially designated butchers were sworn to "serve in butchering and cutting up" the animals. One of these was Asser Levy, who arrived in 1656. He was the first Jewish resident granted permission to own a home and a business in New Amsterdam.

To satisfy their craving for dairy products, most residents now owned at least one cow. New Amsterdam was still open enough to contain a large, centrally located, fenced-in grazing area called "the flat" (now City Hall Park). Every morning the town herdsman, like today's dog walkers, led a procession of cattle from the owners' homes to the field and in the evening returned them, announcing their arrival with a toot of his horn. In dry weather the daily parade created billowing clouds of dust on the dirt streets, which made it impossible for Anneken Van Cortlandt to keep her house clean. In 1657 she convinced her neighbors to sign a petition to the Common Council to cover Brewer Street with pebbles, creating New Amsterdam's first paved road, which quickly took on its current name, Stone Street.

Bread, however, remained the food of contention. The price of a loaf had hardly risen since 1650, while wheat prices were at an all-time high, causing the bakers serious financial strain. They began adding extra bran to white bread or resorting to other money-saving tactics, like shorting the weight of their loaves. The people of New Amsterdam were up in arms. They expected uniform loaves at fair prices. Several of the bakers were arraigned for selling "light" bread. In September 1661 one baker, Hendrick Willemsen, whose shop on Broad Street was around the corner from the more successful de Kay bakery, was summoned to appear before the court. Willemsen was an argumentative man, often in court complaining over supposed wrongs against him. Charged with selling underweight loaves, he turned his defense into a rant against other bakers, whom he accused of lacing their bread with bran and letting their apprentices watch the ovens. His ferocity got him off the hook.

By October, with wheat growing scarce, the bakers banded together—not an easy thing for this group—and resolved to stop making bread or at least to slow production. They wanted more influence over the price of bread, reasoning that if they didn't bake, their protest would be heard. The townspeople were frantic, so was the Council, asking, "how it came that the bakers bake no bread?" Presenting their case, the bakers were adamant that they be permitted to charge more per loaf.

After two weeks the Common Council agreed to "deliberate, so that neither the bakers on the one side nor the community on the other be taken short." Ten days later the Council raised the price of bread 10 percent. However, the Council wanted something in return: bakers had to score their bread with a branding mark to identify their products. The Council also chose two bread inspectors to provide oversight. One was a young merchant, and the other was Hendrick Willemsen. Although only months earlier he had denounced the practices of his competitors, he had a "better knowledge of bread." Now these two men would decide whether a loaf met the specifications.

Brewers generally did better than bakers, and they soon became a who's who of New York City's streets and neighborhoods. Stuyvesant's nephews Nicholas and Balthazar Bayard established a brewery on the future Bayard Street; William Beekman's brewery was at the corner of what are now William and Beekman Streets; Oloff Stevense Van Cortlandt gave Cortlandt Street its name (and his descendents Van Cortlandt Park in the Bronx); Jacob Kip, who had been Stuyvesant's secretary but left to open a very successful brewery, bought a large farm from which Kip's Bay derives its name.

The prosperous traders of New Amsterdam sold wheat, flour, hardbread, beans and peas, salted meat, pickled oysters packed in small casks, butter, and beer to the English colony in Virginia and to the islands of the West Indies. From the Dutch colony in Curaçao, returning ships brought horses, salt, sugar, and slaves; about four hundred Africans arrived in the city between 1660 and 1664. Van Cortlandt owned several, as did one of the city's butchers, and local farmers often traded grain for slaves.

English colonies bordered the Dutch settlement north and south. The English took note of New Amsterdam's flourishing trade and coveted the well-placed port with its deep channels and sheltered waters. Advantageously situated between England and the Caribbean islands, it was in addition the largest city linking them with Boston. The English saw the region's wheat as a potentially valuable asset for their expanding sugar plantations in the West Indies.

In August 1664, British men-of-war sailed into the harbor, seized the soldiers' blockhouse on Staten Island, and landed soldiers on Long Island. The brewer Isaac de Forest, returning from

Virginia inopportunely, was captured by the English and taken aboard one of the ships. When he was freed shortly afterward, he greatly exaggerated the number of troops massing outside the city, terrifying the people of New Amsterdam. There were far fewer British than de Forest represented, but the Dutch were still outnumbered.

Earlier in the summer, a large shipment of grain—the bulk of New Amsterdam's available provisions—was sent to Curaçao. At the time there seemed to be sufficient grain on hand. Once the ship sailed, supplies began running low. The bakers were asked to report how much grain they had stored. Jacob de Kay reported the largest supply, while six others claimed two weeks' worth, and one small baker none. The paltry total left little for the people of New Amsterdam. In addition, "much less peas and meat were remaining in store" and there were "not enough provisions, beef, pork and peas" to feed the small, ill-equipped Dutch army of 150 soldiers, let alone civilian volunteers inclined to fight.

Most of the townspeople leaned toward surrendering. They wanted to harvest their fields, thrash the new crop into flour, brew beer, pickle fish, and generally get on with their lives. The citizens of New Amsterdam felt little allegiance (and often considerable animosity) to Stuyvesant or to the government in Holland, which had long neglected them.

Van Cortlandt was one of four men now appointed to be part of the negotiations to set the terms of New Amsterdam's surrender to Colonel Richard Nicholls. After ten fraught days of talks, the articles of capitulation were signed, and on September 8, 1664, the English took control of the city they named New York.

2

ENGLISH APPETITES

As British citizens, New Yorkers soon began eating and drinking like people in their new country. By 1731 one local writer described how "habitual Tea Drinking . . . universally prevails among us." Even "people that are least able to go to the expence, must have their tea [though] their families want bread. Nay, I am told, often pawn their rings and plate to gratifie themselves in that piece of extravagance."

In the late sixteenth and early seventeenth centuries, most people had never tasted refined sugar; prohibitively expensive, it was reserved for the elite. But by the mid-seventeenth century, increased production lowered the price and put sugar within the reach of a widening group of consumers who used it to sweeten their tea, coffee, and chocolate, contemporary European crazes.

As demand grew, sugar refining became Europe's fastest-growing industry, and when the Netherlands' power ebbed and Britain's ascended, dominance shifted. By 1688 London boasted fifty refineries. Twenty years later England was the world's largest importer of sugar, bringing in fifty times more than it had forty years earlier. The sugar, along with coffee and chocolate, came from expanding British West Indian plantations worked by slaves. Sugar output surged, and British consumption burgeoned to an estimated 4 pounds per person a year.

The "inseparable Companion to Tea" was sugar. New York's first refinery was opened by Robert Hooper, a West Indian merchant. Granted a monopoly to process sugar for local consumption in 1725, he didn't abide by the terms of his agreement and lost his privilege two years later. Nicholas Bayard, the grandnephew of Director General Peter Stuyvesant and the husband of one of Oloff Stevensen Van Cortlandt's daughters, then established "a huge barn-like affair" on the north side of Wall Street between William and Nassau. The ad announcing the opening in the *New York Gazette* for August 17, 1730, said, "PUBLICK NOTICE is hereby given that Nicolas Bayard of the City of New York has erected a Refining House for Refining all sorts of Sugar and Sugar Candy, and has procured from Europe an experienced Artist in the Mystery. At which Refining House all Persons in City and Country may be supplied by Whole-sale and Re-tale with both double and single Refined Loaf-Sugar, also Powder and Shop-Sugars, and Sugar Candy, at Reasonable Rates." His "artist" was probably from London, the world's largest refining center, and expert at the multistage process of extracting the maximum amount of sugar from cane.

As larger plantations in the Caribbean needed more slaves to grow more sugar—Jamaica alone had close to 80,000 slaves—the sale of New York's foodstuffs to the West Indies rose dramatically. With every inch of the sugar islands' arable land devoted to growing cane, those who labored there needed to be fed from abroad. The "Sugar Merchant" John Van Cortlandt (Oloff's great-grandson) boasted a sizable farm in the Bronx which sent peas, pork, and butter to Jamaica, Curaçao, Barbados, and Surinam. The returning ships were laden with 112-pound barrels of muscovado sugar plus cocoa, coffee, and molasses. In 1775 he opened a sugar refinery on the northwest corner of Trinity Churchyard (Church Street), almost adjacent to his elegant English-style townhouse on the west side of Broadway. Fellow merchant Lewis Morris boasted the largest manor in New York City, a 1,900-acre complex called Morrisania, where slaves grew corn, barley, wheat, oats, and livestock to be shipped to the islands. New York's importance in sustaining the British Empire's sugar production prompted King George II to proclaim the city's "considerable sea-port exceedingly necessary and useful to our Kingdom of Great Britain, supplying our Government in the West Indies with Bread, Flour, and Other Provisions."

While New York's foodstuffs were popular in the empire, taxes made importing products less desirable to local refiners and distillers. New York's sugar, cheaper and of better quality, came from the Dutch and French islands, not from the British West Indies. That did not sit well with the British. In 1733, Britain passed the Molasses Act, taxing molasses, sugar, and rum imported from any non-British island at a higher rate than British goods. New York's traders disregarded the act and either smuggled their goods or bribed port inspectors to look the other way. Tea was most often smuggled in from Holland, and "scarce a week passes without an illicit Trader's going out or coming into this Port," one resident noted. Even upstanding citizens like Leonard Lispenard, brewer and distiller, and John

Van Cortlandt became so adept at foxing customs officials that the unenforceable law faded into oblivion by the 1740s.

While fresh and pickled fish were sold to New Yorkers at Coenties Slip on Tuesdays, Thursdays, and Saturdays only, meat was sold daily in "Joynt or in pieces" at licensed stalls at the Butcher's Shamble under the trees at the Old Slip. The British love of meat could easily be satisfied in New York, and cattle from the region's farms, particularly in Brooklyn, supplied the town's fourteen butchers with roast beef, large juicy joints, steaks, and delicate slices of veal, all consumed in quantities so large as to astonish visiting Europeans. Pork was the most commonly eaten meat. Most households kept pigs, who ran wild through the streets and fattened on garbage.

To satisfy the clamor for meat, in 1720 it was proposed that one John Kelly should erect three or more "public slaughterhouses and Penns upon the East River of this City." The old slaughterhouse, a little farther south in a neighborhood turning elegant, had become a "publick Nussance." So long as Kelly built "a sufficient quantity of ground for A Publick Penn" that could hold cattle, supplied "all the Necessary Ropes, trees, & tackle suitable and convenient for the Well and Easy slaughtering and hanging up," and kept the premises "sufficiently scoured and cleansed," the Council agreed that no other facility could be constructed on the East River for twenty-one years. Kelly's plant went up on what is now the intersection of Roosevelt and Water Streets, by the ferries that brought livestock over from Brooklyn. Kelly collected a fee for every animal slaughtered or else took its tongue in payment.

The largest of the four meat markets was Burghers Path Market, soon known as Old Slip Market, open daily except Sunday from sunrise to sunset. Prominent butchers like Isaac Varian ran individual stalls. A recent arrival to the city, Isaac Horsfield, later joined by his brother Timothy, also had a well-placed stand. To avoid fees at Kelly's abattoir, the brothers built their own slaughterhouse on Doughty Street in Brooklyn, where they butchered local cattle. One of their three slaves rowed fresh meat from their wharf across the river to Manhattan each day.

New Yorkers had become more British, but New Amsterdam favorites such as cookies, coleslaw, pancakes, and doughnuts remained in the local diet. The English loved sweets as dearly as the Dutch. There were two confectioners in New York in 1703, and their ingredients—sugar, cocoa beans, and chocolate, even lemons or limes—had long delighted the cargoes of ships stopping in the harbor. The city's small Sephardic Jewish community, using family connections throughout the Caribbean and Europe, presided over the cocoa trade. In 1702, Joseph Bueno de Mesquita began trading both the beans and chocolate (the finished product), and within a few years he, along with Isaac Marquez, Moses Levy, Joseph Nunes, and Nathan Simson, commanded a large share of this market.

As the city adopted English ways, the tide of beer receded from daily life. It was the drink of the "lesser orders," including many of Dutch ancestry. The four remaining breweries still did substantial business, as many workmen and apprentices continued to drink throughout their workday. William Beekman's forty-year-old brewery on Beekman Street was active until his death in 1707. Harman Rutgers Jr. followed in his father's footsteps and established his own brewery on Maiden Lane, producing his first beer in December 1711, and his brother Anthony opened his own brew house in 1717. Those higher up on the social ladder replaced beer with tankards of locally made cider and goblets of wine.

In the city's taverns, rum was the drink of choice, even for the "lesser" classes, because of its cheap price and hard wallop. Rum could be made wherever there was molasses, and while New Yorkers didn't produce as much as Bostonians, they made enough in 1702 that the acrid smells suffused by distilling caused the Common Council to ban its production in the "Citty of New Yorke or within A mile of the Citty Hall." That edict might have slowed down the rate of production, but there were at least two distilleries by 1723.

The food trade nourished a growing elite of merchants and producers. Traders and landowners grew rich off the profits. Those who salted and packed the meats or milled the flour or refined the sugar also prospered. So did some enterprising artisans, like John Vaarck, whose bakery on Broad Street near the Battery wharves employed several workmen baking large orders of hardbread. The Brooklyn butchers Isaac and Timothy Horsfield made a considerable fortune. European visitors professed shock that affluent New Yorkers' "mode of living" was "the same" as that in London. On wide cobblestone streets lined with leafy elm, locust, beech, and lime trees, imported carriages pulled by fine teams of horses were common sights. Elegant ladies in the latest French or English gowns strolled on the graceful sidewalks past Georgian-style brick homes often "several stories high" that lined lush parks.

Artisans, "the middling sort," made up about 60 percent of the city's population in the mid-eighteenth century. The Common Council controlled the number of butchers, and it was difficult to get rich in that trade. However, artisans commanded respect, with many serving as representatives on the Council, and their lives were generally better than those of their equals in England. Certainly they ate better. Food was cheaper and more abundant in New York, especially luxuries like coffee, chocolate, and sugar. Laborers in New York each consumed 14 to 21 pounds a year of sugar; the sweetener was so deeply woven into daily life that even denizens of the almshouses received 7 pounds per year.

Many artisans kept an apprentice in their workspace, a young man between twelve and fourteen who was learning skills that took seven to ten years to master. There were also two thousand enslaved Africans—one out of every five of the ten thousand people in the city. The majority of food producers owned at least one slave. So did almost half of New York's households. Together the brewers owned twenty slaves, the bakers twenty-seven, the bolters eighteen, and the butchers five, the numbers reflecting the collective wealth of the various occupations. Many slaves toiled alongside their owners in their shops, and one slave, named Caesar, possibly owned by John Vaarck, was often seen roaming freely in public. Behind the brewer Harman Rutgers Jr.'s large home and brewery on Maiden Lane was a "Negro kitchen," a small building in the backyard quartering his three slaves. He owned a 1,000-acre farm near today's Chatham Square where the slaves probably harvested hops and barley for the brewery.

In 1736 one of Jacobus Roosevelt's female slaves may have set a blaze that burned his "Bolting-House, Chockalet-Engine-house" (for processing chocolate), and "three dwelling Houses," the *New York Gazette* reported. Millers like Roosevelt often ground cacao beans on the same machinery used for grains, and slaves would have spent days arduously shelling the cacao pods, peeling the thin coating off the beans, and grinding the hard nuts.

Fire was lethal in a city of wooden structures. When a series of unexplained blazes broke out during a frigid winter, with both food and firewood in short supply, New York was gripped by what became notorious as the Negro Plot of 1741. After a shopkeeper was robbed and a cache of stolen linen and silver plate was found hidden under the floor of Vaarck's "Negro kitchen," Caesar (possibly the man who delivered for the bakery) was arrested for the theft. John Vaarck later told the court that Caesar was his best hand and had never caused trouble at work. During Caesar's incarceration, nine more fires erupted. The white population was gripped with terror, and more arrests were made. A trial began in the colony's Supreme Court in April to uncover a suspected conspiracy.

The verdict came down in August. Punishment was severe. Twenty-one slaves were hanged, thirteen men were burned at the stake, one man committed suicide, and eighty-four men and women were transported to the Caribbean. The roster of the food producers whose slaves were implicated included the distiller James DesBrosses; five bakers, including John Vaarck; the butchers Isaac Varian, Isaac and Timothy Horsfield, and three others; three bolters, including John Roosevelt; and the vintner Robert Todd.

Today historians question the validity of the circumstantial evidence and the testimony that proved the "plot."

Altogether the decade of the 1740s was an anxious time in New York. Scores of British soldiers were garrisoned in the city, owing to rising tension with France and French Canada. Feeding troops depleted resources, sending the price of flour and other foods skyward. Those who provisioned them profited handsomely, but

CRYSTAL WHITE

On sugar plantations, iron rollers squeezed the juice from the just-picked cane. The liquid was boiled in copper kettles, then cooled, becoming a moist mixture of molasses and crystals called muscovado sugar (from the Portuguese word meaning "less finished"), which was stable for transportation. This yellow to brown sugar was edible (yet very different from today's product of the same name) but had not reached its most desirable form: the whitest crystals possible. To achieve that perfection, two additional stages of boiling and clarifying were needed.

First the granules of muscovado sugar were melted with quicklime in large open copper boilers. As foam formed, the impurities that rose to the top were skimmed off and the heavier foreign matter dropped to the bottom. Half of the original muscovado was lost during this process. The boiler needed great skill to know the exact moment when the process was completed. If left too long, the molasses wouldn't separate, and either butter or oil would be added to save the less-than-perfect batch. If not boiled long enough, the sugar crystals wouldn't form and would drain away with the molasses. A timing error could also create off odors or tastes that could ruin an entire cauldron. Once the "sweet juice" was properly prepared, it was strained through woolen blankets to extract any remaining debris.

Next, clarification of the liquid further coagulated remaining impurities. The sugar was mixed with ox or bullock blood, the preferred choice of most boilers up until the eighteenth century (they had previously favored crushed whole eggs). New York had a cheap and "plentiful supply of fresh blood" from the Bayard slaughterhouse. After the mixture was baked and the thick syrupy layer of blood and impurities had been skimmed off the top, an off-white crystalline sugar was left. In the heat of the summer months, "the blood underwent a rapid putrefaction and became infected with the larvae of flies. The atmosphere of the refinery was in consequence very offensive and workmen were known to faint from the objectionable odor." The refinery owner Isaac Roosevelt timed his visits for about 10 a.m., before the stench grew unbearable.

The final stage cured the liquid sugar in clay molds, which another writer of the day described as having the "wonderful power over the Sugar, to purge the grosser, flatulent, or treacly Part downward." The "upstairs man" watched over the molded crystals as they dried for several days in the warm upper floors, where small windows reduced air circulation. Over several hours the molasses leached out of a small opening in the bottom of each conical vessel. After drying, white sugar crystals emerged from the molds. If everything went right.

the increased need for meat overburdened the facilities at Kelly's slaughterhouse. Slaughtering was a time-consuming and tricky process: first the animal had to be knocked out with an ax blow to the head, then its throat slit, and finally it was hung upside down by its back legs to drain the blood. Butchers waited in long lines to have their cattle killed at Kelly's congested building, sometimes standing around all night in order to provide meat for their market stall. They began slaughtering at various locales above today's Chambers Street, but as fees were being lost, the Council forbade using any "house, barn, stable, outhouse, yard, orchard, garden, field, or other place in the out ward of New York City" for slaughter, which just about covered any possible place they might want to use. Some butchers moved to Brooklyn; others had no choice but to wait their turn at Kelly's abattoir.

In 1749, New York's traders shipped out a "Great and Unusual Exportation" of grain, flour, fish, and meat. As a result, staples became "most Excessive Dear," especially for the "industrious and Laborious poor." The high cost of grains raised the price of beer. After the brewer Anthony Rutgers's death in 1746, his widow, Cornelia, took over his breweries. Such an executive role was was unusual for a woman in English New York, but Cornelia was Dutch, and she successfully managed the brewery for the next fourteen years while catering to higher-end drinkers with a large wine importing business. Six rum distilleries also helped to ease the stresses of a tense decade.

Other than churches, refineries were the city's tallest buildings. The thick-walled structures harbored the messy "mystery" of transforming molasses-filled sugar from the West Indian islands into sparkling white crystals. There were gradations of sugar for every pocketbook: middling and single refined, not quite pure white; muscovado, tan colored, with more molasses in the crystals, which made it more pungent in taste; and, for those who could not afford crystallized sugar, molasses itself, the syrupy and very sweet by-product of sugar refining. Sugar was sold at the refinery or grocery as "loaf sugar," a large cone-shaped hunk weighing 12 to 14 pounds that was broken into pieces specified by the customer and wrapped in blue paper, lending it a whiter look. A rural farm family might buy one loaf for an entire year. City residents generally consumed more.

3

TOWARD INDEPENDENCE

The French and Indian War (1754–1763) was good for business in New York. City merchants were shipping over 400,000 pounds of hardbread, flour, wheat, and livestock to the islands each year, in addition to sending thousands of bushels of wheat and flour to Boston. With British military headquarters in New York and hundreds of soldiers and sailors still about town, there was plenty of cash (usually in short supply in New York), much of it spent on eating and drinking. The troops wanted meat, but Nicholas Bayard's slaughterhouse could no longer provide enough, so twenty-two butchers signed a petition to the Council asking for permission to build their own slaughterhouse because of "the neglect of Mr. Bayard to provide ropes and other tackle, keep[ing] the houses in repair and clean, the pump having been out of order for six or seven years." The Council rejected the butchers' request, and Bayard maintained his monopoly until 1789.

After England's victory over the French, New York suffered. Army contracts dried up; supplies of illegal molasses were no longer available, as the French island of Martinique was now in British hands; there was a partial crackdown on smuggling; and taxes rose. Business in New York was practically at a standstill. Droughts in 1760 and 1761 caused crop failures. The population grew by 20 percent, and workers outnumbered jobs. The *New-York Mercury* reported that "many families which used to live in comfortable plenty [are] daily falling to decay for want of business."

Then there were rumors about the impending American Revenue Act. The Molasses Act of 1733, a tax on foreign imports, was about to expire, and because the British government's coffers needing refilling after years of war, Parliament decided to squeeze what money it could from the American colonies. The Sugar Act lowered taxes on sugar and molasses from the English Caribbean. That was fine, but the navy strictly enforced new customs regulations, which made it more difficult to get contraband, including sugar from the non-British West Indies, on which the high taxes had traditionally been ignored, into the city. The list of products the colonies could ship only to England was extended and the number of taxable products expanded.

Rum distilleries, sugar refineries, and wine importers were all immediately affected, as were wheat traders, who could no longer trade with any non-English island, including the lucrative markets in Madeira and Tenerife. With shipping almost at a standstill, John Van Cortlandt wrote to a friend that he feared "a Total Prohibition of all foraigne Sugars" would result in "almost a Total Destruction of Sugar Refiners." Raw sugar had become so expensive, Van Cortlandt wrote, that "two of the Principle Sugar houses here have stopped working" (probably Bayard and Livingston), which would likely "be the case with all of them soon." Both the Roosevelt and Van Cortlandt sugarhouses somehow found a way to stay open.

Anger on this side of the Atlantic reached a boiling point when Parliament passed the Stamp Act in March 1765 to defray the cost of stationing troops in America. This notorious law authorized the first direct tax on the colonists enacted without representation, denying a right afforded all British citizens. There was a storm of protests, petitions were circulated, and New York's assembly sent a strong remonstrance to Parliament. Meanwhile the city's merchants agreed to stop importing English goods, and consumers swore to stop buying them. "The Cheaf business here is opposing the Stamp Act with violence," Van Cortlandt militants observed. That same year the Quartering Act was passed, requiring the colonists to supply British troops still stationed in America with munitions and a place to live. The "hosts" of these unwanted boarders were expected to feed and water them with small beer, cider, or rum.

The reviled Stamp Act was repealed in the spring of 1766, and a large public party was held in celebration, with two barbecued oxen, twenty-five barrels of strong beer, and a hogshead of rum (approximately 63 gallons). The reopening of the ports revived business and people replenished their tea supplies. Wheat exports picked up as England and southern Europe experienced droughts, and the city's mood took a more optimistic turn. It didn't last long. In 1767 the Townshend Act placed new taxes on the export of cocoa, an important trade product, and on a variety of imported products, including tea. New York's merchants again joined in a multicity boycott of British products.

Though tea and wine were hard to come by, there was no shortage of alcoholic beverages, what with fifteen rum distilleries operating by 1768. A British naval officer stationed in the city described one that distilled 150 gallons of molasses every day, 300 days a year, for an annual total of 45,000 gallons of rum. Estimates of consumption run as high as 4.6 gallons per person annually.

Richard Deane, recently come from Ireland, opened a distillery in 1766. He advertised to the "Publick, and particularly all true Patriots, who sincerely wish for the Prosperity of AMERICA," that his "Spirituous Liquors and Cordials" were "made from the Produce of this Country, and now has for Sale, at the DISTILLERY" in Brooklyn near the ferry and in Manhattan. The Irish whisky he made was "wholesome," his brandy "considered equal" to French products, but as his distillery was new, he hoped allowances would be made for his "young spirits," which hadn't yet acquired "a Mellownes by Age." He made "Geneva" (gin) using only "Malt and Corn Spirits," which "passes so free through the human body"; Royal Usquebaugh, a cordial made with cinnamon, ginger, coriander, nutmeg, cloves, and cubebs (a peppercorn from Indonesia said to taste like allspice), saffron, raisins, dates, licorice root, and sugar; Red Ratifia, a fusion of black cherries, raspberries, strawberries, sugar, rum, cinnamon, mace, and cloves, and a wide variety of other flavored cordials to cure stomach upsets, nervousness, and headaches. Deane hoped New Yorkers would support his endeavor to keep "Prosperity in this Country." He sought to discourage the drinking of imported products and promoted those made in "our own Country" to allow "large sums of Money kept in the Country at a Time it was so much wanted." New Yorkers must have heeded his patriotic call, for he soon moved to a larger space on Murray Street near the Hudson River.

Deane was voicing a burgeoning sense of local pride and an incipient American nationalism. In March 1770 the British government rescinded all the duties imposed by the Townshend Act except for the tax on tea. As a result, Americans in all the colonies, including New York, renounced English tea. The successful boycott left England's importer, the East India Company, stuck with 18 million pounds of unsold product. To dispose of this surplus, the Tea Act of 1773 allowed the company to sell tea directly to American consumers at rock-bottom prices. The British were confident that they would undersell smuggled Dutch tea and tea-guzzling American colonists would be forever grateful. Instead the move backfired, angering merchants, smugglers, and consumers alike.

New Yorkers warned the captains of trading vessels not to bring tea into the harbor, and the imminent arrival of a huge shipment of East India Company tea became a rallying point. "A SHIP loaded with TEA is now on her Way to this Port, being sent out by the Ministry for the Purpose of *enslaving and poisoning* ALL the AMERICANS," a local newspaper wrote. Three thousand people demonstrated against the tea landing, and when the first ship neared the harbor, the captain got wind of the local sentiment and turned back. But a second ship, the *London*, docked with eighteen chests of tea aboard. On the night of April 22, 1774, New York held its own Tea Party (Boston's had taken place four months earlier) when a band of "Mohawk Indians"—an anonymous group of costumed local men—boarded the ship and heaved the tea into the East River from a wharf at the end of Wall Street. By May, drinking tea was so politically incorrect that neighbors watched each other to make sure that everyone complied. Those who failed to cooperate were met with harassment from vandals and looters. Along with boycotting tea, people stopped buying spices, pickles, mustard, and black pepper. Coffee and chocolate, which could be shipped directly from the West Indies, became the patriot's beverages of choice.

At this time Isaac Roosevelt's sugarhouse had ten people on the payroll. Most, like Dederick Hyer, his foreman, had been contracted to work about four years to pay for their passage to New York. George Dieterich came with his wife from London in 1775; John Lackman and his wife followed in June 1776. It was a strange moment to arrive; troops under George Washington had moved into the city in February 1776 and no one knew what the future would bring.

The majority of New Yorkers were patriots, although many continued to support the king. With Washington in the city, many loyalists fled, but Frederick Rhinelander, a ceramics importer who stayed, bemoaned "the distressed state of this once happy city," where such a "vast number of houses [were] shut up, one would think the city almost evacuated." It was not long until even Rhinelander left for New Jersey.

After Washington's troops were routed in Brooklyn on September 15, the tables were turned and overnight the city was transformed into the center of British forces in America. Unlike many of those in his social milieu, Isaac Roosevelt did not doubt where his allegiance lay; neither did the refiners John Van Cortlandt and Peter Livingston, who closed their sugarhouses and left the city. The brewers Anthony Lispenard and Elizabeth Rutgers and the distillers Charles Tillinghast and Richard Deane were committed to the revolutionary cause. Many suffered losses of equipment and destruction of the property they left behind.

Most of the artisans and laborers joined the fight for independence. Most of the city's butchers followed suit. Richard Varian, the manager of the slaughterhouse and Bull's Head Tavern, served time at sea on a privateer capturing enemy ships; his brothers Michael and James Varian left the family stalls to join the army, as did their father, Isaac. The butcher John Pessenger scoured the countryside to procure meat for the Americans.

In the early years of the Revolutionary War, food was plentiful in occupied New York, but the city was surrounded by water, cut off from the agricultural hinterland, and largely dependent on ships from Ireland or France to supply the essentials. The products that had once been the city's main exports—beef, pork, and flour—were imported at punishing prices. Tories like Frederick Rhinelander returned, while loyalists from other regions streamed into the only British-held city in the north, which swelled the population to 33,000. Joseph Corre arrived from Philadelphia and set up a successful confectionery shop in Hanover Square. Rebecca Gomez, a chocolate-maker, stayed in the city, selling superfine treats on Nassau Street.

The wealthy continued to put on elegant teas, parties, and balls for British officers. But for many, life in New York was "truly deplorable and almost hopeless." Bread was "extravagantly high" and "all the necessities of life . . . dear beyond exception." By 1779 foods in the "markets were raised 800 percent for the necessaries of life," and even a man with a "small fortune could hardly afford" to eat. Supply ships were essential, and when one finally arrived, nearly three months late, the sight of its billowing white sails entering the harbor incited rare jubilation.

Little brewing took place during the occupation. Three breweries housed British troops and probably ended up in as bad shape as Elizabeth Rutgers's substantial brewery, which was "stripped of everything of value," without "a single brewing Utensil left." Benjamin Waddington and Evelyn Pierrepont took over the brewery in 1778 with a royal license to brew and had to "expend a considerable Sum in Repairs of every Nature" before they could begin producing beer. Once operational, Waddington and Pierrepont's brewery made a fortune while the occupation lasted.

Andrew Mercein was a sixteen-year-old apprentice to a baker who supplied the English army. With little interest in politics, Mercein stayed in the city, where he soon opened his own shop. When wheat supplies were scarce, he later recounted, he could sell loaves of bread that had formerly cost six cents for "a hard half-dollar apiece." He also baked hardbread for the English navy. Late in the war Mercein was required to serve in His Majesty's forces, first guarding the fort, then aboard a naval vessel. With no stomach for fighting, he escaped by jumping into the Hudson River and swimming ashore with bullets whizzing past his head, an experience that did not win his heart for the British cause.

New York's imposing refineries found another use during the Revolution, when sugar production ceased. Peter Livingston's five-story Liberty Street sugarhouse, a "dark stone building with small, deep, port-hole looking windows, rising tier above tier, exhibiting a dungeon-like aspect," was converted into an infamous jail for American prisoners of war. Prisoners were herded "like so many hogs" into "the dirtiest and most disagreeable place I ever saw," one captured soldier reported. The water, he said, "was not better than that in the Dock." Their food ration, "4 oz of Pork and as much rotten Biscuit [hardbread] per Man per day and often no more for two Days together," was barely enough to keep them alive. Forty years later Grant Thorburn, who lived across the street from the building, recorded visits of the former prisoners, who told of "sorrows and sufferings" in the "dark hole" where they "were crowded to excess" with "provisions bad, scanty and unwholesome and the fever raged like a pestilence."

John Van Cortlandt's refinery, near what was left of the burned-out Trinity Church, may also have been a prison housing some civilian patriots, but there is scant evidence that the most famous of the refineries, the Cuyler plant, which was later known as the Rhinelander Sugarhouse, ever housed prisoners. During the war it appears to have remained vacant, its loyalist owner, Henry Cuyler Jr., having died shortly after the war began. Roosevelt's sugarhouse was also left vacant. It was wedged between two stylish homes, whose residents were influential enough to keep prisoners out of the neighborhood.

Food—or the lack of it—greatly concerned George Washington. Prices were high, and the Continental Army's troops were often "starving for bread." Washington's letters attest to the difficulty of obtaining salted meats, flour, and especially hardbread. In 1779, writing from West Point, for example, Washington wanted to be sure there was "in stock a considerable quantity of good ship-bread" to feed the American soldiers and to share with the French fleet.

The baker George Fisher left New York to make hardbread for the Continental Army from 1777 to 1779. A baker was expected to locate and buy flour himself, assuming that he would later be reimbursed. Fisher borrowed large sums to purchase the necessary flour, but when he went to settle his accounts in December 1779, he was awarded only a nominal amount. Even then, it took six months to arrive, and by that time the paper currency he had been issued had depreciated. To secure what he was owed, he petitioned a committee formed to rectify situations like his. Congress agreed that all who had furnished supplies for the army should be paid full value, and in 1781 Fisher finally got his due.

After British forces surrendered at Yorktown in October 1781, thousands of Tories who had found refuge in New York thought it wise to leave. A small number went to England, including Benjamin Waddington, who took the fortune he had made at the Rutgers brewery with him. Many left for Canada. Some returned to their former homes around the country, and a few, people like Frederick and Philip Rhinelander, John Varick and Andrew Mercein, remained uneasily in the city, waiting to see whether prospering under the British would be held against them in their new country. For the most part it was not, as New Yorkers turned to building the food networks that would sustain a new nation.

4

FOOD ON PARADE

Forty-six-year-old master butcher John Pessenger had spent the recent years of the Revolutionary War provisioning the American army with meat. Now he stood with the other master butchers under a warm drizzly sky as the thundering sound of thirteen cannons reverberated throughout the city. It was ten o'clock in the morning on July 23, 1788, the start of the Federal Procession celebrating the formation of the United States, an event that had been delayed several times as the country waited for the minimum nine of thirteen states to ratify the Constitution. On June 21, New Hampshire had become that crucial ninth state, followed by Virginia on June 25. New York, bogged down for weeks in bickering, would follow a few days later, on July 26. At dawn Pessenger and his apprentices had walked to the butchers' gathering spot, forming one of many artisan groups, which included almost every master, journeyman, and apprentice in the city. Between five and six thousand craftsmen would march in the well-orchestrated spectacle, along with sprinklings of merchants, physicians, and gentlemen. Anyone not marching got the day off. People hung out of windows, jammed into doorways, and packed the narrow sidewalks along the planned route.

During the chaotic postwar years, prosperity hadn't materialized as quickly as expected. When after six years of fighting the war ended in 1782, the once beautiful city had been ravaged. Weary patriots returning early the next year found widespread desolation. Two major fires had destroyed whole neighborhoods; the leafy thoroughfares, according to George Washington, were "totally stripped of trees," cobblestone streets had been gouged and were impassable, and neglected wharves were rotting in the river. As the last of the British troops took ship on November 25, 1783, the jubilant cheers of most New Yorkers echoed all along the shoreline. But peace came at an economic price, including the closing of the lucrative British-held Caribbean islands to American trade. Although money was scarce, trade resumed, New Yorkers began picking up the pieces of their lives, and the city began to function.

By the morning of the procession almost five years later, the mood was buoyant. A new nation was aborning and the economy was on the upswing. While cannons boomed, women and children, merchants and traders, indentured servants, parlormaids, shopkeepers, slaves, free African Americans, and foreign visitors ignored the rain as the procession solemnly filed down Broadway. Most artisan groups marched in coordinated outfits or in the uniforms of their trade. A small group of master bakers, including John Quackenbos, whose family had been bakers in New Amsterdam, and John's father, Walter, a leader of the Sons of Liberty, led the bread- and biscuit-makers. Following were ten apprentices and ten journeymen, wearing white shirts and blue sashes and carrying the implements of their craft. Next came their flag, which pictured two ovens and the verse "We are well built both sound and tight/We hope to serve the ships in sight/With the best bread, bak'd of good flour/When Congress has the Federal power." The marching bakers supported a strong government that could regulate trade, as more ships in the harbor meant more customers for hardbread.

Just behind another eighty masters, journeymen, and apprentices, all in sparkling white aprons, were four more master bakers riding on a wagon, which carried a 10-foot-long "Federal" loaf of bread with the names of the ten ratifying states and the initials of the three that had not yet voted, including New York.

Most artisans favored ratification, because a central government could, among other things, negotiate trade agreements with Great Britain to reopen the West Indian markets, form a navy to protect American ships, and standardize the country's weights and measurements. Uniform sizes for bushels and barrels would expedite the shipping of New York's products, especially the city's major export, wheat. At the time of the parade the price of wheat had almost quadrupled since the beginning of intensive wheat cultivation in 1720, which buoyed the city's economy. The grain measurers' flag depicted George Washington's face on one side and Alexander Hamilton's on the other, as well as an image of a measuring device, with the word *equality* and the slogan "Federal measures, and measurers true,/Shall measure out justice to us and to you."

Laws covering the inspection of wheat, flour, and bread were issued by the Common Council in 1785 and again in 1788 "to preserve the reputation" of New York's "staple commodities." The flour inspectors, also marching along the route, monitored grain leaving the port, while another group of inspectors in the parade supervised the storing, grading, packing, and branding of beef and pork that was salted or pickled for shipping.

The most precarious display rolling along the parade route was the butchers' wagon, which swayed over the bumpy cobblestone street while John Pessenger, aided by two apprentices, wielded sharp knives to split lambs in half. Behind the wagon a young apprentice, John Perrin, carried their banner, emblazoned with "Federal Butchers," followed by one hundred more butchers in white aprons. Their final flag pictured "three bullock's heads, two axes, a boar's head, an ox and a lamb," plus the verse "Skin me well, dress me neat,/And send me aboard on the Federal fleet," a reference to the commercial advantages of a federal union in regulating foreign trade.

Most flags were decorated with the symbols and images of the workmen's craft. The brewers' banner, "Home brewed," was decorated with barley sheaves, casks of porter wrapped with hop vines, and an eagle with a thermometer in its mouth (hops were heated in the brewing process). The workers marched along with three brewery owners who were staunch patriots: Anthony Lispenard, White Matlack, and George Appleby. Matlack and Appleby had just opened a large brewery at 36 Chatham Street (now Park Row), which made ale and table, ship, and spruce beers. Matlack, a Quaker and an early abolitionist, had painfully forsaken the pacifist tenets of his religion to side with the Revolutionary forces.

Several other breweries had opened, including one run by Samuel Attlee, an Englishman who arrived in New York in 1783, just as most of his countrymen were leaving. Six months later he began brewing porter in the former Harrison brewery on the Hudson River, since the previous owner, the loyalist George Harrison, had left the city. Attlee advertised that his beer was "entirely made of the produce of this Country, and is presumed to be equal" to beer made in London. He hoped to have the "encouragement, which industrious Manufacturers in America deserve." This point was repeatedly reinforced in the parade: making goods in America would protect the country from cheaper English imports and foster the economy.

Each of the three marching brewers had an "elegant gilt mashing oar in hand" and a "barley head" in his hat. One of their wagons carried bags of hops festooned with hop vines. On another, an eight-year-old boy dressed as Bacchus rode on top of a 300-gallon cask of ale emblazoned with the words "Ale, proper drink for Americans." Twenty-three brewers and maltsters followed the wagons on foot.

Behind them were the chocolate-makers, whose scroll included verses extolling the virtues of a united government and an illustration of a hand chocolate mill with two men grinding chocolate. The confectioners' wagon carried a sugar "Bacchus' cup" (probably shaped like a wide-mouthed chalice) that was 4½ feet in diameter and decorated with multicolored sugar letters spelling out "Federal Confectioner," the name of a shop on Broadway run by Adam Pryor.

Most likely watching from the sidelines was the confectioner and former loyalist Joseph Corre, who had come to New York from Philadelphia early in the war and opened a shop popular during the occupation. When the owners of the building returned in 1783, he was booted out, but within six months he opened a new shop and was selling ice cream, jellies, pastries, sugared almonds, and liqueurs and supplying ships' captains with pickled oysters, preserved milk, and "delicious Pyes, warranted to keep good at sea for four weeks." Another confectioner very probably on the sidelines was John Laune, an English soldier (and an aide to an officer hanged in the Benedict Arnold spy case) who had opened a shop on Wall Street where he sold "burnt and sugar Almonds, Orange and Lemon Sugar Plumbs, Ginger and Cinnamon Tablets," ice cream, and "Preserved Milk, warranted to keep for Twelvemonth."

For the most part the parade belonged to the winning side in the Revolution. Many loyalists had chosen to remain in New York, and in the years preceding the parade, former enemies had learned to live together. But for some patriots, merely abiding loyalists stretched the limits of tolerance. So it was a surprise when, shortly after the war ended, the voters elected a loyalist slaughterhouse owner, Nicholas Bayard, to the Council. Also disconcerting to many patriots was the decision of Alexander Hamilton, one of the heroes represented in the procession, to side with loyalists in several unpopular court cases. The first case pitted the seventy-year-old patriot Elizabeth Rutgers against Benjamin Waddington and Evelyn Pierrepont, who had occupied her brewery after 1778. When Mrs. Rutgers made demands for back rent and necessary postwar improvements, Waddington not only refused to pay but fled to England with the fortune he had made in Rutgers's brewery, and two days before British troops were to leave the city the brewery suspiciously burned "to ashes." Mrs. Rutgers filed a lawsuit under New York's Trespass Act to receive compensation, but Hamilton took Waddington's side, arguing that the laws of the country—banning punitive measures against the enemy and mandating clemency for military actions—took precedence over those of the states. Hamilton won, but with anti-British sentiment running high, he urged his client to negotiate a settlement. Waddington agreed but paid barely a tenth of the original claim, and Rutgers's brewery never reopened. Several other patriots, including the baker Walter Quackenbos, lost similar cases to Hamilton. Despite this, his patriotism and "buy American" economic policies made him a hero to most artisans. (Hamilton missed the parade because he was in Albany, along with the sugar refiner Isaac Roosevelt and eight other New York delegates, pushing for ratification of the Constitution.)

As the procession made its way slowly down Broadway to Queen Street (soon renamed Pearl Street), Chatham Street (Park Row), and Bullock Street (the eastern end of Broome), the only sound heard in the normally boisterous city was the "deep rumbling of carriage wheels" as they passed by "numberless crowds . . . pressing on every side"; an "unexpected silence . . . reigned through the city, which gave a solemnity to the whole transaction suited to the singular importance of its cause."

The sense of decorum lasted through the large feast held on Nicholas Bayard's farm (between Bowery and Broadway), where six thousand diners were sheltered from the intermittent rain under enormous tents radiating out from a central colonnade with three pavilions. Diners were seated at ten 440-foot-long tables, each representing a ratifying state. The meal included a 1,000-pound bullock (a young steer), donated by the butchers and roasted whole, also mutton and ham and no doubt the split lambs and the 10-foot "Federal" loaf of bread that had been carried in the parade. Locally made beer was the only spirit served, including the contents of the 300-gallon cask of ale.

The parade was a spectacular success. The strict discipline of the city's craftsmen demonstrated their equal standing in the new nation. This enormous venture must have physically and emotionally exhausted everyone involved. Yet three days later, when news arrived that New York State had finally ratified the Constitution, most New Yorkers were sufficiently game to join in a second round of celebrations. For occasions great or small, in a city of *fressers*, free food and drink were infallible crowd-builders.

II

BREAD

5

THE DARK PROPHECY
OF ADAM SMITH

The confectionery shop at 28 Wall Street stood so close to the spot where, on April 30, 1789, George Washington was sworn in as the first president of United States that the owner, Joseph Corre, could plausibly boast that "Washington shopped here." Corre was a recovering loyalist. The president and the brand-new representatives of the federal government probably felt more comfortable at Adam Pryor's Federal Confectioner at 59 Wall, which sold burnt almonds, sugarplums, peppermint and lemon drops, strings of rock candy, chocolates, and ice cream billed as both "cheaper and much better than can be imported." Alexander Hamilton, the new secretary of the Treasury, should have been pleased by that. Indeed, the words could have been borrowed from his "Report on the Subject of Manufactures" (1791), which urged Americans to buy American. Hamilton's boss needed no such encouragement. When Washington stepped out onto the balcony of Federal Hall to take the oath of office, he was wearing a suit of "superfine American Broad Cloth" manufactured in Hartford. In his speech he expressed the hope that it would soon "be unfashionable for a gentleman to appear in any other dress" than one made in America.

After his early release from his indenture with Isaac Roosevelt, George Dieterich opened a large bakery on Pearl Street during the British occupation. He made bread, doughnuts, cakes, cookies, and tea rusks (today called zwieback or dried toasts). His apprentices, or slaves, along with those of other bakers, were a familiar sight delivering baked goods to local shops throughout the city. Along their route they would try to make a few extra dollars by hawking the baker's wares with cries of "Tea ruk, ruk, ruk, tea ruk." This was illegal: the law stipulated that a baker could sell his bread or crackers only from his shop. But in the larger geographic area of the expanding city, inspectors could not keep an eye on enterprising youths like the eighteen-year-old German immigrant Dieterich hired to shout up his products. Bakery delivery boy was not usually a position from which a young man vaulted ahead in life, but John Jacob Astor managed it.

Released from the constraints of war, New York food producers could now concentrate on cutthroat competition. A group of bakers petitioned the Council for permission to allow their "Servants and Apprentices" to legally "carry & expose to sale about the streets of this City, Cookeys and Rusks," but the request was denied. Jonas Humbert worried that patrons of his Pine Street shop, especially "children and servants," who "might be more gullible," would be intercepted by boys hawking another baker's rusks from a spot near his entranceway. In 1791 he assured his customers in the *New*

York Commercial Advertiser that he did not employ "any boy to carry his rusk and biscuit around the city." The Common Council was also against this practice—it was probably the only issue on which the well-established bakers agreed with them.

In scores of small food workshops master craftsmen toiled alongside their workers. These usually included a journeyman or two, who worked for wages while they perfected their craft and until they could put enough by to open their own shops, and one or two apprentices completing their four- to seven-year contracts. In a three-year period, two apprentices ran away from the hard-bread baker Adam Mount. He seems to have been a difficult man (he was charged with cruelty by one of the boys, which he refuted in a newspaper ad), but with workers needed throughout the country, young men were more mobile than they had been before the war. A seventeen-year-old slave named Andrew also took off from Mount's shop. Described by his owner as a "tolerable good hand at baking," Andrew was luckier than many enslaved people, having learned a trade that might help him survive.

Proving their independence in the matter of tea, in 1784 a group of merchants from New York and Philadelphia financed *The Empress of China*, the first American ship to sail to Canton to trade directly with the Chinese. The ship carried ginseng, which Samuel Shaw, the agent employed to sell the cargo, considered an "otherwise useless produce" from America's "mountains and forests," but the Chinese, who prized ginseng as a cure for impotence, thought otherwise. Shaw exchanged the ginseng for 327, 000 pounds of black tea and 75,000 pounds of green tea, making the investors a handsome profit. By 1785 five more ships had sailed from New York for China, along with one to India, a number that increased every year.

The ships making the fifteen-month round-trip voyage needed large stores of hardbread, as did the many other vessels returning to the harbor. Adam Mount, who had run a bakery for the revolutionary army, opened a shop specializing in these crackers, and Andrew Mercein made them at the bakery. Mercein and Mount supplied "all kinds of SHIP BREAD, etc.," which made up the bulk of their income, but they baked other varieties for New Yorkers, particularly water crackers and butter biscuits.

John Wilson was a partner in a wholesale grocery firm when he and his brother opened a cracker factory at 73 Fulton Street in 1795, five years after they arrived in New York from Scotland. Alexander Wilson was a baker with technical know-how, while John used his wholesale business as an outlet for their product. Theirs was soon the largest cracker bakery in the city.

During the summer of 1790, bakers like Mount and the Wilsons produced 3,323 barrels of biscuits for export. Hardbread bakeries could turn out this unprecedented quantity thanks to rudimentary assembly lines. The first man on the line hand-mixed flour and water to make the dough. Then it was put onto a "dough brake," and another man would "ride the horse" by jumping up and down on one end of a 7-foot-long, 6-inch-wide pole with a lever that moved a triangular paddle in a circular motion, flattening the dough into thin sheets. A third man cut it into cracker-size pieces and stamped it with the baker's name, as in "Adam D. Mount." The next man, using a peel, a long-handled flat shovel like those seen in pizzerias, carefully slipped the biscuits into the oven, while a fifth arranged the baked crackers in the oven's upper chamber to bake a second time, until all the moisture had been removed. (The word *biscuit*, which the English used instead of *cracker*, is derived from the Latin word meaning "twice baked.")

Altogether, the machinery for kneading dough made baking hard-bread so easy that "the principal part of the work maybe done by Boys from 10 to 14 years of age."

In this heady period after the Revolution, wage workers like those toiling in Mount's bakery had lively expectations of one day owning their own shops, but these hopes receded toward the end of the century. Most bakery laborers, it increasingly appeared, would spend their lives working for others and at narrow tasks ("riding the horse") that crimped their capacities.

Adam Smith feelingly limned their plight in *The Wealth of Nations* (1776): "The man whose whole life is spent in performing a few simple operations . . . generally becomes as stupid and ignorant as it is possible for a human creature to become. But in every improved and civilized society, this is the state in which the labouring poor, that is, the great body of the people, must necessarily fall." *Must*, because the increased productivity that lifted the flat line of economic growth for the first time in a thousand years rested on the division of labor. Then Smith adds a caveat that aligns the father of laissez-faire economics with helping-hand liberalism: ". . . unless government takes some pains to prevent it." Smith urged public education as the answer for the martyrs of progress and their progeny.

Work was plentiful during the optimistic postwar years. During busy seasons many shops hired unskilled, low-paid workers. New York's five chocolate mills needed additional hands during the cooler months, when chocolate was ground—grinding was suspended during the summer to avoid melting. (Most mills also ground pepper, mustard, or coffee on the same equipment.) Coffee-roasting was a growing business; seven times more beans were being imported than before the war. Skilled bakers were needed to create good products, but after the turn of the century entrepreneurial master bakers began to think differently about how the work was conducted. Shops took to training apprentices in a few selected skills, creating "half journeymen," who were paid reduced wages. The higher pay of experienced journeymen often made them less desirable hires, and their compensation also fell. The division of labor in the shop was rendering their skills, and them, increasingly unnecessary. And with a continual stream of immigrants arriving from New England, rural New York, Britain, Ireland, and Germany, there was an abundant supply of people willing to work for less. For employers, however, labor costs were only one variable standing between them and success. Thus, when sixty thousand New Yorkers woke up on the morning of November 3, 1801, all the bakeries were closed and there was no fresh bread. The bread assize was at the core of the stoppage; in the changing economic climate of the new century, bakers voiced growing opposition to price controls. But they soon discovered that it wasn't a good idea to deny the public, especially its rich and powerful members, what one commentator called "the principal part of our food."

The bakers had lobbied for the abolition of the assize in 1792, 1793, and 1795 and been rebuffed each time. Making their case again in 1800, they argued that their expenses left little room for profit. While the price of bread was fixed, that of flour, yeast, candles, and firewood was constantly rising. Salaries and rent needed to be paid, and a horse and wagon maintained for deliveries in the spreading city. The Council surprised the bakers by agreeing. It set the standard weight of a loaf at either 1½ or 3 pounds and left the price up to the individual baker. If you can imagine such a thing in New York, the public didn't complain.

The first year went smoothly, but when the cost of flour dropped and that of bread didn't budge, outraged consumers accused the bakers of a "depravity of human nature." Writing anonymously, "A Baker" (possibly Jonas Humbert, who often used a pseudonym) defended his trade. Bakers had bought their flour at least twelve weeks earlier, when it was still dear, he explained, and costs would be adjusted once they began using the cheaper stock. He asked if anyone knew of "one rich loaf-bread maker" (separating bread bakers from those making hardbread and crackers, who often did quite well). Three bakers presented affidavits showing that they lost money on every loaf, but the public insisted that ending the assize was an "evil" that required "a prompt and effectual remedy." With an election scheduled for November, the Council reinstated the assize at the end of October. In less than a year the bakers had lost their foothold in the unregulated market economy, and their good name.

The people had spoken, but the bakers didn't listen. Led by George Dieterich and Jonas Humbert, early in 1801 they banded together in the Society of Bakers to strike back. Humbert, known for his delicious rusks, was also a person of "some authority" as a founder of the General Society of Mechanics (as artisans were called). No stranger to political agitation, he was a close friend of Thomas Paine, the author of the pro-Revolution pamphlet "Common Sense," and he frequently wrote letters to the local newspapers airing his opinions regarding the workingman's dimming prospects for the future. At a secret meeting the society's members voted to shut their bakeries to protest the renewed assize.

Most of the city's shops were small, although few were as bare bones as the Irish immigrant Phillip McCardle's ten-year-old bakery, which, with one poorly paid journeyman, was expected to make about 190 loaves each week. At the top of the trade, the German immigrant George Arcularius's sixteen-year-old bakery, one of the largest in the city, turned out 4,800 loaves weekly. Whereas McCardle rented, Arcularius owned his shop and paid each of his three journeymen four times the salary of McCardle's man. Most bread bakers, including Jonas Humbert, made a decent living and were at the higher end of those considered "middling." A small number became wealthy, although usually from real estate investments.

On the November day the bakeries closed, one newspaper complained that the "unfeeling" bakers were shirking their "duty" because they hadn't given "some kind of public notice" to their customers. Another raged that the bakers had perpetrated this "uncommon occurrence" on the people of New York while "acquiring fortunes at the expense of the poor." The one-day strike was branded the work of a "monopoly" of bakers.

Within twenty-four hours the bakers announced that they would "happily supply their customers again," as a "mutual accommodation" had been reached with the Council. The next day bread was back in the shops. While the Council left the assize in place, it adjusted the formula to link the cost of bread to the price of wheat, tilting it slightly upward in the bakers' favor.

Yet that same day a notice appeared in the local papers that chilled the hearts of the bakers. To "remedy" the "evil" of relying on the fickle bakers, a group of wealthy citizens led by John B. Church, Alexander Hamilton's brother-in-law, proposed the formation of a large bakery to supply the city's needs, to be called the New York Bread Company. They claimed the new competition was the bakers' fault for creating an "inconvenience so serious, and so unexpected," that it "excited general alarm." A meeting, led by Hamilton, was held at the Tontine Coffee House, and shares of the New York Bread Company quickly sold out. Professing to serve the public good, the shareholders sought to corner the market on bread.

Three months later the New York Bread Company opened for business in a large building at 37 Vesey Street. Ovens were installed and bakers put to work making bread and breakfast rolls to be delivered to customers' homes early each morning. The company not only wanted to dominate bread baking, it also entered the lucrative hardbread market.

The bakers were terrified by the threat posed to their livelihood, as were the city's other artisans, who knew this could easily happen in their industries as well. Unfettered free enterprise no longer seemed like such a good idea. Another round of letters appeared in the papers, this time decrying the fate of bakers forced to "abandon their business." The Bread Company might sell cheaper bread to capture the market, the epistolary bakers conceded, but what then was to stop it from increasing prices at whim? Raising an issue of public health, Jonas Humbert warned that the large bakery was much dirtier than small neighborhood shops. Another writer cautioned New Yorkers that if they bought the company's loaves, it would be at "the expense of a class of men who perhaps are as virtuous as the generality of mankind."

When the Bread Company proposed increasing the standard "baker's dozen" from thirteen loaves to fourteen, the small shop owners protested that it would "deprive the bakers from obtaining a living." They hoped that "every good citizen who has the feelings of humanity for tradesmen" would "employ them, rather than

MONOPOLISTS." One sage, who signed his letter "A Bread-Eater," urged everyone to calm down, because "trade will regulate itself," a theory New Yorkers couldn't test just yet.

On May 22, 1803, sometime between five and six in the evening, a pile of wood drying next to an oven in the cellar of the New York Bread Company ignited. The flames quickly climbed a shaft into the upper stories of a building filled with flammable barrels of flour and hardbread. A huge crowd gathered at the scene, making it difficult for the firemen, who unavailingly fought the blaze for four hours, to maneuver equipment. No suspicions were raised about the origins of the fire—bakeries burned with some frequency—but it seems likely that some of those hampering the firefighters on the streets were bakers rooting for the flames. The resulting losses were too great for the bakery to reopen, and the experiment came to an end. By 1806 the city's trade directory listed a total of ninety-seven bakeshops. For the moment New York was safe for competition in bread.

Jonas Humbert continued to rail against the Council for the "stigma" it had cast "on the moral character of Bakers" and its "misguided" notions about the assize, which, he charged, had retarded improvements in wheat and flour production, because new inventions needed the incentive of greater profits. By 1821 the Council had had enough of Humbert's harangues and relinquished its role in legislating the cost of bread, abandoning the assize once and for all.

6

"THE BIG DITCH"

n 1825, after eight years in the building, the Erie Canal was completed; the 363-mile marvel opened up the vast agricultural lands of the Midwest. Before the canal, it took three weeks for barrels of wheat from upstate New York to travel to Albany, where they were loaded onto boats for the remaining 150 miles down the Hudson. After the canal, the trip took seven days and cost ten times less than the overland journey. Within a decade New York became the country's principal flour market and a veritable grain silo for the world.

As tons of inexpensive western wheat, oats, barley, and flour poured into the city, the price of wheat plummeted. About two thirds of the 75 million bushels of grain was for the export trade, but the remainder stayed in New York, where a large portion was processed into flour in the city's mill while 161 bakers milled significant amounts into bread and crackers. Inexpensive grains kept the cost low for feeding the 200,000 cattle and other livestock slaughtered each year in the city. A Mr. Cobbett reported in *American Farmer* that on this side of the Atlantic the price of meat was about half the price in Europe, where, except on special occasions, eating meat was an idle dream.

The influx was also good for the city's twenty-nine breweries and sixteen distilleries. "Good, strong, clear ale," Cobbett recounted, and "all the material for making people drunk," cost much less in New York than in England, and he cautioned a newcomer that for a little money "here you may drink yourself blind." The opening of the canal also opened a quicker route to oblivion than ale: inexpensive grain whiskey made from barley, corn, or rye.

By the second half of the 1840s, grain exports reached new heights. With England lifting tariffs on imported grains, New York's wheat exports were six times what they had been a decade earlier.

Much of the wheat, corn, and rye that floated down the Erie Canal found its way to the Atlantic Basin, built in the early 1840s on 40 acres reclaimed from Red Hook's marshes. Its quadrangular docks, many deep enough to accommodate the largest vessels of the day, could berth a hundred ships. Twenty acres of four-story brick warehouses stored tea, coffee, sugar, molasses, pork, salt, and grain. Corn was deposited in spaces that were open to the "air and sunlight, drying and curing, so that it will be fit to transport." Wheat and rye reached the ceiling of ground-level storage rooms. Hundreds of workers shoveled the grain into the waiting ships.

Some of the Atlantic Basin's grain was destined for the starving Irish, in the death grip of the potato famine. Eight-year-old John Bogal arrived after a six-week transatlantic crossing in 1844, the year before the surge in Irish immigration. The largely Protestant New York of Bogal's childhood was an inhospitable place for a young Irishman, though he attended local public schools and became an apprentice in a cracker bakery. Ten-year-old Thomas S. Ollive, a decades-spanning figure in the saga of Food City, arrived from Liverpool a year later. Young Ollive's English family had an easier time; soon after they were settled, his father opened a small cracker bakery, where Thomas learned the trade. Unusually well documented, his life mapped the vast changes soon to transform food making.

The Irish were the largest contingent of new immigrants, followed by the English, Scottish, and Welsh. Smaller numbers came from Germany, France, Poland, and other European countries, and a smattering from South America and China. By 1850 New York's population reached 370,000 and Brooklyn's 79,000. Over a third were foreign-born.

At the same time American migrants continued to arrive from New England, Pennsylvania, and New Jersey, pulled into the city by the glimmer of opportunity. Thirteen-year-old William Thompson was one of them. His Scottish mother and Irish father were farmers, and he'd left home because "I began to grow tired of working in the potato fields of Long Island. I threw down my hoe one day, tramped to the ferry, where I persuaded the man at the ticket office to let me cross for the only cent I had in the world. I came over to New York, found work with a baker that night," and "commenced an apprenticeship." For five years in the airless cellar of a pie bakery, he labored from seven in the evening until nine or ten the following morning. Apprentices were "slaves then," he later recalled; they worked seven days a week and slept on a hard flour-dusted bench.

When he was eighteen, Thompson, by then a journeyman, opened his own bakery, and since "a dinner without a pie was considered no dinner at all," his apple, lemon, mince, and custard pies were much in demand. Among Thompson's regulars were P. T. Barnum, who wanted pies every day at noon, the newspaper editor Horace Greeley, the millionaire Cornelius Vanderbilt, and Samuel J. Tilden, the governor of New York and an eventual presidential candidate.

Thompson's was one of as many as 550 bakeries in New York in the mid-nineteenth century. The eight specializing in crackers supplied the three thousand ships that anchored in the harbor each year as exports boomed. The demand for hardbread intensified with the discovery of gold in California in 1849. In the frenzy created by the news, thousands set out for the West, where food and other necessities were in short supply. The city's sleek clipper ships sailing around the tip of South America and then to China for tea were rerouted to stop in San Francisco to drop off passengers and supplies. Young Thomas Ollive, now fifteen, left his father's shop and joined Edwin Brinckerhoff's bakery on Madison Street. He later remembered working from four a.m. to four p.m., "helping stock the ships' lockers with these crackers. The extra supply was carried in hogsheads and barrels."

Hardbread was also a necessity on wagon trains traveling on overland routes. Homesteaders hoping to people the lonely spaces between the Mississippi and California were told to carry 16 pounds per person, both as food for the months-long journey and as a hedge against hunger when they got where they were going.

After five years of drudgery in Brinckerhoff's, Ollive—now tall, blue-eyed, and twenty—joined the exodus to the gold fields, where he sought riches by baking crackers for miners. He spent his first two years in San Francisco as the foreman of a new cracker factory, hoping to save up enough money to open his own shop in the hills.

"Two years later I crossed the Sierra Nevada Mountains," he later wrote, "and located at Yreka in the beautiful Valley of the Shasta in Northern California, where I engaged in business for myself." As he anticipated, it proved a "wonderful" opportunity.

In 1860 Ollive returned from the hills of California to an increasingly industrialized New York City. The years he spent out West had been a fertile period for technological innovation. The inventor William R. Nevins designed the "best cracker machine in existence," a steam-powered cutter that could roll out dough and divide it into shapes "much faster," the *New York Times* noted, "than the cook ever did it." By 1859, as demand for both butter and oyster crackers increased, a machine was developed that could duplicate their handmade texture. The largest cracker producer, John T. Wilson, whose Fulton Street bakery employed over three hundred, had machinery that "mixed, kneaded, and cut [the dough] into biscuits, ready for the oven, in one continuous operation," according to the *Scientific American*.

The key innovation was the reel oven, invented in 1860 by Duncan Mackenzie and first installed in Wilson's factory. The hand-cranked circular apparatus revolved like a Ferris wheel throughout the building, passing loaded trays, one at a time, through basement ovens for the eleven or twelve minutes of required baking time. The finished crackers were then rotated to the upper floors, where they were removed and replaced with the next batch, which rotated back into the ovens.

In late 1860, flush from feeding Forty-Niners, Ollive "opened a 'bake shop' of my own" in a busy new neighborhood at "14th Street and Third Avenue" (111 East 14th Street). He hired a team of bakers, and considering what later transpired between the two men, John Bogal, the young Irishman who had beat him to New

York by a year, was probably one of them. Ollive could not have picked a better time to enter the world of New York food production. With the southern states seceding from the Union, a great conflict seemed imminent. No matter what their political leanings, the food-makers of New York could anticipate generous government contracts if the country went to war.

7

WAR BOOM

Weeks before the start of the war at Fort Sumter, those who could supply provisions for the Union Army— meatpackers, coffee roasters, pickle-makers, and other manufacturers—were asked to submit bids. But the largest portion of government funds was reserved for local cracker factories. Bakeries large and small, including Thomas Ollive's new company, soon began cooking for the government. As Ollive later recalled, "We who were engaged in the business of baking crackers were very busy making hardtack for the army. Those were busy times indeed." Hardtack was one of the printable nicknames for the stone-hard tooth-breakers that eventually filled the bellies of more than half a million soldiers. No one could have guessed the vast quantities that would be produced over the next four years.

By the summer of 1861, each soldier was receiving about 1 pound of hardtack, the equivalent of nine or ten 3-inch-square hardbread crackers, in his daily marching rations. Although John Bogal had a valuable trade as a cracker baker, he quickly joined the Seventy-first Regiment of New York, a mostly Irish volunteer unit that saw heavy combat during his four-year hitch. The Seventy-first fought in the war's first battle at Bull Run on July 21, their backpacks heavy with two days' worth of food: salt beef, salt pork, and army bread crackers (which Bogal himself might have made months earlier in Ollive's bakery).

New York fed the Union Army. To fulfill the military's enormous needs, the hardbread factories of the country's leading food producer began baking at full throttle. One firm had an order to produce 200,000 pounds per week, an unimaginable output before the war that quickly became the norm. As the city mobilized and young men joined the army, labor was scarce, and in some of the factories machines replaced men.

By 1862 seventeen bakeries, over half in New York, were mass-producing army bread as well as baking crackers to supply the ships that still crowded the harbor. During the Civil War, wheat became the king of exports, more than filling the gap left in trade revenues when southern cotton ceased to be shipped through New York's harbor. It was a more advantageous crop, as *Hunt's Merchants Magazine*, a leading business publication, drily noted, because "cotton can probably be spared more easily than bread." Europe experienced substantial crop failures in 1860 and 1861. Providentially, those same two years were unusually fruitful for American grain harvests, and 57 million bushels of wheat, corn, and flour flowed into the city in 1861 and, from the protected basin of the Atlantic docks, out to the world.

Grain was moved from silo to ship on the strong backs of Irish laborers until 1861, when seven mechanized floating grain elevators were introduced. The new machinery sucked grain from the

Stereograph showing Union Captain J. W. Forsyth, Provost Marshal, sitting on a crate of hardtack, a cracker-like bread served to soldiers, at Aquia Creek, Virginia. The box says, "50lbs. net. Army Bread from the Union Mechanic Baking Company, 45 Leonard St."

arriving canal barges and spiraled it up through roaring chutes that cleaned the stalks or cobs, expelling a shower of yellow dust. The machinery's "tireless muscles," a reporter noted, worked "day in, day out," greatly reducing the need for human labor. The workforce fell by hundreds of men, and announcements projected more layoffs to come. By July 1862 two thousand workers banded together to form the Grain Workers Protective Association, which declared that the new machinery, now doing two thirds of the work, "must be suppressed." During the doomed strike that followed, workers were replaced by scabs, many of them foreign sailors from ships berthed in the docks.

With large government contracts as well as orders for the export market to fill, New York's food manufacturers relentlessly pursued efficiency. Spear, Ball and Company built a "mammoth

SEA OF GRAIN

Beginning during the war and reaching its height in the Gilded Age, on a "vast stream of life-sustaining wealth, by water and by rail," the *Scientific American* reported, grain flowed into New York. Three hundred railway cars bulging with wheat, oats, corn, rye, or barley arrived daily as barges floated down the Hudson River from the Erie Canal in a massive flotilla numbering 103 vessels, 6 abreast, stretching half a mile up the river.

There were flour mills in all the boroughs, but the three largest included two in Brooklyn, the Kings County Milling Company, at 35 Dunham Place in Williamsburg, and the Jewell Milling Company, at the bottom of Fulton Street, plus Staten Island's Holt and Company, in operation since 1801, which sent large shipments of flour to Brazil. The largest of all was the Croton Flour Mills on Brooklyn's Cherry Street, which had the capacity to turn 3,000 barrels of wheat into "vast quantities of the finest flour" each day, including self-raising flour, buckwheat flour, and griddlecake flour.

Along Manhattan's waterfront were twenty-two stationary grain elevators servicing the export trade. The largest, at the foot of 65th Street on the Hudson River, could hold 2.3 million bushels of grain and transfer 60,000 bushels an hour into a waiting ship. Manhattan also had thirty-three floating grain elevators, "skyscrapers on a tug-boat," which could be floated into position between a barge and a ship, where they could transfer grain without a stop at a warehouse.

The grain elevators on Brooklyn's shoreline had four times the capacity of those in Manhattan. *Frank Leslie's* magazine described the "dull, thunderous rumblings of the powerful machinery" on Brooklyn's docks that scooped the grain from barges and carried buckets full to the upper floors of the elevators. When a ship was ready to receive the grain, it docked alongside the elevator and a chute sent the grain flying down to the ship's deck, where a man opened a valve to fill burlap bags "in a twinkling."

bakery" that occupied the block between Water and Pearl Streets, which, when their large reel oven was going full blast, could bake 400 barrels of flour into hardbread each day. "The recent introduction of machinery into our large bakeries," the *Tribune* reported, "has so cheapened the making of hard bread that thousands of dollars have been saved to the Government in the last few weeks." By March 1863 seventeen bakeries, including Thomas Ollive's, had government contracts and were producing 2.5 million pounds of army bread weekly. Historians estimate that in 1864, 3 to 4 million crackers were eaten each day by Northern soldiers, changing their tastes and habits and becoming part of the daily rhythm of their meals.

Rushing to meet government quotas, the bakeries could be dangerous, and it was not unheard of for a workman to lose a hand or an arm in the gears of a machine. Two men were crushed to death by the newly installed reel oven at the National Cracker Bakery in Brooklyn. But the greatest menace, as always, was fire. Flammable flour dust made cracker factories volatile, and ovens running day and night dangerously dried out the wooden interiors of the brick buildings. During the first two months of 1863, five city bakeries burned, a high number even when fire loss was common. John T. Wilson's factory, which kept twenty-six ovens going around the clock, went up in flames and took ten surrounding buildings with it. Wilson, though, was heavily insured, and with suspicious celerity the factory reopened.

Six weeks later Wilson and eight of his employees were arrested, not only for arson but for the murder of a homeless African American man who had been sleeping inside his building when it burned. At the trial Mrs. Margaret Larkin, whose husband and son had worked in the bakery, alleged that on several different occasions John Wilson had offered to pay her to set a fire. "The bakery that we have is too small for all our orders for the government," she reported him saying, "and by giving this place a torch and burning it down we might be able to get a lot, perhaps on either side of [the building,] and build up and have room to work." She testified that she refused his offer and later saw the foreman setting straw on fire. Only two other witnesses were questioned during the few days of the trial, and the judge, calling the witnesses "utterly unreliable," dismissed all charges as fabricated to "ruin Mr. Wilson." This was not unusual; the courts generally sided with business owners. Wilson went right back to baking crackers for the war effort.

Although crackers were not expensive to bake and most factories kept fairly high standards, some producers used the lowest grades of wheat, either to boost profits or because better grain was unavailable. But even if the crackers that were packed in wooden crates were in perfect condition when they left New York, they were often several months old when they reached the troops. "It was no uncommon sight to see thousands of boxes of hard bread piled up at the railroad station or other place used as a base of supplies," one soldier later remembered, and they sat "only imperfectly sheltered from the weather, and too often not sheltered at all." This invited infestation and mold, and when

A color lithographed Victorian-era trade card using the Statue of Liberty to sell crackers, New York, New York, circa 1880.

they finally got to the soldiers, the crackers often crawled with vermin. In an 1864 article for *Frank Leslie's Popular Weekly*, a correspondent embedded with a New York division fighting in Virginia wrote that he "owed [his] life" to hardtack. Still, "the kind served to the One Hundred and Ninth was alive with 'skippers' [maggots]. Tenderfeet threw the uninviting biscuits away when they saw it garnished with these weevils. The veterans smashed it on a rock, and after giving the animals time to escape ate the fragments with satisfaction."

Local bakeries continued to make fresh bread daily and sell it at shops within a few blocks of customers' homes. Some bakeries went to two shifts of bakers, a night crew preparing loaves by 5:30 in the morning for New Yorkers' breakfasts, and a later shift arriving at 7 a.m. to turn out breads until 11 p.m. Many shops stayed open until midnight on Saturday, and, scandalizing pious New Yorkers, German bakeries did business on Sundays. Most bakeries featured twenty-five varieties of bread, including "wheat bread [white bread], potato bread, Graham bread (unbolted [whole-grain] wheat), corn bread, rye bread (sweet and sour) and rice bread," plus French and German-style breads. There was an assortment of shapes—"round, high round, square, oblong, twist, split"—and "one, two and four pound loaves." There was also a choice of "yeast bread, ferment [sourdough] bread, leavened bread" that had been made either by hand or by machine.

In 1863 the Hecker brothers opened a state-of-the-art bread bakery, their original building having collapsed the previous year. The addition of several new ovens stacked throughout the unsupported five-story structure had buckled the walls. In the

CRACKER BARREL

Robert W. Steele, a salesman for Hetfield and Drucker crackers, recalled that his territory in the 1870s covered Manhattan, Jersey City, and Brooklyn. He rode on horseback from seven a.m. to nine p.m., six days a week, seeing as many as fifty customers a day, carrying his samples in a cigar box. Bakery salesmen visited shop after shop, cajoling store owners to buy their firm's crackers. But if "you sold one merchant on one corner, the opposite corner would not buy from you," Steele remembered. He also tried to persuade grocers to sell his crackers from a box on the counter rather than out of a barrel in the back of the store, where "they lost their flavor."

Grocers generally scooped crackers out of the eponymous barrel into paper bags that held "about a pound or less, generally less." Cracker barrels needed constant replenishing, and wagons carrying boxes stenciled with the manufacturer's name were a familiar sight about town. In 1864, John Morton's Scotch Bakery, a large Brooklyn factory at 128 Fulton Street, was looking for "a young man to drive" one of its wagons, and preference would be given to "returning soldiers." Morton's route had the potential to be very lucrative. The firm's specialty, Balmoral biscuits, sweet biscuits made with almonds and finely ground pastry flour, were sold at fifty-one of the city's bakeries, confectioner's shops, and grocery stores, including three owned by R. H. Macy and Company. Customers generally relied on their grocer to assure that products were of good quality, but Balmoral biscuits were each stamped "Morton" to distinguish them.

About this time Vanderveer and Holmes, another cracker-maker, pioneered an eye-catching display case made of glass with brass trim

continues

that prominently displayed its name. Soon other New York cracker manufacturers began supplying similar cases with ornate gilded lettering, plus tin containers that were similarly adorned. Manufacturers like Holmes and Coutts also began registering the names of each of their varieties, like Sea Foam Biscuits, with the U.S. Patent Office so that others couldn't replicate them.

As better transportation became available (74,000 miles of railroad track had been laid by 1874, 93,000 by 1880, and 128,000 by 1885), cracker bakers took advantage of new distribution channels and began invading each other's territories across the nation. Albany's E. J. Larrabee opened a sales office on Chambers Street in 1875 and thirteen years later moved the company to 15th Street. Vanderveer and Holmes had representatives "from Maine to Oregon to the Gulf States," along with "wide distribution in foreign lands . . . exporting small quantities to South America, Africa and Australia."

Most manufacturers made "no less than seventy-five kinds of fancy biscuits," which had become "indispensable at evening parties, in demand at picnics," and as a part of meals "in every well regulated dining room." Both Vanderveer and Holmes and Hetfield and Drucker made popular animal crackers sold "in dainty tin boxes" or by the pound, as well as many other shapes. One critic complained that crackers were "nibbled constantly by ill-regulated children." By the late 1880s the cracker industry had undergone "a complete revolution," according to George Coutts. By using efficient machinery in all stages of production, manufacturers reduced the price of "fancy" biscuits so significantly that "what was formerly a luxury had become a staple."

new bakery, the bread was made "untouched by human hands," a phrase meant to telegraph superior hygienic quality. In an article about the Heckers' bakery, a reporter contrasted modern production with the practices of a traditional bakery, where the baker's arms were "immersed in the dough" up to his elbows and his exertions caused him to perspire heavily, creating a situation in "regards to cleanliness" that was "not pleasant to speak of or contemplate." At Hecker, which employed 120 men and women, he wrote, the water, flour, and yeast were mechanically mixed to form the dough, which traveled on a conveyer belt to a machine where it was worked until it reached an "exceedingly fine texture." Then the dough moved on rollers to cutting machines that formed it into loaves or strips for braided breads and placed them into the pans they would later be baked in. The machines accomplished this in less than half the time it took a baker and without breaking a sweat.

New Yorkers couldn't throw a brick without hitting a bakery, but bread was sorely missed on the battlefields. The army spent considerable time and expense trying to make "soft bread" available to the troops. At the urging of President Lincoln, two New Yorkers—Duncan Mackenzie, who had created John T. Wilson's groundbreaking reel oven, and the prolific inventor Colonel William R. Nevins—came up with early versions of a portable oven. While Nevins's produced a substantial amount of bread, neither proved satisfactory. When the war ended, in April 1865, their rotting hulks littered army campgrounds.

Thomas Ollive, who had the good fortune to open his business as the war began, grew his bakery on war orders. By 1866 he and a partner had moved into a much larger factory (on the corner of

Second Avenue and 19th Street) with an array of machinery run by a steam engine so large it annoyed the neighbors. When John Bogal returned to New York after four years of service in the Army of the Potomac, he saw Ollive about a job and must have been startled to find a factory that filled a quarter of a city block. Ollive hired him on the spot.

8

THE AGE OF INCORPORATION

"Capitalismus won the Civil War," wrote the poet Delmore Schwartz. War orders gave powerful impetus to the growth of big business. Critics called it the age of monopoly. John D. Rockefeller, whose Standard Oil Trust signaled the new direction, rejected that label. *Monopoly* was a bad word for a good thing—"cooperation"—which saved postwar capitalism from the "ruinous competition" that nearly destroyed the oil industry and Rockefeller's fledgling Cleveland refinery along with it. Only "academic Know-Nothings about business," Rockefeller maintained, could believe that in industries with high operating costs, businesses incessantly "eating each other up" could be good for the economy or society. "Cooperation," by contrast, preserved industries, jobs, and communities. "The struggle for the survival of the fittest, in the sea and on the land the world over, as well as the law of supply and demand, were observed in all the ages past until the Standard Oil Company preached the doctrines of cooperation," Rockefeller told an interviewer in 1917. With risible exaggeration, the seventy-eight-year-old father of corporate capitalism, among the most unpopular men of his time, continued: "It . . . cooperate[d] so successfully and so fairly that its most bitter opponents were won over to its views and made to realize that rational, sane, modern progressive administration was necessary to success." The Standard model spread the gospel of big: "What a blessing it was that the idea of cooperation, with railroads, with telegraph lines, with steel companies, with oil companies, came in and prevailed."

In 1881, the same year that the Standard Oil Trust was formed and for the same reason—to escape from costly price competition—the Diamond Match Company bought out its competitors and merged them into one large company. With scores of firms competing for the same customers, the cracker industry was like oil before Standard and matches before Diamond: ripe for consolidation. In the late 1880s, a group of eight large Manhattan- and Brooklyn-based cracker manufacturers began discussions to form a "combine." Thomas Ollive, the president of Brinckerhoff and Co., a guiding member of the cracker group, consulted a Chicago-based lawyer, William Moore, who helped them obtain substantial capitalization. In 1889 the first modern corporation in the food industry announced that it would "start business under the new regime in a few weeks."

The newly formed New York Biscuit Company was made up of the original eight bakers plus an additional twenty-three of the largest East Coast manufacturers in ten states. Thomas Ollive became an executive of the new company, and a few of the original group, including C. R. Hetfield, stayed in "active management." They were part of an emerging new business class: men (and they were all men) who succeeded the generation of entrepreneur/found-ers as the professional managers of corporations. Ollive told the *Tribune* that "the New-York companies would retain management of the new concern," having received compensation with "stock in the new combination." Like John D. Rockefeller with *monopoly*, Thomas Ollive was at pains to shake off negative labels for what his new corporation represented, telling reporters that he "much disliked the word 'trust,' which generally meant prices would rise," and that if "there should be any change in the price of crackers," it would be to "make it lower than at present."

The New York Biscuit Company was an instant success, but logis-tics were more complicated than expected. The plan was to have each firm produce its specialty crackers in its own bakeries, which were the property of the corporation. But the quality of products made in different locations couldn't be controlled, and the com-pany instituted more uniform production in a state-of-the-art bakery built in 1891 on the southeast corner of 15th Street and Tenth Avenue. One by one the older factories, unable to compete on scale, were closed and their businesses absorbed into the new facility. Thomas Ollive of Brinckerhoff Bakery, one of the few that continued to produce soda crackers at its original location, could often be seen in his coach rushing through the congested streets between the bakery's two locations. Factory-made crackers and bis-cuits had become a staple; even one local family of eleven, who took in three boarders, put store-bought crackers on their weekly shopping list despite a meager budget.

The success of the New York Biscuit Company quickened the formation of two similar regional cracker corporations: New York Biscuit had the eastern market, American Biscuit and Manufactur-ing Company of Chicago the country's midsection, and the United

States Biscuit Company the West. Each built factories in its rivals' territories—New York Biscuit in the Midwest and American Biscuit in Manhattan on Bethune Street and in the Bronx on Tremont Avenue.

In early 1897 a cutthroat price war broke out between New York and American Biscuit. By February each company had slashed prices, and the cost of crackers and biscuits fell by almost 40 percent. At least for a while, the *Times* reported, even those "who cannot afford to buy bread may still have sufficient means to purchase crackers."

By September, as prices reached bottom, rumors circulated of a merger of the cracker giants. Consumers were learning that price wars often ended in consolidation, and when prices began to rise in December, an announcement seemed imminent. Ollive told the *Times*, "It is true we [New York Biscuit Company] have put up our prices, but the increase has simply been from figures that were way below production to something approximating that cost." After much speculation, on January 8, 1898, representatives of the two warring companies, including Thomas Ollive for the New York Biscuit Company, formed the National Biscuit Company, made up of 114 of the country's largest cracker bakeries.

Initially the National Biscuit Company's headquarters were in Chicago (it moved to New York in 1906), but its largest facility was Ollive's mammoth bakery on Tenth Avenue, which occupied the western half of the block between 15th and 16th Streets and employed 1,200. Ollive became a director and vice president of the National Biscuit Company, the only one in its upper echelon who lived in New York and the only member of New York's baking industry to rise so high. Robert Steele, the salesman who had ridden for hours on horseback selling crackers twenty years earlier, headed the sales force. Ollive later described the formation of the National Biscuit Company as "practically a new biscuit industry, so thorough was the revolution which took place."

A soda cracker—a staple in New York and Ollive's specialty— was selected to be the company's first nationally distributed product. Called Uneeda (you need a) Biscuit, it was introduced with a huge nationwide advertising campaign months before it went on sale. On March 10, 1899, the *Brooklyn Eagle* announced the arrival of "a new form of Soda Biscuit, crisp, tender and delicious," but what was most important, it came in a revolutionary "moisture proof package" that was airtight and dust-free. It was so successful that 10 million five-cent boxes of Uneeda Biscuits were sold each month during the first year, a large percentage of them made at the 15th Street bakery in New York.

Five days after the *Brooklyn Eagle* ad ran, similar ads appeared in the Yiddish press: "New in price and entirely new in package. Fresh now, fresh tomorrow, and good all the time." Advertising was persuasive in any language. No matter where shoppers were born or lived, they were concerned with cleanliness and freshness. Within a year Uneeda Biscuits were part of daily life on the Jewish Lower East Side.

While the cracker industry grappled with new business forms, early in the 1880s New York's twelve large-scale wholesale bread factories battled unions. The bakers formed the United Bakers Unions of Brooklyn and New York, which led to boycotts and work stoppages. None were very successful until 1885, when products made by August B. Hersemann's bakery were boycotted. Hersemann, a first-generation German American, had been the superintendent at John H. Shults's factory for many years before he opened his

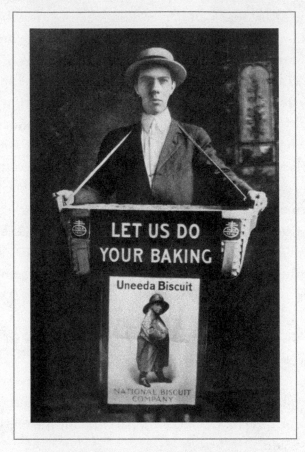

*The first nationally distributed product of the
National Biscuit Company, Uneeda (you-need-a)
Biscuit, launched in 1899.*

own plant on the corner of Graham Avenue and Powers Street
in 1881. George Block, the editor of the union publication, the
Baker's Journal, later explained to the New York State Department
of Labor that after four of his bakers attended a union meeting,
Hersemann "simply discharged them." Soon the bakers in his fac-

tory demanded a reduction of their hours (sixteen hours a day was usual), and when Hersemann refused, the union organized a boycott of the bakery's products "to teach this purse-proud man that lesson he deserves." It was, Block reported, "a pretty effectual boycott; the man was compelled to make peace." Afterward, "all his men" joined the union and "he made an agreement in regards to hours of labor; the agreement is the men should work only twelve hours every day and fifteen on Saturday; that is, you can judge quite a gain for the bakers."

The gain was fragile. By 1889 bakers' strikes had begun to occur with some frequency. First 150 journeymen bakers walked out of the Shults bakery, along with half the drivers of his seventy-two wagons. (The workers at Hersemann's unionized bakery said their boss "grew rich" by stepping in and picking up the extra work.) Also "crippled by a strike" was the O. K. Model Bakery, at 23-37 Jackson Street in Manhattan, a large bakery with sixteen ovens and fifty workers engaged in baking 20,000 loaves of four different kinds of bread. The owner gave his men twenty-four hours to return or lose their jobs. He claimed to have cut their hours to twelve (the goal of most strikers), although the bakers said the number remained closer to fifteen.

To combat the United Bakers Unions of Brooklyn and New York, the bread factory owners formed the Bakers Association of New York and Vicinity. At first they seemed to agree to the union's terms: only union workers would be hired, and they would work no more than eleven hours a day during the week and thirteen on Saturday. But later the owners reversed themselves and the number of hours crept back up. In August 1889 the owners went further and "repudiated" the contract they had signed earlier, so 360 men called a boycott. The workers said they would "leave their

THE BREAD OF CHARITY

Fighting for room on the crowded streets with horse-drawn omnibuses and carriages were the delivery wagons of the large factory bakeries, carrying bread and rolls to groceries, restaurants, and hotels. Fleischmann's Model Vienna Bakery sent out thirty-eight bread wagons on the roads. Louis Fleischmann had started his bakery, as well as a popular cafe at 10th Street and Broadway near Grace Church, in the late 1870s. Fleischmann was born in America and came from a German Jewish family whose business, Fleischmann Brothers in Cincinnati, manufactured compressed yeast. They had introduced Vienna bread, a delicate, slightly sweet, yeast-raised butter loaf, at the Centennial Exhibition in Philadelphia in 1876. Afterward Louis opened the New York shop, where the bread quickly became a favorite. In two "immense" baking factories on 10th Street and 13th Street, each day 210 men baked 15,000 Vienna loaves in 13 large ovens. Each loaf was labeled with the bakery's name to assure authenticity. At night, after the café closed, Fleischmann gave away free loaves of leftover bread and coffee to those who waited on the "bread line." "Night after night, in any weather, a queue of men stood patiently on the sidewalk." In good times the line was short, but when work was scarce, "up to 500 people" waited for "the daily dole of bread given by the Fleischmann Bakery to all who came."

case to the people to decide," and they urged the public not to buy bread from Brooklyn's A. B. Hersemann, John H. Shults and Co., and others, along with the O. K. Model Bakery and P. Rockwell in Manhattan.

Percy Rockwell predicted that the union would lose because "the inhabitants of New-York and Brooklyn must have bread to eat." Another factory owner told a reporter that "the public need have no fear"—there would be no shortage of bread. "We bosses are all practical bakers ourselves and we will go into our shops and roll up our sleeves if need be. And we will put our wives, our sons, and our daughters at work." While the bosses could "bake all the bread that is wanted for a while," New Yorkers might have to do without "rolls and buns and cakes and fancy things" for a few days, but there would always be "ordinary bread," especially with a multitude of non-union men willing to work. The boycott faltered, the strikers were replaced, and the union was weakened by infighting among its leaders.

Unions had even less luck organizing workers in the city's many small local bakeries. To make even a basic living, most boss bakers, as the owners were called, worked as long and hard as their journeymen, for up to one hundred hours a week. In a situation familiar to John D. Rockefeller, intense price competition among the increased number of shops—Manhattan alone was home to 1,177 "baking establishments, large and small, by 1900"—lowered profits and wages.

By 1890, 60 percent of New York's 5,778 bakers were German-born, and many worked "in a state of absolute slavery." The *Sun* reported that "there is scarcely a trade in existence whose members are worked as hard as this, their hours usually being sixteen,

FROM ENGLISH MUFFINS TO MATZOH

Baker C. B. Decker boasted in 1887 that there were only fourteen journeymen bakers in New York (the number in his shop) who knew how to make English muffins and crumpets—something he, an American-born baker, had been doing since 1868. Today Decker's smaller competitor is much better known. Six years after arriving from Plymouth, England, in 1874, Samuel Bath Thomas opened a shop at 163 Ninth Avenue between 19th and 20th Streets. Using a recipe brought from England, he made Thomas's "toaster crumpets," with "nooks and crannies"; he didn't use the name "English muffin" until 1894.

English crumpets would have been an exotic novelty to the Jewish immigrants living on the Lower East Side, where bakeries made more familiar dark ryes, pumpernickel, and challah. The 2.5 million Jews who came to the city between 1870 and 1920 shared a religion but were from different countries with different food traditions. With foods involving Jewish dietary guidelines, confidence in the producer was essential, and a baker from the same town or region as his customers was often the most trusted.

When Jacob Horowitz arrived from Hungary in 1883, maintaining his observant lifestyle was vital to him, so he baked his own matzoh in the small grocery store he rented on Willett Street. The following January his four sons, joined by his newly married and pregnant daughter, Regina, and her husband, Ignatz Margareten, arrived. That spring they hand-baked 50 pounds of flour into matzoh in a small rented bakery. Twenty-year-old Regina worked as hard as the men, lighting the fires, working the dough, and rounding up customers in their Hungarian community. Years later she told her children that she had to work so hard because her brothers were in school and she "never saw the light of day except on the Sabbath," when her twenty-four-year-old husband, "a fine looking man" with "a Van Dyke beard and clear cut features," would dress up in a frock coat and high silk hat.

By 1910, Horowitz Brothers and Margareten had moved into a large matzoh bakery on East 4th Street and filled it with machinery to mix, knead, roll, and stamp the dough. They added matzoh meal and egg matzoh to their product line and employed about thirty-four workers, plus a rabbi to certify that their products were kosher. They were one of "ten or twelve" matzoh bakeries in New York "shipping great quantities to all parts of the United States."

When Ignatz Margareten died in 1923, Regina joined the board of directors and became the company's treasurer. The *New York Times* would eventually call her the "matriarch of the kosher food industry." Throughout the Depression, Regina fed anyone who came to the downtown matzoh baker Horowitz and Margareten's factory asking for food.

and in many instances twenty-four hours for a day's work." Their wages were less than those of unskilled laborers in bread factories, a third of those of bricklayers, half those of millers. In one march of two thousand workers, banners read "Down with Slavery," but their wretched hours made unionization next to impossible, since they simply had no time to meet and debate. Many bakers even slept in their places of work, constantly toiling under their bosses' supervision instead of organizing.

NATIVE PASTA

On the sidewalks of Elizabeth, Bleecker, Mulberry, Roosevelt, and James Streets, wooden racks of drying pasta marked the location of small pasta-makers. In the mid-nineteenth century, a secondhand macaroni mill cost about $150, making it relatively easy to set up business in a back room, living space, or cellar, where six workers could produce 875 pounds of pasta a day. To expand, a pasta-maker would have to buy expensive individual copper disks that extruded different shapes and forms, each costing almost as much as the mill. Motto, Novelli and Company, located in the back of a five-story tenement at 51 Crosby Street, invested several thousand dollars in its machinery. The more prosperous firms had a separate indoor drying room, where rods extending from wall to wall near the ceiling were draped with ribbons of dough hardening for two to four days.

Local macaroni-makers began moving beyond the Italian and French communities as consumption of pasta products increased. Antoine Zerega, an Italian born in France, founded the A. Zerega macaroni factory sometime after his arrival in 1848 or 1850. The thirty-two-year-old Zerega had spent years making pasta in Lyons before settling in Brooklyn, and he opened his macaroni factory on Front Street with machinery imported from Europe. For power to turn the rotary mill that rolled the dough he used a horse in the cellar walking in circles. Initially, he had little competition and sold his products mainly to Italian, French, and German clients. Imported pasta, however, was regarded as of better quality, even by native-born Americans, who considered French food (and French immigrants) to be more refined than American ones, although the majority of what was sold, especially outside of Italian neighbor-hoods, was made domestically.

Thirty years after his arrival, Zerega had two steam-powered macaroni presses, including one that was probably "the largest in the United States." The machinery ran continuously because, Zerega told a reporter, "the taste for macaroni is becoming more and more general and the demand in the United States increases year to year."

In 1890 twelve large pasta factories in the New York area employed several hundred men and together produced 10 mil-lion pounds of spaghetti, vermicelli, and other varieties a year. The prejudice against domestic pasta began to fade when tariffs were imposed on imported products in the 1890s to help boost U.S. industry. Production expanded about 200 percent, particularly when suitable gluten-rich wheat began to be grown in the Dakotas. Demand was so high that, for example, sixty men worked sixteen hours a day at V. Savarese & Brothers' macaroni factory in Brooklyn. American-made macaroni was beginning to be hailed as "better and cheaper" than imported pasta and, more important, "cleaner." At the turn of the century there were an estimated one hundred pasta-makers in New York, and some branched out, making egg noodles, which were popular with German and Jewish customers. In Italian neighborhoods the imported variety was preferred, but New York–made pasta must have been very close in taste and texture; it was a common practice for local producers to fill cardboard boxes from Italy with their own pasta, reaping the extra two cents charged for the imported variety.

9

DIRTY BREAD

With a series of sensational investigations in 1880, muckraking reporters revealed that for many food producers, adulteration was part of doing business. In their wake national advertising campaigns began to tout sanitary production of products, standardization, and uniformity. People were confused about the safety of what they were eating. New York's Board of Health, university chemists (many on company payrolls), sanitarians, and outright quacks issued so many contradictory opinions it was enough to make a consumer's head spin. The food-processing industry had vastly expanded since the Civil War. But there was little oversight. Depending on who produced them, products could be either safe or toxic.

Into the 1890s, most immigrant women baked their family's bread at home. If their cramped tenement kitchen didn't have a large enough oven, they paid the local baker to use space in his. "Store bread" was only for emergencies. However, families quickly realized that they could buy inexpensive bread from one of the hundreds of neighborhood bakeries for only a fraction more than the cost of breadmaking ingredients. Most immigrants were likely to find a countryman, a Jewish baker from Hungary or Russia or a Norwegian from Oslo, who spoke their language and made familiar loaves in the cellars of low-rent Lower East Side tenements, where the rent was cheap. Within a short time new arrivals were buying their family's bread just like other New Yorkers. Bread was vital to the neighborhood because it often accounted for half of an immigrant's diet.

Henry S. Levy's bakery at 115 Thames Street in Williamsburg sold dark pumpernickels and big loaves of rye with or without caraway seeds. When he arrived in 1888, Levy brought with him a bit of dough from Russia, a "sour starter" that bakers use for leavening, to keep alive the taste of the shtetl in New York. Elias Gottfried's rye bread had its own special flavor and texture because he fermented it for thirteen hours in wooden troughs in his small Lower East Side bakery. Moses Pechter took out a five-year lease in 1899 to open a bakery at 75 Pitt Street in Manhattan, where rye and egg breads were his specialties. Other bakers made "great twists" of challahs, loaves "sweetened and sprinkled with raisins," or pumpernickel that was "as good, as hard, as digestible and as genuine as any that is baked in Germany." Enormous loaves of Italian breads were sold by the pound in the neighborhoods around Elizabeth and Mulberry Streets. For those who wanted to eat like a native New Yorker, white breads were also available.

In the morning crowds gathered around vendors' pushcarts clamoring for fresh bread. Fresh, but clean? Not so much. The loaves had often been baked in dingy underground bakeries over-

TWO STRIKES

At seven o'clock on a blustery March morning in 1886, fifteen teenage boys gathered on the sidewalk outside the Elizabeth Street entrance to Brinckerhoff's cracker factory. Normally they would have been inside packing crackers, but on this day they stayed outside in the cold, where they formed a committee to declare they were dissatisfied with their pay and hours and "would not return to work until matters were arranged to suit them." The boys, all between thirteen and sixteen years old, had no doubt been influenced by the boycotts, strikes, and demonstrations that laborers in many industries were staging for better pay and working conditions. Thomas Ollive, the president of the cracker factory, found the affair "ridiculous," especially since the boys had never before expressed any discontent and, hired only when needed, worked irregular hours. The boys picketed all day, chasing away teenagers who didn't join and pelting those who crossed their picket line with rocks.

The next day boys from other bakeries met outside Brinckerhoff's and marched about carrying large placards with hand-drawn pictures of hardbread crackers mounted on broomsticks until one o'clock, when the strike abruptly ended. Why? Because Ollive had contacted the strikers' mothers and fathers, who told the boys to stop the "nonsense" and get back on the job. Many of the families depended on the income the boys brought home, no matter how irregular or meager.

The Brinckerhoff boys went back to work without any repercussions, but a strike at the Hetfield and Drucker factory in Brooklyn backfired.

In the competitive cracker business, each piece had to arrive at its destination in good condition. To keep biscuits crisp inside their tins, women wrapped each layer in vegetable-fiber papers that didn't absorb grease. One local factory employed sixty female workers for this task. Large groups of unskilled men and boys were paid by the barrel to package hardier crackers into heavy barrels that held about five hundred pieces.

In 1880, Hetfield and Drucker began receiving complaints about broken crackers. The company discovered that its packers would neatly fill the bottoms of the barrels, then "shovel in a mass of crackers loosely until the barrel was nearly filled" and carefully arrange those sitting on top. C. R. Hetfield and William Drucker established a new protocol: no worker was "allowed to more than half fill a barrel," and only after lunch could a second hand fill the remainder. This was "anything but acceptable" to the packers, whose daily output shrank, and they struck for higher wages. Although Hetfield and Drucker offered a slight increase per barrel, the workers rejected the offer. The bakery then "engaged a number of new hands [to replace them] and they have gone quietly to work."

night, and most customers were unaware of the conditions inside, which a candid baker said were "entirely unfit for the manufacture of wholesome bread." They would, he went on, "lose their appetites altogether . . . if they could go into the shops at night." In 1892 an official from the bakers' union warned that although "consumers like clean, wholesome bread," that wasn't what they were buying. "Unkempt and dirty, because tired and sleepy, the bakers do not feel like washing their hands five times in the course of a night." The union had made little progress in its five-year fight for a ten-hour day; the journeymen bakers in most bakeries still worked twelve to sixteen hours a day, sometimes seven days a week, sweating into the bread alongside the boss baker.

New Yorkers were shocked to learn just how revolting these bakeries were when the *New York Press* ran an 1894 exposé called "Bread and Filth Cooked Together." An 1895 report by the state factory inspector delved deeper and found that the "physical spaces were appalling." Most had "leaky pipes, open sewers, filthy closets [toilets]," clogged sinks, festering puddles, and open sewage. "The men chew, smoke and many use stimulants to brace them" for their grueling night's work. The report described one journeyman baker in an Italian bakeshop, "situated in a cellar in Mulberry Street," who was "required to work nineteen hours a day, seven days a week." This "woe-stricken" man virtually lived in the bakery with four other bakers. The situation was no better in "French, German, or Jewish" cellar bakeries, where depleted bakers were often on call twenty-four hours a day. Before the weekend rush, some worked thirty-six hours straight and got to sleep only while the bread was baking. Their beds were "damp and moldy" mattresses "in a nauseatingly filthy condition." By comparison, flopping down on one of the sacks of flour that filled every spare inch of the tiny spaces was like sleeping on a Sealy Posturepedic.

In the 100-degree heat of the unventilated cellars, the "partially clad" men had "evidence of vermin on their bodies which dropped into the dough underneath." Without any fresh air, they were exposed to "poisonous gases," dust, and flour powder and often developed respiratory and eye diseases, or a repulsive skin ailment, "baker's itch." Their mortality rate was high. With "no fear," rats roamed freely through the bakeries. One inspector described a "dense population of cockroaches, many of them the size of grasshoppers, who, not wanting to be disturbed in their unlimited reign about the oven and water closet, flew at me like birds, and, I can assure you, caused my immediate retreat from that part of the shop." The report termed such bakeries "a disgrace to civilization."

The public demanded reforms. Sensing the shift in opinion, the Journeymen Bakers' and Confectioners' International Union condemned these non-union shops in the *Baker's Journal*. Cynics suspected that the union might have inspired the *Press* exposé. And the union was hardly disinterested when it castigated boss bakers for using the "cheap labor of the green hand from foreign shores." Petrified of losing their jobs, immigrants just off the boat were chary of unions.

The New York State Senate in Albany responded to the mounting indignation by unanimously passing the Bakeshop Act, which mandated a ten-hour workday and a six-day week (owners were exempt and could work as long as they wanted), plus standards for hygiene and sleeping conditions. Passing the act was easy; enforcing it was another matter. Between 1895 and 1897, only eight arrests were made in the state, a few cellar bakeries were closed, and some bakeries received small fines.

The owners treated this toothless law as a threat to their existence. To fight the limitation on the hours their journeymen could work, in 1902 the owners formed the American Master Bakers Association and challenged the act in court. Their test case was a Utica, New York, baker, Joseph Lochner, who had been fined twice for violations. The association argued that the government had no right to tell bakers how to run their businesses. *Lochner vs. New York* was heard before the Supreme Court in 1905. In a decision "still shorthand in

THE HORSE KNOWS THE WAY

In 1898, the year that New York City was incorporated, 2,000 bakeries employed 8,300 bakers to feed the 3,437,000 people of Manhattan, the Bronx, Queens, Brooklyn, and Staten Island, four out of five of whom were either foreign-born or first-generation Americans. Not all bakeries were in a cellar; there were many street-level shops in affluent neighborhoods where native-born New Yorkers predominated. B. F. Smith opened one on Hudson Street in the early 1890s and baked between 3,000 and 8,500 loaves a day to supply the neighborhood (the usual output of cellar bakeries was about 1,700). A standard loaf weighed about 1 pound 3 ounces and sold for a nickel. The baking areas in these shops were generally clean and well ventilated, and most used dough-mixing machines. On Eighth Avenue and 130th Street, ten clerks leaned over the marble counters of the H. S. Ware First-Class Variety Bakery to wait on their "high-class trade." The twenty-year-old bakery had elaborate glass display cases that showcased bread and rolls, loaf and fancy cakes, doughnuts, pies, and the "toothsome dainties" that were the standard fare of New York bakeries.

"Dainties" faced competition from groceries and delicatessens selling packaged cakes, many made by Drake Baking Company, whose first bakery, at 1006 Wallabout Market in Brooklyn, opened in 1896. Newman E. Drake had moved from New Jersey in 1881 and seven years later began selling pound cakes by the slice. The new factory branched out to include marble, citron, and raisin pound cakes as well as other types of cakes. In about 1900 the company built a new factory at 77 Clinton Avenue in Brooklyn and changed its name to Drake Brothers Bakery.

By 1891 the New York Pie Baking Company had become, as its ads said, "the world's largest pie bakers," with 150 people baking the pies in the factory's four buildings on Sullivan Street. A group of twelve pie bakeries, most located in Brooklyn and Manhattan, consolidated in 1898 as the American Pastry and Manufacturing Company. In 1903 the firm built a bakery on East 15th Street that was the height of modernity, using electrical power to run its dough-mixing machinery, lights, and elevators.

Some small bakeries, like David H. Dugan's in Brooklyn, expanded into wholesale operations. Dugan had begun selling bread from a pushcart in Brooklyn as a twenty-year-old in 1878, and after a year, along with his younger brother Edward, moved into a shop on Broadway, where they hung a sign that said HOME BAKING. Dugan soon bought a horse and wagon to take bread and rolls to his customers' doors six days a week. Home delivery became his forte, and his horses grew so familiar with their daily routes that they would stop and start at each house while the driver carried the baked goods to the door. By about 1900, Dugan had roughly 10,000 customers and 700 horses.

constitutional law for the worst sins of subjective judicial activism," attacked by liberal justices like William O. Douglas and by conservatives like William Rehnquist, a closely divided Court ruled for the owners. The Bakeshop Act's provision establishing the ten-hour day and sixty-hour week "violated the liberty of person and freedom of contract . . . of master and employee alike." For "the general right to make a contract in relation to his business is . . . protected by the Fourteenth Amendment to the Constitution." The right to contract was a judicial construct of the age of incorporation, when the business lawyers appointed to the Supreme Court served as the last redoubt of reaction against reform. In a historic 1937 ruling upholding a Washington State minimum wage law, Chief Justice Charles Evans Hughes made the decisive point: "In each case the violation alleged by those attacking minimum wage regulation for women is deprivation of freedom of contract. What is this freedom? The Constitution does not speak of freedom to contract." *Lochner* left the journeyman bakers in the same miserable situation that the Bakeshop Act had been passed to remedy.

In 1911 a state report, "On the Sanitary Conditions of Bakeries in New York," found that conditions in the bulk of the city's small bakeshops hadn't improved since the investigations of 1895. Eight hundred bakers were given physical examinations and 57 percent were found to have tuberculosis or venereal or skin diseases. Descriptions of three bakers from a 1913 survey would churn anyone's stomach: rashes "due to body lice," bronchitis, acne "even on his arms, so that the part that necessarily makes the dough was also infected," and tuberculosis were rampant. The 1911 report did find that wages had risen slightly since the 1895 inquiry, but hours in non-union bakeries "were not less than 12" and bakers often worked all night.

10

CLEAN BREAD

As newspapers and government reports continued to expose filthy conditions in small bakeries, supposedly salubrious factory-made bread was an idea whose time had come. In 1911 the Ward Baking Company announced that it would "supply the people of Greater New York with bread that surpassed all other kinds in quality and purity and above all, in cleanliness." Meanwhile, following the biscuit company model of co-operation, twenty-one factory bakers in seventeen cities between New Orleans and Boston were amalgamated into the New York–based General Baking Company. Their plant was Fleischmann's Vienna Bakery on 81st Street and East End Avenue.

The following year Ward Baking built two six-story bakeries, each with thirty ovens able to produce 250,000 loaves a day. The Bronx unit usurped an entire block; the other, at 800 Pacific Street in Brooklyn, was called "the first sanitary and scientific bakery in America" and a "snow-white temple of bread-making cleanliness."

New factories were built with better ventilation, interiors lined with easy-to-clean tiled surfaces, and woodwork covered in washable white paint. By 1912, 60 percent of the city's bakers worked in such establishments.

Robert B. Ward had been born in New York above his family's bakery on Broome Street in 1851, two years after his father and grandfather had arrived from Ireland. By age eight he had begun helping in the bakery, and during the Civil War he delivered bread around the city. When his father died, his younger brother, George S. Ward, inherited the family bakery, and the two brothers combined forces as R. B. Ward and Co., making sheet cakes and bread, particularly an inexpensive loaf that combined good flour with a coarser grade to make a larger-than-average, "rather dark-colored" bread for "the poorer classes." Within three months of setting up, the Ward Baking Company, as it was now called, was selling "hundreds of thousands of loaves" each day, bread the "human hand never touches." It featured a whole wheat bread, Wheat-Heart; a sweet rye, Kron Prinze; and Cottage Buns; but its bestseller was a white loaf, the brilliantly branded Tip-Top Bread.

"Since the bread was made amid surroundings of spotless cleanliness," Ward's ads claimed, the same standard should apply to its delivery: "horses, harness and stables had no place in the Ward way of delivering the staff of life." The symbols of Ward's modernity and efficiency were the new electric trucks that were making New York's streets cleaner. (As late as the 1890s, New York's 60,000 horses were dropping 1,250 tons of manure and 60,000 gallons of urine on the streets *every day*.) The cabs of the trucks were identical to the old wagons (minus the horse) and were remarkably similar in use. They both had a range of about 10 miles and were easy to start and stop. Even Pechter's bakery on the Lower East

Side bought trucks, and Thomas Alva Edison was watching when the first Edison electric trucks rolled out of their garage. Ward Baking became so enamored of "electric motor vehicles driven by clean-cut, healthy salesmen, uniformed and gloved in white," that it began a division to manufacture trucks in 1914. Robert Ward ran Ward Baking until his sudden death the following year.

Factory-made baked goods were not only "cleaner" than the bread and pastry sold in mom-and-pop bakeries but cheaper. Newman E. Drake ran the largest commercial cake bakery in the Northeast, and his packaged products could be purchased in "thousands of grocery and delicatessen stores in greater New York and vicinity," at "prices within the reach of everybody" and considerably lower than the "prohibitive" prices charged at a local bakery. "Every vestige of dirt or dust" was banished from the factory-made "finished cake." At the new factory at 77 Clinton Avenue, employees were clad in pristine white uniforms and gloves, washed in the bakery's rooftop laundry. Human hands didn't touch the packaged cake until "you take it home," and such was the demand for clean, cheap food that by 1914 Drake Brothers Bakery was cooking 15 tons of pound cake every day.

Unions saw the big bakeries as fertile grounds for organizing, and they were often the targets of strikes. One of the largest began at Fleischmann's factory bakery on 81st Street and East End Avenue in 1910. While the bakers wanted shorter hours and higher wages, the main issue was unionization. Most owners agreed with Otto Fleischmann, the son of the founder of the Vienna Bakery, who said the question was "unarbitratable"; his bakery wouldn't "put [itself] in the hands of the union." On May 2, the first day of the strike, six thousand bakers from several factory bakeries walked out, and they were joined the next day by an additional two thousand. A newspaper headline declared, "Bread Famine Here," although most small bakeshops had ample supplies. Six hundred French bakers, mainly in hotel kitchens, swelled the strike on May 4, joined the following day by two thousand Italian bakers. Citywide, only 10 percent of the factory bakers reported for work.

In a visual and social novelty, women appeared on the picket lines, while others urged neighbors to buy only union-made bread, distinguished by a label on the packaging. The *Tribune* described "a little dot of a German woman, with determined black eyes and two union buttons" pinned onto her dress, which was "badly faded, but very neatly laundered." She had little money and an exhausted and "cross" husband who left for work at three in the afternoon, before his children were home from school, and was asleep when they left in the morning. He got to see them only on Sundays. Despite justified complaints by bakery workers, little progress was made in any area of contention by the time, shortly afterward, the bakers returned to work.

Working conditions were harsh in all the food industries, according to W. Gilman Thompson, a physician who studied occupational diseases. In 1914, New York's "complex modern civilization," involving "the evolution of new machinery and apparatus, new varieties of food and drink, new occupations and habits of life," was causing a variety of physical problems. As vats and mixers grew to industrial scale, they could easily swallow men. Complex machinery—conveyor belts, grinders, generators—could catch a limb or a hank of hair and mangle a worker's body before others could disengage him. Searing steam heat could burn flesh in seconds. Unions might have made such dangerous conditions the subject of collective bargaining, but in decades of protest they had failed to breach the bread industry's wall of resistance.

Hand-packing cookies and crackers at the turn of the century.

Large grocery chains were proliferating. Jones Brothers Tea Company, which opened its first store in New York in 1872, went national, as did the Great American Tea Company, which opened in 1859, selling tea, coffee, and spices. In 1869 the company's name was changed to the Great Atlantic & Pacific Tea Company (A&P), and it also operated a large manufacturing facility in Brooklyn. Every one of these chains stocked Uneeda Biscuits.

The red and gold A&P wagon was a traveling store, selling tea, coffee, and spices in the early 1900s.

The National Biscuit Company's new factory was billed as the most technologically advanced in the country. The complex encompassed the square block bounded by 15th and 16th Streets and Ninth and Tenth Avenues (today the Chelsea Market). To celebrate the opening in February 1904, a luncheon was held for five hundred guests. Afterward they took a tour of the six-story, fireproof building with 21 acres of floor space. The "complicated machinery" had the capacity to produce 6,375,000 biscuits a day, enough to fill 255,000 packages with 25 crackers of each of National's brands: Uneeda Biscuits, Cheese Sandwiches, Butter

FEEDING THE DOUGHBOYS

In July 1917 an army recruiting officer stood outside the Uneeda Biscuit building and exhorted the 1,500 white-suited workers who were hanging out of the windows listening to his pitch to join up. He left with forty-six new army bakers. As employees from all New York's food companies entered the armed forces—eight hundred male Loose-Wiles workers went overseas—women were allowed onto the baking floors for the first time, "steadily increasing their output" and proving both "their efficiency and patriotism." Married women were hired part-time, since they had to "look after their babies and households," and could choose their own hours. At American Sugar Refining, six hundred women, 15 percent of the workforce, were employed in jobs usually reserved for men.

Both National Biscuit and Loose-Wiles were producing truckloads of hardbread for the doughboys. To distinguish this generation of "modern" crackers from the "slabs of concrete" of the Civil War, with a failure of euphemistic imagination the army renamed them "hard bread." Loose-Wiles devoted one third of its production to these crackers, produced mostly by women bakers.

By July 1918, National Biscuit's 15th Street bakery operated three shifts working around the clock and twenty ovens running day and night baking hard bread. An army private in France wrote to the company that his "hard bread is an unsalted white cracker, like Uneeda Biscuit, though smaller, and is put up in cardboard cartons and tin boxes to keep it dry and clean. I have eaten a lot of N.B.C. Hard Bread both up front and behind the lines. Many a time I have

continues

been glad to salvage it from wounded men going back and from the packs of men who have been killed." National's specialty was moisture-proof packaging. Fresh bread absorbed poisonous gases, so the company was asked to devise a new formula for the waterproof paper that went inside a protective tin box to shield the crackers from the nerve gas used by the Germans.

Thin Biscuits, Nabisco Sugar Wafers in vanilla, lemon, orange, chocolate, and mint, ZuZus, and Oysterettes.

The *Chicago Tribune* pronounced the bakery "the largest concern of its kind in the world and the largest manufacturing plant in New York City." The *Herald Tribune* admired its floors, which "were as clean as your dining table," the screened windows to keep out insects, and the filtered water flowing through its pipes. The bakers were clad in "spotless uniforms," and each female employee wore "a full-length overdress." There were showers and lunchrooms for the two thousand workers.

A formidable competitor, Loose-Wiles, a Kansas City baking company, entered New York's biscuit market in 1912. Beginning with a few floors in a building on Hudson Street, within a few years it had built a ten-story building that covered an entire block in Long Island City, a part of the Degnon Terminal complex, an industrial park in a reclaimed marsh. The Thousand Window Bakery, which eventually employed 2,500 people, the majority young women, opened in 1913. It was so big that messengers roller-skated between departments.

Loose-Wiles named its signature crackers "Sunshine" to play up the bakery's light-filled atmosphere. It installed eighty-four ovens on the top floor, an innovation that allowed heat to dissipate through skylights in the roof. The company made 352 different varieties, including Krispy Crackers (the first saltine cracker), Hydrox cookies (introduced in 1908, beating National Biscuit's Oreos by four years), and Tak-Homa (take home a) soda crackers, its answer to Uneeda Biscuits. In the modern bakery, the dough of one variety was mixed in three minutes, then was pressed, stamped, cut, and delivered to a 54-foot oven, undoubtedly "without being touched by human hands." To publicize both its product and its modernity, in 1914 Loose-Wiles topped the building with a 586-foot-long electric sign, the largest in the world, its four thousand light bulbs

A Nabisco worker shows off a 1970s-era Oreo press mold.

blazing LOOSE-WILES SUNSHINE BISCUITS. The sign was visible 7 miles out at sea. (Today the scaffolding holds the letters IDCNY on the rooftop sign.)

The traditional cracker industry shunned the new electric trucks because managers feared that battery odors would permeate the goods. New York's cracker bakers had a long history with their colorfully decorated wagons, an innovative advertising tool when they began to use them thirty years earlier, and like National Biscuit, they resisted abandoning their large fleet of horses. Unencumbered by that equine legacy, Loose-Wiles bought a fleet of twenty-five electric trucks. By 1912 there were 1,400 on the streets and each one, reported a trade magazine, did the work of two horses. By 1916 the number of electric trucks had increased fivefold.

Along with those making crackers, bread, and cake, macaroni-makers increased their use of flour to meet a near-doubling of demand. Half of what was eaten in New York was locally made; the rest was imported from Italy, where wages were low and pasta cheaper to produce. By 1906 imports had put at least thirty smaller firms out of business. Three large factories dominated local production, but they claimed they hadn't made a profit "in years," and by 1909 they successfully lobbied Congress for a one-cent tariff on imported pasta.

The largest domestic producer was Atlantic Macaroni. The company was started in a small factory on Canal Street in 1895 by several partners, including Emanuele Ronzoni. Eleven years old when he arrived from Italy in 1881, as a young man he worked in several of the city's macaroni companies before starting a small company with a partner in 1892. Three years later he joined Atlantic Macaroni, where he long oversaw production. The fully mechanized plant on Vernon Avenue near the Queensboro Bridge, he explained, was thoroughly scrubbed three times a week, and was "the cleanest in the world." During the pasta's weeklong stay in the plant's steam-heated drying room, it was covered and carefully watched to prevent mold, then packed into sealed, airtight boxes.

This description starkly contrasted with a National Consumers League report in 1906 that investigated the sanitary abuses in food production in tenements, which included shoestring pasta-making operations in Italian neighborhoods. A vignette describes macaroni being made in the crowded front room of an apartment during the day, while at night, as it hung drying from every available doorway and window, the space metamorphosed into a sleeping area for the family and their lodgers. The report also included a touching yet unsettling scene of a father making pasta in the front room of an Elizabeth Street tenement while his child lay ill with diphtheria in the back. After tending to his sick daughter, soothing her in his arms, the father went back to the "macaroni machine, pulling the macaroni with his hands, hanging it over racks to dry." The report acknowledged that those struggling in immigrant neighborhoods had scant choice about where they bought their pasta.

These families, however, were eating much more food, including pasta, than ever before. In Italy pasta wasn't an everyday food, but in New York macaroni, spaghetti, or vermicelli was served most days of the week, along with a wider variety of foods and certainly more meat. The National Consumers League report concluded by demanding that everyone, regardless of economic status, have access to cleaner food.

11

"AMONG GREAT INDUSTRIES . . ."

The 1920s were boom years for many New Yorkers, but not for young women employed in the city's factories. Over 82,500 workers were employed in food production in 1924; the number had climbed by 70 percent between 1900 and 1922. Thousands of women toiled in 1,127 food factories, including those that refined half the country's sugar, made one quarter of its chewing gum, a sixth of all its bakery products, and one seventh of its confections. While the local coffee and spice industries had declined over the previous two decades, the companies that remained still ground and roasted 13 percent of the country's products. The three hundred wholesale butchers ranked third in the country's beef-slaughtering industry. Together these companies produced $1.3 million worth of food.

A diary written by Anna Saitta gives a bleak account of her days at the National Biscuit Company, beginning at 7:30 on the morning of June 21, 1928, when, unhappy with her job and in a foul mood, she left her home at 509 East 79th Street. She was miserable that her shoes were "torn, my dress is dirty, shabby," and with "a melancholy look" she deposited her fare in the Second Avenue elevated train's turnstile, thinking "Goodbye my nickel I'll never see you again." After leaving the crowded train she walked down 14th Street and crossed the intersection at Eighth Avenue, where trolley cars fought for space. Automobiles and trucks made the streets treacherous for the horse-drawn wagons leaving National Biscuit's stables on West 15th Street for their morning deliveries.

Turning onto West 15th Street, Anna reached the sprawling Uneeda Biscuit manufacturing complex, where she was an insignificant pebble in a workforce of eight thousand at what she called N.B.C. College. "The heat is terrible," she wrote of that day. "The foreman was every five minutes hollering at us today, because we couldn't work fast. Our fingers were bleeding from the hot crackers that stick to the pans, and nearly every one of us had to go for plaster to the nurse. One girl fainted in Building A."

Lunch was signaled when the wail of the "hot whistles of the National Biscuit Company broke the simmering hush at noon," as F. Scott Fitzgerald wrote in *The Great Gatsby*. Anna had a few minutes to get a breath of fresh air, eat the sandwiches brought from home, and swap stories with her coworkers: "Spanish Mary got fired in spite of the busy season, because she danced the Tango during the lunch hour—lifted up her skirts above her knees—the girls clapped and the men workers hollered. But the foreman, that old joy-killer, came in, and later we heard she got the air."

They were a mixed group. "Jewish Shirley, Irish Gertie, and German Erna," along with "Lithuanian Rose" and "Slovak Mary," spent the nine-hour days discussing their own good-for-nothing boyfriends and the hard-luck romances of others. Most were single; the

Holy Grail for most female factory workers was marriage, because women in almost all ethnic groups stopped working outside the home once married. A wife would work alongside her husband if he owned a shop or business, or take in piecework, but rarely would she continue in a factory.

According to Anna's diary, her coworkers didn't get along well and, their cultures clashing, spent much of the time arguing. On that day Shirley and Gertie were embroiled in a fight about religion.

Anna's account picked up two days later on Friday, June 23, when the "forelady" told Anna, "You'll work in the Ninth Avenue building today . . . across the street." With thirty-five other girls, all in "uniforms, white caps, and we all look alike," Anna walked to the second building. Employers believed that the incessant chatter of female workers slowed them down, so the foreman yelled, "Dry up there, stop your babbling, less talking and more work. What the hell is this, a picnic or a factory?" Later he lit into them again: "Girls, I want you to stop your noise. You understand! All the work is broken—don't break so many crackers." The saving grace was that it was Friday, the end of the week. "Girls, tomorrow no work," Anna said, although no one needed to be reminded that Saturday work had been eliminated earlier that month. "This afternoon, we received our little but well-deserved wages, $14. Again to the machine to pick up the hot crackers, sweating and quarrelling as usual with the men workers because they put too much work on, and before we get our wages, the foreman is always snooping around telling us to work faster or we will get canned today. Gertie was cursing, she said she would spit in the jaw of the foreman next time he said something to her."

Crackers had their best year ever in 1920, thanks to returning doughboys who had gotten used to eating biscuits. Industry executives, however, saw room for growth: per capita consumption came to only 20 boxes of Uneeda Biscuits, or 500 crackers, a year. Both National Biscuit and Loose-Wiles knew that the best way to add new customers was to turn the city's immigrants into American consumers, or, as National Biscuit delicately termed it, to take the "foreigner" the "rest of the way." In 1922, of New York City's 6 million residents, a third were foreign-born. It had the largest Italian community in the United States. Seventy percent of New Yorkers were Catholic, and a third were Jewish. There were substantial German and Irish populations, 150,000 African Americans, and communities of Puerto Ricans, Greeks, Chinese, Poles, Turks, Czechoslovakians, Norwegians, Romanians, and a multitude of others. One grocery that sold to "various alien races" said that "Uneeda Biscuits were a sort of springboard which starts them on the way to Americanize their buying habits." A good route was through their children. National Biscuit supplied classrooms in local schools with miniature cracker departments identical to those in grocery stores, which included cash registers, play money, and small packages of sixty of its products. Accustomed to eating crackers in school, the kids nagged their parents to buy them for the home. To National Biscuit, eating crackers made them real Americans.

The cracker firms also helped their employees become Americans. After work, between five and six p.m., National Biscuit held Americanization classes: English classes taught by Board of Education teachers that included reading and writing, plus classes in geography, U.S. history, government, and "inspirational" subjects. On completion of the course the students filled out citizenship papers.

Both cracker giants catered to immigrants with special products. National Biscuit began producing matzoh in 1922, but its executives didn't think the "light and delicate as gossamer" cracker should be confined to "people of any class or creed" but should be eaten by all, at any time. They suggested serving it with Welsh rarebit, a combination to horrify a rabbi.

Loose-Wiles was more serious about creating a special market. After being approached by the Union of Orthodox Jewish Congregations of America, it established a kosher department in its New York bakery in 1925. No lard was used, and a rabbi was always on hand to supervise. The first product was a kosher version of Tak-Homa soda crackers, and its red-and-white label had a prominent Star of David and a pledge by the Union, in both English and Yiddish, that it was "kosher in every respect." Mainstream manufacturers who didn't want to offend their non-Jewish customers soon began using a series of small letter symbols to discreetly denote kosher food.

When it came to matzoh, the cracker behemoths had stiff competition from the well-established Jewish bakers. Horowitz and Margareten was grossing "millions of dollars" and baking so much matzoh—and after 1927 so many noodles—that it went through 45,000 barrels of flour annually (compared to 50 during its first year, 1891).

In 1925 the *Times* announced, "Bread Takes Its Place Among Great Industries": technology had finally conquered all stages of the breadmaking process. Machinery could sift, knead, rise, and proof the dough and pack the finished loaf. No whiff of hyperbole now attached to the claim "untouched by human hands." Along with mechanization, consolidation was the big trend in the industry. The largest was the formation of the General Baking Company, spearheaded by William B. Ward, who spent three years assembling the constituent companies.

William had run Ward Baking Company's Bronx factory until 1912, when he struck out on his own to form the Rochester-based United Bakeries Corporation. By 1922 that company operated forty bakeries in thirty cities, including New York, where it had acquired the twelve factories owned by the Schults bakery in Brooklyn, the largest wholesale bakery in the metropolitan area, with one thousand bakers. Its Cream Bread was delivered daily to 500,000 families.

When Ward completed the formation of the General Baking Company, it included three of the country's four largest bakery conglomerates: Ward Baking Company, with 18 bakeries in 14 cities

Shults electric bread delivery truck, 1910.

and the marquee brand Tip-Top Bread; Continental Baking Company, which had acquired United Bakeries for a total of 106 bakeries in 80 different cities, with Wonder Bread; and the 33 bakeries in 25 cities of New York–headquartered General Baking Company and its brand Bond Bread. General Baking's consolidation now controlled 20 percent of the bread market.

General Baking's factory in the Bronx could bake 5,000 loaves an hour. After machines had prepared and shaped the dough, each loaf was mechanically transferred to a movable tray that carried it through the ovens. Machines then cooled and sliced the loaves before another apparatus wrapped them in wax paper. A reporter visiting the bakery was surprised that "inside the whirring plant" it was "deserted." "Occasionally, here and there, a man or woman employee turns a handle or inspects the process or gives a push or poke, but they all seem incidental." He surmised that the "plant nearly runs itself," which wasn't actually the case, though the number of workers had indeed declined with mechanization.

The same reporter went on to admire the way "scientists constantly watch food values and calories to protect the health of the public they serve." Ward made "super-bread Vitovim, a creamy white wheat bread" packed with vitamins A and B and minerals, as nutritional science entered food processing and advertising. The company's ad read: "Ward's Vitovim Bread: The Key to Good Health," and each loaf came with a key on the wrapper.

William Ward intended to buy up even more companies, but in 1926 the Justice Department found that the megacompany had broken antitrust laws, and General Baking was dissolved.

Outside of Ward's conglomerate, another large New York baking concern was Purity Bakeries Corporation, which ran 9 plants

A GENTLEMAN

In 1920, as New York took its place as the capital of the twentieth century, Thomas Ollive, the grand old man of the National Biscuit Company, died at the age of eighty-five. In the preceding years his old-fashioned muttonchops had turned white, but he was still a tall, distinguished-looking man. While going into the office less frequently, he continued to fulfill his duties as a vice president, director, and member of the company's Executive Committee. He had witnessed momentous changes over his seventy years in the cracker industry. Thomas Ollive had reached the top of his field, successfully navigating the transformation of the food industry from shop to factory and ascending to the heights of a national corporation, something few men in his occupation—or his generation—accomplished, all while remaining every inch a gentleman.

and 186 retail stores in the New York area. Lewis A. Cushman Jr., son of one of the founding brothers of Cushman Sons, Inc., formed Purity in 1924. In 1922 Cushman's stores had begun selling "Grade A" bread, which they advertised as higher in "protein food value" than ten other New York breads. A "million New Yorkers" tasted the bread on its first day.

Bread had become "a filler-in instead of the basis of every meal," as the American palate expanded to include a wider variety of food. People at all economic levels were eating many more fruits and vegetables, as large companies devised better methods of freezing, canning, shipping, and advertising these foods. The increased use of dairy products meant more cheese on plates and milk in glasses. People cut back on potatoes, grains, and bread. As work became more sedentary, Americans generally began to eat less. With slimmer silhouettes becoming stylish, women tried to adapt their bodies to the thin, boyish flapper look that was all the rage in the 1920s. Dieting was in vogue, and the food industry had to adapt.

Yet not everyone was dieting, to judge by sales of coffeecakes, muffins, crullers, and sweet and raisin breads often topped with glazed sugar. One large bakery made thirty-six different pastries. In 1923 a merger of the Wagner Pastry Company of Newark with the Brooklyn firms Jochum Brothers and Consumer's Pie and Baking Company formed Wagner's Pastries Inc. As a result of the merger, the two Brooklyn firms moved to a large factory in Long Island City and began using the Mrs. Wagner brand name.

In 1929 Loose-Wiles changed the sign on top of its building to read SUNSHINE BISCUITS, the bright red *S* and *B* contrasting with the yellow of the other letters, which stretched over a 383-foot span (20 feet longer than a football field). A smaller sign facing Manhattan outlined the company name in red, yellow, and green. The light of both equaled 8,700 25-watt-bulbs and was visible 15 miles out to sea, its glow used for navigation by the ships in the East River and as a beacon for pilots at local airports.

12

"BROTHER, CAN YOU SPARE
A DOUGHNUT?"

n the hot summer of 1931, special fans blew the mouthwatering aromas of frying doughnuts over the crowds gathered outside a storefront window on Broadway and West 45th Street. According to *The New Yorker*, people stood mesmerized as puffs of dough "float dreamily through a grease canal in a glass-enclosed machine" in the new contraption in the window of the Mayflower Doughnut Shop. The five-cent doughnuts popping out of the machine at a rate of 480 per hour were within the reach even of those with only a few pennies to spare, which, in that Depression year, included many in threadbare white flannel sports jackets and frayed, frilly sleeveless dresses watching the pastries "walk dreamily up a moving ramp, and tumble dreamily into an outgoing basket."

When Adolph Levitt invented the doughnut machine eleven years earlier, New York had been on top of the world, the vibrant center of modernity, where everything, including its doughnut

Summer afternoon crowd, National Headquarters Mayflower Doughnuts, 45th Street and Broadway.

machines, was bigger, faster, and more up-to-date than anywhere else. The crash of 1929 had slowed the pace of business to a crawl.

During the first few years of the Depression, grocery sales had leveled off, with luxury items the first to be scratched off shopping lists. Sales of expensive cookies declined to about a quarter of National Biscuit business, while crackers, particularly soda and graham crackers, seemed Depression-proof. Several independent bakers made lower-priced, poorer-quality crackers, and both Loose-Wiles and National Biscuit responded: three boxes of Uneeda sold for a dime, whereas only a few years earlier one had gone for a nickel.

National Biscuit expanded in the early 1930s, although most changes were in the works before the crash. The company bought Wheatsworth Inc., makers of whole wheat crackers, and in 1931 Milk-Bone dog biscuits, taking over its recently built seven-story bakery at 444 East 10th Street, between Avenues C and D, which tripled the bakery's capacity. It also completed renovating a new headquarters at 449 West 14th Street, in a building bought from the American Can Company that spanned the block through to 15th Street and was decorated with wood-paneled offices, well-stuffed chairs, and large, plush oriental rugs covering highly polished floors. A pedestrian bridge several stories above the street connected the offices to the bakeries.

National Biscuit demolished the original bakery built by the New York Biscuit Company on the southeast corner of 16th Street and Tenth Avenue to erect a building that allowed trains on the newly built elevated freight route (today's High Line) to roll inside. The railway replaced the tracks that ran along Tenth Avenue, known as Death Avenue for its incidents of fatal accidents. The new tracks could facilitate the one thousand rail cars that arrived at National Biscuit each month to deposit the flour, butter, sugar, spices, and nuts used in hundreds of products. Baked and boxed, the products filled the empty rail cars to be shipped across the country, where they accounted for 50 percent of all the crackers eaten in America. Independent bakeries sold the other 35 percent, and Loose-Wiles the remaining 15 percent.

In the grim spring of 1934, simmering anger at National Biscuit came to a head as two thousand struck. The incident was settled amicably, according to the company, but it was just a prelude to another strike, which began on January 9, 1935, when three

MATZOHS IN COURT

In 1930, Rabbi Moses Weinberger charged Horowitz and Margareten and B. Manishewitz with restraint of trade, claiming that his jobber, the man selling his matzoh to grocery stores, was being strong-armed into being an exclusive dealer for the two large firms. He also charged that about a month before Passover began they had colluded on the price of matzoh.

Regina Margareten's sons, Frederick and Jacob, were now both vice presidents of the firm. Frederick also served as treasurer of the Associated Matzoh Bakers of America, a trade group whose three largest members included their firm, B. Manishewitz of Cincinnati, and New York's A. Goodman and Sons. Together they were believed to control 85 percent of the matzoh market.

Rabbi Weinberger had been hand-making matzoh at a small shop since 1916, at first with a partner, Aron Streit, though Streit left in 1925 and with his two sons opened a more modern and profitable machine-made matzoh factory on the first floor of a rented building at the corner of Rivington and Stanton Streets. Streit was so successful—customers lined up around the block at Passover—that the police needed to control traffic, so the company soon needed more room and purchased the Rivington Street building plus three adjoining properties.

The trial initiated by Rabbi Weinberger against Horowitz and Margareten and B. Manishewitz lasted about a week. On the final day, samples of the various brands of matzoh were brought into the courtroom to determine their similarities. A long morning ensued during which the judge sampled crackers until the jury, who took what matzoh remained, finally retired to deliberate. The jury ended up deadlocked and the case was dismissed, but their unanimous opinion was that all the matzoh had been very tasty, and before they were discharged they ate every last crumb.

thousand National Biscuit Company workers—almost the entire workforce (reduced from an earlier eight thousand)—in sympathy with fellow workers in Philadelphia again walked off the job. National Biscuit's management claimed to be "in the dark," saying they thought workers were "eminently satisfied with their conditions of employment and their scale of wages."

After eleven days of picketing the factory, 2,800 of the striking workers staged a huge parade up Eighth Avenue to 86th Street to make their cause known to the public. They also protested at local grocery stores to dissuade shoppers from buying the company's products. Their slogan: "Until the strike is done, U-Don't-Needa biscuit!"

Only two days after the peaceful parade on Eighth Avenue, fights erupted between the picketers, strikebreakers, and police and the wail of police sirens and ambulances could be heard above the chants of strikers. Over the next two weeks "sluggings, stabbings, and broken heads" were reported in the blocks surrounding the factory. The neighborhood was a "war zone"; each night the precinct jails bulged with angry strikers. In the weeks that followed, mass demonstrations, skirmishes, and arrests continued.

Even though the strike lasted ninety-five days, New York was never in danger of running short of crackers; supplies from non-union bakeries in other parts of the country were shipped in and other cracker bakeries, including Loose-Wiles, kept operating. In April the trade press reported that after a yearlong slump, biscuit sales had begun to pick up.

When the strike ended on April 29, employees expected to return to work. The "immediate needs" of the company, however, dictated the number of people hired. Later statistics compiled by the union revealed that only one thousand of the original 3,000 striking workers were rehired, with women hit the hardest. Wages remained at prestrike levels and in some cases were cut.

Many sought an escape from their troubles at the movies. Bert Weil of Devon Bakery loved going to the movies, but "for years I was disturbed by people sitting next to me and cracking peanut shells whenever the movie got good, like Joan Crawford walking out on Clark Gable or something. Suddenly the idea came to me— why not a cracker guaranteed to be absolutely silent." He devised Kracker Nuts, a nut surrounded with a cracker instead of a shell, and packaged it in small cellophane bags, just right for eating quietly in the dark, but also in tins "for the harried but discriminating hostess." This, he thought, would be Devon Bakery's biggest seller. He was wrong.

He and his wife opened the bakery in the early 1930s after his knitwear business went under, leaving him with $500. In telling the story, Weil said that the bakery cost $450 and they blew the remainder on a celebratory dinner at Delmonico's. Weil's Devon Bakery eventually became famous not for Kracker Nuts but for Melba Toast, a delicate cracker originated by the esteemed French chef August Escoffier for the opera singer Dame Nellie Melba. Marjorie Weil loved the crackers and struggled to devise a way to make them without having the edges of the very thinly sliced bread curl up as it was toasted. Her grandson explained: "Margie solved the problem. She sliced the bread thinly and baked it in the oven with her own heavy clothes iron on top. The toast stayed flat, and could be wrapped, boxed and shipped to stores and restaurants."

By 1932, Bert Weil had devised and patented machinery that could do the same job as his wife's iron. The Weils turned the product into a "big seller" by giving a Bulova watch to any storeowner who ordered them, and started a publicity campaign that touted Melba Toast as a diet food. By 1937, Melba Toast had become synonymous with weight loss and was sold up and down the eastern seaboard. The company name was changed to Devonsheer Melba Company, and it moved to a factory in West New York, New Jersey, where it employed 150 people. Two years later the Weils introduced Melba Toast Rounds, which became even more popular.

While crackers and snacks seemed to gain in popularity, bread was becoming less of a staple, though it remained a large and prosperous industry. In 1932, Brooklyn alone employed 6,200 men and 124 women in breadmaking. Sliced bread had been introduced in 1928, and the white version outsold whole wheat six to one. Wonder Bread was made in the Jamaica factory of Continental Baking Company, built by the Schults Bread Company in 1906. One baker estimated that 6 million rolls—frankfurter, hard, Vienna, and seeded—were sold each week. Still, pasta was pushing bread off the tables of struggling families, especially after the macaroni-makers' trade association, along with flour millers, launched a $1.3 million ad campaign to tell cash-strapped consumers how healthful their product was. Production had increased 100 percent in the fifteen years since the start of World War I, and spaghetti was a dinner staple even before it became a necessity for filling bellies in lean economic times.

ROSIE THE BAKER

On April 27, 1942, the enormous Loose-Wiles Sunshine Biscuit sign went dark. The friendly beacon had been shut down to prevent its lights from guiding German submarines into the harbor. Yet local cracker factories were working at a record pace making enormous quantities of the rations needed in World War II. Loose-Wiles employed at least two thousand workers, mostly women, at its Long Island City bakery, where approximately 25 percent of production was set aside for the nutritionally balanced ration or defense biscuits, scientifically configured to contain concentrated calories for optimal nutrition. National Biscuit Company's four thousand workers, also mainly women, devoted the same share of production to ration biscuits, as did many smaller, independent biscuit companies. By the time the war ended, National Biscuit and Loose-Wiles had sold a total of $90 million worth of biscuits to the armed forces. While the American military was the best-fed fighting force in World War II, one soldier resonantly commented that it "took a hungry man to eat the orange-colored biscuits."

At National Biscuit a specially trained group of women packed the hermetically sealed cans of K rations that were used during continuous combat. These came in several varieties, including one that contained five biscuits made by National Biscuit and Loose-Wiles, packages of instant coffee supplied by one of three local companies, three cubes of sugar from one of Brooklyn's refineries, and a handful of hard candy from New York's Henry Heide Candy (which received four Navy "E" awards for outstanding achievement in war production) or Huyler's Candy, whose executive John S.

Swersey, as a consultant to the army quartermaster general, helped to develop the ration packages.

The biscuit companies continued to make their usual consumer products, although wartime shortages of key ingredients—not only sugar and fats but also cartons and workers—meant there were fewer crackers. Nevertheless, consumer consumption didn't slow down. Indeed, per capita consumption of crackers in 1944 was twice that of 1939 (these figures included government purchases of "more than 250 million packages of crackers and cookies" sent to army post exchanges).

Driving up cracker sales were purchases made by the time-pressed women who filled the jobs vacated by men at war. Many spent the days and nights in overalls building ships and packing ammunition, but women also drove milk delivery trucks or worked in bakeries, refineries, and other food industries. As salaries rose, women had more money in their pockets, though there was little to spend it on other than food. Although the taste of the crackers and cookies made during the war did not match that of peacetime products, they could easily be used for piecrusts or in other baking preparations once sugar rationing went into effect (supply was limited owing to the Japanese), and many exhausted women were willing to splurge on extras to get dinner on the table quickly.

The cost of feeding a family had risen 25 percent by 1943, which resulted in strikes for higher wages by bakers, sugar refinery workers, and biscuit-makers. Still, wartime regulations held prices for bread products at low levels. As the war continued, the bulk of the wheat harvested in America went to feed the troops;

continues

reduced supplies were allotted to bakers, and availability was erratic. Sometimes bread was easy to buy; sometimes it was in short supply.

Large factory bakeries, like Continental and the General Baking Company, could weather the restrictions, but it was more difficult for small baking companies, which felt the pinch, and some simply had to close. The Brown Bomber Baking Company, a three-and-a-half-year-old, black-owned bakery on Prospect Avenue in the Bronx, cited "the increasing labor shortage and problems acquiring materials due to the war program" as the reason it shut its doors in 1943. The bakery was named for the prizefighter Joe Louis (it used his nickname, but "he wasn't involved in the bakery"). The "100% Negro owned and operated" bakery had been opened by Macy Mac O'Neal in 1939, although the publishers of the *Amsterdam News* soon bought into the company and took control. The paper reported that with its ninety-two employees, it was the largest African American–owned bakery in the country. It had twenty-four trucks making deliveries to four hundred restaurants and lunchrooms around the city, and in one week in 1943, the paper reported, the company sold 65,000 dozen rolls. Not bad, but not enough to survive during the war years.

New Yorkers were in luck that noodles, macaroni, and spaghetti were in good supply at "fairly reasonable" prices. In 1941, La Rosa Macaroni sold about 1 million pounds of pasta a week, 40 percent of it in Brooklyn, the rest distributed as far west as Chicago. The company had seen a 15 percent rise in sales each year because, according to its publicists, macaroni was "fast becoming an American dish," especially during the days of rationing.

By 1939 the La Rosa Macaroni Company was New York's largest producer, with 300 workers manufacturing an estimated $4 million worth of pasta. The company had added a factory in Connecticut nine years earlier, but most of its product was made in New York. After founder Vincenzo La Rosa's death in 1936 the business was run by his five sons, and sales continued to mount throughout the decade. Atlantic Macaroni, with 250 workers, was the second largest local producer, with the Ronzoni Macaroni Company in third place. In 1938 its 200 workers turned out about 12 million pounds of macaroni, and it was planning an ad campaign to take on its competitors.

Although many people cut back on costly pies, cakes, and cookies in the 1930s, industrial goodies fared better than those made in small bakeshops. In 1932, Drake's Bakery, which had been bought out by Ward Baking Company, had fifty-seven drivers delivering products throughout the region. Adolph Levitt's doughnuts, billed as "the food hit of the Century of Progress" at the 1934 World's Fair in Chicago, were priced for the times at fifteen cents a dozen. Levitt, a Russian-born Jewish immigrant, first made doughnuts by hand in a small Broadway shop, but he knew that speed and mass production were the way to a fortune. After inventing the "Wonderful Almost Human Doughnut Machine," he founded the Doughnut Machine Company in 1920. During his first year in business from his warehouse in Brooklyn he sold 128 machines to shops across the country, and it was estimated that the company was making an estimated $25 million a year. It also manufactured standardized mixes for the machines, so that any baker could turn out a perfectly uniform "light, puffy product."

Levitt's Mayflower Doughnut Shop in Times Square was the first link in the country's pioneer doughnut chain. The name was changed to the Doughnut Corporation of America, and the company continued to expand its line of machinery and products. At the 1939 World's Fair, held in Flushing Meadows in Queens, it expected to sell 20 million doughnuts. Another food-related highlight of the fair was the Wonder Bread pavilion, its exterior configured to look like a polka-dotted Wonder Bread wrapper.

13

EXODUS

The Stella D'Oro Biscuit Company, a small family-run factory in the Bronx, was changing rapidly in the 1950s. Early in the decade many small firms were moving beyond their local neighborhoods to reach a wider market. Anything seemed possible. In the late 1940s, Joseph Kresivich, a native of Trieste, Italy, opened a new Stella D'Oro factory three blocks from the original bakery in the Kingsbridge section, which he had started in 1932 with his wife, Angela, and where they baked anisette cookies, breadsticks, biscuits, and biscotti for the local Italian community. After the war the cookies and breadsticks caught on with dieters, a growing consumer group eager to buy products that cut calories. Stella D'Oro did not, however, spare the calories in their Swiss Fudge cookies, which enjoyed a large and loyal Jewish following because they were made without milk or butter and thus were kosher.

Stella D'Oro's European-style baked goods were not very sweet and were geared toward adult tastes. In the new factory the company's workers (who joined the 98,000 other New Yorkers who, as late as the 1950s, were manufacturing all types of food) could produce larger quantities to supply the many new customers. By midcentury, even though the sons and daughters of immigrants were leaving the old neighborhoods for other parts of the city or the suburbs, they had not left the tastes of their childhood behind. Over the decade Stella D'Oro products, like other ethnic specialties, appeared on more and more greater New York supermarket shelves.

The trend toward eating less bread continued in postwar America. Higher incomes and increased spending power allowed for more varied purchases, and with all the processed products beckoning from the supermarket shelves and freezers, bread had new competition. And new troubles.

The factory bread industry was roiled by labor issues throughout the 1950s. Helped by the New Deal, unions had finally organized big bread. Two large strikes were averted in the first two years of the decade, when, in one of their first real victories in three hundred years, bakery workers won a five-day workweek. By then most of the 22,000 New Yorkers making bakery products were union members, and the Bakery and Confectionery Workers numbered 2,500 members working in 9 of the city's largest companies. A two-week strike in 1954 won them further wage increases.

During the early 1950s wheat prices were rising. The causes were varied. The United States was sending wheat to war-ravaged countries, and bread bakers faced competition from macaroni-makers, whose preferred durum wheat, decimated by disease and bad weather, was in short supply. By mid-decade prices for shortenings had risen almost 100 percent. S. B. Thomas was the first bakery to increase the price of its bread, and all the other manufacturers soon followed. Drake's Bakery, one of the largest companies devoted exclusively to cake baking, discontinued several types of doughnuts in the 1950s. It was narrowing its line to those varieties that weren't too expensive to make and "developing items we can live with." Its main plant was at 77 Clinton Street in Brooklyn, but it also built two factories outside the city. That was a sign of things to come.

In the 1950s, Jewish rye and bagels, Danish pumpernickel, Norwegian grisle, Irish soda bread, Swedish limpa, and German Kaiser rolls, plus hearth-baked bread, were all made in automated factories by small specialty bakers in neighborhoods mainly scattered throughout Brooklyn. After closing its original bakery in Manhattan, the Pechter Baking Company bought a former Ward Baking plant at 800 Pacific Street, between Vanderbilt and Carlton Avenues in Brooklyn, in 1953. It opened additional plants in the Bronx and Westchester County and ran the Harrison Baking Company in New Jersey. Pechter made dark, heavy ryes and pumpernickels, white bread, Kaiser rolls, egg bread, layer cakes, bialys, and bagels. Hard to believe, but bagels were still considered exotic fare. In an article about a strike at the factory in 1957, the *New York Times* assumed Gentile readers had never seen a bagel before, describing it as "a kind of hard roll with a hole in the center."

The Larsen Baking Company had opened in 1900 in Red Hook to make grisle, a sour rye bread baked in an oven with bonfires on each side that gave the crust a smoky flavor and made the bakers look "like coal miners." The smoky flavor was sacrificed when the bakery automated and the dough was baked with steam heat. In the 1950s the bakery made a wide variety of Norwegian breads and cakes, but as with many ethnic bakeries, demand for grisle was dwindling as the neighborhoods changed. By the end of the

THE QUEEN PASSES

In 1953, Horowitz and Margareten sold out its Passover production during the hectic week leading up to the holiday as "people come in cars from all over the city to the bakery to buy 'hot' matzohs." One of the family explained, "Everyone expects them fresh from the griddle." This was still a family-run business, and "children and grandchildren and great-grandchildren" were expected to pitch in during the Passover rush. The ninety-year-old matriarch, Regina Margareten, still made daily visits to the block-long Long Island City plant. She rarely sat at her glass-topped desk, because she was too busy overseeing every stage of the baking process.

In 1945 she had been instrumental in making the decision to move Horowitz and Margareten from the Lower East Side to the larger Long Island City plant. In truth the company hadn't had much choice; the old neighborhood had been condemned to make way for a housing project, part of mayor Fiorello La Guardia's plan to build a more modern and efficient city. The company's employees followed it to the new factory; they were family. "My people have been with me for years, and many of their children work here now," Regina said. "In fact, I'm godmother to about twenty-five and have attended many of their weddings."

As a grandmotherly businesswoman and the company spokesperson, Regina made an annual radio broadcast during Passover in the 1940s and 1950s. First she gave a Yiddish greeting, which she would repeat in English "for the sake of the children who may be listening in." In 1952, in her final talk, she thanked the United

decade most of Larsen's business was in cakes, sweet breads, and
green soda bread for Saint Patrick's Day.

As the 1950s came to a close, it was clear that for the largest
factories there were greener pastures than New York City. Like
many corporations, National Biscuit had gone on a building spree
following the war, when it could finally begin construction after
years of pent-up desire to expand. But National's New York complex, "the largest cracker bakery in the world," wasn't included in
the nine factories around the country that the company renovated
during the 1950s. Multistory structures couldn't house advanced
machinery—they had become obsolete.

The first National Biscuit plant to leave New York was Hills Brothers Dromedary Dates near the Brooklyn entrance to the Brooklyn
Battery Tunnel. The complex of fourteen buildings was deemed
outmoded, and production was moved to a plant in upstate New
York almost 300 miles away. For the four hundred employees,
mostly women, it might as well have been Tibet.

The National Biscuit compound in Manhattan—New York's largest factory, which included 7 acres between 14th and 16th Streets
and Ninth and Eleventh Avenues, multiple bakery buildings, railroad and pedestrian bridges, a cafeteria seating 500, a research
lab for 125, plus a huge parking garage on 14th Street—was sold

in 1956. But before National closed shop, hardbread crackers had one last role to play in the city where they had been invented. In 1957, New York's government amassed stores of crackers made by National Biscuit on 15th Street. It was the height of the Cold War, a period when both government agencies and private citizens bought "survival crackers" to stock fallout shelters in the event of a nuclear attack. A cache of 352,000 crackers was packed in airtight containers under the Brooklyn Bridge and forgotten, only to be discovered in 2006 during a routine structural inspection. An official who sampled the forty-nine-year-old crackers said they "tasted like cardboard."

The company was moving to a new location in Fair Lawn, New Jersey, about 12 miles north of the George Washington Bridge. Its 40 acres could accommodate a sleek horizontal factory where the operations would be performed by the latest automated machinery, including a new "electronic brain" that could direct a myriad of ingredients in sixteen giant mixing machines. Machine-driven systems would handle many of the tasks performed on standardized production lines, making New York's large pool of skilled workers unnecessary. National Biscuit's corporate offices stayed in the city, moving into a newly constructed skyscraper at 435 Park Avenue.

The company and its executives were welcome in the suburban community, but its workers were not. Maxwell Lehman, the deputy city administrator, reported that the "feeling in Fair Lawn as in other communities [is] that the type of worker who would come out of New York was 'not wanted.'" The mayor declared that the town "welcomes all who can find a home." But that was just a politic way of saying the same thing, as most of the towns in the adjacent areas had banned the building of apartments or "look-alike" tract housing. The mayor did concede that "many workers might find it economically difficult to obtain homes priced within their budgets." As there was nowhere affordable for the New York employees to live, in the end the "great majority" of workers in the new National Biscuit plant already lived in New Jersey.

Some companies supplied buses to ferry their workers to far-off factories. That option usually petered out. Many just couldn't afford to make the time-consuming commute. When a factory relocated to a distant state, moving was out of the question. The hard truth was that companies were happy to shed their New York workers, most of whom, organized in labor's New Deal banquet years, were paid a union wage.

III

SUGAR

14

THE HEADLESS HELMSMAN

The early 1800s were good years for New York food exporters. War in Europe, where Napoleon was confronting a shifting coalition of nations led by Britain, buoyed American trade. This lucrative neutrality ended in 1805, after Admiral Horatio Nelson destroyed the French fleet at Trafalgar and the British mounted a blockade that shut American commerce out of French-held ports on the continent. Then, to crew its busy frigates, the Royal Navy stopped American ships and impressed—seized—American sailors. Especially galling to New Yorkers was an incident off Sandy Hook in April 1806. The *Leander,* a sixty-gun British frigate, fired a warning shot across the bow of an American schooner, the *Richard,* suspected of harboring deserters from the Royal Navy. The *Richard* hove to, but the *Leander* fired two more shots, one of which decapitated the *Richard*'s helmsman. His headless corpse was displayed at the Tontine Coffee House, which inflamed feelings against the British. A "prodigious mob—huzzaing" seized the boats the *Leander* had sent into port for supplies and gifted their contents to the almshouse. A few months later a crowd of dockers and sailors forcibly stopped six British deserters from being sent back to their ship.

As such incidents multiplied, President Thomas Jefferson acted to check the drift toward another war with Britain by banning all exports and thus keeping American ships and sailors out of harm's way. It was, one critic wrote, an effort to "cure the corns by cutting off the toes."

Signed into law three days before Christmas 1807, the Embargo Act ended the prosperity New York had enjoyed since independence. With the port shut down, soup kitchens were opened to feed hungry idle sailors and stevedores. Returning from abroad in April 1808, a New Yorker found the city "gloomy and forlorn . . . Not a box, bale, cask, barrel, or package was to be seen upon the wharfs . . . Instead of sixty or a hundred carts that used to stand in the street for hire, scarcely a dozen appeared, and they were unemployed."

No national policy would so damage New York's food industry as the "Dambargo," which cut exports by 80 percent in one year (smuggling accounted for most of the remaining 20 percent). The city of plenty would not soon forget the sight of six thousand men lined up at the almshouse for bread. The embargo won no friends for Jefferson in New York. Nor did it prevent war, in 1812, with Britain.

When that war finally ended, "the door of the concert-room was thrown open and in rushed a man breathless with excitement," a witness at City Hall that February evening in 1815 recalled. "He mounted on a table and swinging a white handkerchief aloft, cried out 'Peace! Peace! Peace!' . . . I rushed into the street, and oh, what a scene! In a few minutes thousands and tens of thousands of people were marching about with candles, lamps, torches, making the street appear like a gay and gorgeous procession."

With peace New Yorkers began to eat well again. In 1820, Mr. Cobbett, the British traveler writing in the *American Farmer*, was astonished by the profusion of luxuries in the city. "Tea, sugar, coffee, spices, chocolate, cocoa" were "so cheap as to be within the reach of everyone." Cobbett was particularly struck by the low cost of chocolate, "a *treat* for the *rich*, in England," but so reasonable in New York that it was "used even by negroes." Considering that New York did not abolish slavery until 1827, he meant "used even by *slaves*."

Sugar in New York was indissolubly associated with the name Roosevelt. In 1783, when the last British troops boarded ships for home, patriots such as Isaac Roosevelt and his twenty-three-year-old son James, the great-grandfather of FDR, returned to the city after years of serving with George Washington's army. Wending their way through garbage-strewn streets, they were stunned by the desolation. East of Broadway two terrible fires had left walls of gutted buildings "cast[ing] grim shadows upon the pavement." Churches and public buildings, recently used as stables or barracks, were in grim condition; private homes "looked as if they has been inhabited by savages or wild beasts." Expecting the worst, Isaac was no doubt elated when, turning onto Pearl Street, he saw that both his home and his sugar refinery were in relatively good condition. He wasted no time reconstituting his business, recruiting a new sugar boiler (a well-paid craftsman) from London. By 1785, with his refinery up and running, Roosevelt posted a notice in the *Daily Advertiser* that "having had his Sugar-House repaired,

SWEET MEMORY

New Yorkers consumed almost two times as much sugar as the sweet-toothed French. The proximity to sugar—by the late 1820s there were eleven refineries—kept the cost of candy-making low for the city's confectioners. One pioneer candyman was thirty-year-old Kinloch Stuart, who had arrived from Edinburgh with his wife, Agnes, in 1806. In Scotland, Stuart had incurred a large debt from a building scheme gone awry. Facing debtor's prison but swearing to make good on his obligations, he fled to New York.

Stuart set up shop on the ground floor of a two-story brick building at 40 Barclay Street, where his pure sugar candy (made by using the same technique as sugar refining) quickly caught on. Family and shop soon moved to the corner of Chambers and Greenwich, where his sons, Robert and Alexander, were born and where Kinloch reputedly worked fifteen-hour days to make a go of his business (most workmen labored for ten). Though somewhat out of the way, the new shop "attracted the pennies of schoolchildren by underselling" other confectioners. One young woman's memory of his shop was recorded in a diary written in 1849 by her ten-year-old daughter, Catherine Havens. "My mother," she wrote, "says Stuart's candy store . . . used to be *the* store in her day. When she was a little girl in 1810, old Kinloch Stuart [he was thirty-five!] and his wife Agnes made the candy in a little bit of a back room and sold it in the front room, and sometimes they used to let my mother go in and stir it." Stuart's slogan, "Low prices and fair dealing," plus a product esteemed for its purity made his enterprise flourish. By 1812 he had paid back every cent of his Scottish debt.

[he] is now carrying on his BUSINESS of SUGAR REFINING as formerly, and has ready for Sale (by him and his Son), all grades of loaf and lump sugar." This was possible because the French, Spanish, Dutch, and Danish islands in the West Indies had reopened their ports to American ships, and American wheat, flour, and beef were once again being traded for raw sugar and molasses. By the time of the Federal Procession, there were eight refineries in the city.

Reserving his afternoons for his duties as president of the year-old Bank of New York, Isaac Roosevelt spent his mornings in the sugarhouse; James handled the day-to-day operations. Over the next few years the refinery was staffed by a rotating cast of eight workers, most from London (some accompanied by their wives), who generally stayed for their two-year indenture. The refinery's sugar molds also came from London, but the other supplies—rolls of blue wrapping paper, lime produced by burning local oyster shells, and clay—were from New York. The Roosevelts also had a monthly "blood account" with a city butcher for bullock's blood, used in sugar's clarification process. James continued running the family's large establishment after Isaac's death in 1794. The Roosevelt family knew a good thing when they saw one. In 1803 another Roosevelt, Cornelius C. (great-grandfather of Teddy), opened a sugarhouse near City Hall.

15

CANDY GETS TECHNICAL

When the confectioner Kinloch Stuart died at fifty-one in 1826, he was one of New York's wealthier men. Kinloch's sons, Robert and Alexander, opened a refinery that produced 3,000 pounds of sugar a day using traditional methods. Although presiding over a large and profitable industry, most of the city's refiners ignored the technological advances revolutionizing sugar-making in Europe. One local firm unsuccessfully tried one or two of the new techniques, but after they failed to work, New York's sugar men rejected the fervor for innovation that gripped many other industries. Robert and Alexander Stuart were the exceptions. They grasped the potential for transforming refining. Using their sizable fortune, they spent a year working out a steam-powered process that yielded more sugar at lower cost.

On a hot summer morning in 1831, workers were enlarging the three wooden buildings housing the R. L. and A. Stuart Com-

The Old Sugar House and Middle Dutch Church, Liberty Street, 1830.

pany to accommodate an enormous steam engine. While Robert, the more outgoing brother, managed the financial side of their venture, Alexander, the younger and more introspective of the brothers, was out on the sidewalk supervising, since his grasp of technology had helped the brothers design their new equipment. In the midst of the commotion Frederick C. Havemeyer, walking up Greenwich Street from his own nearby refinery, happened to pass by. Stopping to watch the steam boiler's installation, he became agitated, grabbed Alexander by the arm, and bellowed, "Don't do it—it will ruin you." The Stuart brothers were undeterred. Though only slightly younger, they were far more progressive than Havemeyer and wanted to create the most technologically advanced refinery in America.

Newspaper ads in 1832 claimed that the R. L. and A. Stuart Company had adopted a new way of making "sirop, or sugar, purified by steam process." Their white, red, yellow, and brown rock candy would have "a lighter color" and "better flavor" and be produced with "a greater degree of purity," all at the existing low prices. At the 1834 American Institute Fair, the Stuarts exhibited the sugar produced with steam power. The sparkling white crystals elicited "the wonder and admiration of the public" and were "the envy of the other refiners." Subsequently, their competitors did partially upgrade their factories, but only partially. The refiners still used blood for clarification—1,800 gallons a year—a method a Treasury Department report on sugar refining termed "revolting to the feelings."

By 1836, having outgrown their wooden buildings, the Stuarts spared no expense building "the most complete six-story, fireproof buildings in the city." One newspaper said it was "well worth a visit to the establishment" to see the "machinery and fixtures, most of them being the invention of the ingenious and enterprising proprietors." Their up-to-date equipment made it possible to process 12,000 pounds of sugar a day while giving "permanent employment" to only "about thirty persons."

Almost a hundred employees worked at Congress Sugar Refinery's six-story building on the southwest corner of Duane and Reade. The English refiner Samuel Blackwell had opened it several years earlier, but when it was rebuilt after a spectacular fire in late 1836, Blackwell, facing enormous debts, sold it to his foreman, Dennis Harris. Though he ran it successfully, refining was an odd profession for an abolitionist like Harris, since sugar was grown by slave labor in both the southern states and the Caribbean islands. Each day must have tried his conscience.

New York had abolished slavery only ten years earlier, and many African Americans struggled in menial jobs. Thomas Downing was an exception. Downing's Oyster House, a plush, mirrored cellar restaurant at 5 Broad Street, served bankers, politicians, and visiting dignitaries, including Charles Dickens and his wife. Downing also sold oysters in various forms, announcing "TO MERCHANTS AND OTHERS" in the *New York American* in 1837 that "having received a very superior lot of fine oysters, which I have pickled in that superior style which I have been accustomed to do for my customers for a number of years, I have them already for exportation or family use and shall be happy to fulfill all orders you may please to favor me with." Downing shipped his pickled oysters to the West Indies, a fried variety to Paris, and fresh oysters across America and around the world, including a batch to Queen Victoria in England, who reciprocated with a gold watch.

The Panic of 1837, caused by both domestic and foreign events, abruptly ended the city's postwar run of prosperity. Within weeks banks closed, businesses failed, and one third of New York's workers were jobless. Many "who but two years since considered themselves rich" were suddenly poor, the Common Council observed. In *The Adventures of Harry Franco, a Tale of the Panic of 1837*, Charles Francis Briggs likened the overnight "collapse of a businessman to the shutting of a wild bird in a cage while its fellows soared above." Insolvency, a visitor noted, "changes at once New Yorkers' friends, their associates, and often their nearest relations, into strangers."

16

BONE CHAR AND OTHER "NUISANCES"

The growing nation had a sweet tooth that required ever-larger refineries to satisfy it. By 1842 the R. L. and A. Stuart refinery had moved into a new "lofty" building made "of brick, stone and iron," with "one hundred . . . small windows." It inspired a feature, "A Day at a Sugar Refinery," in *New World*.

To this sugar castle thousands of hogsheads of muscavado sugar were carted daily from the docks, and cranes hauled the barrels into the refinery. Workmen then shoveled the sugar into cisterns that were "six to seven feet in diameter, and about five feet high." Water was piped in, lime added, and the mixture heated and spun, the steam dissolving the sugar and separating out impurities. The liquid was filtered through several layers of cloth bags, yielding a transparent "juice" with a reddish or yellowish tinge. The colored juice was then piped into "square vessels" whose bottoms were lined with several feet of bone char, the only substance that could remove the stain left by the steam.

Bone char was made from the bones of beef and pigs. This least refined ingredient in sugar refining was supplied by "bone boilers." One graced what is now Central Park, though most were located in an area in lower Manhattan bounded by Fifth Avenue and the Hudson River—a neighborhood of wooden shanties called "pig town" for its piggeries. Outside the one-story wooden bone boilers sat piles of festering bones "collected from the retail butchers whenever it best suited convenience regardless of whether they had remained a week or a month in the shops." The piles teemed with bugs and vermin. It was a wonder the creatures could stand the stench.

Though airtight ovens existed, few companies used them, and the incineration emitted a noxious odor. Pig town encompassed many other "nuisance" industries: fat boilers and renderers of other animal by-products, such as those who collected gelatin (used by Peter Cooper, the founder of Cooper Union, who in 1845 received a patent for his "transparent concentrated or solidified jelly dessert mix," today known as Jell-O). New York's sanitation regulations were lax in the nineteenth century, and "nuisance" businesses operated without interference.

Two thirds of the bones used to make char were collected by children, "without whom we could not have one of our commonest luxuries," the *Friends Review,* a Quaker magazine, reported. Scavenged from the city's garbage heaps, the bones were often first taken home and boiled for soup, then stored in the corners of crowded apartments. As a thirteen-year-old girl explained to the *New York Times* in January 1853, with the two shillings she made each day from bone collecting she helped her mother pay the four-dollar-a-month rent. Sorted bones were heaped high in the courtyard of her Third Street tenement waiting to be picked up by men

Scavenging a garbage dump for rags, coal, and bones, on a barge docked at the foot of Beach Street, 1866.

who paid thirty cents a bushel for them. Still, the girl lamented that "bones is hard business now, there is so much snow and people use *so much poultry.*"

After the sugar "juice" percolated through the charcoal, "a colorless transparency almost equal to that of pure water" emerged and was "proof of the success of modern improvements in this branch of manufacture." First it was boiled; then an air pump created a vacuum to remove a portion of the water from the sugar, which was thickened, turned back into granules, and reliquefied. Next a "large number of men, each stripped to the waist," filled scoops with the hot viscous sugar and "walked, or rather ran, with a quick elastic motion"—their skill the only thing that kept them from being scorched—to fill "hundreds, and probably thousands" of 2-foot "conical moulds." The sugar cooled and solidified for several days in the upper floors of the building, and each resulting loaf was put through a machine whose conical blades shaved the surface until it was smooth. The loaves were finally baked in an oven until "thoroughly dried" and then wrapped in the traditional blue paper.

In 1849 the Stuarts once again enlarged their refinery. The nine-story building featured a colonnade along the front of its white façade that stretched over four lots on Greenwich Street. Underground passages led to three additional buildings and enormous steam engines that heated 1,000 gallons of water a day and burned tons of coal a year. The new complex, employing three hundred workers, dwarfed the city's other refineries both in size and in the mountain of sugar produced (44 million pounds a year) by refining 1,100 pounds of sugar "every 11½ minutes of the six working days."

The Stuarts lived comfortably, Robert in a large home on fashionable Fifth Avenue, where he was amassing a large collection of paintings, coins, and rare books, and Alexander in a brownstone near the refinery. Neither brother had any children. Both were devout Presbyterians and liberal philanthropists. They were in the upper echelons of a city whose lifeblood was commerce, and people were astonished when in 1856 the brothers transferred their entire candy business, along with the building and the land it sat on, to seven longtime employees, free and clear, with no strings attached. The lucky recipients had been working at the company from eighteen to forty-two years, the man with the longest tenure, Robert A. Ridley, having apprenticed with old Kinloch Stuart. The foreman since 1821, Ridley had "almost exclusive management" for several years. The *Tribune* registered amazement that the city's largest candy company had been given as a "present outright."

The new venture, Ridley and Company, assured the public that it would "continue to supply young people and old people with the sweets of life in the form of candy and confectionery, plums and horns, and kisses, and all sorts of sugar things." The original company had been renowned for using pure ingredients, and the new owners stressed that they would meet that standard in all their "several hundred different styles of candy." Their products would continue to be sold in "all parts of the United States, and many other countries besides, as various parts of South America, London, Paris, China, etc. etc.," and Queen Victoria would remain a steady customer.

By the 1850s refining was the city's largest industry, producing a 190-million-pound sugar mountain yearly, making New York one of the "foremost among sugar markets of the world." Sugar refining in the United States continued to grow throughout the century, with major refineries in Philadelphia and Baltimore, though the majority remained in New York.

Frederick C. Havemeyer's opinion of technology had changed in the thirty years since he had tried to stop the Stuart brothers from modernizing their refinery. After taking a two-decade hiatus from the industry and traveling in Europe, where he witnessed the latest advances, he returned to New York and in 1857 opened a seven-story, state-of-the-art refinery. Its initial production of 300,000 pounds of sugar per day exceeded the *monthly* output of all the other New York refiners, including Stuart's, combined. Not

CANDY-MAKING WOMEN

Women workers slowly began entering food factories during the 1840s, and their numbers surged by midcentury. Usually in their late teens or twenties, unmarried and without children, they needed stamina to stand at their workstations for ten hours a day.

Candy-makers employed the largest number of women. Virginia Penny, the author of *The Employments of Women,* estimated that during the busy fall season between 25 and 50 percent of the five thousand workers making sweets were women. "The city of New York is the headquarters of the confectionery trade," she wrote. Twelve large candy manufacturers made sweets for "all parts of the United States" and for export to "Canada, most of the West Indies, Mexico, Chili [*sic*], and many other places."

At Ridley's, the city's largest candy-maker, women earned a meager monthly salary but were assured year-round work and could sit for the ten hours they spent painting candies. That was not a privilege to be taken for granted; the second largest manufacturer, Struelens and Palmers, or S & P, at 68 Duane Street, employed at least ninety "girls" who stood until ten at night making French confections of "every description." Penny observed a small child there sugaring gumdrops.

Another confectioner employed fifteen women to roll nuts in chocolate, separate gumdrops, paint decorations on individual pieces, and especially turn out chocolate cream-filled candies, for which the demand was "very great." After making the candies, the women wrapped them in paper or metallic foil and placed them in decorated boxes. Some confectioners complained that the women wasted too much time "laughing and talking and carrying on."

only were the building, machinery, and processes cutting-edge, but the refinery's Williamsburg, Brooklyn, location possessed another advantage. Built directly on the East River, the refinery had a dock where ships could unload hogsheads of sugar directly into the waterside warehouses. This not only saved carting fees and cut down on delivery delays, but a loophole allowed Havemeyer to avoid import duties.

17

WAR AND SUGAR

Frederick Havemeyer was not the only refiner opposed to the Civil War because slavery was good for his business. He was aligned with "the shipowners who hauled cotton, the bankers who accepted slave property as collateral for loans, the brokers of southern railroad and state bonds, the dealers in tobacco, rice, and cotton"; New York's sugar men "had come to profitable terms with the slave economy." A New York merchant candidly acknowledged as much in conversation with the abolitionist Samuel L. May: "Mr. May, we are not such fools as not to know that slavery is a great evil . . . But . . . there are millions of dollars due from Southerners to the merchants and mechanics alone, the payment of which would be jeopardized by any rupture between the North and the South. We cannot afford, sir, to let you and your associates endeavor to overthrow slavery."

Given the interests binding New York businesses to the southern plantations, it was appropriate that Dan Emmett's "I Wish I Was in Dixie's Land" premiered in Manhattan on April 4, 1859, in a performance by Bryant's Minstrels at Mechanics Hall. New York businessmen tamped down abolitionist sentiment by raising fears of disunion, but when the new Confederate government sharply cut duties on imports arriving through New Orleans, Charleston, and Savannah, the *New York Times* was horrified: "We shall not only cease to see marble palaces rising along Broadway but . . . our shipping will rot at the wharves, and grass will grow in the streets." With southern papers like the *Charleston Mercury* editorializing that planters could now bypass the "New York money changers" and "trade directly with our customers," New York businessmen "virtually overnight" backed war to restore the Union.

One confectioner cut his staff by half in January 1861 because he had not received any southern orders. A pickle manufacturer who usually hired 125 women for the busy two-month summer season feared that he might lose his largest market. Yet with the start of the war, as "new industries arose, old ones took on new proportions," said the *New York Times*, and both the confectioner and the pickle-maker probably made more money selling their products to the Union Army than they had selling to southerners before the war. One confectioner later said that during the war "we could hardly keep up with demand," because soldiers "must have spent most of their pay in mint-stick."

No matter their political leanings, for manufacturers the prospect of generous government contracts soon created an atmosphere of great expectations. In the rush to fill government orders, fraudulent or adulterated food—tainted meat, rotten flour, and substituted ingredients—was regularly shipped to the troops by "small-souled creatures," the "rascally, thieving contractors" whose greed measured their patriotism. At the army's procurement center, at the foot of Spring Street on the Hudson, inspectors emptied the contents of wooden barrels and scraped the salt covering off pork to certify that the meat was edible, which did not mean it was safe.

The soldiers weren't alone in eating adulterated food. Additives were routinely used as enhancements or fillers. Pickles were made greener by tincture of copper. Hard candies were colored with poisonous dyes, giving the city's children, the *Daily Tribune* noted, "blue and red and white poison by the pennyworth." What passed for cayenne pepper often contained only cornmeal and salt colored with toxic red lead, and chicory or any variety of trash and waste might lurk in ground coffee beans. Such additives, a medical writer found, were bad enough to "weaken the digestive organs of an ostrich."

Each soldier enjoyed a sugar ration of 15 pounds a month, far more than the average person consumed (per capita consumption was 30 to 40 pounds a year). However, supplies of raw sugar from Louisiana became scarce once the war began, and although there were supplies from the Caribbean, the government made huge purchases of the available refined sugar, and prices tripled. Sugar refiners reaped huge rewards. Though their refinery was running at 50 percent of capacity, Robert and Alexander Stuart were earning larger profits than before the war.

As the few dozen millionaires of 1860 were joined at war's end by several hundred more, the gulf between rich and poor (which included most laborers) grew wider. In 1863, 1,600 New York families held 61 percent of the city's wealth. They flaunted war profits on shopping binges at Tiffany's, paraded them in splendid equipages in Central Park, wore them in velvet carriage cloaks, dis-

FRAPPUCCINO FOR THE TROOPS?

Gail Borden's New York Condensed Milk was the best known of several companies that supplied canned or evaporated milk products to the troops, and wagonloads of the large cans traveled from the city to the military encampments, where it was a greatly desired item. Soldiers were willing to pay $2.50 a can to "sutlers"—shopkeepers who followed the troops—when the wholesale cost was only three cents! The troops used it to lighten their coffee, which they drank "*at* meals and *between* meals . . . and at all hours of the night," one soldier recalled, because it kept them alert, filled their empty stomachs, and served as a warm liquid in which to soak their stone-hard army bread.

The soldiers received some of their coffee roasted, but most beans arrived green and needed to be roasted over an open fire, a skill few acquired. To make coffee-drinking more convenient, three companies, including Borden's, tried to make a canned coffee drink—a combination of evaporated milk, coffee, and sugar, like a primitive Starbucks bottled Frappuccino. Samuel J. Tilden, the future governor of New York and brother of one of the competitors, claimed that this new product would "promote the health and comfort of the soldiers." Borden won the six-month bidding contest, but when the concoction was actually prepared and shipped, it ended up being oily and undrinkable, leaving soldiers with coffee redeemable only with heaps of sugar.

played them in the livery of their servants, and dined on them in belly-breaking dinners at Delmonico's that *Harper's* reckoned could feed a soldier's family for "a good portion of the year." The festering resentments of working men and women boiled over at the inception of the draft lottery in 1863. This law allowed a man of means to avoid conscription by paying a $300 fee to a substitute to take his place. "Gentlemen will be furnished promptly with substitutes by forwarding their orders to the office of the Merchant, Bankers and General Volunteer Association," read a notice appearing daily in the city's papers.

In July 1863, two weeks after the fate of the Union had hung in the balance at Gettysburg, the city erupted in five days of violence known as the Draft Riots, targeted the wealthy (who could hire substitutes to replace them in the draft) and African Americans (who were blamed for causing the hated war). Shop and factory owners closed to avoid confrontations, while others were intimidated into taking no action against workers who joined the mobs. All of the sugar refineries closed except R. L. and A. Stuart. The Stuarts had been warned that their "buildings would be in ashes before morning," but, refusing to be bullied, they decided to fight back.

Before he left home on the tense morning of July 14, Robert Stuart probably assured his wife that she had nothing to fear, although his vocal support of the Union put a bull's-eye on his residence and business. Traveling to the refinery through the eerily quiet streets was unnerving, but as Stuart pulled up to the white portico façade of the block-long building on Greenwich Street, steam was pouring out of the lofty chimneys as usual. Inside, his brother, Alexander, normally would have been directing the steam-powered iron wagons that raised and lowered tons of sugar through the floors of the building. But this morning the factory floor was still, the wagons standing ready in case they were needed. The brawny workers— "faithful to a man"—stood by, having already moved 30,000 heavy metal sugar molds to the roof of the nine-story building where, if necessary, they could be dropped onto rioters. To further protect the refinery, the brothers armed their men with heavy hickory bludgeons, and as a last resort they planned to use their immense steam boilers to shoot a torrent of scalding vapor at any rioter foolish enough to try to enter the building.

When the rioters were a few blocks away, they got word of what was in store for them and gave the refinery a wide berth. Once the danger had passed, Robert Stuart jumped back into his carriage to check on his wife and servants. He was taking a chance. Rioters shouting, "There goes a three-hundred-dollar man!" targeted the white rich. Surprisingly, although several nearby houses were burned, Stuart's was spared. Possibly his reputation as a generous philanthropist helped, or his well-known piety (he gave each new worker a Bible) put him above the fray.

Most businesses could not count on similar loyalty from their workers. To protect themselves, some, including several slaughterhouses and cattle yards, paid the rioters to skirt their premises. When the Bull's Head Tavern adjoining the huge Allerton stockyards on 44th Street refused to serve them alcohol, they ransacked it, smoked all its cigars, and then burned it to the ground. In Brooklyn news of the Draft Riots may have been the spark that ignited the pent-up bitterness of grain shovelers over the failure of a recent strike. A mob of two hundred "reckless and desperate characters," their anger boiling over, destroyed two grain elevators, at great cost to their owners.

CANNING CAPITAL

Canned goods, sparingly used before the war, became more commonplace as prices dropped. Thousands of troops received these products courtesy of the Union Army, and although some canned goods were better left on the battlefields, canned fruit and especially condensed milk won many new converts. The men told their families about them, and by the end of the war civilian customers were asking for products made by Borden's and American Solidified Milk. A woman told the *Tribune* in 1864 that her doctor had recommended condensed milk and "I had never heard of it before—and now I would not be without it for any money."

Canned food usage grew sixfold between 1860 and 1870, and over the following decade it jumped by 200 percent. Condensed milk became a "grocery staple," "finding its way in to almost every family's repertoire." Familiarity with it made all canned products more acceptable, and the output of the city's canning companies expanded from a "mere trifle" to an "enormous amount." As the prices dropped, a more varied diet was available to a broader range of New Yorkers, especially during the winter months.

In 1875 there were six major canning companies in New York City, one of them producing 50,000 three-pound cans of peaches (more than half the peaches canned nationally) and 20,000 cans of green-gage plums, along with similar quantities of ten other fruits and berries. This same firm also canned 20,000 bunches of asparagus (the majority of the country's asparagus was canned in New York), 125,000 quarts of tomatoes, and 12,000 cans of lobsters. Pickles—7 million a year—were its major product, though it still canned only 20 percent of the nation's 35 million pickles.

Once it became clear that General Robert E. Lee, reeling from his defeat at Gettysburg, had escaped south across the Potomac, five fire-tested regiments of Union soldiers were sent by rail from Pennsylvania to New York. Firing cannon loaded with grapeshot into crowds of rioters, they put down the "largest single incident of civil disorder in the history of the United States."

18

KING HARRY

B y the early 1870s, Brooklyn, refining 500,000 to 1 million pounds a day, was on its way to becoming the "greatest sugar manufacturing city in the world." Havemeyer and Elder, the largest refinery in the world, loomed across the river from Manhattan, where many of the smaller and older companies were located. While all the refineries had made money during the Civil War, the industry modernized after the war, requiring bigger physical plants, and space-cramped Manhattan refineries couldn't compete. By mid-decade almost all had been forced out of business or gone bankrupt.

The Stuarts' forty-year-old refinery closed in 1872, and the brothers retired with their fortune intact. Alexander lived quietly in his brownstone on Chambers Street until his death in 1879. Robert, a founder of the Museum of Natural History, died in 1882, aged seventy-six. When his equally pious wife died some years later, she left his collection of art, coins, and rare books to the New

York Public Library because it was the only institution in New York that closed on Sunday.

During the second half of the 1880s, workers in the remaining sugar refineries (primarily in Brooklyn) began agitating for better working conditions. Refinery jobs were grueling and dangerous, with little security, as hands were let go during slow periods. The Sugar House Workingman's Union presented the refiners with demands for a ten-hour day, dinner breaks, higher wages, Sundays off, bimonthly wage payments (as opposed to one paycheck a month), and recognition of the union. The refiners refused these terms, and 2,500 workers from most of the Brooklyn plants went on strike. "Germans, Austrians and Polanders" began picketing across the street from the Havemeyer and Elder sugarhouse.

Much of the animosity was directed at Henry O. Havemeyer, known as King Harry, a gruff, brutish, secretive, and unyielding man who got his way or else. The youngest of Frederick C. Havemeyer's four sons, he entered the business at fifteen, just as the Civil War began, and "early mastered the mercantile" side of sugar. He took over the running of the large refinery in 1885, having been selected over his older brother Theodore, who remarked, "Get it down as a *fact*, Harry is the king of the sugar market." Not only did King Harry dominate his sibling, but his iron fist ruled the industry.

Ships arriving from "Pernambuco [Brazil], Manila, Hawaii, Cuba, Egypt, and Java" unloaded raw sugar at the Havemeyer and Elder wharf on the East River, "hardly thirty steps" from the refinery. The company's storage sheds held up to 1,000 hogsheads of sugar, and a constant stream of donkeys could be seen hauling them into the refinery. In 1882 the refinery comprised a formidable complex of buildings, including on the north end a "bone-black house," on the south end a cooperage that made between two and three thousand barrels a day. The "colossal pile of masonry between them" was the Yellow Sugar House refinery.

Just inside its door stood "half a dozen tall, muscular men" dumping raw sugar into "a black-looking well," where it was mixed with a "wine-colored fluid called sweet water" spouting from a pipe in the wall. Improved technology had significantly shortened the processing procedure. Bone black to filter the sugar was transferred from the bone-black house next door on a leather conveyor belt. Several floors of the building held from forty to sixty huge drying molds filled by men "stripped to the waist, showing sinews and muscles." Then the molds went into floor-to-ceiling ovens for baking. The finished sugar was crushed to make either granulated or powdered sugar, or sliced by machinery into cubes. The firm's H&E Eagle brand was well known around the country and fetched premium prices.

On January 9, 1882, at about four o'clock in the afternoon, the nine-story Yellow Sugar House was engulfed by fire. The flames jumped from floor to floor, igniting the sugar dust in the air and setting off a series of explosions. The wooden floors burned, sending huge machinery downward. Fire engines quickly surrounded the building, but "floods of water" couldn't save it, and it collapsed into "a great mass of smoldering ruins." No one was killed, but the "doomed refinery" shed a thousand workers.

Shortages pushed the price of sugar up during the eighteen months it took to build a new $7 million complex. It covered 16 acres, subsuming the adjacent De Castro and Donner refinery. The brick walls were 4 feet thick on the lower floors and 2 feet thick at the top. The interior had "unending rows of iron columns, brick arched ceilings, and asphalt pavements." Three hundred electric

The Havemeyer and Brooklyn Houses, Refineries in Brooklyn offices, Wall and South Streets, 1882.

lights lit the space, which had "hundreds of windows" for "perfect ventilation" to keep the temperature down to 100 degrees in warm weather. The building was constructed so that raw sugar entered from the dock and the finished product exited into railway cars waiting on tracks ready to receive it and carry it across the country. Once up and running, the refinery could process 3 million pounds of sugar a day, double the amount of the country's second largest refinery, in New Jersey, and do it "cheaper than anyone else."

Even with so many windows, the new refinery was still a miserable place to work. An article in the *New York Tribune* described the conditions in the "forbidding, fortress-like" buildings, where the heat, "severe enough during ordinary conditions of temperature," was punishing during the summer. The majority of the three thousand men employed in two twelve-hour shifts were newly arrived immigrants from Germany, Poland, or Hungary, "thin and stooped" men "rarely above middle age." Their work areas were "veritable infernos," and workers couldn't "stay in them over ten minutes without falling down utterly prostrated by the terrible heat." To help them get through the day, some refineries were known to give (or sell) their workers up to fifty glasses of beer a day.

The temperature was worst in the drying rooms, where the windows were kept closed. It was so hot that the men worked naked except for shoes and a loincloth, their bodies "as wet as if they had been plunged into the East River." Ambulances were summoned so frequently that the company employed its own doctors to avoid drawing attention to its own private hell. Working in the broil, "many have died, and others have had their minds so affected as to be unable to return to work." Some became so overheated that they suffered from hallucinations that they were "burning up," which often sent them "in a mad rush to the nearest water," the East River, where most drowned.

During a strike in the mid-1880s, Havemeyer and Elder had "very much less than one tenth" of their employees working. H. O. Havemeyer offered a slight pay increase but also issued a statement that "no trades union will be recognized by our firm." Havemeyer was confident that the men would be back in "twenty-four hours" or "as soon as they had spent all their money on beer."

The strikers, however, were prepared to "starve before they [would] give in." They began picketing peacefully, but as the police presence grew over the following weeks, the strikers got angrier. Rocks and punches were thrown, skirmishes erupted, delivery wagons were attacked, and shots were fired on both sides. The strikers

A CONFLAGRATION OF GUMDROPS

E. Greenfield and Son's factory on Barclay and Greenwich Streets sold candy, including its specialty, gumdrops, in "every town in the United States and South America." On the morning of December 21, 1877, the first floor of the shop was bustling with salesmen filling orders for the pre-Christmas rush." Suddenly a huge explosion tore through the building, knocking everyone down and shattering the plate-glass window overlooking the street. Those in the shop escaped through the gaping front wall, including the owner, Ernest Greenfield, with a gumdrop buried in his ear.

The explosion crumbled walls and then the wreckage caught fire. Thirteen employees were killed, among them twenty-nine-year-old Thomas J. Grissich, who had been boiling gumdrop ingredients in open copper pans on the second floor, and Frederick Kerber, who had been arranging candies in the 200-degree drying room on the third. (Grissich had boarded with Kerber and his family in their apartment on 96 Orchard Street, across the street from today's Tenement Museum.)

In another room on the second floor three German boys, brothers George and Albert Krumery, aged sixteen and thirteen, and August Droxler, thirteen, were rolling gumdrops in sugar when death came. Most of Greenfield's thirty workers were Germans (along with Italians, they made up the majority in candy factories). German immigrant children typically entered the workforce at fourteen, but depending on a family's circumstances, some began even earlier. Many of those seriously burned in the tragic fire were teenagers.

stood their ground, although many were penniless and hungry. (A. B. Hersemann's factory bakery sent "a cartload of bread," probably a gesture to mollify Hersemann's own disgruntled workers.) With no progress in sight, desperate to put food on the table, a trickle of workers accepted a ten-cent pay increase.

As more men returned to work, Havemeyer and Elder prepared to process sugar but still refused to recognize the union. "No man can serve two masters," one manager said, and "any of our old hands who want to return must first get out of the union." The need to work won out. The men settled for a ten-cent pay increase, bimonthly paychecks, and a ten-hour day (although often only on paper), but barely half the strikers were rehired.

Not content with lording it over his workers, King Harry extended his rule over his industry. He opened negotiations with 80 percent of the country's refineries to join a trust, the Sugar Refineries Company, a consolidation that required each refinery to exchange private ownership for shares in the new company. The trust was a monopoly that would control labor agreements, production quotas, and sugar prices. Many smaller firms joined rather than be forced into bankruptcy. After a year of talks, seven New York refiners joined the trust, which comprised twenty companies nationwide. A board of trustees was formed, with Henry O. Havemeyer as its president. The *Louisiana Planter*, a trade magazine, warned that Havemeyer had gained "despotic power in the management of the Trust's business."

The Sugar Refineries Company closed half its members' facilities, putting thousands out of work. Sugar went "up in price, and is still going up, and there is no certainty that it will not go up a good deal higher than it is now," the *New York Times* reported. These increases came when the cost of raw sugar had fallen, which "aroused a great deal of enmity on the part of the public," which liked "sugar cheap and plenty."

New York's candy-makers all felt the effects. One told a reporter that he would not raise his prices. "I get a fair price. I give good goods. You can say for me that the beautiful ladies of New York shall not have the price of their bonbons increased. Never! Never! Never!" He soon broke that pledge, however, passing the higher cost of his raw material on to his customers.

Most people were unclear how a trust differed from a combine or a corporation. Laborers and small businessmen saw them all as conspiracies to squash competition. The public's greatest fear, however, was that consolidation would boost prices, which the formation of the sugar trust confirmed. In 1890 the New York State attorney general brought a suit against one of the trust's entities, North River Sugar Refining Company in Manhattan, saying that its shares had been transferred illegally. Simultaneously another suit charged that the trust stifled competition and inflated prices "at the consumers' expense." Over the next few months the refiners testified in court, and during one exchange Havemeyer admitted that the trust's "principal object" was to control prices. The trust lost both cases and was found to be illegal. Appeals in the state's highest court upheld the verdicts, and the Sugar Refineries Company was forced to reorganize. (Shortly afterward the U.S. Congress passed the Sherman Antitrust Act.) In 1891 the trust was renamed the American Sugar Refining Company, but only the name and the legal status had changed. King Harry still ruled.

TREATS

Ice cream manufacturing began in New York in 1863, when Jacob Fussell opened his factory on 23rd Street and Fourth Avenue (Madison Avenue). Fussell took on three partners, among them James M. Horton, a big man in the milk trade. Horton bought out the other partners and named the company after himself. Soon the city's premier brand, J. M. Horton Ice Cream, was made in ice-filled cellars, where gallon cans of flavored fresh cream were fitted with blades and attached to machines. Then, "a rasping squeak, a subdued roar, a crushing grinding noise of ice, and the cans [were] whirling furiously in their icy beds." After hardening in a bed of ice and salt, the cream mixtures were packed into zinc molds. A local favorite was made by pouring first strawberry, than chocolate, and then vanilla to create multicolored bricks that were frozen, sliced, and wrapped in white paper. By the new century, every steamship bound for Europe carried four hundred 2-pound bricks of Horton's ice cream. Commercial refrigeration had begun by the mid-1800s and progressed quickly. The first ship to transport refrigerated meat successfully in 1881, the *Dunedin*, had launched a movement of refrigerated shipments of foods.

In 1874 twenty-two-year-old John S. Huyler opened a store on 18th Street near Broadway where he sold ice cream and then added "an old-fashioned molasses candy." "Huyler's Taffy, Fresh Every Hour" caught on fast; within a few years Huyler launched a second store in Manhattan, one in Brooklyn, and another in Albany. Ridley and Company's candies included "rocks, sticks, bars, lumps, braids, crystallized, plums, kisses, comfits, drops, lozenges, nonpareils." The company also made

continues

"conversation lozenges," flat disks that had "a brief remark, question, or answer printed upon its face in bright red letters," and some even had "a kind of small torpedo that goes off when pulled, with a delicate pop just loud enough to please a young lady."

New Yorkers starting chewing gum after Thomas Adams opened the world's first gum factory in 1870, where he produced Adams New York No. 1. The inventor had met Mexican general Antonio de Santa Anna, the bloodthirsty victor of the Battle of the Alamo and a former president of Mexico. Living in exile on Staten Island, the general was trying to sell chicle, a natural gum from a tropical evergreen tree, as a replacement for rubber. The story goes that Adams, who was having no luck experimenting with chicle, put a piece of it into his mouth, as Mexicans did, and began to chew. He sold his first batch of unflavored gum to a drugstore, and within a few days orders began

to arrive. Within a year demand was so great that he patented a machine to speed up production. Four years later he added licorice flavoring to create Black Jack gum, the first offered in sticks.

Adams Black Jack Gum ad, 1918.

Another New York treat was soda water; the bubbly drink was sold in drugstores, at hotels, from street stands, and in specialty shops. On a summer day an estimated 10,000 glasses were quaffed in Manhattan, and when the temperature hit 90 that number doubled. One mid-nineteenth-century memoir describes a long line of bankers and brokers on the sidewalk outside A. J. Delatour's soda fountain at 25½ Wall Street. A counterman took an order, filled an ice-cold glass with syrup, and infused it with a "long glassful" of the effervescent water. This popular shop was owned by the banker John Gelston, whose soda-water factory on 5th Street was one of twenty-one in the city. The largest belonged to the inventor John Matthews, who was active in the business from 1832 to 1865. Matthews's one hundred workers made "everything in the soda-water line," including siphon bottles. In Brooklyn, Robert Robinson was reputed to be one of the first New Yorkers to make ginger soda, or ginger ale, as well as plain soda water and lemon, cream, and sarsaparilla sodas. Four delivery wagons filled orders in Manhattan, Brooklyn, and that new summer mecca, Coney Island.

19

PRICE WAR

"The cheaper we can furnish sugar to the consumer, the more he will eat and the more we will refine," Henry O. Havemeyer told the House Committee on Manufactures in 1888. American Sugar Refining intended "to provide all the sugar the consumers of this country will take." Four years later Americans had increased their consumption to almost 64 pounds a year, a 10-pound rise since Havemeyer's testimony. American Sugar controlled about 98 percent of the eastern market, and its Brooklyn refineries represented 80 percent of the country's refining capacity. American Sugar also set the prices followed by all other refiners. Clearly it was a monopoly. But in 1894, in *United States vs. E. C. Knight Co.*, the Supreme Court ruled that Congress could not prohibit a monopoly in manufacturing. On the eve of a war that threatened his reign, King Harry looked invincible.

Arbuckle Brothers, the largest coffee packager in the country in 1892, sold twice as much coffee as its two closest competitors combined. Its machinery filled a continuous stream of paper bags with 16 ounces of ground coffee and mechanically sealed up the packages. Using the same process, Arbuckle began to pack 2-pound bags of sugar bought from Havemeyer's American Sugar. Consumers liked the bags because they kept the sugar cleaner than sugar scooped from a grocer's barrel.

Unhappy over the Arbuckles' success, Havemeyer tried to buy the patent for the machinery, which was bagging 250,000 pounds of sugar a year. Having prudently purchased it from the inventor, the brothers refused to sell. Havemeyer retaliated. First he raised the price of the sugar sold to Arbuckle, and then he bought the Woolson Spice Company, a coffee-roasting company in Pennsylvania (the Arbuckles were surreptitious investors), to package his own coffee. Once amiable business partners, the Arbuckles and Havemeyer "parted as bitter and implacable enemies."

Harry Havemeyer entered the battle with "the enthusiasm of a schoolboy," but he had met his match in John Arbuckle, a plump man with a high, ruddy forehead and a long graying beard covering a thick, square jaw. A contemporary described him as looking like a country bumpkin. However, he had a sharp mind and was a "mighty factor" in business dealings. With "his blood boiling," Arbuckle announced in 1896 that "we were going to build a refinery ourselves," and during the time it took to put up three buildings at the foot of Plymouth Street, a price war was joined on the battlefield of grocery-store shelves.

Havemeyer launched his opening round of "heavy artillery" in January 1897 with a steep five-cents-a-pound cut in the price of his Lion Brand coffee. Within ten hours shops in Manhattan had sold 10,000 packages. Arbuckle took up the challenge. "Well, we mean business, too," he told reporters. "Fighting is right in our line." Shoppers were delighted when Arbuckle set his price even lower. By September a pound of coffee went for ten cents, twelve cents less than a decade earlier. If Havemeyer was trying to scare him, John Arbuckle said, the price cut wasn't "going to change the decision of Arbuckle Brothers to go into the sugar refining business," and if his competitors thought so, "they are mistaken." A "battle to the death" was expected. While American Sugar had much greater sugar-refining capacity, Arbuckle could roast twice the amount of coffee. Prices fell again in April 1898, and both companies were practically giving their coffee away while losing millions every day.

Arbuckle's foray into sugar created an opening for others to enter Havemeyer's realm. Frederick Mollenhauer and his two brothers converted their father's molasses house on Rush Street in Brooklyn into a three-thousand-barrels-a-day refinery. The California refiner Carl Doscher, who retired when he sold his business to the sugar trust, decided to open another refinery. A known enemy of Havemeyer, who had fired Doscher's three sons after the trust took over his business, Doscher began operating the New York Sugar Refining Company in 1898 on Newtown Creek in Long Island City. A short distance north of New York City, in Yonkers, another competitor launched the National Sugar Refining Company.

Fitted out with the latest equipment, these three refineries shaved American Sugar's share of the market to 80 percent. Working furiously behind the scenes to control the industry, Havemeyer eventually secured 30 percent ownership of Mollenhauer's stock. It took a little longer to come to terms with the other two, but once they agreed to follow his lead in setting prices, he left them alone and negotiated preferential deals with the railroads and grocery wholesalers.

Completed in September 1898, the Arbuckle sugar refinery had only a quarter of the capacity of a single American Sugar factory. Nevertheless, a sugar price war broke out. Sugar was produced on slim margins, and even the slightest price dip affected the bottom line. To the benefit of everyone except the refiners, sugar eventually sold for about five cents less a pound, as a direct result of the price war.

While Arbuckle was invading sugar, Havemeyer was raiding coffee, building a roasting facility in a defunct sugar refinery in Williamsburg. The American Coffee Company, when it opened in 1899, filled a block; with twenty-two roasting machines, it was "the largest roasting plant in the country." Initially American packaged its coffee in 5-pound cloth bags, but when consumers balked, it switched to the more convenient 2-pound packages.

By March 1899, with the price of sugar ticking up, it was believed that the war looked to be over; but in August, American Sugar cut prices again. An executive at John Mollenhauer's refinery, forced to close during the winter months of 1900, said that American Sugar's plan was "to make business so unprofitable that some companies will be forced out of existence." American Sugar's stock price was dropping, and even Henry Havemeyer sounded deflated when he told reporters, "There is no money to be made in sugar refining at the present prices. The consumer is the only one benefited. Things look pretty shaky, don't they?"

Soon prices crept upward. By June 1900, Henry Havemeyer was encouraging the three independent refineries—National Sugar Refining, New York Sugar Refining, and Mollenhauer—to form the National Sugar Refining Company of New Jersey. When they did, the new company became the country's second largest refiner. Technically a separate company, National Sugar Refining worked

. . . AND SPICE

Late-nineteenth-century New Yorkers liked their salads dressed with a variety of sauces and their tables laid with piquant condiments. According to *King's Handbook*, E. R. Durkee was "synonymous with . . . fine spices, salad dressing and kindred appetizing condiments," along with flavoring extracts, meat sauces, and celery salt. Eugene R. Durkee had founded the firm in 1850 and seven years later introduced Durkee Famous Sauce, the first bottled salad dressing. His son, Eugene W. Durkee, took over in 1884. With "very extensive" mills in Brooklyn, "the largest in the country," the company also had a factory, laboratories, and offices in Manhattan.

Mustard was one of the most popular condiments. It had been used as a spice like turmeric until a nineteen-year-old German immigrant, Charles J. Gulden, began adding vinegar to mustard powder at his first factory on Elizabeth Street. Under his son, Charles Jr., Gulden's made thirty different products, including various types of mustard, catsup, and Warwickshire sauce (a condiment similar to Worcestershire sauce but less pungent). It also packaged capers and olives, as did the Seville Packing Company on Franklin Street, which employed eighty people, three quarters of them women, who packaged Pim-olas, large green olives from Spain that they stuffed with pimentos. Robert T. French began making French's Mustard in 1876 (his son relocated the company to Rochester, New York, at the end of the century).

Louis Funke Jr. inherited Boker's Bitters in 1860 from his father. Originally crafted by the German immigrants John G. and E. [Emily] Boker, who in 1828 began making the bitters from various botanicals —most likely cassia, also known as true cinnamon, cardamom, and orange peel. By Funke's time, the drink additive was sold around the world. Funke suggested that it was best used with curaçao or anisette, or "vermouth, wines, or liquors, as well as for the preparation of the refined drinks of the bar." The product was prominently featured in an 1862 bartender's guide, *How to Mix Drinks, or the Bon Vivant's Companion.*

in concert with Havemeyer, who set both price and production schedules.

In January 1901 rumors circulated that the price war, having cost Havemeyer and Arbuckle close to $25 million, was about to end. On January 8 sugar prices went up. Both sides denied any collusion, saying that the increase was purely a matter of supply and demand. There was nothing pure about it. The price change suggests that Havemeyer and Arbuckle must finally have verbally agreed to a truce, though they left no written documents to incriminate them in any future government investigation.

"A ROTTEN JOB"

Working conditions were harsh in all the food industries, concluded W. Gilman Thompson, a physician who studied occupational diseases. In his 1914 report, Dr. Thompson found that constant exposure to industrial contaminants and a "lack of variety in work" was causing new ailments. Sugar refinery workers contracted "sugar refiner's itch," an inflamed rash on their hands. Bakers exposed to flour dust and those who ground mustard and pepper or bottled vinegar could develop nasal catarrh, an inflammation of the nose and throat. Millers and grain handlers courted asthma. Tea and coffee tasters got buzzed on caffeine, and chocolate tasters risked developing a "chocolate habit" that led to obesity and diabetes. Along with cuts and gashes inflicted by weary men wielding sharp knives, "speeding up" in slaughterhouses caused back problems. Slaughterers and bone boilers toiling in "gross and unpleasant surroundings" were often heavy drinkers. For brewery workers, "easy access to the product" often ended in alcoholism.

Factories were particularly brutal on women. Most female candy workers were fourteen to eighteen years old, perhaps because young women were apt to have the stamina to stand all day, sometimes until nine or ten o'clock at night. They worked in rooms with little ventilation that were chilled by large fans blowing ice-cooled air to keep the chocolate from melting. They would "come home exhausted," tumble into bed, and be "so tired in the morning their mothers [would] have to throw water in their faces." In 1914 the State Factory Investigating Commission found women laboring seventy hours a week or more. Although laws limited their hours, most put in for illegal overtime because they needed the money. The work was usually steady once a woman got her foot in the door. The confectionery industry was one of New York's largest food categories and there were hundreds of candy factories, each with more than one hundred employees, plus an uncounted number of smaller firms.

Half the candy workers were young Italian women whose families did not want them venturing outside the neighborhood, so they often worked at factories near Italian communities. But even close to home there was discrimination in hiring. One candy company only took on women who came to apply wearing a hat, rejecting the bareheaded or those wearing shawls. Women who didn't speak English were given the worst jobs, like peeling coconuts or almonds. American-born Italian women usually worked as packers but could advance to become dippers. One of these women, a Mrs. Santori, who had done time in a factory before her marriage and had returned as a dipper, was not alone in hoping that her daughters would find better jobs.

May Malone was a typical candy worker: nineteen years old, the eldest of nine children, still living with her family in a four-room flat on West 20th Street. Her longshoreman father, an Irish immigrant, earned $10 to $12 a week when he could find work. May made $6.50 in the candy factory and gave half to her mother. She spent a mite on entertainment but somehow managed to save enough to buy good shoes, since standing all day in a cheap pair was too painful. Near her home was the Maillard Chocolate Company, at 112 West 25th Street, run by the founder's son, Henry Maillard Jr., where 76 men made After Dinner Mints and other candies and 130 women packed them. Huyler's Candy built a ten-

Confectionary, Maillard Chocolate Company, 1902.

story addition to its large factory on 18th Street and Irving Place in 1910. It had a regular workforce of six hundred, and during the holiday rush, from August to December, put on an additional five hundred "girls."

The "less the public knows about candy making, the better," said a manager of one of the factories under investigation in "Behind the Scenes in Candy Factories," a 1928 exposé undertaken by the Consumers League of New York. The industry had been battling image problems for decades, and while it had made strides in cleaning up ingredients, cleanliness and working conditions were another story.

During the 1927 Easter and Christmas seasons, undercover members of the league worked "elbow to elbow with expert candy makers" to research "Behind the Scenes." The report included firsthand accounts of conversations with factory workers and interviews with the fourteen managers (out of twenty-five) who agreed to talk. The investigators found work in both the "little loft" in a "dirty side street turning out the cheapest grade of lollipop" and in the large "model" factories making "nationally advertised" candy. By the end of the assignment, Lillian Symes, the lead investigator, who worked in twenty different factories, had to be hospitalized, the terrible working conditions having hurt her health.

One of the league's findings was that "outside interests"—conglomerates often connected to tobacco companies—had bought some of the city's largest candy firms, although most continued operating under their own names. In at least five cases the conditions, equipment, and quality of the candy under new ownership had deteriorated.

The report found that approximately 61 percent of candy workers were young women. Their bone-wearying jobs paid little but were in great demand, with a line of hopefuls always willing to take their place. The backbone of these workforces continued to be Italian or Italian American girls, with smaller numbers of Irish Americans, a few Jews, and a new influx of Puerto Ricans. Only four of the factories in the survey hired African Americans, usually as janitors.

The aristocrat of candy workers was the skilled chocolate dipper. Usually a bit older, between twenty and thirty, she could earn $35 or $40 a week, with a guaranteed year-round job, and she could sit while working. Most factories employed a few older workers, though Emma Hoenkamp, a self-supporting widow for nineteen years, said, "It's hard to work in a candy factory when you're sixty-three years old." These women usually shelled nuts or pitted dates, sit-down work but much lower-paying.

Packers made up the largest group. Packing was an unskilled job that paid an average of $12 to $14 a week and required the "girls" to stand until ten at night during the peak season, from September to Christmas. The most recently hired (or someone who had annoyed the boss) scooped bulk hard candy into boxes, a painful job because their "palms were punctured full of holes from the sharp edges." To keep the chocolate cool, the "best plants" held the temperature at 65 degrees, but the investigators discovered some at an uncomfortable 45 degrees. The women worked swaddled in "frequently dirty" sweaters and had constant colds, and at the end of the day most were "fairly blue with cold." Fancy packing involved putting pieces of candy into paper cups before placing them into ordered spots in boxes. "You hold a pile of cups like this between your thumb and forefinger," one woman demonstrated, and when the papers stuck together, "you lick your middle finger like this, slide out the bottom one and put the candy into it." Asked if some more sanitary method could be used, the woman said, "It'd take too long," because volume meant profit.

Sanitation practices in many of the smallest companies were "appalling"—rest rooms often "disgusting," aprons filthy, and candies routinely packed after falling on dirty floors. "On one occasion," an investigator witnessed, "some old chocolates were taken out of stock to fill a rush order. Tiny worms on the top of the chocolates were industriously brushed off with the same brush [that had just fallen on the dirty floor]."

A persuasive tool to push manufacturers to clean up their factories was the December 1929 publication of "Do You Know How Your Candy Is Made? Buy White List Candy and Be Sure," prepared by the National Consumers League of New York. To make the list, employers needed to meet the league's criteria: female employees couldn't work more than fifty hours a week, for which their pay had to be at least $14, the workspace "clean" and "well-lighted," and the temperature kept at "at least 64 degrees." In addition, "sufficient toilets and washrooms" and a chair for each worker must be provided. The personal cleanliness of workers was to be enforced and medical examinations maintained, since the candy investigators had found that the twice-yearly health exams mandated by law rarely happened.

When the list came out, it received tremendous publicity and companies on it saw their sales increase significantly. Among them were Henry Heide, Loft Candy, Maillard, Huyler, Wallace and Company, and Repetti, plus the smaller firms Hills Brothers Dromedary Dates, Mells Manufacturing (a company started by Leo Hirschfeld of Tootsie Roll fame), and Phoenix Candy.

PURE FOOD

The practices of manufacturers of "brightly colored and cheap candies" cast a pall over the industry. New York enjoyed a brisk trade in these candies, sold in towns throughout the country at such low prices that there was no incentive to make them anywhere else. To sell them so cheaply, some businesses cut corners, substituting ingredients that were poisonous, and poisoned candy was regularly implicated in the deaths of children. Peppermint flavor might come from turpentine or the taste of pineapple from a mixture of sulfuric acid. Coloring materials were particularly deadly; yellow was made from extremely toxic chromate of lead, and bright red from red lead. The attitude of the Board of Health was not to impose "unnecessary burdens" on businesses, no matter how badly a business might sicken the public, and there was no way to prosecute offenders for things not forbidden by law. One sanitary inspector suggested that injurious substances were added as the "result of ignorance rather than intent," because even the "most depraved candy-maker can have no object to kill his customers outright."

From 1884 to 1904 candy manufacturers led a campaign to clean up the confectionery industry, long rife with adulteration scandals. John S. Hawley of Hawley and Hoops was active in the National Confectioners Association, a trade group formed in 1884 "to stamp out the use of adulterants and injurious coloring matter from confectionery." Many states had no laws at all. The association sought a national law to ban the use of harmful additives, and it was aided by "those who are working in Congress" for the passage of a national pure food bill to protect the whole country from "the fraud of adulterated foods of every description."

Medical associations and women's groups, food and beverage manufacturers and their trade organizations, magazines and newspapers agitated for passage of the Pure Food and Drug Act. It took the publication of Upton Sinclair's bestseller, *The Jungle*, an exposé that turned American stomachs with its descriptions of Chicago's meatpacking plants, to get the law passed in 1906. It set standards for "the manufacture, sale, or transportation of adulterated or misbranded or poisonous or deleterious foods, drugs, medicines, and liquors." A companion measure, the Meat Inspection Act, required that all animals for human consumption pass an inspection before they were slaughtered and that their carcasses be inspected afterward. Cleanliness standards for slaughterhouses and processing plants were established.

Within weeks of the passage of the Pure Food and Drug Act, ads like those of one local soda company began to appear: "The Pure Food Law goes into effect Jan. 1. The New York Bottling Co.'s Ginger Ale and Carbonated Beverages ARE ALWAYS PURE." Pure, clean, and untouched—those were the qualities consumers came to expect from food products.

Manufacturers not included pleaded to get on the list. To stay there, they had to submit to biannual inspections. The Sweets Company of America, makers of Tootsie Rolls, was dropped from the second edition because it refused to allow inspection of its payroll ledgers. Its lawyer responded with a "very drastic letter," and after a phone call that didn't get him the results he wanted, he threatened to sue for libel. The league held firm. Mason, Au, & Magenhimer and E. Greenfield were both dropped from

DRINKS IN A DRY TIME

Prohibition sent soda sales soaring. New Yorkers often drank soft drinks as a substitute for beer, but soda's true surge in popularity came in its use as a mixer to blunt the taste of the cheap liquor in speakeasy cocktails. Ginger ale, long a local favorite, was especially popular for mixed drinks.

Two years after a Canadian product, Pale Dry Ginger Ale, was introduced to New York in 1921, it was eagerly taken up, because some said it hid the acrid flavors of illegal alcohol better than any other ginger ale. Canada Dry Ginger Ale, Inc. built a huge facility on West 38th Street in Manhattan, which the *Wall Street Journal* called the "most modern and best-equipped plant in the beverage industry."

Brooklyn's largest soft-drink maker, H. Kirsch and Co., was considerably smaller, yet its seven delivery trucks, each topped with a large replica of a soda bottle, delivered five thousand cases each day of its Golden Dwarf ginger ale, sarsparilla, lemon, cream, and celery sodas. A few years later it boasted in newspapers that "no human hand" touched the beverages made in its "up-to-date plant" on Flushing Avenue.

Kirsch was only one of Brooklyn's many soda producers. United Soda opened in 1912 with the slogan "Made with Pure Sugar." It was one of the first to make a chocolate soda. Espresso soda was made in Manhattan Special Bottling Corporation's barnlike wooden building at 342 Manhattan Avenue in Brooklyn, where the aroma of the coffee beans brewed for the drink filled the neighborhood. The company's open-sided delivery truck ferried the bottled soda to Italian communities in the surrounding boroughs.

the White List for the same reason. Greenfield began a public relations blitz to counter its demotion with newspaper articles describing the amenities the company provided for its employees: dressing rooms, showers, rest rooms, a library, a restaurant, and a hospital with nurses in attendance. The articles said nothing about the workers' salaries. When the league learned that the National Licorice Company planned to drop wages, fear of falling off the list moved the company to reverse itself. G. Cella and Company, makers of chocolate-covered cherries, was dropped for underpaying its workers plus racking up fourteen sanitary "discredits." P. Margarella was found to be "dirty" but agreed to follow a league plan to clean its factory and "submit to inspection without warning." The White List lasted for four years, but low wages and dicey sanitary practices lasted much longer.

After Mother's Day, the largest candy-selling holiday, the slow season began. Many women were unemployed during the summer, but a lucky few got jobs in the cracker industry. Once September rolled around, the candy factories began hiring again, even though one worker told the league investigators, "Candy's a rotten job, in which you never know what you're going to make or how long you'll be working."

SWEETS IN SOUR TIMES

n the 1920s, D. Auerbach's Candy Company occupied the east side of Eleventh Avenue between 46th and 47th Streets and perfumed the neighborhood with the "sweetest and most intriguing scent in the city," the aroma of its chocolate bars, both "with almonds and without." In 1930 the company filed for bankruptcy. Its president, Joseph S. Auerbach, son of the founder, was mired in almost $2 million worth of debts, and by 1932, when he was sentenced to three years in jail for falsifying financial records, he was penniless and the firm's factory had to be sold.

The first few years of the Depression were tough on candy manufacturers. Only after 1933, as consumers resumed buying a bit of chocolate or a fistful of penny candies, did the city's substantial industry—three hundred factories, ranging from tiny backroom spaces to thousand-worker plants—begin to recover. Profits ticked up, often because the labor force had been reduced and the average female worker's salary cut by 30 percent. Still, those who had jobs considered themselves lucky.

Spurring sales were men, who had previously tended to buy candy not for themselves but for their wives and kids. During the First World War chocolate had been part of the doughboys' rations, which made men more accustomed to eating sweets. In the 1930s fancy candies that a man might buy for his sweetheart were still popular, but nudging elaborate treats aside were wrapped candy bars. Manufacturers began to design their grab-and-go bars to suit men's preferences, selling them at tobacconists, newsstands, and drugstores. While many candy bars were made in Chicago, in 1935 New York's Sweets Company of America was selling $1.25 million worth of Tootsie Rolls. Henry Heide introduced twenty new candies each year, hoping one would be a winner, and some were, such as Jujyfruits and Jujubes. Heide also sold Red Hots, a macho-sounding treat that was actually a raspberry-flavored candy. Mason, Au, & Magenhiemer in Brooklyn made Mason's Peaks, a chocolate-covered candy bar; Mason Mint, a round, chocolate-covered mint patty, a more bracing and less sweet treat; and Mason's Dots and Crows, chewy candies appealing to men.

In the 1910s Loft Candy operated "the largest candy-making organization in the world," according to Standard and Poor's. At its block-long plant on Fortieth Avenue and 9th Street, across the East River in Queens, it transformed 3 million cocoa beans, 2 million pounds of nuts, and 12 million pounds of sugar, along with multiple tons of butter, vanilla, and cream, into candy and ice cream for the chain's 186 nationwide stores. Company profits had slipped in the late 1920s, and in 1929 shareholders wrested control away from George W. Loft and his son (the founder's son and grandson). But it was Pepsi-Cola, not candy, that helped Loft survive the Depression.

Charles G. Guth had been Loft's president for a year when he bought the twice-bankrupt Pepsi-Cola Company in 1931. The acquisition included the soft-drink company's trademark and syrup recipe, which Guth directed a chemist at Loft's Long Island City factory to change so it was "more to his liking." The production of the base syrup was moved to the Queens facility, and the liquid was then shipped to Baltimore, where sugar and water were added before the beverage was sent off to bottlers and Loft soda fountains. First sold in a 6-ounce bottle, it didn't catch on until Guth switched to a 12-ounce size, offering twice the cola for the same price.

By 1934 the new management had opened many additional candy stores and acquired two local chains, Happiness Candy Stores, with seventy-five retail shops, and the Mirror, with twenty-five soda shops. Loft had made no layoffs during "the so called 'depressions,'" and increased the number of employees to six thousand men and women (including those who worked in the stores). When confronted with a bias suit in 1935, a company press release said that its labor force was made up of "Jews and Gentiles, Italians, Hungarians, Germans, and in fact all nationalities, and the colored race is represented with about 150 representatives." It was true that Loft did hire people of color, but only as janitors or in the stockrooms.

Guth presented a rosy picture to the Loft stockholders—Pepsi-Cola, his main interest, had become an international success—but he kept silent about the candy company, which was not doing well. The board of directors backed Guth until 1935, when he decided to lower the salaries of Loft Candy employees at the Long Island City factory. A strike ensued; besides picketing the plant, the strikers trapped Guth in his office. It took a phalanx of policemen to get him out of the building.

Charles Guth resigned with the board's approval shortly afterward, and then his legal battles began. Loft sued him for a tangle of financial dealings, including appropriating the Pepsi syrup formula for himself and using Loft's assets, facilities, and employees to build up Pepsi for his personal gain. The three-year court case concluded in 1939 in Loft's favor. Guth not only lost his controlling interest in the Pepsi-Cola Company but he was ordered to stay out of the soft-drink industry for five years.

By 1936 the Barricini Candy chain had moved to Queens, its third move in eleven years and a world away from the small shop on Broadway near West 158th Street where it had started. In its little back room, the two partners made candies by hand with the help of their wives, who were sisters. New York had many little shops like theirs, but these partners had big plans. Jack and Regina and Mac and Jean Barricini were Jews who had changed their names to sound more European. They incorporated the company in 1931, and sales started to take off. Moving into ever-larger manufacturing spaces, by 1936 they had 10,000 square feet on the second floor of a building on Northern Boulevard in Long Island City.

One of the Barricini "brothers" (as the partners described themselves), who was in charge of production, had a "mad passion" for cleanliness and had the "girls" in the factory scrub their arms and hands "until the skin turned scarlet" before dipping chocolates. Each day a chemist sampled and examined all their ingredients. The other Barricini "brother" was the businessman,

HEROES AND ROGUES

In 1934 two Polish American brothers from New York, the newly trained amateur pilots Joe and Benjamin Adamowicz, won acclaim after they left Floyd Bennett Field on June 28 in a secondhand plane and—after several emergency stops, a couple of near-fatal crises, and one wrong turn—landed in Warsaw on July 2 to the cheers of thousands.

The brothers had opened a soda company, Adamowicz Brothers, in 1920 on Conselyea Street, after Bronislaw, forty-six, the oldest brother, left his job at a sugar refinery. By 1924 they needed four trucks to deliver their A. B. brand sodas. They were the city's only Polish American soda-makers and so supplied all their countrymen's clubs, picnics, and special events. However, soft drinks may actually have had little to do with their firm's meteoric rise. While the aviators were being feted in Poland, federal agents raided their soda factory and found a 10,000-gallon working still in the back room. It had probably been producing moonshine since Prohibition and had continued to do so a year after repeal, depriving the government of $700,000 in taxes. Joe and Benjamin, arriving home as heroes, were almost immediately arrested and were soon in court fighting the moonshine charges. While they were on trial, they lost their soda factory. Convicted, they appealed. They insisted that an apparition named Jack Schwartz owned the still, but Schwartz was never located. The brothers were sentenced to fifteen months in a federal penitentiary.

and he credited their success, fifteen stores in ten years, to "the perfect harmony in which we worked together."

Out in Coney Island, Victor A. Bonomo was fighting for the reputation of his family's candy company, Bonomo Candy and Nut Corporation. In 1938 it was found guilty of shipping polluted one-cent candies throughout the eastern states. One of the 350 varieties the company made contained a "filthy vegetable substance" and "rodent hairs, bits of paper, sections of mouse pelts and fragments of glass." During his trial, Bonomo claimed that his factory had had been credited by "the Department of Health and by inspectors of the Federal Department of Agriculture with being better than the average candy factory in our standard of cleanliness," but the judge issued the maximum sentence, a $600 fine and three years probation, and said, "If this was an average factory, then God help the children of America." (Ten years earlier, Bonomo was dropped from the second edition of the White List for questionable sanitation.)

Bonomo claimed an "injustice" had been done, which "could have happened to any manufacturer in the country." He insisted that he had been tricked into confessing on the witness stand and that it was all a "terrible misunderstanding," as he had received contaminated fig paste from what he believed was a reputable source. He made these comments to his employees at the company's second annual dinner dance, awkwardly scheduled three days after the conviction. He wasn't thinking of the rodent hairs or glass when he said, "You who work in the Bonomo plant know how rigid our sanitary regulations are. You know how meticulous we are as to care of the plant and personal cleanliness of employees." Our "doors are wide open," he said to anyone who wanted to inspect the factory. (The negative publicity might have been what prompted the firm to change its name to Gold Medal Candy in the early 1940s.)

By 1937 the number of candy firms citywide had fallen by about half from the start of the decade. Perhaps consumers had begun to cut back on candy consumption to protect their health as well as their wallets. Certainly the Depression years drove not just closures but mergers and relocations, like that of the Sweets Company of America (makers of Tootsie Rolls) to Hoboken.

WAR, RATIONING, AND YOGURT

W hile many things were in short supply during the Second World War—grain, coffee, meat, oil, metal, tires, and the men who made them—sugar, both on kitchen tables and as an essential ingredient, was the scarcest and perhaps the most missed.

Following the attack on Pearl Harbor, sugar from Hawaii and the Philippines became unattainable. In February 1942 the government's War Production Board took charge of the raw sugar supplies, controlling the amount received by each refiner. By March prices had begun to climb, and the amount refined in New York dropped by a third.

Sugar rationing for consumers began on May 6, 1942. Each person was allotted 50 pounds of sugar a year (a significant cutback from the average 74 pounds consumed in 1941). This equaled about half a pound a week, with an extra allowance of 5 pounds per year for canning fruits and vegetables.

SEGREGATED CANDY, VICTORY GUM

With so many men away fighting the war, there was a shortage of workers, and in 1944 Loft Candy Stores desperately needed employees. The candy business had been spun off from the Pepsi-Cola Company in 1941, when the company changed its name and focus. Because Loft was short of staff, "working below capacity," it couldn't "turn out as much candy" as it once had. In advertisements it promised a sweet deal for workers, but it was competing against much higher-paying defense jobs. In addition, Loft wanted only white workers. "We have always hired colored people," the company said, "as long as we've been in existence [since 1871], but we put them in certain types of jobs." Loft was "proud to say that there are at least fifteen colored stock men who have been working for us for more than ten years" and "one or two who have been on the payroll for as long as twenty-three years." The company also hired African American men as porters and dishwashers, but never to work in the company's stores or make candy in its factories. Unable to fill all the openings, Loft clung to its discriminatory hiring policy, and its all-white factory continued to work below capacity.

At least 20 to 25 percent of American Chicle's output was earmarked for the armed forces. Gum was in every ration and food packet and every navy lifeboat and sold in all military stores. Gum was believed to be therapeutic and enhance relaxation in times of tension—sailors on a destroyer could chew 10,000 sticks in a week—and some said it even helped build courage. Chewing stimulated the flow of saliva and staved off hunger and thirst, making it essential in jungle rations. American Chicle's raw materials, which came from "the far corners of the globe," rose in price as the war progressed, and profits declined, but the company made gum for the duration, signing a $5 million contract with the army for gum in K rations, on which it made no profit.

Gum companies found that "consumption [was] up while production [was] down," and civilian shortages were severe. The workers in arms plants, where smoking was banned because it was dangerous, had plenty of gum, however. Topps Chewing Gum Company, founded in 1938 by four brothers, Abram, Ira, Philip, and Joseph Shorin, at a factory at 60 Broadway in Brooklyn, used the slogan "Don't Talk Chum; Chew Topps Gum," an allusion to the silence urged in war-related factories to increase worker productivity. It was also a reminder not to leak secrets.

Drake's Bakery had wanted to expand, but its additional space would sit idle if it couldn't obtain enough sugar, said Ralph D. Ward, the bakery president and a member of the second generation of Ward Baking's founding family. By June 1945, Drake's announced that it was cutting back production of cakes, cookies, pies, doughnuts, cinnamon rolls, and crullers. Fillings inside and icing on top of its products would disappear. The Gottfried Baking Company, on Eleventh Avenue, a large wholesale baker, also suspended its line of crullers, jelly and chocolate rolls, jelly cupcakes, and butterflies (a type of sugar bun).

Sugar was reserved for the military, not only to feed the troops but to make munitions (molasses was used in explosives). There was a "gloomy outlook" ahead for those with a sweet tooth, said Ward in 1945, as companies making sodas, candies, and biscuits slashed consumer production. National Biscuit Company cut the number of Fig Newtons, sugar wafers, and other cookies by almost 50 percent.

Sugar quotas were particularly difficult for candy-makers, unless they had contracts to produce candy for the military. One 1942 headline explained that "Candy Goes with the Army," along with chewing gum and soft drinks. Candy and gum were included in ration packages and available in large quantities in military stores. All through the war, "wherever American soldiers and sailors go," sweets went with them. In 1942, before the second wartime Christmas, a "great, gray Navy transport" left Brooklyn for the naval and air bases in Iceland carrying 350,000 candy bars. Whatever chocolate was available (cocoa was even scarcer than sugar) went into candy for the soldiers. The government told businessmen what products were needed, and if they volunteered to supply them, their sugar quotas were raised.

The wave of war refugees arriving in New York from Europe included many seasoned businessmen. Daniel Carasso, who had run the French branch of his family's yogurt company, Danone, reached the Bronx two weeks before Pearl Harbor was bombed. His father had opened Danone (his son's nickname) in Spain in the early 1900s. Daniel was sent to France to study business and bacteriology in the early 1920s and then began the French branch of the firm. After the Nazis occupied France, he was told by the Spanish embassy in Paris that it couldn't assure his safety because he was Jewish, so he and his wife left for New York. There, in the early 1940s, he bought one of the few small companies that produced yogurt in the city. His friend Joe Metzger left Spain to join him in the business, as did Joe's son, Juan.

BLACK MARKET SUGAR

While most Americans gladly sacrificed for the war effort, rationing brought a thriving black market. Money could be made in industrial theft, and sugar was a prime target. Black marketeers sold large amounts to bakers, confectioners, and especially soda-makers. Early in the war, Waxey Gordon, the cognomen for the former bootlegger Irving Wexler, set up a sham soft-drink company, Vita Cola. For show it produced a minuscule amount of soda, but it sold almost all its allotment of 30,000 pounds of sugar to other companies at inflated prices. Wexler, who had just finished serving eight years of a ten-year sentence for tax evasion, got another year in prison.

Sugar was stolen from National Sugar's refinery, and several American Sugar trucks were hijacked. Black market sugar drew criminals like flies.

Toward the end of the war, two brothers, Murray and Irwin Greenberg, diverted 25 million pounds of sugar from army and navy hospitals and sold it to soft-drink and crushed-fruit companies. The Greenberg brothers were convicted of tax evasion, having failed to pay $1 million in tax on their illicit sugar sales, and served jail time. Most of their customers got off on technicalities.

Maurice Gottfried, of the Hanscom Firm, which had fifty-eight bakeries in its chain, was indicted for receiving black market sugar. His brother Harold Gottfried masterminded a scheme that falsified records from previous years so he could receive 750,000 pounds of sugar rather than the 350,000 pounds his upstate soda com-

continues

pany could legally obtain. Over several years the brothers diverted 1 million pounds of sugar illegally and obtained machinery using false statements. Maurice got off scot-free, but Harold Gottfried and two other defendants were found guilty and sentenced to three years in a federal penitentiary.

A year after opening, the Dannon Milk Company was producing two hundred 8-ounce glass jars of yogurt a day. In 1942 yogurt was unfamiliar to most New Yorkers, and Juan Metzger spent $2,000 on an ad campaign to promote it as a substitute for meat, which was scarce and expensive. Juan soon left to serve in the army. Although some found yogurt unpalatable and exotic, with a slightly sour taste, by the time Juan returned at the end of the war the company had moved to a larger plant in Long Island City and operated seven delivery trucks.

Dairy products were abundant and milk consumption rose appreciably, although to save gasoline, home delivery of milk had been curtailed. J. M. Horton and Breyers were making vanilla and strawberry ice cream, but not chocolate, because cocoa beans were too scarce.

Rationing eased after VJ Day, but because of the cocoa bean shortage, there was nary a chocolate Easter bunny to be found in the city that year.

"GREATEST MANUFACTURING TOWN ON EARTH"

n 1945, National Biscuit's factory produced 18.4 million cheese tidbits in eight hours and baked 60,000 molasses cookies in one hour, along with sixty other varieties of crackers and cookies traveling on conveyor belts through 250-foot ovens. When rationing (except for sugar) ended in November 1945, people wanted plenty.

During the war base pay rose and overtime flourished for New York's workers. But the cost of living was rising, and workers didn't want to see their wartime gains evaporate in peacetime. While most companies had made large profits, they worried about government price controls and were loath to raise wages. By this time women were making way for returning soldiers, relinquishing their high-paying jobs and returning either to the home or to lower-paid packing and icing jobs.

In 1946 sugar workers went on strike at American Sugar Refining, National Sugar Refining, and SuCrest and won an hourly increase almost 40 percent above their 1941 salaries. But then 15,000 truckers went on strike and the ports were closed, and American Sugar Refining laid off 1,200 workers because it didn't have enough raw sugar to refine. By the time the truckers went back to work fifty-eight days later, shoppers were so eager to restock that they swarmed the grocery stores. They bought every available box of crackers and cookies, products that had "virtually disappeared from the diet of millions of persons living in New York City" during the previous two months. During the strike truckers had made no local deliveries, keeping crackers and cookies off the shelves. A simultaneous strike was waged by 1,500 workers at the Sunshine bakery (Loose-Wiles took the name of its best-selling cracker in 1946), adding to the shortage. Although National Biscuit stayed up and running, its output was sent to other parts of the country.

The truck drivers won a thirty-one-cent hourly increase and a forty-hour week. The striking Sunshine workers also gained a salary increase. Wages began to rise, and New Yorkers' salaries generally outpaced those in other locales.

By the end of the decade food was more plentiful and employment was rising. The city boasted more manufacturing jobs than Philadelphia, Detroit, Los Angeles, and Boston combined. John Gunther's 1947 bestseller, *Inside U.S.A.*, described New York as "incomparably the greatest manufacturing town on earth."

While New York was returning to normal, in June 1948 Soviet troups blockaded Berlin, stopping the flow of food over highways and rails. More than 2 million people faced starvation. The Americans, English, and French began a massive airlift, flying in staple foods. One of the pilots on these missions, First Lieutenant Gail

Halvorsen, started dropping candy tied up in handkerchief parachutes for famished German children. They gathered in parks as he flew by, wiggling his wings so they would recognize his plane. He became known as the Chocolate Flyer or the Candy Bomber, grabbing the attention of the military brass.

Halvorsen was sent to New York to appear on radio and television to publicize Operation Little Vittles. While in the city he received an invitation to join John S. Swersey, of Huyler's Candy, for lunch. Swersey had been with Huyler's since 1937, where he had done everything from putting sticks into lollipops to helping develop K rations.

At the lunch, Halvorsen later wrote, "a large, well-proportioned man warmly greeted me. 'I'm Mr. Swersey,' he announced. 'Have a seat. I represent the confectioners of the United States. We are really excited about what is going on over there and want to do more. What can we do?'" When Swersey asked how much candy Halvorsen needed, the airman replied with "a number that I thought would give him indigestion." Swersey however, "didn't bat an eye." He offered Halvorsen all the chocolate he wanted. "Mr. Swersey's proposition was staggering. Who said businessmen weren't interested in anyone else?"

In a taxi on the way to have drinks at the home of Huyler's president, Swersey told Halvorsen that as a Jew he was conflicted about dropping his candy to Germans, but he believed that children were the country's future, and if sweets could brighten their lives, he was willing to help. Within days of Halvorsen's return, 3,500 pounds of chocolate candy bars and gum were delivered, followed shortly by another 3,000 pounds of chocolate, much of it from Huyler's factory.

Sugar took longer than most commodities to return to prewar levels, but by 1950 supplies were once again widely available. Another Jewish-run family business, Barton's Bonbonniere, had opened its first candy store in 1940 and within ten years operated forty shops and planned to add more. Barton's sold about $8 million worth of candy in 1952. After the war it had begun advertising that its ice cream and confections, including the chocolate Santa Clauses and Easter bunnies that were its bestsellers, were kosher, attracting the city's large Jewish population. To appeal to all New Yorkers, however, the company adopted a contemporary and continental image. When Barton's opened its fiftieth shop in the mid-1950s, the design was inspired by current trends in art, including Alexander Calder's mobiles. The shop was painted in vibrant modernist colors—the signature hues were yellow and magenta—and Barton's candy packages were a riot of multitoned abstract shapes.

The factory was as up-to-date as the stores, with air conditioning, fluorescent lighting, and glass brick interior walls. Three floors were given over to machinery; huge vats mixed chocolate and assorted fillings, assembly lines half a block long carried metal molds of liquid chocolate, which were frozen, then squirted with a filling, turned upside down, and coated with chocolate on the opposite side. Long-stemmed cherries were hand-dipped in a bath of cordial-flavored cream coating before traveling along another assembly line, where a machine covered them with liquid chocolate. Rolled out by hand, marizpan was put into a machine that squirted pellets of the almond paste into molds that rode a conveyor belt to their chocolate rendezvous.

Candy workers were older than before the war, as labor laws were now stricter and teenagers stayed in school longer. Rows of

CLORETS AND TRIDENT

Chlorophyll, reputed to freshen breath, was introduced as a food additive in 1951, stimulating a rash of new products. Also in 1951, American Chicle Company, whose five-story, block-long building in Long Island City sported rooftop signs in the logos of both Dentyne and Chiclets, introduced Clorets, one of the few new gum products of the era. Soon the gritty Queens neighborhood around 31st Street and Thompson Avenue smelled of freshly cut grass. The company continued to produce Trident gum and mints long after Dentyne, Chiclets, Clorets, and Adams Sour Gums moved to other plants around the country.

In 1961 American Chicle introduced Trident gum, first billed as a tartar reducer but by 1964 refigured as a sugarless gum using saccharine that was "good for your teeth." Sticks of gum traveled into outer space when NASA chose Dentyne to go with the astronauts on the second set of manned space flights, the Gemini missions, in 1965. Two sticks were in each meal packet. Interviewed on the subject, the astronauts said that when they finished chewing, they swallowed the gum.

women in their twenties and thirties, "standing elbow to elbow" in white uniforms and small caps, packed boxes with finished candies, weighed them, and then sent them into machines that wrapped them up and tied them with a ribbon. In another part of the factory machines wrapped chocolate bars in tinfoil and paper.

Monthly visits by a rabbi kept everything kosher. Before Passover the factory was closed and thoroughly cleaned. Then it began producing confections that included chocolate-covered matzoh, which Barton's claimed to have invented. Passover, however, was only the second largest holiday; Christmas sales were bigger.

In 1951, Barton's rival, Barricini Candy, began publicizing that its confections had the seal of approval of the Union of Orthodox Jewish Congregations. Its "somewhat tarter" candy was also kosher, and its shops stayed open on Sunday to counter sales lost to Barton's, which stayed open on Saturday, the Jewish Sabbath.

Huyler's Candy, however, was in bankruptcy in 1951, a drastic reversal from only three years earlier, when the firm, which had moved to Long Island City, had turned out 21.5 million pounds of candy. After being acquired by a syndicate in 1947, the company operated three New York candy firms and two in Boston. Nonetheless, most of Huyler's profits came from its twenty-four soda fountains and lunch counters, nine of which were in New York.

All was well until Huyler's experienced a serious financial setback after a backlog of candy amassed for the 1950 Christmas holiday was left unsold because of an overestimate of demand. Before the addition of stabilizers, chocolate did not keep well, and retailers would not let it sit on the shelves. The company filed for bankruptcy but continued to operate until early 1953, when the trademarks were sold to John Swersey, who had worked at Huyler's for decades but left in 1950 to start his own firm, Swersey's Chocolate Company, in Maspeth. He incorporated Huyler's into his new company. Three years later Swersey suddenly died, and for a while the firm continued to be run by his wife, Esther. But by the early 1960s the Huyler name had vanished.

Meanwhile, low-brow candy marketing was getting pretty sophisticated. Candy bars were flourishing in the 1950s. Snickers were touted on the *Super Circus* TV show, an animated television ad about the Three Musketeers was used to promote the candy bar of the same name, and a Super Secret Video Ranger ring and decoder could be had by mailing in a PowerHouse candy bar wrapper, a magnet for kids.

Gold Medal Candy Company reaped huge success when it packaged Bonomo's Turkish Taffy. The taffy had been invented by an Austrian, Herman Herer, who had come to New York to be an apprentice candy-maker, while making a batch of marshmallow candy for M. Schwartz & Sons of Newark, New Jersey. Herer made the mistake of adding too many egg whites, which resulted in a sticky concoction that was hard to chew. The Bonomo family of Coney Island bought Schwartz & Sons, along with the recipe for Turkish Taffy, which they made in four flavors: vanilla, chocolate, strawberry, and banana. An illustration of men in fezzes adorned the label, and purchasers were instructed to crack the bar against a flat surface and then let the pieces "melt in your mouth."

About 11,700 vending machines now helped distribute candy and gum across the city. First built in 1888 by the Thomas Adams Gum Company to sell gum on subway platforms, the machines sold 134 million pieces of gum in 1953, accounting for about three quarters of all underground sales. American Chicle held the contract with the city to manage the machines, and at the end of each day its trucks transported 150 bags, each holding about $50 worth of pennies, to the Federal Reserve in Lower Manhattan.

Other vending favorites were bags of peanuts and Chunky bars, a distinctive squat, flat-topped trapezoidal chunk of chocolate filled with raisins, cashews, and Brazil nuts, developed in the late 1930s by the candy-maker Philip Silvershein and distributed by the Wrigley Gum Company. A new owner, Jeff Jaffe, acquired Chunky in 1950, and the company expanded rapidly, soon selling the bars nationally.

A woman buys gum from a wall-mounted vending machine, 1950s.

In 1953, Jaffe's company bought a four-story building at 655 Dean Street, one of the Ward Baking Company's bakeries, and converted it into a candy factory. It also launched a "nonfattening" candy bar called Sweet 'n Low that included "non-calorie substances" (never specified) as sweetening agents. The bar didn't set the world on fire, but it may have lent its name to another product that did.

Rockwood & Company was the second largest cocoa and chocolate company in the country, with sales of $30 million (to Hershey's $150 million). Merged with a Milwaukee grain company in 1947, it was sold to a Chicago industrialist in 1954. Rockwood discontin-

TOPPS IN GUM

Flavors and products popular before the war continued to sell afterward, although bubble gum had become more popular, and as the *Brooklyn Daily Eagle* put it, "When the guns stopped shooting, kids began to pop bubble gum." Topps Chewing Gum Company developed squat pieces of Bazooka Bubble Gum (not, if you can believe the company, named after the weapon) and Atomic Bubble Gum (nor for the bomb). In 1951 it also began selling thin strips of bubble gum packaged with cardboard trading cards. Not the first to do this, it designed a better card and was the earliest to be successful at it. By 1955, Topps was the largest manufacturer of bubble gum and baseball trading cards, both made in two buildings across the street from the Bush Terminal in Brooklyn.

Topps's control of the bubble gum trading card market made its competitors unhappy. No doubt at their urging, in 1962 the Federal Trade Commission charged the company with illegally monopolizing a "growing industry." Collecting baseball cards was an obsessive "hobby with young boys" from five to fifteen, and Topps had an unfair advantage, the FTC alleged, because it had contracts with all but 7 of the 421 major league players. After two years of testimony, captured in a four-thousand-page transcript, the "world's largest manufacturer of bubble gum" was cleared of all charges. In 1964 Topps sold an estimated $14 million worth of gum, $3 million of that attributed to baseball trading cards. Its huge success, however, created a demand that was too great for the Brooklyn factory, and in 1966 the company moved the production of the gum, trading cards, and wrappers to Pennsylvania.

LOW-CAL SODA

The biggest news of the fifties in the soft-drink industry was the introduction of diet soda. Hyman Kirsch of Kirsch Beverages, the large Brooklyn soda company, was on the board of the Jewish Sanitarium for Chronic Diseases (today Kingsbrook Jewish Medical Center), and after repeated requests from diabetic patients to "make a soft drink we can drink," he and a research scientist at the soda company set to work on a sugar-free beverage. After two years of fiddling with synthetic sweeteners, in 1953 they produced No-Cal ginger ale, which contained 1½ calories in an 8-ounce glass. They expected modest sales, at most 100,000 cases nationwide, since it was available only at drugstores and hospitals. But, Kirsch later said, once it was released "the storm hit" and "the public jumped all over it" and "flooded stores everywhere." Kirsch's ad agency soon realized that most buyers were dieters, and the soda was made more available. Sales exploded, and the company had a hard time keeping up with deliveries, which grew from 300,000 cases in the second year to 2 million in the third, double the amount of its regular soft drinks. More flavors followed: cream, black cherry, cola, and root beer. At least one hundred bottlers were selling their own versions of diet soda within a year.

Hoffman Beverages, a Newark-based company, which had just built a $3 million Long Island City plant, made 2-calorie LoLo Cola and in 1954 introduced Tap-A-Cola, in both a "nonfattening" variety and a regular version, intended to compete locally with Pepsi and Coke. The soda-maker, a subsidiary of Pabst Brewery, was an early packager of soda in flat flip-top cans like beer.

ued its wholesale cocoa-butter business to focus on manufacturing cocoa and chocolates, and the following year sold 55 million pounds of these products. The factory employed eight hundred workers, mostly residents of Brooklyn, including over one hundred African American men and women, an unusually progressive position at the time. By 1957 Rockwood had become part of the Selby Shoe Company, and though the mayor, the governor, and the union all intervened to try to save the candy company, Rockwood ceased production. Members of the racially mixed union rejoiced when the Sweets Company bought the factory, moved Tootsie Roll production into the plant, and filled four hundred jobs. Invented in New York, Tootsie Rolls were made here until 1967, when the factory closed its doors for good. Today the building, in Brooklyn's Fort Greene neighborhood, has been converted to loft apartments.

24

CHEMICAL AND OTHER
CHALLENGES TO SUGAR

n 1954 more than 1,500 New Yorkers worked at the National Sugar Refining Company, the second largest refiner in the country. It was not afraid to throw its weight around in the city, and had in the not too distant past received permission from City Hall to close streets to expand operations. Consequently, when National decided to erect a neon sign to advertise Jack Frost sugar on its waterfront property facing Manhattan, it anticipated no resistance. Two bright signs already promoted American Sugar Refining Company's Domino Sugar, and Pepsi-Cola's logo was up in lights. So National was shocked when its proposal stirred strong negative reactions. Robert Moses, the powerful city planner, registered "strenuous objections" to the spectacle of Jack Frost in 25-foot letters. Officials at the newly built United Nations were among many outraged over the sign, which, "cast[ing] a multihued glow on the United Nations buildings," would "light [them] up like a Las Vegas honky-tonk."

New York's attitude toward manufacturers was changing. Manhattanites didn't want another huge sign glorifying the city's factories. A city of ideas where world peace might be achieved had bigger things on its mind. It didn't want ceaseless reminders of sugar. Large manufacturing in the food industry increasingly jarred with New York's new image of itself. National Sugar, which said its only motive was "one shared by every American business—to advertise and promote our products," abandoned the proposal and made an atoning donation to a riverside park.

National was not some hidebound visual polluter. It was the most progressive firm in the industry, a pioneer in enlightened postwar labor relations, the first to offer workers in its Long Island City plant a guaranteed annual wage, in 1950. Employment in sugar refineries had been erratic; seasonal layoffs were the rule, and a man wouldn't know until Monday evening if he would work on Tuesday.

National's new policy wasn't purely altruistic. Industrial users making scheduled purchases stabilized the refiner's production schedule and made the annual guarantee more feasible. In the 1950s, confectioners, soft-drink companies, and bakers began buying bulk sugar on a regular basis. Most sugar was consumed in processed foods, not from the sugar bowl.

Soon after National Sugar adopted the guaranteed annual wage, American Sugar followed suit. The world's largest sugar refinery could afford it. By 1959 the Brooklyn plant employed 1,500, and a major reconstruction was planned for the following year to expand its packaging, warehousing, and shipping facilities.

Only a few miles from these humming refineries, three men were working on a formula that would cut more deeply into the profits of New York's sugar industry than anything since Jefferson's Dambargo. On this quest was Benjamin Eisenstadt, a lawyer who had worked as a short-order cook in his father-in-law's diner across from the Brooklyn Navy Yard in the 1940s. After the war Eisenstadt put all his energies into starting the Cumberland Packing Company. In 1945 he bought a machine that filled tea bags, then decided to use the same technique to fill small packets of sugar. This was a novel idea, and such a good one that when he tried to sign up American's Domino Sugar as a client, Domino built its own machines from his unpatented idea. Cumberland Packing stayed in business filling sugar packets for National's Jack Frost sugar, along with packets of soy sauce, duck sauce, catsup, and a few other products.

In 1956 a pharmaceutical company approached Eisenstadt. It wanted to fill packets with an artificial sweetener, but he would have to devise a product that would work. Together with his son Marvin and Dr. Paul Kracauer, a chemist, he devised a powdered sweetener that poured like sugar. By the time they took their idea to the pharmaceutical company, it had lost interest. Eisenstadt and Kracauer decided to produce the new sweetener on their own. They patented their formula, wrapped the sweet-tasting, no-calorie powder in a distinctive pink packet, and called it Sweet'N Low. Company lore has it that the name came from Eisenstadt's favorite Tennyson poem, "From the Princess: Sweet and Low," with the opening lines

Sweet and low, sweet and low,
Wind of the western sea,
Low, low, breathe and blow,
Wind of the western sea!

Unlike the unsuccessful diet candy bar of the same name made by the Chunky Corporation in 1953, the product took off. When the first packets left the factory, they were sold to hospitals and restaurants for diabetics, but, like Kirsch's No-Cal sodas, Sweet'N Low caught on fast with dieters, a vastly larger audience.

In 1977 the FDA proposed a ban on saccharin, and production at the factory was halted while the company, which commanded 60 percent of the market for artificial sweeteners, fought the ban. The five hundred workers, mostly African American and Puerto Rican women, were put on vacation with pay.

Even though new products were being developed, new plants opened, and new companies formed in the city's food industry, by 1960 the clock was ticking on large factories in New York.

In 1963 National Sugar integrated its workforce: people of color made up almost 50 percent of the employees both in the Wall Street offices and in the Long Island City refinery. According to the *Amsterdam News*, an "appreciable segment" of African Americans and Hispanics were in supervisory and technical sections of the plant. A year later National Sugar announced a $9 million modernization of the plant, but it soon reversed course, despite having already sunk about $3 million into updating parts of the operation. In 1965 National Sugar closed the 24-acre site, deeming the seventy-two-year-old refinery's twenty-building complex "inefficient" and "uneconomical," and all activities shifted to Philadelphia.

With the makers of beet sugar waging a bitter fight for dominance in the mid-1960s, Big Sugar was no longer invincible. Many cane-sugar refineries were operating at only 50 to 80 percent capacity. And liquid corn syrup and artificial sweeteners were just around the corner.

YOGURT GOES MAINSTREAM

After nine years in New York, Daniel Carasso, the founder of the Dannon Milk Company, returned to Europe to run the family yogurt business. He sold his stake in the company to his partner, Joe Metzger, and in 1950 Joe and his son introduced yogurt to a wider audience. They placed small ads in the *New York Times* that asked, "What Is Yogurt?" Since most people had no idea, the ads explained that it was "made from pure, fresh milk PLUS lactic strains, invaluable for digestion. Ask your doctor. Eat Dannon daily; it's delightfully refreshing—plain, as in the jar, or with jams, sweetening or fruit." To make the taste more palatable to a wider audience, in 1947 Dannon began adding a layer of strawberry preserves to the bottom of some containers. Waxed cups replaced glass jars, and soon the product with the strange name and unusual taste grew more familiar. In 1958 Juan Metzger said, "We knew we were over the hump two years ago, when Bob Hope told a joke about yogurt and nobody laughed." Dannon began producing a low-fat version, and soon a fleet of fifty-five trucks delivered yogurt to almost every supermarket and the approximately 15,000 delicatessens in the city.

In 1959 Dannon Milk Products was sold to Beatrice Foods, the country's second largest food corporation. Beatrice began a much larger advertising campaign and expanded the line, adding hard and soft frozen yogurt. Both were made in the Louis Sherry plant in Long Island City, using Dannon's ingredients.

Sweet'N Low was catching on fast, and legions of dieters had begun to regard sugar as the enemy. In 1963, Cumberland Packing got a call from the head buyer of A&P. Marvin Eisenstadt later explained, "Manufacturers would kill to get their product in there. They told us they wanted to start stocking Sweet'N Low. That's when we knew this was really going to be something big." Three years later Cumberland stopped packing sugar entirely. In 1969 the FDA banned cyclamates, because large doses were found to cause cancer in rats, and Sweet'N Low beat competitors in reformulating. As Marvin's brother Benjamin recalled, "Early the next morning six of us dusted off the formula for the saccharin-based Sweet'N Low. We retooled the machines, designed new packages, and we dumped about $2 million worth of [the old] inventory into about a dozen landfills around the country." Sweet'N Low tripled sales.

Although sugar refining had competitors on all sides, in 1969 American Sugar cast a vote of confidence in the future and in New York. Rather than move its five hundred office workers to the suburbs, it announced that they would stay in Manhattan, and management signed a new contract with the 1,400 workers at the Brooklyn plant.

25

CANDY ON THE ROCKS

During the 1960s all the candy-shop chains began seeing losses as city dwellers moved to the suburbs. Loft opened stores in the communities ringing the city, but shopping patterns were changing as people drove to their destinations. With little foot traffic to put customers in the way of temptation, suburban candy stores saw only a fraction of the sales Loft was accustomed to in the city.

At the beginning of the decade, Barton's Bonbonniere was thriving in Brooklyn. Ninety percent of its 850 employees, a "cross-section of all races and nations," lived in Brooklyn, where Barton's was one of the larger employers. Barton's sold its candy in sixty-two company-owned shops. In 1965 it began offering franchises both for its retail candy shops and for in-store counters. Soon its candy was being sold in thirty-six states and Canada, in individual stores and in departments in three hundred pharmacies, pastry shops, and greeting card stores.

In 1961 the 1,400 employees of Loft Candy made 35 million pounds of candy in its Long Island City factory. Loft too began offering franchises, but most of its sales came from its 275 company-operated candy shops.

African Americans weren't heading for the suburbs in large numbers, and it became advantageous for Loft, known for discriminatory hiring practices, to try to court them as customers. In 1963 the *Amsterdam News* ran a long story about Tracey Sam, a rarity as an African American supervisor, who ran the bulk stock and packing department. When the reporter asked Sam, then in his mid-sixties, what he did to look so young, he replied, "I eat a lot of Loft's candy." He had been eating it for a long time: he had started as a stock boy at the company in 1920, when he was a nineteen-year-old immigrant from St. Vincent.

By the end of the 1960s, Barton's and Barricini began closing stores and, along with Loft, switching to wholesaling, mainly selling their candy in department stores, greeting card stores, and drugstores. Neither the volume nor the freshness was the same. Restaurants and Waldorf Associates (later known as Restaurants Associates) acquired Barricini's 128 stores in 1967, and in 1970 the company was sold to the Southland Corporation, best known as the parent company of 7-Eleven. A year later Barricini's Stores, Inc., as a wholly owned subsidiary of the Southland Corporation, bought all Loft Candy's trademarks, machinery, and seventy retail stores. By the end of the decade the company was out of business. Barton's large workforce in the Brooklyn factory still made a tremendous amount of candy, but tastes and customs were changing. Giving a box of fancy candy to a sweetheart was becoming a quaint tradition.

After ninety-two years in Manhattan, the Henry Heide Candy Company, one of the country's largest candy-makers, moved to

New Brunswick, New Jersey, in 1961. Its new factory covered 4 acres set inside a large industrial park. Like many of the companies leaving for the suburbs, Heide offered the jobs to employees at the Hudson Street candy factory. In this case it was fairly easy for some long-time employees to follow the work, because that area of New Jersey had reasonably priced housing.

Candy-making, once a mighty industry in New York City, had employed 4,100 workers in 1969. Just seven years later that number had dwindled to 1,600. In 1972 the three-year-old Candy Corporation of America sold Mason Dots and Crows and Bonomo Turkish Taffy to the Sweets Company of America, and the following year it moved production to Chicago.

Early in the 1970s there were a few bright spots in this dim picture. Madelaine Chocolate Novelties in Rockaway Beach employed one hundred women in its one-story factory. Most were wives and mothers supplementing family incomes with their five-dollar-an-hour wages wrapping Easter bunnies, Valentine hearts, Thanksgiving turkeys, and Santas in colorful foils. Madelaine's 100 and the 750 employees at Barton's made up more than half the city's candy workers. Stephen Klein's factory in downtown Brooklyn continued to make candy for franchises in department stores and drug and card shops, especially for its thriving Passover candy business, but this niche was not so robust as in past years. Klein wasn't moving, however. "Our primary need is good labor," he told the *New York Times,* "and no place in America has a better labor force than New York. We have excellent relations with the three unions we deal with. Thirty-six years in business and not one strike, not one lockout."

In 1970, Cella's Cherries, known as G. Cella when the company began making chocolate-covered cherries back in 1864, moved into three floors of a large building on West Broadway, just south of Grand Street, in Manhattan. Most businesses were leaving an area that would soon be known as SoHo, and artists were moving into recently vacated lofts. The year before, Candy Corporation of America had bought Cella's Cherries, the Rolls-Royce of manufacturers of the product because it used 100 percent liquid filling, a "real fruit cherry," and chocolate made with a patented process that sealed the liquid in without any leakage. In 1985, Tootsie Roll acquired Cella, although Cella remained in the neighborhood until 2005, when it moved to Chicago, where it is still based.

PepsiCo, the parent company of Pepsi-Cola, bought its New York bottling plants from General Cinema, which had owned them since 1968. In 1974, Pepsi-Cola's sugar refinery plant in Brooklyn closed. Pepsi found that it could make sugar more cheaply elsewhere. The Long Island City plant operated under the control of the parent company until 1999, when it too closed. The ruby-red neon Pepsi-Cola sign on top of the factory was dismantled when the structure was demolished, but it has been resurrected at a location slightly north of the original building and still shines over the East River.

CLOSING TIME

n 1976 the 1,600 workers making Trident mints and gum at American Chicle began producing Freshen-Up, a gum that had flavored gel inside. The new gum was made on the fourth floor of the five-story factory, which operated twenty-four hours a day. During the overnight shift, from 11 p.m. to 7:30 a.m., only 150 people worked on the assembly lines. At 2:40 a.m. on November 22, about seventy workers were making Freshen-Up when a "thunderous explosion" tore through four floors of the building. Large windows and the walls on three sides were blown out; huge pieces of glass, concrete, and machinery landed in the deserted streets. One chunk of debris crushed a car. Over two blocks away, windows were shattered and buildings were "shaken from side to side." Even at that distance people heard workers screaming.

One nineteen-year-old said that the blast "threw me clear across the room. It was truly terrible. I saw men with their clothing and skin burned off. It was like a cloud of dust coming right at us."

The few that were unharmed—forty-eight people suffered burns, twenty-eight of them critically—got out using fire extinguishers to keep the flames at bay. "It's a miracle they survived," reported a fireman on the scene.

The injured, many running down the street with second- and third-degree burns "still smoldering," were loaded into a van from a nearby prison, police vehicles, and cars passing by and rushed to Elmhurst Hospital. Recent budget cuts had slashed the capacity of the hospital's burn unit, and soon ambulances were carrying patients to hospitals around the city and out to Long Island. A few of the most serious cases were flown by helicopter to Philadelphia. Eight days after the blast, fifteen workers were struggling to survive. Six ultimately died of their burns.

Arson was ruled out. But reports surfaced that a year earlier American Chicle had been warned that a volatile chemical, magnesium stearate, applied as a dry powder to strips of jelly-filled Freshen-Up and parts of the machinery to prevent sticking, could cause an explosion. The fire was believed to have started when sparks from a malfunctioning machine ignited the chemical dust, which was dense enough in part of the factory that some workers wore masks.

Repairs were made quickly and the company was ready to reopen by mid-December 1976, but the fire department wouldn't give its authorization. As of December 29, the American Chicle plant was still closed, and the workers were informed that 1,400 of them would be laid off the next day. All the employees had continued to be paid since the blast, but that was to end. Miraculously, the day after the threatened layoffs, the factory was cleared to reopen and 1,000 employees were called back to work.

The rumors began as soon as the Long Island City plant reopened. Some parts of the facility had been reconstructed and even enlarged, but two huge new factories had just been built in Illinois and California, both long, sleek buildings built for efficient production of 40 million boxes of gum a year. In the sixty-year-old Queens building, production lines weren't running as smoothly as they once had.

In 1977 the Queens district attorney charged executives at the parent company, Warner Lambert, with "reckless and conscious disregard for the lives, safety, and security of their employees." The company then announced it was ready to "vigorously defend itself." In 1978 the charges were dropped for insufficient evidence, then reinstated on appeal in 1979, charging that the company had failed to take measures that might have prevented the blast. Those charges too were dropped. Finally, in 1980, New York's highest court ruled that the danger was not foreseeable and the company and its executives couldn't be prosecuted.

During the four years following the blast, as the court cases were pursued, the number of workers steadily fell. By 1980 only 455 were left making three products: Crewels, another gum with a liquid center; Trident mints; and the four flavors of Trident gum. Even though there had been several omens, on the morning of April 21, 1981, when the production lines at the American Chicle factory in Long Island City were stopped and workers were gathered in the cafeteria, most were devastated when told that the plant would close at the end of the year.

Despite the terrible fire and the fatalities, 98 percent of the employees surveyed said that they loved their jobs and felt close to their coworkers. "It's a beautiful place to work," said sixteen-year veteran Rose Kear. "I've enjoyed every minute of it. Everybody got along like family," which was often the case, as nearly the "entire workforce was made up of family members, husbands and wives, fathers and sons, sisters and brothers." Ms. Kear had told her son fifteen years earlier, "You're going to work at Chiclets," and he had begun right after high school, working his way up to a supervisory position. The large majority of the line workers were first- and second-generation Poles, Italians, and Hispanics, and many had bought small homes close to the factory. Most workers weren't about to accept the suggested transfers to other company locations: One third were at least fifty-four years old, and the moves were just too far to contemplate. "I went home and cried," said a machine operator with thirteen years of service. "You tell me where I'm going to get a job," lamented a ten-year veteran leaving the plant for the last time.

Warner Lambert offered the employees a year's salary, extended medical benefits, and job counseling. Nevertheless, with manufacturing jobs disappearing with depressing regularity, only one of a group of twenty-five friends had found a job a few months later. Others eventually did get work, but most had to take a significant cut in salary.

"American Chicle is not typical of what's happening in Long Island City," said a spokesman for the Chamber of Commerce, but he was just blowing smoke, as this was exactly what had been happening to many of the city's food production companies over the previous two decades, a trend that accelerated between 1979 and the early 1990s, when there were an increasing number of departures of large factories and closures of small ones. The city and state did little to stop the outward flow; some officials were happy to see New York become a city of service industries. Food companies were a big part of the general exodus of manufacturing firms. The five-story American Chicle factory with peeling cream-colored paint and cracked tiles was slated to become an office complex.

27

DEPARTURES AND ARRIVALS

New Yorkers loved sugar but did not want it refined in their backyard. In 1971 an anonymous company proposed building a $35 million sugar refinery in Sunset Park, Brooklyn. But once the word leaked, people living nearby registered vehement opposition, because the "character of the neighborhood would be changed from primarily residential to industrial," and the plans were scuttled.

Two years later the anonymous company—Columbia Sugar, a Michigan beet-sugar refinery—proposed building a $40 million four-hundred-job cane-sugar refinery in the Stapleton section of Staten Island. By 1975 the project was awaiting approval, as Columbia wanted the least restrictive zoning classification and the Community Planning Board, concerned about increased truck traffic and pollution, was reluctant to grant it. The Staten Island refinery was never built. By then the city was down to two refiners, Amstar and SuCrest.

As mergers and acquisitions in the food industry continued, SuCrest (formerly American Molasses Company) sold Grandma's Molasses, bought Revere Sugar, a Boston-based company, and adopted that name for its two refineries. In 1977 the publicly traded company asked the Securities and Exchange Commission for more time to file its annual statement. The delay was needed to complete an internal investigation into raw sugar transactions. After its own investigation, the SEC accused SuCrest of making "false and misleading statements" to lower its tax liability. Without admitting liability, the firm ultimately agreed to the entry of a permanent injunction.

During this period SuCrest sold the sweetener division, the Revere Sugar Refinery, to a Filipino businessman. Revere had accounted for two thirds of the company's total assets, and what was left of SuCrest changed its name to Ingredient Technology, Inc. By 1985, amid charges that the deposed Philippine president Ferdinand Marcos and his wife, Imelda, were illegally linked to the company, Revere was in bankruptcy court. The refinery closed for good. Most of the buildings in the SuCrest/Revere Sugar Refinery complex in Red Hook were demolished in 2006.

And then there was one, Amstar. Its large complex on the East River in Williamsburg was one of five plants. The company, begun by Frederick Havemeyer, had dominated the sugar industry through most of the twentieth century because of its access to the Brooklyn waterfront, which made its products perfect for export. Domino Sugar, named by Henry Havemeyer in the early 1900s, was still one of the best-selling brands. In the late 1970s, Amstar had diversified into high-fructose corn syrup as a cheaper alternative to sugar, which was widely used in soft drinks like Coke and Pepsi, and by 1982, Amstar was the country's largest producer and distributor of sugar and other sweeteners. In 1986, Amstar's Brooklyn refinery was taken private in a leveraged buyout by Kohlberg, Kravis, Roberts and Company. Two years later Amstar Sugar changed its name to the Domino Sugar Corporation. Its sugar division, with its three refineries in Brooklyn, Baltimore, and New Orleans, was sold to the British refiner Tate & Lyle.

After a five-month strike in the mid-1990s, the Williamsburg refinery, one of the last of New York's large manufacturing plants, resumed operation, but in renegotiating union contracts in June 1999, Tate & Lyle announced that it was going to eliminate one hundred jobs. It also planned to end guaranteed full-time employment and weaken seniority rules, rolling back fifty years of hard-won advances.

The union struck again, and 286 workers—African Americans, Hispanics, and immigrants from Egypt, Italy, Poland, Yugoslavia, the Caribbean, and Russia, most with more than fifteen years on the job—walked out of the factory. Nine months passed; not a single striker returned to work. As the one-year anniversary arrived, fifty of the workers, discouraged at seeing so little progress, went back to work. One striker, despairing of ever finding another job, committed suicide.

Throughout the strike the refinery continued operating, using supervisors and workers from the Baltimore and New Orleans facilities but producing only "one tenth of its normal output of four million pounds of sugar a day." Domino claimed that since the Brooklyn plant had mainly produced specialty sugars, no customers were being affected by the strike.

For twenty months a group of workers continued picketing in the freezing winds blowing off the East River and under the broiling summer sun. After another 104 workers returned to work, the remaining diehards told the *Daily News* they would rather see the company close than have the contract "shoved down their throats." At this juncture the company announced that the plant would no longer refine sugar from raw cane. Instead semiprocessed liquid sugar would be shipped from Baltimore in barges that would dock next to the plant and the liquid would be pumped inside, where it would be crystallized into granules. The air in the Williamsburg neighborhood would never again carry the smell of molasses.

Finally, by a slim margin, the union voted to approve basically the same contract that had been offered almost two years earlier. The workers received a 5 percent increase in pay but lost full-time job rights and seniority and had to accept reduced sick and vacation time. In addition, more jobs were cut. According to a Tate & Lyle spokesperson, those let go received "a generous enhanced severance package." Six months later Tate & Lyle sold its American sugar operations to Florida Crystals, which renamed the parent company Domino Foods in 2001. In 2012, eight years after it closed, the former refinery in Brooklyn was bought by the real estate developing company Two Trees Management, which proposed mixed creative office space, community facilities, and affordable housing. In 2014 it was the site of a giant female sphinx—80 feet long by 40 feet high, with a core of polystyrene and a coating of sugar, created by the artist Kara Walker and commissioned by Creative Inc. Domino Foods donated the necessary 80 tons of sugar. Slated for demolition after the art event, it was the last connection to sugar the plant would have.

While the industrial food business in New York was shrinking, a revolution in taste was gathering force: a movement in both restaurants and food production to use first-class ingredients in better-crafted foods fostered dozens of small food companies that stressed either the quality of their product or its freshness and healthfulness. In 1977, two twenty-one-year-old childhood friends, Sophia Collier and Connie Best, began experimenting with soda in Collier's Brooklyn kitchen. After creating all-natural pink Fruit Punch Soho Natural Soda from seltzer water, orange juice, and assorted fruit, Collier explained, the young women "went from store to store to get people to buy it." It was a hard sell, "because no one ever heard of it" and the product was different from what most deli owners were used to. The women kept pounding the pavement, and by the end of their first year in business had sold 72,000 bottles of the carbonated fruit beverage, all of it delivered from the trunk of Collier's Jeep. It wasn't a roaring financial success. Their first fiscal year they earned "exactly one dollar," and by February 1979 revenues had risen only to $928. Yet Soho Soda had entered the market at a propitious time. Natural foods were catching on. Soho's high-quality beverage was less sweet and more complex in taste than the national brands—just what a growing band of consumers wanted in new products.

By 1984, Soho Soda, officially named the American Natural Beverage Corporation, had sold 4 million bottles of Soho Natural Soda, which now came in eight flavors: cream soda, orange soda with real orange juice, black cherry, lemon-lime, ginseng, ginger, blueberry, and root beer, all made with cane sugar and without preservatives, artificial colors, or artificial flavors. In the beginning the soda was made at "a little kosher bottling plant in the East New York section of Brooklyn owned by Alvin Schoenfeld," Collier later wrote in the *New York Times*. "He had started his own business with nothing, and I think he saw us as his spiritual heirs. Alvin bottled our first fifty cases on credit. Only afterward did he ask, with his special combination of practicality and Old World courtesy, 'And when will I be paid?' " When Schonfeld's small company could no longer handle the volume, Soho Soda was bottled by a Pennsylvania company, which it also outgrew. In 1987 the company employed thirty-eight workers and sold 14 million soda bottles a year, bottled at two different plants.

Soho Soda had reached $30 million in retail sales, but to expand it needed more capital, which its owners didn't have. "After eleven years of duking it out in the New York market," Sophia Collier told the *Wall Street Journal* in 1989, "I think I need a break." American Natural Beverage Corporation sold the company to Seagram for $15 million. Seagram hoped to grow sales by "four or five times," but it changed the formula, the soda flopped, and Seagram sold the brand in 1991.

In Brooklyn another young woman, twenty-year-old Aurora Passaro, had been thrown into the job of running her family's struggling eighty-eight-year-old business, the Manhattan Special Bottling Corporation, which made espresso-based Manhattan Special soda, when her father, Albert Passaro, was murdered in 1983. Aurora left college to step into his shoes. Her father had bought out his relatives to consolidate the company. During the 1980s, younger New Yorkers began looking for the richer and more robust flavors found in ethnic foods, made with older methods and good ingredients. This audience welcomed Manhattan Special and other community producers, including bakers, brewers, and butchers, whose original customers had either moved away or died off. "What celery soda was to Jews," Albert once said, "Manhattan Special was to the Italians." Albert Passaro was probably referring to Dr. Brown's Celery Tonic, which according to a 1984 *New York Times* article originated in 1869 in Williamsburg and was so popular among the Jewish community that it was referred to as "Jewish champagne."

Aurora Passaro had been working in the Manhattan Special factory since she was twelve, sweeping floors and making cartons, doing "whatever Daddy says." Together with her younger brother, Louis, she continued to produce the soda in its original nineteenth-century location, although the barnlike wooden structure had been remodeled in brick in the 1950s. They used the labor-intensive recipe with real-brewed espresso handed down from their brewmaster great-grandfather, Gaetano. Learning on the job, the fourth generation kept the company going with their close-knit neighborhood pulling for them.

IV

DRINK

28

SWILL MILK

n 1840 the city's milk came from an estimated 18,000 cows in Manhattan and Brooklyn, half housed in 500 small dairies. The rest were kept in crowded shanties attached to distilleries whose waste—swill—doubled as their feed. During the early 1840s, William Johnson Son's Distillery, the largest of these cruel operations, used ten times the amount of grain it had consumed ten years earlier. Each day, after 1,400 bushels of wheat had been soaked and fermented and the alcohol extracted in the distilling process, the leftover "distillery-slop" or swill was shoveled steaming hot into feeding troughs. Each cow consumed about 32 gallons daily. Fed this way, they produced large quantities of milk so thin and lacking in fats that it could not be churned into butter. A steady diet of swill milk, without the addition of any natural grains, destroyed the health of the cow and eventually killed it.

In an *Essay on Milk*, Robert Milham Hartley, a prohibitionist, exposed the horrors of the distilling industry. The "cattle are packed in rows of seven to ten across the building, head to head and tail to tail alternately." The cows had little fresh air and no water to drink, and their stalls were not cleaned. An "intolerable stench" sometimes fouled the air over a mile away. "Here in the stagnant and empoisoned atmosphere that is saturated with the hot steam of whiskey slop, and loaded with carbonic acid gas, and other impurities arising from the breath, the perspiration, and excrements of hundreds of sickly cattle, they are condemned to live, or rather die on rum-slush. For the space of nine months they are usually tied to the same spot, from which, if they live so long, they are not permitted to stir, excepting, indeed, they become so diseased as to be utterly useless for the dairy." A few unlucky ones "have stood in the same stalls for fifteen or eighteen months," although most never lasted that long.

Dead cows too obviously diseased were thrown in the river, while the carcasses of those not visibly damaged were bought by the "slop-beef dealer," a disreputable butcher who hastily sold the meat before it spoiled or stank. Health inspectors found swill meat in shops in poorer neighborhoods. When cooked, the "sickening odor" of the dairies was "perceptible in the meat on the table." Hartley said he had heard it "was a little darker" than healthy beef but was "very juicy, and sometimes well flavored," although "unwholesome!" That was also the word for a blue-tinged milk adulterated with "starch, burnt sugar, flour, plaster of Paris, chalk, eggs, annatto, etc." to make it whiter. This passed as milk for most of the city's children. Farm-fresh milk was reserved for the wealthy.

In 1851 Manhattan's twelve distilleries pumped out 3,000 gallons of rum from molasses each day; from Brooklyn's six distilleries flowed 5,459,300 gallons of whiskey. Charles Wilson's "extensive

COFFEE CATCHES TEA

The influx of inexpensive grains from the Erie Canal buoyed the city's twenty-nine breweries and sixteen distilleries. "Good, strong, clear ale," Mr. Cobbett recounted in his *American Farmer* article, and "all the material for making people drunk," cost considerably less in New York than in England.

The city's heavy drinking habits came under fire from the burgeoning temperance movement. By the 1830s master craftsmen began joining the ranks of those calling for New Yorkers to sober up. Some believed in total abstinence, while others would settle for a ban on drinking in workshops and factories, and workplace drinking waned.

Carbonated soda water was one popular substitute for booze. First produced in the century's opening decade by Noyes Darling & Co., by 1832 the John Matthews Soda Fountain Company at 55 Gold Street was thriving. Matthews had devised a method to produce bubbles by "agitating" marble dust or chips with water. Matthews gathered the leftover bits of marble from the construction site of St. Patrick's Cathedral on Mulberry Street, and his company produced 25 million gallons of effervescent liquid from the churchyard refuse. His rudimentary soda-fountain setup used different-flavored syrups to create peach, orange, cherry, lemon, and teaberry (similar to root beer) drinks.

Another substitute for alcohol was coffee: by as early as 1780, consumption had increased five times since the Revolution. Having eclipsed tea in popularity, coffee was becoming thought of as American's national hot beverage. A "good cup of hot coffee" with "sugar and fresh milk" was "exhilarating," exclaimed an article about a new shop in the basement of the Merchants Exchange. More important, it could free a man from the "worm of the still."

distillery" on the corner of Flushing Avenue and Skillman Street used 16-foot-wide and 4-foot-deep washtubs to hold a "mash machine" filled with hot water; corn was added and left to stand, then rye, heated and cooled; then yeast and the "mass" run off into "fermenting cisterns, producing alcohol." Wilson produced 480,000 gallons of whiskey a year made from 120,000 bushels of grain and extruded enough swill to feed eight hundred cows. Birdsall, Schenck & Sneaden's distillery needed eighty-seven wagons to cart away over 8,000 gallons of swill each *week*.

When *Frank Leslie's Illustrated Newspaper* ran a series of articles called "Our Exposure of the Swill Milk Trade" in 1858, it revived the crusade against bad milk that had stalled in the sixteen years since Robert Milham Hartley's earlier report. This time the public was given a full dose of the "sickening details," with illustrations and text describing the barns and the handling of the milk. The series lingered on the details: cows' tails truncated by useless inoculations, ulcerated sores, disintegrated teeth, diseased organs, and the contraptions used to hoist those too weak to stand for milking.

The worst offender remained Johnson's Distillery on 16th Street in Manhattan, along with two in Brooklyn, the Wilson Distillery and S. L. Husted. The latter was portrayed by the *Brooklyn Eagle* as the "largest, nastiest, the most offensive in every respect," a place where two hundred cows perished because they were too weak to flee the barn during a fire. The *Leslie* series described the revolting state of the milk, drawn from cows whose udders were covered with manure and urine "in which [they] had been lying"; the grimy "milkmaids" were men with long, greasy beards and hands "seldom or never washed before milking," and the milk pails, from

KLEINDEUTSCHLAND BEER

Just as more efficient systems for transporting grain altered eating and drinking habits, so new systems for providing clean water changed the quality of New York's number-one beverage, beer. In 1836, Sebastian Sommers was short a hand in his brewery and hired twenty-one-year-old Frederick Schaefer, a recent immigrant from Prussia. His brother, Maximilian, joined him, bringing along a recipe for lager beer. About the time that the two Schaefer brothers purchased Sommers's lower Broadway brewery and began producing their own beer, the Croton Aqueduct was completed, bringing clean water from the Hudson Valley to a huge reservoir on Fifth Avenue and 42nd Street with 38-foot walls holding back 24 million gallons of water. The F & M Schaefer Brewery was doing so well after two years that it moved into a larger building at Seventh Avenue and 17th Street (site of the Rubin Museum) and in 1849 moved again, to Park Avenue (then called Fourth Avenue) and 51st Street, a largely vacant area where it could continue to grow. Another brewer, George Gillig, who opened at about the same time, was also part of the lager wave.

Lighter in body, with a lower alcohol content than English-style beers, the German brew had a longer shelf life. There was a growing market for the beer as more Germans immigrated to New York. Many lived in Kleindeutschland (Little Germany), later called the Lower East Side: a mix of workshops, factories, bakeries, slaughterhouses, and breweries "in continuous operation, and this necessitated the practice of living-in for the workers"—code for working around the clock in little more than "sheds or shanties which they also called home."

which at least one thirsty horse drank, were filthy. Johnson's Distillery, which produced "twenty four thousand quarts" of swill milk a day, stretched that to 30,000 "by the addition of six thousand quarts of water."

The 59 million quarts of swill milk consumed annually harmed children and were blamed for New York's high infant mortality rate. Dr. S. Conant Foster wrote that the dairy owners had "amassed fortunes, built palaces, clothed their wives and daughters in diamonds, . . . purchas[ing these trappings of wealth] with the blood of slaughtered innocents."

Reporters followed the milkmen's wagons, "gorgeous in gold and blue and red paint," and watched the men fill their filthy pails with watered-down swill milk. Each route was printed in *Frank Leslie's* magazine, alerting families, bakeries, and grocers throughout the city of the "liquid poison" many were unaware they were buying. A cart belonging to B. Mullen had "Westchester Milk," "grass fed Milk," and "Pure Country Milk" boldly painted on its side, but what it deposited at the homes of unsuspecting residents between West 19th and West 26th Streets was swill. After the exposé customers dropped the services of the offenders and officials voiced outrage but took no action.

29

THE BRADY BUNCH

axes on alcohol have long been a politically acceptable way to fill the public coffers. Cash-strapped after the Civil War, the federal government raised taxes on distillery products from seventy cents per gallon in 1866 to two dollars in 1872, rendering spirits so unprofitable that a distiller could make more money off swill than rum or gin. The licit liquor industry, particularly in Brooklyn, was just about obliterated, but illegal production boomed. Wedged into backyards and hidden in cellars all over the city were mom-and-pop stills making mostly low-grade rum. A post–Civil War congressional report estimated that "the chances are nine out of ten, perhaps nineteen out of twenty," that an outlaw distillery could operate in New York without interference, and possibly "with the tacit support of the local government."

The federal government did notice that taxes were not being paid and sent federal agents and troops into New York to stamp out illegal distilleries. Early on the snowy morning of December 3,

1869, 1,500 soldiers, guarding about 70 revenue officers, marched into what was then Irishtown (now Vinegar Hill). The awakening residents "were somewhat astonished at hearing the tread of an army under their windows" as troops converged on the area, which *Frank Leslie's Illustrated* colorfully called "Bourbon Avenue and Lightning Alley" (John and Little Streets). The soldiers' mission was to destroy the area's many stills and confiscate any illegal spirits during what was later called the Whiskey War. "Buildings were ripped up, and tumbled down; floors were raised to find beneath more evidence." Troops seized "smoking hot" mash tubs and the "apparatus of the trade" as "rivers of rum ran through the gutters." The officers destroyed thirteen distilleries, seized 35 barrels of "bad rum," and washed gallons of the bubbling fermenting brew down sewers.

But the production of illegal rum was profitable and hard to stop. Within two years at least fourteen stills were cooking hooch. The Brady family opened their first still, ostensibly a molasses distillery, at 46-48 Green Lane. Like most large operators, the Bradys hid their shady activities behind a legitimate enterprise that emitted strong masking odors. The "kings of the moonshiners" were the five Brady brothers. The two eldest, John and Edward, ran the business; Hugh, Patrick, and Thomas manned the distilleries.

The Bradys also operated a protection racket that extorted fees from other moonshiners, forcing them to sell their products through the brothers' distribution network. Their stranglehold on the moonshiners may have caused a disgruntled competitor to turn them in, as their Green Lane still was confiscated during an 1871 raid. Between 1870 and 1874 there were numerous large-scale government forays into the neighborhood, but scouts kept an eye out for revenue officers and the wily moonshiners could quickly dismantle their apparatus or escape into the alleyways, and their businesses were usually back up and running within a week.

As the Bradys' operations expanded to "all of New-York and its vicinity," they acquired a rectifying factory on Gold Street, on the waterfront, that made legal chemical-grade alcohol. Next the "gang of roughs from Irishtown" set up an even more audacious venture, producing 1,000 gallons of rum per day in a bone-boiling factory on a desolate island in Jamaica Bay (now part of Floyd Bennett Field). They took molasses out to the island by boat, and on its return trip the boat sailed around the edge of Brooklyn and unloaded the rum into the Gold Street building, their main distribution center. The island was raided in 1874 and all the rum destroyed, but the brothers escaped. Escaping a second raid at their Gold Street operation, Edward Brady fled to Canada. Upon his return to New York about two years later, he was arrested and sent to prison for thirteen months. Halfway through his sentence, in January 1877, he injured his arm in an accident, and because he was a "poor" man with a "dependent and destitute" family, President Ulysses S. Grant pardoned him. No sooner was Edward Brady free than he opened a still on Delancey Street.

In about 1877, John Brady moved their operations to 45th Street in Manhattan, between Tenth and Eleventh Avenues, where they again used a rectifying factory as a front for a 1,000-gallon rum-distilling facility. Even though the place had underground pipes that moved the rum to a building across the street to avoid detection, it was raided. Arrests were made, but the four Bradys involved escaped.

John and Edward then opened their largest distillery, on the Jersey side of the Hudson River, under the Palisades. The three younger brothers were there when it was raided in the spring of

1879, and Hugh and Thomas were arrested. Patrick escaped to Canada. Edward went into hiding, but by December he was feeling cocky and went out partying at a saloon on 45th Street, where he was captured and taken into custody. John was arrested a few days later. During their trial Edward tried to shield his brothers by pleading guilty. Having already been behind bars for six months, Hugh, Thomas, and Patrick avoided further jail time. In 1880 John and Edward were found guilty of manufacturing illegal rum for fourteen years "in and around different dives of Manhattan and Brooklyn." John served one year, Edward two, with hard labor.

By the time they got out, large-scale illegal operations seem to have been prosecuted out of existence. As for the legal stuff, cheaper imports from Tennessee, Kentucky, Indiana, and Illinois had undercut local producers so substantially that the majority of hard liquor bought in the city's bars and saloons was no longer made in New York.

THE LAGER CRAZE

eer was what everyone wanted, the *Sun* reported, and what filled people's steins and glasses was overwhelmingly lager. After the Civil War its popularity overtook that of other kinds of beer because of its sparkling effervescence and fresher taste. Owing to its lower alcohol content, it was taxed more lightly and sold more cheaply than heavier beers. By 1880, Manhattan's fifty-seven breweries made 1.5 million barrels of beer, about 80 percent of it lager.

The country's largest brewer was George Ehret's Hell Gate Brewery, opened in 1866. Ehret had arrived from Germany sixteen years earlier, apprenticed at A. Hupfel's brewery, risen to foreman, and then, with help from Hupfel, opened his own brewery. As with biscuits, canned foods, and condensed milk, tastes were changing, and the wide variety of new products found a population ready to experiment. In Gilded Age New York, where different ethnic groups lived in close proximity, it was easy to see what the other guy was eating or drinking; an Irishman might discover a fondness for lager at work, where his German mates were drinking it.

Named for a particularly treacherous section of the East River, the Hell Gate was located between 92nd and 93rd Streets and Second and Third Avenues, a "bucolic" area with a "decidedly rural character," and it was here that Ehret's brewery flourished. The first beer was put into deep underground caverns in January 1867. The caves had been dug out of the rock beneath Manhattan; there the beer would "lager," or ferment, for three months in a stable, cool, humid environment. Within five years Ehret was selling

Entrances to the Central Park Brewery rock vaults (started 1866) on East 56-57th Streets.

33,512 barrels a year, and by 1874 that number had tripled. An enormous fire in the brewery was "not an unmixed evil," because demand had far outstripped the capacity of the original brewery and Ehret could now build a larger one outfitted with the latest machinery.

By the end of the 1870s the 1,800 men employed in Brooklyn's thirty-eight breweries rolled out 1.1 million barrels a year. Eight establishments manufactured Weiss beer, which, at only 2 to 4 per-cent alcohol, was so mild that many saloons considered it a temper-ance drink.

A Brooklyn brewer, William Ulmer, arrived in New York from Germany in 1850 while in his late teens and became the brew-master at his uncle Clausen's East 47th Street brewery. By 1871 he had formed the Vigelius & Ulmer Continental Lagerbier Brewery in Bushwick. Between 1880 and 1885 the brewery occupied more than half the block and Ulmer became the sole owner. The brew-ery's collection of brick buildings was given landmark status in 2010. Today the owners' names and the 1872 date are still visible etched into the marble on the building's façade.

On Staten Island, George Bechtel led a large brewery started by his father. He boasted that he was "know[n] the world over as being the producer of the best beer made in the United States." After he won first prize in an international exposition in Sydney in 1880, with beer that had traveled for fourteen months but remained "as sweet, clear and full of life as when first bottled," he sold 10,000 barrels a year to an Australian distributor. Later some of his beer made it to Manila, where it withstood the tropi-cal heat, and then traveled on to Japan, to which he soon shipped 1.2 million bottles.

RULERS AND RULED

The brewery princes, who became fabulously wealthy, modeled their buildings on European castles and ruled their breweries like kingdoms. They hired immigrant men fresh off the boat and forced them to rent apartments in company-owned housing. This labor force worked marathon hours six days a week, with a shorter six-hour day on Sunday mornings. Even with the introduction of machinery, the work was one of the most arduous in food processing. The men had to endure constant temperature changes as they moved between the heat of the brewhouse and the icy storage areas, which made them susceptible to a variety of bronchial and joint diseases. Most were burned out by the age of forty-five.

Eight percent of the men were German, most of them factory workers; only one or two skilled brewers were needed in any brewery. In January 1881 four hands in Peter Doelger's brewery died while varnishing the inside of a barrel, an unnecessarily dangerous activity. A grand jury investigated, and while it placed no blame on either Doelger or his drunken foreman, the publicity galvanized the workers. By June the Union of Journeymen Brewers had been formed and demanded that brewery owners in "New York [Manhattan], Williamsburgh, Morrisania, Union Hill, Staten Island . . . limit the hours of work (including mealtimes) to twelve" and "cease entirely on Sunday."

Determined to maintain the status quo, the United Lager Beer Brewers of Greater New York made a show of negotiating. Fourteen smaller breweries agreed to the workers' demands, but the rest refused, and the workers struck just as brewing entered its busiest season. After two weeks, while recruiting replacements, the owners made noises about accepting the shorter hours, and many strikers returned to work for fear of losing their jobs permanently. By July, with the men again working sixteen-hour days, the breweries were running at full capacity.

GROWLER

New Yorkers drank beer at home as well as in taverns, saloons, restaurants, and factories. "In New York a can brought in [and] filled with beer at a bar-room is called a *growler*, and the act of sending this can from the private house to the public-house and back is called *working* [or rushing] *the growler*," *Harper's Magazine* noted in July 1893. Children as young as five mastered the task of carrying the galvanized pail of beer without spilling it, scurrying back and forth between the local brewery or saloon and the factory floors or apartment kitchens. The word *growler* likely came from the sound of carbon dioxide seeping out of beer sloshing inside a moving pail.

Even though lager was the most popular beer, the mainly English and Irish workforce in Manhattan's twenty breweries stuck with ale or porter. The David Jones brewery filling East 6th Street between Avenues A and B turned out a variety of ales: India Pale Ale, Amber and Burton (a dark, aged ale), fresh porter, and ale brewed expressly for the southern market. The Milbank Brothers Brewery, originally owned by John Murray, operated in its original location on Madison Street, but in a new five-story building modernized with steam engines and a refrigeration system. One of its fans wrote that only "ale from that time-stained brewery is ale," and a "pewter mug full of that is more precious than a big Missouri river of Lager."

31

BREWERY PRINCESS

hough it's unlikely that he expected to die suddenly at forty-six, August Schmid so believed in the business acumen of his thirty-six-year-old wife that he bequeathed her his half of the Lion Brewery and his enormous estate, which she was to manage until their two daughters came of age and the estate was equally divided between them. A woman heading any large business, especially a brewery, was an anomaly in 1889. The Lion Brewery, a sprawling group of buildings between 107th and 109th Streets and Amsterdam Avenue to Central Park West, employed 230 men and not a single woman. When Josephine Schmid incorporated the brewery, she made herself president and treasurer and showed up at the plant every day. She also ran the fifty saloons her husband had accumulated over the years, though her work was exclusively on the executive side. She "never attempted to brew beer in person," she later explained, and the "mending of beer pumps was always relegated to employees." During this time she also expanded August's real estate holdings and six years after his death built a limestone mansion in a style reminiscent of a Loire Valley château at Fifth Avenue and 62nd Street.

Her daughter Pauline later recounted that during the period when Josephine was trying to work with her partner, Simon E. Bernheimer, she had "business difficulties" and was "rather bitter against everybody." Bernheimer wanted to move the Lion Brewery closer to the Hudson River and was undoubtedly shocked when Josephine objected. In 1900 he initiated a suit to declare that all the Lion Brewery's assets—the land, buildings, and capital—belonged to the partnership and should be sold. Josephine countersued, stating that half the land under the brewery was hers. And she won. By 1903 she had bought out Bernheimer's interest for $3 million and was solely in charge of the brewery.

It was a good time to own a large brewery; beer consumption had risen steadily, as a 1905 headline in the *New York Sun*, "Beer Drives Out Hard Liquor," testified. Mechanization and refrigeration were speeding up brewing, and the total number of breweries declined as several of the larger ones expanded and smaller operations were forced out of business. By 1910, Brooklyn was down to thirty-one breweries, and by 1915 to twenty-three.

By the second decade of the twentieth century, most large breweries had bottling facilities, and about 20 percent of their output was earmarked for pint and quart bottles of pasteurized, clear, pale, and mellow beers distinguished by branded labels. Once the top was popped, creamy white foam formed as the liquid cascaded into a glass. New Yorkers could now chill bottles in the icebox and drink beer at home.

When Pauline Schmid turned twenty-one in 1894 (her older sister had died two years earlier at the same age), Josephine offered to buy out her portion of the inheritance for a lump sum of $342,748, promising to manage the money and pay her daughter 5 percent of its profits annually. What Josephine didn't tell her daughter was that the estate was worth about $10 million. Asked later why she agreed to sign away her fortune so easily, Pauline replied, "I signed anything she wanted me to sign," because she believed any profits "were for both of us" and eventually everything would be hers.

Pauline's attitude obviously changed by 1908, when she sued to receive her fair share of the estate and to remove her mother from management of the brewery, where most of the profits went to pay Josephine's $500,000 salary as treasurer. During the trial, which lasted for almost a year, fifty-five-year-old Josephine married in a quiet ceremony in Brooklyn. The groom, Don Giovanni Del Drago, who claimed to be twenty-seven and an Italian prince, was actually forty-seven, twice divorced, and had a twenty-year-old son in Switzerland, and he was no prince. Four days after her wedding Josephine settled the lawsuit, agreeing to step down as

JEWISH MOONSHINE

In the early years of the twentieth century, plebian New Yorkers were making money from making booze. While beer drinking continued to grow at the expense of hard liquor, there was still a market for the cheap, illegal version. Moonshiners are often pictured as rifle-toting, bearded mountain men, but distilling illegal beverages was more widespread and profitable in the canyons of New York than in the hills of West Virginia. Most city raids were completed without gunshots or bloodshed, and the pragmatic city distiller, who knew he would soon be back in business, paid his fine or did his (short) time. Even though New York had a large contingent of revenue officers, they were the first to concede that "there was little hope of suppressing the illicit distilling in New York" as long as it turned a dollar.

In poorer neighborhoods, stills were often found in tenements, usually near a saloon where the product (and evidence) could quickly be quaffed. One ingenious Lower East Side setup impressed even the jaded revenue agents who had long searched for it. A trapdoor behind the bar in a saloon led to a ladder into an underground passageway. Deep beneath the streets was a block-long labyrinth of rooms full of stored liquor casks, and 100 feet down the path was the still . . . under a synagogue. The congregants of First United Podhaycer, which had opened in 1903 at 126 Rivington Street, worshiped right over this underground still. On the building's ground floor was Sam Schapiro's legal winery.

Schapiro had arrived from the Austro-Hungarian Empire in the late 1800s and by 1899 began producing kosher wine as a sideline for his restaurant on Attorney Street, where diners were served a free glass of mead, or honey wine. On the days before the Jewish holidays, people lined up to buy the wine, which his ads described as "so thick you can cut it with a knife." Concord grapes from upstate were crushed in the shop and fermented under the supervision of a rabbi. Belowground, either Schapiro or someone with his blessing was making well-crafted whiskey. The moonshiner was probably a Russian Jewish immigrant, since Jews had operated about 89 percent of Russia's distilleries in the 1870s, drink being one of the few areas where they could legally work. In the 1920s Schapiro's family reminisced that he sold "the good stuff" out of his back room.

treasurer but not as president. Pauline now became a director of the brewery.

Even though Princess Josephine Schmid Del Drago, as she was now known, spent much of her time with her husband in Italy, she retained tight control of the brewery, to the detriment of the business. After the brewery experienced several years of significant losses, Pauline sued her mother for neglect and mismanagement. Josephine won, and she and her husband, possibly chastened, took charge of day-to-day operations.

After years of further legal wrangling with her mother, Pauline Schmid Murray emerged as the sole shareholder of the Lion Brewery in 1925, and her husband was named president. The brewery survived Prohibition and continued to operate after the Murrays were killed in a car crash in 1931. The wealthiest woman in the American brewing industry, Pauline was worth over $4 million at the time of her death—$3 million attributed to shares in the brewery.

32

THE THIRSTY HOME FRONT

Taking a rest cure in Germany, George Ehret was trapped there when World War I broke out. While he was away the U.S. government confiscated his $40 million brewery as alien property. After the United States declared war on Germany in April 1917, not only the government but vigilante patriots targeted German brewers. Sales suffered.

The war was not the only problem for brewers. Three years earlier the Anti-Saloon League, the major force lobbying for Prohibition, launched a campaign to amend the Constitution and swayed a large portion of the House of Representatives to their "dry" side.

At first brewers doubted that the temperance legislation would affect them. Forty-eight-year-old Rudolph J. Schaefer, an unmistakable character with a handlebar mustache that tapered off into thin curls that reached halfway to his ears, had worked his way up through the ranks for thirty years to become "one of the best-known and most popular men in the business." He had taken over his family's F & M Schaefer Brewery in 1912, after his uncle Frederick and his father, Maximilian, died, then he bought out his cousins and began looking for a new location.

In 1859 the founders had moved the brewery to midtown, when it was still undeveloped, and expanded until their buildings covered 50th to 52nd Streets and from Park to Lexington Avenues. As the city moved north, the land under the brewery became a goldmine, and the sale of a parcel on Park Avenue to St. Bartholomew's Church financed Rudolph's decision to move the facility to a state-of-the art brewery in Brooklyn, on the East River. With the average adult's consumption of beer topping 30 gallons a year, F & M Schaefer was in an excellent position to expand and modernize.

As the movement to outlaw drinking gathered strength, Josephine Schmid Del Drago's Lion Brewery advertised its beer as "Pure Wholesome Nutritious," made in "the most modern way and under absolutely sanitary conditions." Other ads were more to the point. In 1916, with the "drys" holding a majority in both houses of Congress, Peter Doelger's Brewery, on 55th to 56th Streets between Third Avenue and Avenue A (now Sutton Place), advertised that "Beer is the Pure Temperance Drink."

The ads for S. Liebmann Sons Brewery's Rheingold beer ads ventured a subtle distinction: "Temperance was one thing; abstinence is another." The third generation of the family presided over the fifty-year-old Brooklyn brewery. Six Liebmann grandsons, groomed by their fathers, were producing about 21.7 million gallons of Rheingold beer and buying up neighboring breweries. They were active in beer associations, which published articles pointing out how the industry employed thousands not only in the

HOOCH

To preserve grain for bread, whiskey distilling ceased in September 1917, a few months after the declaration of war. The ban didn't affect New York, where there was very little of the legal industry, and indeed buoyed the underground network. Once the restrictions on distilling went into effect, only those with permits could buy non-beverage-grade alcohol, used in products ranging from hair tonics to flavor extracts. Soon five thousand permits were issued to new "manufacturers" in New York, and while some actually made legal products, overnight "cologne-makers," whose products weren't daubed behind anyone's ears, pulled most of the permits. Revenue agents estimated there were about fifty illegal stills in operation. One garage in the Bronx turned out 200 to 300 gallons of liquor a day before two of its four moonshiners were caught; the other two fled. Saloonkeepers poured the 150-proof hooch into empty bottles of legitimate products to disguise their illicit contents, dispensing to customers drinks that would "scorch their innards."

breweries but in businesses catering to the industry, and paid significant water and real estate taxes.

When a wartime Congress prohibited the production of distilled spirits and severely restricted the supply of grain, the beer-makers were taken by surprise. Josephine Schmid Del Drago's lawyer complained that the "Lion Brewery, like other large brewing concerns, [was] suffering from the present wave of prohibition now rolling over the country, coupled with the increased cost of barley, hops, and other material used in the manufacture of beer" and was losing money because it couldn't "raise the price of beer above 5

COFFEE IN AN INSTANT

After the government bought a Brooklyn company's entire stock of soluble coffee, its ads exclaimed, "G. Washington's Refined Coffee has gone to war." Soldiers could enjoy instant coffee, heatable over a small fire that wouldn't attract the enemy, without the fuss of brewing. One soldier wrote, "I am very happy despite the rats, the rain, the mud, the draughts, the roar of the cannon and the scream of shells. It takes only a minute to light my little oil heater and make some George Washington Coffee ... Every night I offer up a special petition to the health and well-being of Mr. Washington."

The ads for G. Washington's instant coffee, introduced in July 1910, urged, "Make your coffee in a cup" without "a pot, bags, grounds, or eggs when you used Red E coffee" (as it was initially called). It was "always ready," required "no cooking," and made the "best iced coffee you ever drank." While George Constant Louis Washington, the company's founder, didn't invent instant coffee—a Japanese scientist, Dr. Satori Kato, had done that in Chicago in 1901, but his Kato Coffee was unsuccessful—he had his own secret process and was the first to market it successfully.

cents a glass." Desperation fathering invention, the brewers came up with "war beer," which was 2.75 percent alcohol.

After the armistice, the brewers pledged their allegiance to the country, though the Eighteenth Amendment, which banned the manufacture, transportation, and sale of intoxicating liquors, was before the states for ratification, and they were powerless to stop it. Samuel Gompers, the labor leader, was outraged over dry activism. Beer was the "workingman's drink at the noon hour with the rough sandwich he brings from home," and he wouldn't be made "a total abstainer" by law "in a day."

German-born George F. Trommer, of the Evergreen Brewery in Brooklyn, testified at a Senate hearing in 1919 that it was his company's policy to allow workers to drink their fill of brews with only 2.75 percent alcohol. His men took full advantage of this perk, which had "never made them intoxicated, nor has it in any degree decreased their efficiency." Trommer also ran a restaurant, banquet halls, and a summer garden that could accommodate four thousand people where at least 75 percent of the liquid refreshments served—approximately 1,881,500 glasses—was 2.75 percent alcoholic beer. From his "personal observation" at gatherings of "young and old assembled around the same table eating and drinking," it was "practically impossible for one to become intoxicated by drinking the beer as it is now brewed." Yet rural nativist drys felt beer gardens had no place in America.

33

"CITY ON A STILL"

One day in 1920, thirty-year-old Fannie Cohn answered the door of her Bronx apartment to find the police. Responding to a tip, they had caught her with a 50-gallon copper still, 5 gallons of mash, and 150 gallons of homemade whiskey. On East 79th Street, detectives entered Bertha Weber's kitchen, and although no whiskey was brewing, the stove held a red-hot still and a quantity of sugar, potatoes, and mash. Bertha bottled a barrel of whiskey a day, swaddling her deliveries inside a baby carriage. Across town, opposite the Cathedral of St. John the Divine, the air was filled with the pungent fumes of moonshine. Police only had to follow their noses to find Charles Hofman's cellar distillery. Downtown, at 215 Mulberry Street, one cabinetmaker was caught with 120 gallons of red wine aging in the cellar of his apartment building. Italian immigrants had regularly made wine before Prohibition and legally still could for their family's personal consumption. The cabinetmaker, however, was selling his wine to the restaurant next door, and *that* was illegal. In Brooklyn, the "master moon-shiner" Simon Nosowitz was accused of manufacturing stills that he installed for his customers, then instructing them in the art of making whiskey. Found guilty, he was given a sentence of thirty days in jail, but the judge, learning that he had children, cut it to one day.

During Prohibition New Yorkers cooked up vast amounts of moonshine, earning the city the nickname "City on a Still." Just about anyone with enough chutzpah could make money manufacturing illegal alcohol, and although many were caught during the first year, few moonshiners served prison time. Whether uptown or down, a $500 still paid for itself in a few days. New Yorkers had all the booze they could drink.

It was harder to get a good glass of beer.

The Anti-Saloon League, which had spearheaded passage of Prohibition's Volstead Act, estimated that each week before the law went into effect New Yorkers drank 30 million quarts of draft beer, plus a million quarts of bottled beer and ale, along with hundreds of thousands of gallons of various whiskies and wine—three and a half times more than the rest of the country. Considering its source, that figure should be shaved, but New Yorkers *were* big drinkers.

Once Prohibition began, the city's approximately seventy breweries struggled to stay in business. Before 1920, Brooklyn alone had twenty-three, a number that dwindled to twelve in 1929 and to ten by 1931. To survive, thirty breweries, including Lion, Liebmann, and F & M Schaefer, obtained licenses to make "near beer," a legal brew containing less than one half of 1 percent alcohol. Some breweries switched to soft drinks, ice, or malt syrup for confections. Several made malt extract from a brewery by-product; F & M Schaefer's product was called Malt Vita. After suing the government in late 1920 to test the constitutionality of Prohibition, a case that went nowhere, the Lion Brewery turned to dry pursuits, running a garage and a dyeing plant.

During the first few years of Prohibition many smaller breweries were sold. Part of George Ehret's mighty Hell Gate Brewery complex, occupying the block between 63rd and 64th Street, went to a holding company owned by John D. Rockefeller Jr. for the future enlargement of the Rockefeller Institute for Medical Research. In his will, Ehret, who died in 1927, asked his children to keep the brewery going, making near beer until they could resume regular production, but eventually they had to sell. The manager of the Peter Doelger Brewery on 55th Street and what is now Sutton Place offered $10,000 to "anyone who can show us a successful use for this brewery." No one could, and in 1929 the family sold it.

Bernheimer and Schwartz Pilsner Brewery closed in 1923 after a raid by federal agents, a cruel day for the city's beer drinkers. The brewery had moved and the new owners of the building wanted all its contents destroyed. Resting in the cellars of the twenty-year-old brewery were 836,000 oak barrels filled with lager, plus 4,000 barrels of twelve-year-old ale kept at the perfect temperature by optimistic employees. The brewmaster, his assistant, and twenty men silently watched as federal agents opened the valves on one barrel after another and the golden liquid sloshed into a drainage pipe that ran into sewers that emptied into the Hudson River at 129th Street.

Watching years of their labor go down the drain, the men were overcome and burst into song: "Beer, beer, glorious old-fashioned beer/Up with the sale of it, down with the pail of it/Glorious

Dry agents seize alcohol in barrels stored in a perfume establishment at Hudson and 11th Street.

old-fashioned beer." As the drainage pipe could hold only so much liquid, it took several days to empty all the barrels, the men standing by, watching. On the final day a sign was put on an empty keg with the epitaph "Rest in Peace Until We Meet Again," which would be many years in the future.

New Yorkers could still get their hands on a bottle of beer with 4 percent alcohol, and in the early years those who were making this illegal beer were rarely caught. In 1923 federal agents staged a simultaneous raid at many of the city's breweries and found that the alcohol content of the beer was higher than was legal. The manufacturers blamed it on the weather, and this must have been accepted, as no action was taken.

As Prohibition ground on, government agents got cannier, but they were in short supply. In 1925 a few agents discovered that the new owners of the David Mayer Brewery, in business since 1882, made "day beer," the legal near-beer variety, but also a surreptitious "night beer" shipped out after midnight, and the brewery was closed and padlocked.

Similarly, when agents found bottles of full-strength beer in an Ebling brewery delivery truck, there was no alibi. Further, when the Ebling brewery was searched and 120 cases of old-time beer were found, the owners offered a $4,000 bribe, but it didn't help them evade fines (although bribes often did help). Two years later another Ebling truck carrying illegal beer was searched and the brewery was temporarily closed and padlocked. The owners pled guilty and paid fines, and after four months the brewery reopened. The Ringler Brewery, caught in a similar situation, lost its license, and its officers and employees were "forever prohibited from manufacturing even near beer."

Near beer could easily be made at home, as representative Fiorello La Guardia demonstrated in his Washington office in 1926. Mixing two parts malt extract (3.76 percent alcohol) with one part near beer (half of 1 percent) "knocked the 'near' clean out of the near beer." This concoction raised a "thick, rich foam" and tasted like pre-Prohibition lager. The Queens *Daily Star* reported that malt extract producers saw their sales "increase materially," providing ingredients for parties held across the borough.

While most breweries limped through Prohibition, George F. Trommer in Brooklyn sold more near beer that he ever had real

SACRED AND PROFANE WINE

During the early years of Prohibition, Schapiro's House of Kosher Wine operated legally because sacramental wine was exempt from the Volstead Act. Likewise, priests in Catholic churches could dispense wine during mass. Jewish users were allotted 10 yearly gallons per family. This was often more than enough. The *Atlantic Monthly* quoted a woman who lived on the Lower East Side whose father "used to buy a gallon and have it for a whole year." The federal government wasn't sure who was or wasn't a rabbi, but all anyone needed for a rabbinical permit to distribute the wine was a list of the congregation. Not surprisingly, many new congregations sprang up overnight, with a host of decidedly non-Jewish names, and many abuses were perpetrated in rabbis' names, and occasionally with their help. A rabbi might, for a fee, let a bootlegger handle the paperwork, transportation, and storage of the sacramental wine, which these middlemen then often used as a cover to peddle the profane variety. Between 1922 and 1924 the amount of sacramental wine "withdrawn on permit from bonded warehouses" increased by about 800,000 suspicious gallons a year.

beer, making him one of the few brewers in the country to increase sales in the dry years. He brought it off by financing 965 lunch counters that exclusively sold his *White Label Near Beer,* and he had to enlarge his brewery to supply them all. His success might have influenced Edward B. Hittleman, a Russian Jewish immigrant, who in a quixotic act bought the Otto Huber brewery in 1925, changed the name to the Edward B. Hittleman Brewery, and survived Prohibition by making near beer.

Man with kosher wine in New York, circa 1930.

The manager of the Lion Brewery said that the "flavor and quality of this [near] beer" was "being improved," but people were
drinking 50 percent less than before Prohibition because it didn't
taste as good and people felt full before feeling any buzz. Another
said brewers were trying to make "near-beer taste something—but
not very much—like a good brew." As one saloonkeeper explained,
near beer "had little appeal as a beverage" and was usually only
"taken as a 'chaser' for some contraband drink." Beer drinkers
who had "never drunk anything stronger," he said, were turning
to whiskey, which was easier to make illegally and, because of its
smaller packages, smuggled better.

34

THE BATTLE FOR
PASTEURIZED MILK

M ilk was New York's second favorite beverage (after beer), and by 1925 milk processing was a big industrialized business. The largest consolidation in the dairy industry took place in 1926, when the National Dairy Products Company bought New York's Sheffield Farms Company, one of the largest U.S. processors and distributors of dairy products. Sheffield continued to operate under its own well-known name and by the mid-1920s ran two thousand delivery routes in Manhattan, Brooklyn, Queens, and the Bronx. Three of its New York pasteurizing and bottling plants were among the nation's largest.

The company that became Sheffield Farms had roots stretching back to 1841, when Thompson W. Decker left his job as a Manhattan deliveryman for a dairy on the Morris family's estate to sell fresh milk from his own Morrisania Dairy. His slogan, "Quality & Purity—on these rocks I mean to build my business," resonated with New Yorkers during the swill-milk scandals of the 1850s and

HEWITT 10 TON TRUCK
ONE OF FLEET OF 3 HEWITT TRUCKS IN SERVICE OF THIS COMPANY

Hewitt along with Saurer were sister brands to Mack when the International Motor Co. was formed in 1911. Hewitt trucks were high-capacity vehicles used mainly in the New York City area.

1860s. As his business expanded, he convinced the railroads to run special trains to carry his milk into Manhattan and opened a milk store on East 27th Street.

In 1902, Decker merged with two other large dairies to form the Sheffield Farms-Slawson-Decker Company. The city's largest milk processor, it brought together three men who transformed milk production. The company's president was Loton Horton, owner of the Slawson dairy, a family business, and the third partner was Lewis B. Halsey of Sheffield Farms, an early advocate of pasteurization.

Halsey admired the work of Nathan Straus, the co-owner of

Macy's Department Stores, who had championed pasteurization after one of his children died from milk possibly contaminated with diphtheria. In the 1890s the city's infant mortality rate was high, especially during the summer, when it was hard to keep milk chilled. Warm milk was a fertile environment for the bacteria that caused typhoid, diphtheria, scarlet fever, and septic sore throat, along with tuberculosis from infected cows. Although Louis Pasteur had discovered in the 1860s that milk heated to 145 to 162 degrees Fahrenheit killed the bacteria, New York lagged in accepting a theory still questioned by the local medical and scientific communities. Nathan Straus, however, could and did fund his conviction that pasteurization would save New York's children.

In 1890 he joined with a few like-minded pediatricians to stop the "slaughter of babies." First he bought pasteurized milk from a processor in Dutchess County, and by summer's end he had distributed 34,400 bottles of inexpensive or free milk from a depot on the East 3rd Street pier. The second summer, with five additional depots, the number rose to 306,446 bottles. Three years later he financed his own pasteurization and bottling plant on East 3rd Street and opened eighteen strategically placed milk pavilions to acquaint the public with "the best possible milk for children." One hot summer afternoon in City Hall Park a reporter watched as 8 glasses a minute were sold. By 1916 these stands were serving over 1.5 million glasses of pasteurized milk.

For $1.50 New Yorkers could make their own clean milk with the Nathan Straus Home Pasteurizer. It contained a pot with a lid and a rack to hold milk bottles so they could be submerged in hot water for 40 minutes and pasteurized "to a degree of exactness that is almost unbelievable," said Straus. Lewis Halsey, the president of

Sheffield Farms, studied Pasteur's and Straus's work and in 1891 set up a commercial pasteurization plant at his New Jersey dairy for distribution in New York.

Other groups, however, opposed pasteurization and championed "certified" raw milk, a system that inspected "every drop of milk consumed in the city" from cow to consumer. Although the inspections reduced bacteria, certified raw milk was too expensive for the majority of New Yorkers.

The two factions opposed each other for several years, but the economics of producing the vast quantities of milk consumed by the city led inexorably to pasteurization, which could be industrialized. By 1906, as Straus's work expanded, infant mortality rates were drastically cut in neighborhoods near the milk stations. Nevertheless, the Board of Health continued to back certified raw milk.

By 1905, Halsey was the vice president of the merged Sheffield Farms-Slawson-Decker Company and was one of the "principal movers" encouraging "authorities to secure an unadulterated milk supply for the city." The merged company, which had shortened its name to Sheffield Farms, built the first large-scale pasteurization plant in America, at 524 West 57th Street at Tenth Avenue. Producing pasteurized milk was expensive and a bottle cost one cent more than unpasteurized milk, but it was so desirable that thousands were willing to pay extra. The new plant's output of 10,000 quarts a day was almost immediately insufficient, and in 1909 a second plant producing 75,000 quarts was built on 125th Street near Broadway.

Seven days a week, at about 11:30 p.m., cans of milk packed under chunks of ice arrived by rail next to the Sheffield factory. There it was pasteurized and then shipped to staging areas throughout the

HAPPY DAYS ARE HERE AGAIN

On the night of April 6, 1933, when the clock struck midnight and Prohibition ended, people were lined up for hours under sheets of icy rain to witness the first kegs of legal beer being loaded onto trucks at local breweries. They had to wait an extra twelve hours while a delivery contract dispute was settled, but by noon the rain eased to drizzle and beer wagons and trucks—123 from Trommer's brewery, 120 from Ruppert's, 100 from Piels, and about 96 each from Liebmann, Peter Doelger, and F & M Schaefer—rolled out of the breweries.

New beer was less potent than the old, with slightly less than 4 percent alcohol for beer and 5 or 6 percent for ales, but the throngs were eager to drink legally and queued up outside restaurants and piled three deep in bars, where they pronounced the beer "at least as good" as what they remembered from before Prohibition. Chain drugstores, delicatessens, and groceries were selling as many bottles as they could get their hands on. By two o'clock in the afternoon many venues had exhausted their supplies. The only other damper on the day was that early in the evening most drinking spots ran out of pretzels, and for the next few days bakers couldn't keep up with the demand.

Jacob Ruppert's brewery sold more beer in the first two days of repeal than at any other time in its history. It probably would have sold twice that amount, but it couldn't get the empties back quickly enough to pace the demand. Ruppert declared that America would once again be a "beer-drinking country."

F & M Schaefer Brewery adopted the slogan "Our hand has never lost its skill," and both it and the Liebmann Brewery did especially well during this period. Liebmann had hired the manager of a renowned German brewery, Dr. Hermann Schulein, driven from his homeland by Nazi persecution of Jews. Soon their slogan, "Rheingold, the dry beer—think of Rheingold whenever you buy beer," was ubiquitous.

In 1941, 3.2 percent beer was declared legal on military bases, and once the war began, consumption soared, especially in New York, a staging area for tens of thousands of troops being sent overseas. Not every brewery opted to make GI beer, since it had to be done in small batches, but that didn't deter big boys like the Liebmann Brewery and F & M Schaefer Brewery (which celebrated its hundredth anniversary in 1942).

New York's breweries placed high in the national ranking: Schaefer and Ruppert breweries were fifth and sixth, and Liebmann was seventh. But many breweries couldn't brew to capacity because there were restrictions on grain, equipment was difficult to replace, and workers were scarce. By the mid-1940s, Manhattan's Lion Brewery had been sold, its buildings on the Upper West Side dismantled, and their several tons of steel recycled for the war effort.

city. By 2 a.m. the dark, quiet streets were filled with milk wagons beginning their rounds, delivering dairy products to 400,000 families. This was just a portion of the 1.25 million quarts of milk consumed in 1905; the rest was distributed by wholesalers to grocery stores and delicatessens.

In 1914, following Chicago, New York mandated pasteurization. The next year Sheffield Farms expanded again, building the most expensive milk-processing plant with the largest capacity in the country. The Bronx Milk Plant was covered with gleaming white tiles glazed "like pieces of china or pottery." It featured a long row of delivery bays, the center of each decorated with the sculpted head of a Jersey cow. White molded letters spelled out "Sheffield Farms" on a glazed green background, and the posts between the arches each held a white ceramic milk bottle on a green tile background.

The interior was lined with easy-to-clean white tiles on the walls and translucent green glass ones on the ceiling. Large windows were built into the interior walls of the second and fifth floors to enable viewing of the pasteurization process. A maze of pipes used gravity to carry the milk from the top floor down through the building, passing the various stages of filtering, heating, and refrigerating until it reached the bottling area, where 15,000 bottles were filled each hour. Then the milk was loaded onto wagons lined up under the arches. The company employed 2,200 workers and operated 94 retail stores, and its milk routes blanketed Manhattan, Brooklyn, and the Bronx.

One of Sheffield Farms' products was Dr. Spieker's Bulgarian Yoghurt, of which "a jar a day keeps the blues away." There was no Dr. Spieker, but the sixty-year-old Loton Horton, president of the company, had married twenty-four-year-old Lucy Tillie Spieker in 1915. Horton met Lucy when she was in her early teens, during a European visit with her father, a Danish-Russian businessman, who was a longtime friend of Horton's. After she expressed an interest in improving her English, Horton arranged a 1914 visit to New York. Stranded in the city during World War I, she had obviously learned enough of the language to say yes when Horton proposed marriage. Possibly Lucy liked yogurt, and Horton obliged by giving it her family name.

Dr. Spieker's Bulgarian Yoghurt was made in New York with cultures shipped each week from Bulgaria. Billed as a "soothing balm to a rebellious stomach," it was sold at Sheffield Farms stores. Although the Horton marriage had become strained, when Loton died in 1927 he left Lucy one hundred shares of the company.

35

ROLLS-ROYCE COFFEE

offee suppliers worried that the return of beer might lessen demand for their product. During the 1930s coffee consumption was erratic, not because of competition from beer but because coffee cost too much. When the price was right, New Yorkers made it their beverage of choice.

In 1935 local coffee consumption was at an all-time high, averaging 20 gallons per person a year. Arbuckle Brothers covered a dozen city blocks on the Brooklyn waterfront, where the company roasted about 1.26 million pounds of coffee per day and prepared 800,000 packages of moderately priced Ariosa coffee. Each day it filled over one hundred railroad cars with sugar and coffee, and the Jay Street terminal teemed with locomotives, tugboats, ships, and barges.

But the company was in trouble. In 1929 "the world's greatest coffee business" had sold the Yuban brand to shore up its finances, but selling Yuban hadn't helped the bottom line, and its other brands—Arbuckle's Breakfast, Drinksum, Certified Java, and Mocha—weren't so popular as they had been. Many grocery chains were packaging their own brands, and national brands with large advertising campaigns were becoming more popular. The downward slide picked up speed. Seven years earlier the three Arbuckle heirs had made the fateful decision not to fund a national ad campaign for their premium coffee. They advertised locally, but at this time national brands were gaining ground, and Maxwell House became New York's favorite coffee. By the late 1930s the company was selling off whatever it could. In 1937, General Foods bought several of Arbuckle's coffee brands—Ariosa, Seven Day, A-B Certified, and Plainsman—then discontinued all of them. It also bought some of Arbuckle's Brooklyn property to be used by the Maxwell House division of the corporation. General Foods later bought Yuban, then made it in its original factory. In 1940 the sugar division was sold to National Sugar Refining.

When Margaret Jamison, the last heir, died in 1942, the Arbuckle brothers' fortune, once estimated at $40 million, was gone, and the assets didn't even cover the bequests she left to various charities. In 1945 the 16 acres covering thirteen blocks of warehouses, factories, railroads, and docks of the Arbuckle Brothers complex was sold for $1.5 million; of that, $800,000 was owed to the city in back taxes. The rest covered the administrative costs of Jamison's will.

Joe Martinson bragged that his premium brand was the "highest-priced coffee on the market" and "we are very careful about every bag of it." In a 1932 interview in the *Pittsburgh Press*, Martinson claimed that he drank forty cups a day. He said he had been drinking "gallons" since 1902, when he'd started in the business, and it

CHICORY'S FATE

Arriving in Flushing in 1895 with chicory seeds, Eugene Beitter soon discovered that the plant grew well in the area. Thousands of pounds of dried chicory had been imported in 1894, so it was worth trying to cultivate it domestically. Beitter set up a planting demonstration in Queens, and it took farmers a few years to master the crop, but by 1900 they grew 400 to 500 tons. At the same time George Floto built a roast house on Bushwick Avenue in Williamsburg, where farmers from East Williamsburg, Flushing, and Newtown brought their supply of chicory. In 1916, Beitter bought an additional 45-acre meadow in Corona to site a second factory. During World War I the government seized the German-owned firm, but when Eugene Beitter became a naturalized citizen, he was allowed to continue operating.

In 1935, Heinrich Franck and Sons still operated chicory farms and factories in Corona and Flushing, but fewer people were buying the drink. In 1936 the city opened negotiations—over the company's objections—to buy the 31 acres in Flushing that Heinrich Franck and Sons had acquired over the years. It was slated to become part of the 1939 World's Fair grounds. Eugene Beitter, the company's secretary and treasurer, sued to stop the city from confiscating the land, but with his death in 1938, the fight lost its leader and the factory, soon to be part of the fairground, was closed.

had become "part of my life." Martinson spent afternoons buying coffee beans and creating the blend that "always tastes the same." After work he returned home for dinner, where he might be having a family favorite, "steak baked in coffee sauce."

After breakfast (six cups) Martinson was picked up in his chauffeur-driven Rolls-Royce and began his rounds, visiting thirty to forty of his customers in their coffee shops, chain restaurants, and luxury hotels. At each stop he tested half a cup of coffee to see how well the customer had prepared his product. Martinson, who personally blended and tested each batch of coffee, believed that how it was brewed was just as important as how the coffee beans tasted: "The only way I can be sure the restaurants are making it right is to get around and drink coffee." Martinson's was too choice for trucks; instead liveried chauffeurs delivered the coffee in Rolls-Royces with the company logo painted on the side and the back seats removed.

In the early 1920s Martinson coffee was sold exclusively in restaurants and hotels, but people wanted to drink it at home. After vacuum-packed tins became available, Martinson bought a six-story building at 85 Water Street to roast his coffee and expanded into the retail business.

On the eve of World War II, coffee was a $42 million industry in Brooklyn, with seven steamship lines bringing beans from Brazil, Colombia, Africa, Asia, and the Caribbean. Most beans stayed for only a day or two before being shipped to other parts of the country, but 250,000 tons remained for local coffee roasters. Maxwell House, Albert Ehler, and Martinson had a major share of the business in 1941, but none was so big as

A&P, with the largest roasting plant in the country in Brooklyn. The roasting facility at the Navy Yard was a close second.

War boosted coffee prices before Pearl Harbor was attacked. South American beans were plentiful, but with enemy submarines plying the Atlantic, most merchant ships would risk the dangerous voyage only to transport arms or aluminum. Once the United States entered the war, the armed forces bought coffee in enormous quantities. Civilian supplies shrank to 75 percent of the prewar level, and when coffee was rationed in November 1942, a second morning cup became a memory. A New York woman said that one cup a day, when most people had been used to three, was "the wartime measure to have affected one the most." To stretch a pot by two cups, chicory was added to roasted beans. The S. A. Schonbrunn company suggested adding a quarter pound of its dark roast Medaglia D'Oro to a pound of regular coffee to make the equivalent of 2 pounds of coffee. There was little choice in substitutions. Tea was even scarcer than coffee. Black tea consumption was cut in half, and green tea was "virtually unobtainable."

By 1944 the Brooklyn Navy Yard was roasting 2 million pounds of coffee a month, every drop for the navy.

One of The Great Atlantic & Pacific Tea Company's store fronts around 1900. Better known as A&P, this was the country's first grocery store chain.

THE COFFEE THIEF

Fred L. Soufert of Woodside, Queens, didn't let his infirmities—a wooden leg and a bad heart—stop him from using his position as an executive of the coffee firm S. A. Schonbrunn to steal over 133 tons of coffee. He sold it out of his grocery store in Jackson Heights. Soufert's scam exploited Schonbrunn's customers, who knew him well, as he had worked there for twenty-five years. When they ordered 100 pounds of coffee, he delivered 200, and after the customer complained about the excess, Soufert sent a truck to pick it up and reroute it to his store for sale at war-inflated black market prices. Caught red-handed with 267,000 pounds of coffee, 14,000 pounds of tea, and 800 pounds of rice, he pled guilty and got eighteen to thirty-six months in prison.

HEAVENLY COFFEE,
EARTHLY BEER

rom the 1880s to the 1950s, the smell of roasting coffee wafted over Water Street in Manhattan, where many smaller roasters had congregated. Gillies Coffee, one of the oldest roasters in the city, had been in business for 112 years when it moved into larger quarters on Water Street in 1953. Four years later the city decided to widen the street, displacing most of the firms. Some tried to stay in the area, but to meet new regulations any plant needed to install expensive "devices to eliminate . . . heavy, oily smoke." Instead many roasters simply went out of business. S. A. Schonbrunn, which made Savarin and Medaglia D'Oro, left for New Jersey, where a new factory doubled its capacity. Just a bit earlier, in 1949, Martinson's premium moved to a large new roasting and blending warehouse at the corner of Franklin and Greenwich Streets; others of the newer, larger operations had already set up in Brooklyn. Most adults drank a little over three cups of coffee a day, usually at mealtimes. According to a Chock full o'Nuts survey, only 3 percent of New Yorkers drank their coffee black (and 95 percent smoked a cigarette with it).

William Black, the founder and president of Chock full o'Nuts, was a natural at self-promotion. When the Brooklyn native couldn't find a job after graduating from Columbia in 1926, he pounded the pavement and came across a tiny 6-foot-by-20-foot space under a stairway in the basement at Broadway and 43rd Street, where he began selling nuts to nearby theatergoers. Within a few years he had opened eighteen shops. When nuts became a luxury during the Depression, Black switched to selling coffee, along with a walnut and cream cheese sandwich on raisin bread, charging a nickel for each. Black converted one of his nut shops into a quick-service restaurant, the idea caught on, and the restaurant became the first in a chain serving 100,000 cups of coffee a day across five states. In 1954 the Chock full o'Nuts Company gambled that its reputation for making excellent coffee in its restaurants would induce shoppers to buy its new packaged coffee. The company leased a one-story building in Brooklyn to set up a roasting plant to make Chock full o'Nuts Coffee, an all-purpose grind for all coffeemakers—regular, drip, and percolator. (Most coffee companies sold each in a separate package.) The gamble paid off. Within a year Chock full o'Nuts was the third largest-selling coffee in the city, with the factory humming nineteen hours a day, six days a week. The plant installed $500,000 worth of new machinery to meet the demand.

In 1957, in an era when African Americans were struggling to enter the workforce in many different industries, William Black hired Jackie Robinson, who broke the color line in baseball, as vice president for personnel. Robinson had just left the Dodgers in a disagreement over being traded. Black later said, "I needed a personnel manager and I heard Jackie was quitting baseball. I figured he would be a natural. It worked out that way. The employees idolize him."

The African American community was concerned over the "almost complete absence" of people of color in many food industries, especially in the lily-white city breweries. According to the Greater New York Urban League, of New York's eight thousand brewery workers, fewer than fifty were African Americans, most in menial positions. Even with city and state officials pushing integration, in 1953 only four minority men had found work through the unions' complicated hiring-hall system. Only ten were hired in 1954. After five years of campaigning, an agreement on hiring practices was signed with Liebmann, F & M Schaefer, Schlitz, Piel Brothers, and Jacob Ruppert, but by then fewer jobs were available in the industry.

The future had seemed bright in the early 1950s. Philip Liebmann, the fourth-generation head of Liebmann Brewery, explained that people were drinking more because the "public taste for beer has definitely changed during recent years. Fifty or sixty years ago less than 50 percent of the population were regular beer drinkers. These consumers were confined to manual labor classes. Now, however, about 85 percent of the people drink beer." Much of it was consumed at home, as more families acquired television sets and stayed put to watch them. In 1953 three times more beer was consumed from bottles and cans than on tap.

Encouraged by the trend, the Liebmann Brewery expanded its plant, spending "eight figures" building onto its 17 acres in Brooklyn. The company had recently bought the John Eichler brewery in the Bronx and John F. Trommer's brewery in Orange,

New Jersey. While it had record sales in 1953, brewers who focused on national sales were doing better, and Liebmann dropped from fourth to sixth in the ranking of the top twenty-five breweries. To grow nationally, in 1954 it bought plants in Los Angeles and San Francisco to brew Rheingold.

The Ruppert Brewery also ranked in the top ten. In its thirty-five fortresslike buildings filling four blocks on Third Avenue from 90th to 94th Streets, six thousand men produced 3 million barrels of beer a year. In 1951 the outfit introduced Knickerbocker Beer,

A brewery worker drawing a sample glass after filtration at the Jacob Ruppert & Company Brewery in 1933.

"extra light and frosty-dry," and erected a 75-foot electric sign that blazed the beer's name over Bruckner Boulevard at 132nd Street in the Bronx. Its glow could be seen in Manhattan, Long Island City, and northern Brooklyn. The brewery did a large business in New England, making it one of the East Coast's leaders, and placing it ninth nationally.

There were only five breweries left in the city in the early 1950s, after larger had swallowed smaller companies. Both Ruppert and Liebmann expanded that way, as did Piel Brothers, which had ingested John F. Trommer's Brooklyn brewery and the Staten Island plant of Rubsam and Horrmann. (Local drinkers referred to R & H as "rotten and horrible." When Piel examined the leftover beer, it found that it contained "beetles, ants, moths and cockroaches, pigeon feathers" and had to be destroyed.) F & M Schaefer bought a brewery in Albany. The fifth brewery, Schlitz, a Milwaukee-based company, was one of the top three national brewers. New Yorkers weren't far wrong in regarding it as a local brand: virtually all of the 1.25 million cases of beer produced in its Brooklyn plant—the former Ehret Brewery—were consumed in the metro area.

The decline of the New York beer industry dates from an eighty-two-day strike in 1949 against fourteen local breweries. Truckers refused to deliver their beer but supplied customers with products from large out-of-state breweries. New Yorkers began to drink those brews, and many didn't give up the habit once the strike ended. By then local breweries had lost $75 million in sales, and many of the smaller companies were put out of business. During this period Pabst expanded its Newark facilities, and Anheuser-Busch announced that it would build a $20 million brewery in Newark. The frequent strikes, delivery stoppages, periodic work slowdowns, and lockouts caused local breweries to halt production, weakening them financially and giving the big national brands a clear field to infiltrate the market.

After the PepsiCo bottlers bought the Liebmann Brewery and changed its name to Rheingold in 1973, they immediately tried to unload it; word in the industry was that they wanted only its lucrative soft-drink franchises. A year later, unable to find a buyer in the United States, Japan, or Europe, they closed the 119-year-old brewery. City officials, the union, and the workers were all stunned when the staff of 1,500 was abruptly laid off. PepsiCo's decision to pump 100,000 gallons of unfinished beer into the East River sparked angry demonstrations.

Into the fray stepped William Black of Chock full o'Nuts. He arranged a lunch with the brewery owners at the Four Seasons and arrived with a one-dollar bill in his pocket—the price of the brewery—and a credit statement showing he was good for its $20 million debt. When he left he was Rheingold's new owner.

A week later, even more bad beer news surfaced. F & M Schaefer Brewery announced it was shuttering its Brooklyn plant and moving to an automated facility in Pennsylvania, putting another 850 men out of work. The country's seventh largest brewing company said the decision had been "dictated by financial losses caused by the excessive and increasingly rising cost of brewing beer at the Brooklyn plant." The Kent Avenue brewery, opened in 1916, would soon be up for sale. Four years earlier the Brooklyn plant of Piel Brothers had closed. By 1977—for the first time since 1626—not a single drop of the beer New Yorkers drank was made in New York.

THE KOSHER AFTERGLOW

Among the city's high-flying companies in the 1950s was Monarch Wine; its sweet wines made from Concord grapes were fast becoming a nondenominational product. Kosher-style wine had been about the only choice available during Prohibition, and because these were fortified with sugar, the sweetness could mask inept production. On the plus side, the drink lasted for months. During the war not much wine was available, but kosher caught on big-time afterward with non-Jews, who accounted for roughly 65 percent of sales.

George Robinson and Leo Star used Concord grapes grown In upstate New York. To be kosher, all phases of the production had to be carried out by observant Jews, and harvests in the Hudson Valley and later in the Finger Lakes could easily be supervised. Monarch Wine Company expanded in 1940 through a leasing agreement and began making wine under the Manischewitz label, benefiting from its well-known name and large distribution network. A decade later it was producing close to 5 million gallons a year, and Monarch was one of the top four privately held winemakers in the country.

Even though Monarch Wine knew that non-Jews were buying its product, its executives were surprised in the 1950s to see sales spike when there were no Jewish holidays. Investigating, they discovered that these sales were in mostly African American neighborhoods, and they began advertising in African American newspapers around the country with endorsements by celebrities such as Lionel Hampton ("I really go for Manischewitz Kosher Wine") and the Ink Spots ("It harmonizes with us—sweetly"). Monarch then produced an original

continues

creation called Half and Half, equal parts port and sherry, which also flew off the shelves in these neighborhoods. "Officials consider the influence of the Negro in discovering Manischewitz as one of the most important single reasons for the market for this fine wine beyond its base Jewish consumption," reported the *New York Age*.

Of course, Monarch's Manischwitz wine was also still found on seder tables throughout New York, across the country, and from Moscow to Buenos Aires. But the largest sales were at Christmastime, and the company anticipated that the wine would become an all-year drink. In 1954 it added thirteen redwood wine tanks, each holding 500,000 gallons, at the Bush Terminal winery and spent $2 million on advertising.

Manischewitz's jingle became part of everyday life. When the astronaut Eugene A. Cernan stepped out of the space shuttle onto the moon in 1972, he blurted out "Man-O-Manischewitz" in awe at the spectacular sight around him. He didn't repeat the line that followed: "What a Wine!"

GOODBYE TO ALL THAT

The 1970s were fraught with problems for coffee roasters. In 1975 coffee drinking was at its lowest level in years; the average number of cups had slipped from slightly over three to two and a quarter a day. Young people, the coffee drinkers of the future, showed the deepest decline. Among the contributing factors were the medical fears about caffeine that filled the media. In response, Chock full o'Nuts introduced a decaffeinated version of its ground coffee. But declining consumption of coffee was partly the coffee-makers' own fault: the big brands tasted flat, bland, and uninteresting.

New Yorkers remained loyal to their more robust regional brands. Chock full o'Nuts held on to 16 percent of the market, followed by Jersey-made Savarin, with 13 percent, and Martinson, with 7 percent. Old Dutch remained a favorite in Brooklyn. Maxwell House, a national brand with a more middle-of-the-road taste, was the exception, because it had long been made in New York and had a local following.

For decades, each morning at 6 a.m. the Martinson coffee factory on Franklin Street began its daily roasting and the fragrant smell filled the streets of a neighborhood soon to be famous as Tribeca. Its last aroma-filled morning came in early 1984, when production was moved out of the city.

Chock full o'Nuts was the third largest coffee company in the country, behind Maxwell House and Folgers. But after William Black's death, in 1983, the company foundered. The restaurant chain was sold; planned acquisitions fell through; several company presidents filtered in and out in quick succession. Only the coffee operations in Brooklyn still made money.

Chock full o'Nuts in 1969; 135 Broadway at Cedar Street (what is now Zuccotti Park).

By 1989 local coffee-bar chains, usually with only a few shops, began to open as specialty coffee became popular. Chock full o'Nuts, which was the nation's fourth largest roaster, entered the field. "We have a name in this area that means something to people," said its president at that time, but the people patronizing coffee shops were too young to remember the original stores, and the chain didn't last long.

The rise of specialty coffee was good for the dozen or so small roasters, like Gillies Coffee Company, which had moved to Sunset Park, Brooklyn, in 1991, where it prepared beans for coffee bars, restaurants, and hotels, as did the family-owned roaster Dallis Coffee. And then came Starbucks, which opened its first New York store in 1991. Today Starbucks has 283 stores in New York City, dominating the coffee-to-go market in all five boroughs.

One of the few growing milk processors in the city in the 1970s was the Elmhurst Dairy. In 1975, to the consternation of the small businesses, junkyards, and owners of empty lots that surrounded the dairy, thirty-two properties in Queens were condemned by the city so the dairy could expand. The City Planning Commission, calling the "preservation of the dairy industry . . . an important goal of New York City," gave its blessing. Elmhurst pasteurized and bottled milk that was trucked from farms in the Hudson Valley to the Queens dairy every day. By 1978 it had begun to branch out, because "you can't put milk in a carton and sell it anymore. Milk sales are down; consumption is down," said Henry Schwartz, Elmhurst's owner, and so the company introduced a yogurt drink with added pureed fruit called Le Shake.

Milk consumption continued to fall. When John Labatt Ltd., a Canadian conglomerate, bought the Queens Farm Dairy in Ozone

VIOLENT YOGURT?

Dairy industry jobs in New York were quickly evaporating while labor disputes were rife. The workforce at Dannon, which was producing a total of 400 million cups of yogurt a day in eight factories across the country, waged five strikes between 1979 and 1983 at Dannon's Long Island City plant. The longest and most violent was in 1983, when five people were hospitalized in fights, more than a dozen on both sides arrested, and one Dannon worker charged with attempted murder. The cause was summed up by the union's lawyer: "The real point in this dispute is that the company has told us they want to close the plant here, shrink delivery routes, and get rid of more than one hundred jobs. Our position is that, yes, you may be able to produce yogurt cheaper elsewhere, but this is far and away the company's major market, and if you're going to sell here, you have an obligation to keep jobs here." While the company responded by saying that moving wasn't "that absolute," in fact it did close the strikebound plant and move the New York production to Ohio.

Park, one union official said it was the beginning of the end of "an already deteriorating New York–based milk industry." Farmland Dairies, New Jersey's third largest processor, had just won a court ruling ending a fifty-year restriction on the sale of out-of-state milk, which opened up the city's milk market. It took Labatt only a month to close the Queens Farm plant and dismiss the 350 workers. Milk would now be processed at plants outside the city and trucked in.

In 1987, Sunnydale, Queens Farm Dairy, and Elmhurst Dairy were the only local dairies still thriving. Along with Dellwood, based in Yonkers, and Tuscan Industries (owned by Labatt), they controlled 44 percent of New York's milk. The other dairies were laying off workers, eliminating routes, and consolidating operations. That same year, *Inc.* magazine said that it was "clear that nobody is getting rich selling milk in New York."

V

MEAT

MANHATTAN CATTLE DRIVE

The butchers of New York, a guild of the cleaver, wielded political influence to maintain apprenticeship standards that kept out immigrant competitors. Scions of the notables who had marched in the Federal Procession in 1788, including grandsons of Isaac Varian and John Pessenger, were prominent among those butchers applying for stalls in the new Fulton Market, established in 1822. In addition to the 174 New Yorkers holding a butcher's license, five sausage-makers and a meat smoker added variety to the city's meat-heavy diet. Meat cost about half what it cost in Europe, where most people ate beef or pork only on special occasions.

On rooming house tables, meals meant meat. "Ham and beefsteaks," the English visitor Mrs. Trollope wrote, "appeared morning, noon, and night." Even on working families' tables, "butcher's meat"—roasts, chops, and beefsteaks—were constants; lesser cuts were for the dogs and cats. New Yorkers probably tended toward the higher side of the national average of 150 to 200 pounds of meat consumed per person per year. Pork loins, veal, racks of mutton, salted, smoked, or pickled hams, and sausages were part of many a New Yorker's weekly cycle of meals. But beef, and especially steak, filled more plates than any other kind of meat.

To satisfy New York's appetite for beef, which nearly doubled in the 1820s, Daniel Drew, owner of the Bull's Head Tavern, journeyed to Ohio and Kentucky to buy two thousand animals and led a seven-week, 1,000-mile cattle drive to New York. Drew lost five hundred head along the way but still made money. Through the 1830s, drovers from as far away as Illinois showed up at the city limits with herds of up to 1,200 cattle, timing their arrival for a Sunday afternoon, the designated day of entry.

Herding the cattle within the city fell to butchers' apprentices, usually teenagers. "Armed with a large stick, or club, with hooting and shouts," they rushed the bewildered beasts through the unfamiliar streets, poking them to speed them up or whacking their noses to slow them down. Traveling in groups of up to one hundred head, the cattle often were spooked and stampeded. As the *Times* reported, a terrified animal might "trample and gore every one he meets in his headlong desperation." One enraged bull charged into the basement of a house on Christopher Street just as the family was sitting down for breakfast. In the 1840s, New York echoed with the reverberations of hooves and the plangent braying of thirsty animals. In 1850 a city ordinance barred mass herding below 42nd Street during daylight hours. Thereafter the animals were moved at night, piles of manure marking their path.

A new Bull's Head Tavern, a "spacious, airy" hotel, opened in 1848, and beside it the proprietor, George W. Allerton, built "thirty to forty" cattle yards "of various shapes and sizes" at 44th

Street between Fifth and Park Avenues. There were pastures on its northern and western sides, the Croton Reservoir to the south (today the location of the New York Public Library at 42nd Street), and the main depot of the New York and Harlem River Railroad nearby. The *New York Times* called it the most "commodious" location for this "extensive business" within "sight of our city steeples." Up to two hundred city butchers roamed the lots looking for the best animals to purchase, and few were left at the end of the day.

New Yorkers liked their steaks and chops fresh, and butchers obliged by slaughtering animals in yards "scattered over many populous districts of the city." The blood and guts of eviscerated beasts were often left in the streets, scenting "the surrounding atmosphere during the long hot summers with the most noxious effluvia," one English visitor noted. "An East-side Sufferer" wrote in the *New-York Daily Tribune* in 1844 that the "stenches" emanating from the butchers' slaughtering yards in "densely populated portions of the city . . . *must be dealt with*." Though the butchers hotly denied accusations of parlous sanitation, the labor leader Samuel Gompers, who as a boy in the late 1850s lived across the street from a Lower East Side slaughterhouse, had a different recollection: "All day long we could see the animals being driven into the slaughter pens and could hear the turmoil and the cries . . . The neighborhood was filled with the penetrating and sickening odor." Unremitting exposure to the "nauseating" smell rendered him unable to eat meat for "many months" after his family moved out of the area.

Neighborhood slaughterhouses, in the words of a market inspector, were "a great and a perpetual nuisance to many of the inhabitants

Thomas Nast cartoon of New York City's Wall Street in ruins with dead bulls piled behind a sign reading, "This 'street' is closed for repairs."

of New York." By 1846 the city inspector's report urged the "establishment of a public-slaughterhouse in the upper part of the city." New Yorkers agreed, hoping it would be located in a less "inhabited part of the city."

By 1853, 375,000 cattle, sheep, and hogs were butchered at 206 slaughterhouses and sold at 531 meat shops and 11 public markets. Accounts of those markets vary. The *Daily Tribune* wrote that a strong stomach was needed just to walk through "these filthy and revolting stink-holes," which supplied "some eighty-thousand households" every day. Another suggested "the need of pickles or sudden stimulants for the appetite" after a visit because of the filth and offal on the floor.

On the other hand, Thomas F. De Voe, butcher and superintendent of markets, waxed improbable on the "gorgeous avenues of flesh, all garnished with masses, and quarters, and ribs, and loins of the finest beef, in streaks of mellow meat imbedded with layers of golden fat," which sat alongside "the whitest marble-fatted mutton" and "milk-white veal." When the Fulton Market, which had long housed prominent New York City butchers, proved inconvenient to the dispersed population of the growing city, the butchers abandoned their stalls and looked for ways to bring meat closer to their customers' mouths. As a result, unlicensed and illegal meat shops proliferated in the 1840s, particularly above 14th Street. When prosecuted, the proprietors were rarely convicted, owing to sympathetic juries. City-run markets like Fulton were increasingly perceived as a restrictive system that kept prices high, and the city comptroller voiced majority sentiment when he said that New Yorkers hated monopolies, especially "one concerning the meats they consume daily." Emptied of butchers, Fulton Market became, and remained, New York's central fish market until 2005.

In 1843 the Common Council declared that the market laws "no longer serve people's interests," and independent meat shops were legalized. Shop owners needed a license but were spared the hurdle of apprenticeship to obtain one. This opened the field for Irish and German immigrants; two years later, they made up half the

"WANTON CRUELTY"

The lack of standards in the unregulated market prompted the medical community to investigate the safety of the city's meat. In an 1853 report for the New York Academy of Medicine on the state of the cattle market and the city's slaughterhouses, Dr. Augustus K. Gardner found the meat "eaten in New-York [to be] generally of an excellent quality." While the 2,500 cattle and the thousands of calves, sheep, and pigs that arrived each week were generally "well-fatted, driven with care and in the vigor of health," he documented "wanton cruelty" in the slaughter of calves, some "but three days old," butchered by young apprentices who "delight in inflicting unnecessary suffering."

Gardner entertained a high opinion of the pigs. Only "one in ten thousand" was diseased, and this "measly pork" was not wasted but "barreled up and sent to the West Indies, there to furnish food for the plantation negroes, who are said to prefer it to healthy meat." "Hams not sufficiently salted or smoked" were sold at reduced prices to Irish or German immigrants, or found their way "to the Southern market." The doctor's attitude was not unusual; New York had strong financial ties to the Caribbean islands and the southern states. The slave labor in these regions kept sugar refiners' costs low and profits high.

city's six hundred butchers. New Yorkers had found the "numerous Private Meat Shops throughout the City" a more convenient way to obtain meat.

Some butchers even began acting as wholesalers, buying up large numbers of animals at yards like Allerton's and then selling cuts to small meat shops. Lacking the space to keep the animals in their yards, the butchers often confined them in pens for days without food or water, and the "lowing and bellowing of the poor beasts" could be heard "a half mile" away.

FOOLING MRS. EASTMAN

Timothy C. Eastman's slaughterhouse on 60th Street, just next to the Hudson River, was one of the city's more modern abattoirs. In 1875 Eastman sent the first "vessel with dressed beef" from New York to England, "land[ing] the cargo in good condition." His low-cost meat "put a piece of good beef steak" on "poor men's tables" in England. "The exportation of dressed meat and livestock from America to Europe," a journal reported in 1877, had "suddenly grown into an extensive business" that was "confined almost exclusively to New York."

A successful dairy farmer in Cleveland, Eastman had moved to New York to take advantage of the Civil War boom. By the 1870s he had become "one of the most extensive and successful dealers in cattle in the city," bringing herds from St. Louis and Chicago not by overland cattle drives but on the New York Central, Pennsylvania Central, and Erie railroads.

In his abattoir Eastman's cattle were "converted into four quarters of good beef," according to an account in *Scientific American*, then "enclosed in canvas to keep it clean and prevent it from being bruised." His "chilling rooms" were kept at a constant 38 degrees, which retained the meat's taste better than freezing. The canvas-wrapped packages were quickly loaded into vast refrigerated rooms in steamships. He bought the patent for ice-cooled circulating fans for refrigerated shipping rooms or chill rooms in 1876, which further enhanced the quality of his meat. (At the same time the Chicago meatpacker Gustavus Swift invented the refrigerated railway car and began shipping dressed beef to the East Coast.)

After a ten-day voyage, the meat arrived in Liverpool in a state of "perfect preservation." Eastman increased his shipments to 3 million pounds a year and opened a chain of three hundred butcher shops in Ireland, England, and Scotland. He advised American farmers and ranchers to raise "better and larger cattle, and I will sell them all over the world at a better price." Its wide-open spaces made the United States the world's ranch.

Eastman's hold on the meat-shipping trade didn't last. Soon Lehman, Samuels & Brother, a competing slaughterhouse on 44th Street and First Avenue, shipped "the first cargo of [live] beef cattle ever sent across the ocean," although only four of the twenty-six animals survived. The second shipment was more successful, because the animals were given several hours of fresh air en route—the equivalent of a passenger's promenade around the deck—and they arrived alive. In short order New York firms were "shipping nearly 1,000 head of cattle, or about 750,000 pounds of beef," abroad each week, much more than their rivals in other cities.

Ever resourceful, Eastman made good use of the by-products in his slaughterhouse, producing fertilizer from blood and oleomargarine from beef fat. A few years earlier his Commercial Manufacturing Company in New York had begun making "artificial butter" with a patented French process that used the "choicest" stomach, or caul, fat. While still warm, it was processed to eliminate fiber, tissue, and the solid portion of the fat, leaving oleomargarine oil. This was combined with milk, salt, and annatto (a natural yellow food coloring) and churned into margarine, a substance indistinguishable from butter.

"Eastman had an especial room where he manufactured the oleomargarine," a cattleman wrote, reached by passing "through two or three doors before you got into the enclosed room," which kept it "sweet and clean—sanitary." He watched Eastman, wearing "a big rubber coat, . . . put his finger in the tallow that was being made into the oleomargarine and . . . taste it." His visitor couldn't bring himself to join in, but Eastman thought his product was so good that "I am fooling the old lady. She is eating oleomargarine and I am calling it Connecticut butter." And clearly Eastman was right, as the dairy industry soon began losing money on butter, more costly to produce than the imitation.

By 1877 laws required oleomargarine to have an identifying "stamp, brand or mark on every tub" so as "to prevent deception in the sale of butter." But since grocers usually scooped oleomargarine from a large container into smaller packages, the law was unenforceable. Later legislation made it mandatory for margarine to be either left white or colored some color other than yellow. In the 1880s the Commercial Manufacturing Company was producing five times more oleomargarine than a decade earlier and exporting 250,000 pounds of oleomargarine oil to European factories.

FRAGILE REFORM

An 1866 cholera epidemic ended New York's regime of unregulated butchery: the two hundred wholesale butchers who slaughtered 1.62 million animals in their yards had to clean up their act for the sake of public health. To combat the disease, the state government established the New York Metropolitan Board of Health and empowered it to reform the "nuisance" industries: slaughtering, bone boiling, and fat rendering, whose "mephitic" odors were believed to cause cholera. Board members met with the Butchers Hide and Melting Association, a wholesale butchers' group, which assured them that the "mass of butchers will go to any length to keep their places clean." As proof that their meat was salubrious, the butchers displayed their "portly bodies."

Though a butcher might keep his slaughterhouse spotless, blood still permeated wooden walls and floors and feculence seeped into the soil of yards. A board member singled out as "abominable" the establishments on First Avenue between 3rd and 4th Streets, where a quarter of the city's meat was butchered in blood-soaked shacks "so utterly filthy that it is impossible for a man to pass them some mornings without the loss of his breakfast."

By summer 1866, with cholera spreading, the board gave up cajoling the butchers to move farther uptown, away from residential areas, and ordered the worst offenders closed. Fat renderers and bone boilers, lacking their own association, were pursued with more zeal than the butchers. Most moved to less populated areas, especially in Brooklyn. By 1870 the Metropolitan Board of Health had

continues

prevailed. Most of the fifty independent wholesale butchers were ordered to move above 40th Street. Clustering around 44th Street on First Avenue, they hugged the shoreline of the East River.

Within a year of the butchers' move uptown, the city elected a new mayor, Abraham Oakey Hall, friendly to the slaughterhouse interest, and he appointed a more pliant Board of Health. Soon sheds appeared uptown as foul as the ones lately abandoned downtown.

NOISE POLLUTION

Animals unloaded from trains or steamboats at the Washington Drove Yard at 44th Street on the Hudson River could cross Manhattan to the East Side slaughterhouses from eight in the evening until two hours before sunrise, but only on specified streets. A memoirist recalled that "late at night you would frequently hear them coming, from side streets, even on those lined with brownstone houses adjacent to Fifth Avenue, on their way to the hog yards or slaughterhouses." The noise could not be escaped; by 1874 the city's slaughterhouses were processing over 1.6 million animals. Hogs were unloaded at the foot of 40th Street on the Hudson River, close to where the pork processors had built a new slaughterhouse. Pork packing, along with ham and bacon curing, was big business. Having seen Chicago's packers become enormously wealthy, New York porkmen consolidated their killing under one roof and processed every part of the pig "but the squeal." To mitigate vocal public reaction to noise—and nose—pollution, their Manhattan facility operated between six in the evening and two in morning.

40

THE MILITANT

n 1884, Mathilde Wendt finally had enough of the stench waft-
ing into her spacious townhouse on Beekman Place in Manhattan. The large windows of her drawing room had to be tightly
shut, and she couldn't even think about venturing out onto her
expansive lawn overlooking the East River.

Wendt's neighborhood was a mix of well-to-do homes and
middle-class brownstones. Abutting the area were fifty-five dilapi-
dated "dirty little pens" squeezed between 41st and 47th Streets
in the East Side slaughterhouse district. These businesses consistently flouted regulations regarding sewage and building materials, and the air of the surrounding blocks, including Mrs. Wendt's
parlor, was redolent of blood, excrement, offal, and rotting flesh.

For decades the stench had tormented the people of New York,
and Mrs. Wendt, spurred on by her husband, thought a petition
might force the Health Department into action. She enlisted a
group of friends and within three days had gathered two hundred

signatures. A month later the Ladies Health Protective Association of New York was founded "to protect the people living in the neighborhood." Spearhead by Wendt and ten other upper-middle-class women (all married to influential men), they were prepared to face down opposition that might have intimidated reformers with less social power.

Their first target was Michael Kane's fertilizer company, whose operation was virtually adjacent to their backyards. It stockpiled mountains of manure on a barge in the East River—about 20,000 tons, "steaming and fermenting in the sun," with one pile rising 30 feet high. The politically connected Kane (his brother was a state senator) thought he could easily beat the women, but to his amazement, they pursued him through the courts until he was convicted of violating sanitation laws.

The Ladies Health Protective Association of New York next focused on the city's meat-processing establishments. The slaughterers had no idea what was in store for them. In January 1885 a fact-finding tour was arranged for a group of women swathed in silk and fur. When Mrs. Wendt entered Solinger and McCarthy's slaughterhouse on East 44th Street, the wooden floors oozed with the stomach contents of a just-butchered bullock. Covering her mouth with a lace handkerchief, she pulled out a copy of the city code and read aloud to the owners the section mandating that slaughterhouses install cement floors that drained into city sewers. As she read, two small boys were hard at work scraping the offal off the floor and dumping it into a barrel. Solinger and McCarthy politely showed Mrs. Wendt out to the blood-soaked sidewalk and thought the worst was over.

Initially few butchers took seriously what the newspapers dubbed the "Committee on Smells." When the ladies' associa-

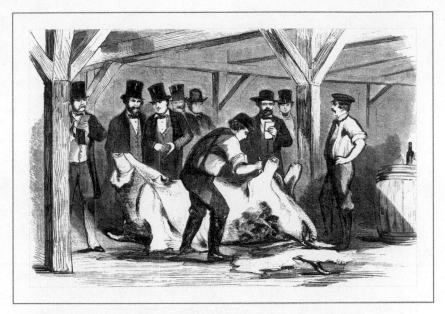

"Our Exposure of the Swill Milk Trade." Dissecting a cow brought from the 16th Street stables, before the city health wardens and Frank Leslie. 45th Street on the East River, 1858.

tion demanded that the health commissioner take action, a local inspector truthfully reported that the slaughterhouses had committed no violations for the unanswerable reason that the city had stopped inspecting them. Undaunted, the association, sustained by 150 dues-paying members, enlisted more recruits for a war they knew would be "long and bitter."

Exposing the filthy backstory of the city's meat, the mothers and homemakers of the association had touched a nerve. New Yorkers expected their steak to be treated better than this. Over the next year squads of angry women swooped down on the worst offenders. Police escorts were needed to protect the women from irate

CLEAN KILL

One of the cleaner slaughterhouses was Schwarzschild & Sulzberger on 45th Street. Joseph Schwarzschild had begun his business in a small kosher plant on Eldridge Street in about 1853. Ten years later he took on a partner, Ferdinand Sulzberger, who had spent his early years on his father's farm in Germany and arrived in New York around 1861 at age twenty. "Full of ambition and of an indefatigable energy," Sulzberger worked "from early dawn until late into the night." That is, when he wasn't in a nearby tavern drinking beer with his workers.

Schwarzschild & Sulzberger's slaughterhouse was one of the few the Ladies Health Protective Association pronounced "well-regulated." It dressed both nonkosher and kosher meat, the latter for the burgeoning Jewish population. (The half million Jewish immigrants who arrived between 1881 and 1895 kept New York's wholesale meat businesses viable as Chicago became the nation's leading meatpacker.) Schwarzschild & Sulzberger's block-long slaughterhouse, built in 1870 at the foot of East 45th Street, was the city's first meatpacking plant to use electrified cooling rooms. The partners planned to build others like it across the country, but they hadn't created the model slaughterhouse simply because they wanted to. "It was all the work of the ladies," Joseph Schwarzschild admitted. "We fought pretty hard at first, and we should perhaps have fought it longer had we known the tune of half a million of dollars which this abattoir was going to cost. But we are not sorry now; it is a good thing and we are glad the Ladies Health Protective Association made us do it."

owners, foul-mouthed workers, and neighborhood "hoodlums" incited to pelt them with garbage or rocks. But the women persevered, horrified by what they saw: cattle confined to cellars so stifling they would climb on top of one another to reach a small grate to breathe fresh air, or piles of butchered meat on filthy tables covered with flies, or groups of neighborhood children laughing while watching a cow's throat being slit and its blood running in the street.

The ladies took their fight to the mayor, but their proposals languished. A mellowed Mathilde Wendt softened the tone of their campaign, saying, "We don't want the slaughterhouses removed, but we want them kept clean. If we don't insist on this we'll all die of cholera." A few slaughterhouses attempted to clean up, but most carried on as usual.

Stonewalled by City Hall, without "sacrificing one iota of feminine refinement," the women lobbied the notoriously corrupt state legislature in Albany. Their bills were defeated, but the president of the Butchers Hide and Melting Association decided it was just too expensive to keep fighting. "If we have to pay out all this money" to lawyers and lobbyists and politicians, he reasoned, "we may as well put it into what the women want"—slaughterhouses that complied with the city code. In return the butchers asked for (and received) the assurances of the Ladies Health Protective Association that they could remain in the city.

41

THE BEEF TRUST

n 1910 a bulletin from the federal Census Bureau called New York the "greatest manufacturing centre on earth." Five of its twenty-one largest industries, employing 65,000 people, were food-related: sugar refining, slaughtering and meatpacking, baking bread and other products, malt liquor manufacturing, and candy-making. All except butchering held "first place" in their respective fields.

While Chicago, "Hog Butcher to the World," boasted a bigger meat industry than New York, thousands of cattle were still slaughtered daily in the city. Trains transported them from the western United States to New Jersey, where they rested for a day before crossing the Hudson River by boat to Manhattan or Brooklyn. The city's "chief abattoirs" were United Dressed Beef Company, which prepared 80 percent of its meat for the kosher market, and Schwarzschild & Sulzberger.

In 1895, Chicago's Big Four meatpackers—Swift, Armour, Wilson, and Cudahy—formed the Beef Trust, and New York's Schwarzschild & Sulzberger "joined hands" with these "Westerners." The packers banded up to stiff ranchers and gouge consumers. Though meat prices climbed to their highest level since the start of the Civil War, the companies denied collusion. Ferdinand Sulzberger "declared that prices were high because farmers of the West were not able to supply the packers."

When the Beef Trust hiked prices by 50 percent in 1902, the city's retail kosher butchers, selling an average of 600,000 pounds of meat weekly, closed their shops to force the wholesalers to cut prices. But talks went nowhere. "It makes no difference to us whatsoever," Ferdinand Sulzberger told the *Times*. "If the butchers do not require the meat, then we will not be obliged to ship so many cattle. If they want to reduce the price they will have to go out West and try to do it. We cannot help them in any way." That cavalier attitude came easily to him because there was "scarcely a town that is not reached by [our] branch houses, distributing points and sales agencies . . . throughout the United States and at many European points."

The wholesalers wouldn't budge, and at the end of a week the butchers reopened their shops, saying that their customers had been "besieging" them and it was "useless" to stay closed. But they badly misread public opinion. Rather than rushing into the shops to buy meat that had just risen six cents a pound, neighborhood women engaged in a spontaneous riot that spread beyond the Lower East Side to Jewish neighborhoods in upper Manhattan, Brooklyn, and the Bronx. During the three-week boycott, women doused meat in the shops with carbolic acid and dragged carcasses into the street. To cross boycott lines was to take your life in your hands, and neighbors who continued to buy meat were shunned.

The Germanic name Sulzberger became a liability during the early years of World War I. Although Sulzberger and Sons (previously named Schwarzschild & Sulzberger) had been doing business in England and France for decades, both governments confiscated meat shipments exported by it, questioning the origin of its meat. Sweden, once a huge market for the company, was cut off, and the firm's foreign market evaporated.

Loss of its European business substantially weakened the company. In both 1913 and 1914 there were negotiations with the Chicago meatpackers Swift (which owned a large chunk of stock) and Armour over carving up the company between them. By 1915 the company, the family's fortune, and the livelihood of its 750 workers were in jeopardy. At the last minute a group of New York bankers stepped in to save it. The Sulzberger family still owned a large block of stock but had lost control of the company.

Some extremists even entered people's kitchens, "picking up whatever meat they could find to throw on the street, where it was caught and pitched about and trampled upon."

Rioting women were injured in scuffles with police, and hundreds were arrested in the "great struggle for cheap meat." The police and the *Times* both deplored this "dangerous class" of protesters, who "mostly speak a foreign tongue." "Let the blows fall instantly and effectively," an editorial demanded. During one of the many meetings held by the boycotters, a flier was distributed that said, "The people feel very justly that they are being ground down, not only by the Beef Trust of the country, but also by the Jewish Beef Trust of the City." Boycotting proved futile in the face of such power; when the boycott ended on June 5, meat cost two cents *more* a pound.

Later that year, the government investigated the Beef Trust, particularly the practices of United Dressed Beef and Schwarzschild & Sulzberger, whose vice president, Samuel Weil, told the *Tribune* in 1903 that the company had "no connection with the meat merger [of the Big Four]" and was "perfectly independent." Four executives from Schwarzschild & Sulzberger eventually pled guilty to charges of accepting kickbacks from the railroad companies but settled just as they were about to go to trial, paying a hefty fine. The firm then severed the connections with the "combination" that it denied it had made.

42

THE SAUSAGE MILLIONAIRES

Five hundred sausage companies of all sizes graced New York in 1926. One of the largest, Hygrade Products, had been opened by Samuel Slotkin on South Street in Brooklyn in 1914, with $15,000 and twelve employees. When the fifteen-year-old Slotkin left Russia, he couldn't decide whether to study art in Paris or go to America, where two of his six brothers were living. He chose New York but traveled on to Buffalo, where one brother had settled, and worked as a photographer and painter. After a few years he returned to New York and took a job curing meats in the cellar of the Zimmerman Provision Company on Houston Street, where, working from five in the morning until eight at night, he eventually rose to clerk. Slotkin moved on to a salesman position for the Gomprecht Sausage Company on Columbus Avenue because the owners, he claimed, were "a nice bunch" making "a high-class sausage," and he built up a huge clientele, including Gimbel's and Bloomingdale's.

The 1906 publication of Upton Sinclair's *The Jungle* hit the sausage business hard; the book's graphic descriptions of Chicago's meatpacking plants shocked everyone. Slotkin carefully studied Gomprecht's sausages, deemed them sanitary, and set about rebuilding sales, but a power struggle within the Gomprecht family prompted him to return to Zimmerman's. Over the next four years he stayed at home, fielding telephone orders from clients up and down the eastern seaboard. In his silk top hat and cape, he and his dolled-up wife were a familiar sight at the opera, museums, and tony cafés. Zimmerman's didn't care for his flashy lifestyle, however, and the dapper dresser left to start his own meat-processing business, Hygrade.

Slotkin's clients all followed him to his new enterprise, which made a variety of meats, though his "first loyalty" was to his first product, the frankfurter. His were always all beef and came with a skin, because otherwise "all the juice leaks out."

In 1927 Hygrade merged with eight other companies to form Hygrade Food Products Company. According to the *Washington Post*, it was "the first consolidation of delicatessen food properties ever effected" and included some of the biggest sausage-makers in New York and Philadelphia. The combined company manufactured frankfurters, bologna, salami, smoked and cured tongue, spiced, pickled, and corned beef, and other ready-to-serve meat products and sold them to over five thousand delicatessens, chain stores, meat markets, clubs, grocers, hotels, restaurants, and steamship and railroad companies throughout the United States and around the world. It had plants in Europe, South America, Ireland, French Morocco, Australia, and New Zealand. Slotkin was the firm's president, and within two years the company recorded sales of $9 million. But the restless Slotkin was ready to expand further. His first purchase was Chicago's Allied Packers, which had sales six times greater than Hygrade's but was in bankruptcy. The vertically integrated Hygrade could now "transfer meat from the prairie to the retail butcher." Hygrade Foods cleverly weathered the Depression by making cheap food—packaged beef and pork products, especially frankfurters—at its offshore plants.

Another New York sausage millionaire, with factories throughout America, was Adolf Göbel (also spelled Adolph Goebel), maker of sausages, fresh and smoked meats, ham, bologna, corned beef, bacon, and lard. The German immigrant, who began in New York as a peddler with a straw basket, opened a factory on Morgan Avenue in Brooklyn and by 1921 employed 220 men and ran 75 delivery trucks.

After Adolf Göbel died, in 1924, his wife, Ottilie, was named the sole executor of his $3 million estate, including his company. His will stipulated that his son, Adolf Jr., should become the firm's president. The younger Göbel opened a second packing plant next door to the New York Butchers Dressed Meat Company on 39th Street, doubled the number of employees, and expanded his fleet to ninety-six trucks. All went smoothly for about a year, until Ottilie married Dr. Sigwart J. Reed, a sculptor hired to design a mausoleum for her husband. Ottilie and her new husband fired Adolf Jr., but he and his older sister did not take the firing, or the marriage, lying down. Together they hired a private investigator, who discovered that Reed, whose real name was Josef Rittmier, was a serial bigamist, with one wife in Philadelphia and another in Germany. The mortified Mrs. Göbel filed for an annulment but was ousted as executor of the estate by her children, and the duplicitous Dr. Reed vanished. The company was then sold to a group of bankers.

In 1927, the new firm, called Adolf Göbel, Inc., went on a buying spree, acquiring four local companies. It added another local company in 1928, plus four large firms in different parts of the country. In 1930, "Göbel's—Quality First—Pure Meat Products" sold a record 243,715,995 pounds of meat. By the 1940s the company had moved to North Bergen, New Jersey, and been bought by a notorious swindler, Tino De Angelis, who, among other criminal exploits, sold over 2 million pounds of uninspected meat to the New York school lunch program.

One of Göbel's competitors, Stahl-Meyer, was formed when three sausage companies, each with its own specialties, merged in 1928. Otto Stahl, opened in 1895, was famous for its bologna. Louis Meyer, Inc., which was also formed in 1895 in Brooklyn, made bacon, ham, and European-style canned frankfurters. The third company, F. A. Ferris, founded in 1836, had an international market for hams. Together they produced a full line of prepared meat products. The merged Stahl-Meyer claimed to have over 9,800 delicatessens and butchers as their customers and over $9 million in annual sales.

In 1928, Isadore Pinckowitz, a Romanian immigrant who worked for a butcher on the Lower East Side, bought the Hebrew National Kosher Sausage Factory at 155 East Broadway from the bankrupt previous owners. Pinckowitz sold the firm's kosher sausages and hot dogs to delicatessens, restaurants, and grocery stores. After the 1929 crash, many sausage companies struggled, but Hebrew National flourished. The products made by the Hebrew National Kosher Sausage Factory were filling and cheaper than steak, which was just what people wanted in the Depression.

HOT DOGS CAN'T STRIKE

By 1900 sausages were so popular that a city district was known as the "great sausage belt." The area, east of the Bowery between Canal and Houston Streets, was home to several dozen small manufacturers, including Hebrew National Kosher Sausage. The city's two hundred sausage-makers prepared kosher and nonkosher versions in long, short, fat, and thin links. Ingredients included smoked liver, beef, lamb, pork, and ham. Products included blood pudding, head cheese, garlic sausages, salamis, cervelat, Hungarian sausages, Polish kielbasa, bratwurst, knockwurst, and weisswurst.

Over six thousand sausage-makers worked in these factories, and when they went on strike for higher wages and better working conditions in 1901, Coney Island feared a hot dog famine. Charles Feltman, impresario of the island's German Gardens restaurant, must have been close to panic. His 1,200 waiters served 8,000 meals a day, including millions of hot dogs—so many that seven grills were needed to cook them all.

43

FROM DEPRESSION TO WAR

n 1934 Helen Worden published an account of the neighborhoods abutting the city's waterfront, *Round Manhattan's Rim.* Worden's tour took her past the "packing plant at 816 First Avenue," the former Schwarzschild & Sulzberger slaughterhouse, part of the Wilson Packing Company of Chicago. It covered "the entire block between Forty-Fifth and Forty-Sixth Streets; that half fronting on Forty-Sixth Street takes in the big seven-story building with the killing-beds (we didn't go in to see them; though people can), chill-rooms and sales coolers on the ground floor." The slaughterhouses were "within waving distance of New York's Gold Coast," the fashionable apartments on Sutton and Beekman Places to the north and Tudor City to the south. The side facing the slaughterhouses had no windows, to hide the grisly view within.

Between 1932 and 1941 kosher abattoirs processed 90 percent of the 400,000 cattle slaughtered in New York. Worden was fascinated to discover that "everything comes under rabbinical inspection. Even after the animal is dressed, it is constantly under the eagle eyes of those bearded gentlemen." All their products were "stamped or sealed by the Rabbis as proof and protection for the Jewish butcher." Fewer people than before adhered to strict kosher laws in the 1930s, but ingrained food habits kept kosher meat in demand. Because of the kosher market, slaughtering and meat-packing was the second largest food industry in the city in 1930.

By law the slaughterhouses were forced to hug the shoreline on either side of Manhattan. Both cattle and smaller animals were butchered there. In addition, the slaughterhouse district served as a distribution center for refrigerated meats arriving from the Midwest. Butchering was also done on Tenth Avenue, between 11th and 14th Streets, later known as the meatpacking district. Several small or midsized firms opened there during the first and second decades of the twentieth century. By the 1930s, however, the overhead of running large abattoirs in New York was becoming prohibitive and the problems of disposing waste so onerous that slaughtering was moving out of the city.

The processed meat industry was growing during the 1930s, and Worden noted that Wilson & Company "runs modern smoke-houses and refinery units in a large building on Forty-Seventh Street, where tons of smoked meats are processed every year." Local manufacturers claimed that the city's consumption of hot dogs was "the largest of any community in the country." On a hot summer weekend, Coney Island, the "hot dog capital of the world," sold 100,000 pounds.

As the Depression dragged on, the hot dog mutated from a snack gulped down on the run into a staple on the dinner table.

Sailor sharing a hot dog with his girlfriend. Coney Island, July 18, 1943.

The local standard was eight links to a pound, enough for a family meal. Isadore Pinckowitz's Hebrew National Kosher Sausage was doing so well that he ran a soup kitchen that fed "thousands of men and women of various races and creeds" in the hard-pressed Lower East Side neighborhood where his factory was located.

In 1943 GIs voted hot dogs their "favorite meat." Despite soldiers' preference for the cheap stuff, 60 percent of U.S. Choice meat was reserved for the military. The steak missing from butcher shops was to be found only on the black market. By 1945 wartime meat shortages were so acute that even processed meat in delicatessens was running low.

Gulden's Mustard ad from 1918 in the Brooklyn
Daily Eagle.

During the war meat processors faced problems with transportation, with finding experienced workers, and with a black market that was siphoning sales. Then too, civilian cattle were scarce. To find animals, Sam Slotkin sent Hygrade's salesmen out West with instructions to camp out on the range until ranchers sold them cattle. In this way Hygrade cornered many of the available animals and company sales grew to $111 million in 1945, more than double the total for 1940.

THE RUNNING OF THE BULLS

Well into the 1930s, the most modern city in the world came to a standstill when beasts arriving at the riverside slaughterhouses broke loose, terrorizing pedestrians and snarling traffic. The journalist Helen Worden was "astonished to learn that the live cattle, sheep and lambs are floated in cattle cars from Jersey and driven off of the boats directly into the plant where they are rested, fed and watered until transferred to the killing floor." New Yorkers continued to prefer freshly slaughtered meat, both kosher and non-kosher. Fresh pork was also in demand. Pork butchered in the Midwest and shipped east turned slightly gray, which disgusted local shoppers.

But it was the large demand for kosher beef that necessitated the heavy traffic in live cattle, who occasionally ran amok. In 1930 four 1,200-pound bulls got loose while being unloaded at the New York Dressed Meat Company on 38th Street and Eleventh Avenue. A group of policemen jumped onto trucks and commandeered taxis in hot pursuit. Two of the bulls made it downtown to Desbrosses Street before they were shot. A few months later a young steer bolted from the same slaughterhouse and ran into Herald Square, knocking over several pedestrians before pausing in front of the statue of Horace Greeley in Greeley Park. The terrified beast then smashed through the plate-glass window of a tailor shop. Another animal made it all the way to Lord & Taylor on Fifth Avenue before being shot in front of speechless shoppers.

THE UN RISES OVER THE SLAUGHTERHOUSES

In 1946 the slaughterhouse district, the 8 acres between 40th and 43rd Streets and First and Second Avenues, was on sale for an exorbitant $6 million. At seventeen dollars per square foot, this land was selling for over three times the price of the surrounding slums. The first real estate person approached on the deal was the developer William Zeckendorf. He recognized that the surrounding land was so cheap only because "the slaughterhouses are there," and without the meatpackers the parcel was "the greatest opportunity I have ever seen in my life." He bought up the slaughterhouse district and quietly acquired 9 more acres, extending the parcel to 49th Street. He envisioned building a huge futuristic project called X-City that would contain forty-story office towers, thirty-story apartments, a cultural center, a hotel, a yacht marina, a heliport, and elevated highways.

Coincidentally, the United Nations, created two years earlier, was seeking a permanent home. New York was the first choice of the secretary general, Trygve Lie, but the city didn't have a large enough piece of land in a good location. By 1946 the UN announced that it would relocate to Philadelphia if New York could not find a suitable site. Zeckendorf called mayor William O'Dwyer to offer the land to the UN for "whatever it wanted to pay." A few days later Nelson Rockefeller called Zeckendorf to say that his father, John D. Rockefeller Jr., was interested in his proposal. They made the deal on the phone for $8.5 million, and on December 12, 1946, the United Nations was offered the site. It took the UN three days to accept.

Three weeks before demolition was to begin, United Dressed Beef asked for an extension. It could not move out until at least October, "the earliest practical time," and preferably later, because it supplied much of the city's kosher meat. UN officials "made no effort to hide their chagrin and resentment," the *Times* reported. United Dressed Beef was holding up the building plans, and although the abattoir didn't "wish to retard construction," the UN project couldn't move ahead on schedule. A deal was struck: the United Nations would grant United Meat an extension if it moved its operations into the rear part of its plant so the demolition of surrounding structures could begin. Soon underground tunnels were being dug and buildings bulldozed. United Dressed Beef Company moved later in 1947. Construction of the glass-walled Secretariat building began in 1949. By 1950 the United Nations complex had replaced the stockyards and slaughterhouses on the banks of the East River.

When peace returned, wholesale butchers were soon processing 25 million pounds of meat a year, and more than two thousand men were back at work in New York's slaughterhouses. There had been two good grain harvests, but after the second one the United States sent large shipments overseas, causing feed shortages that reduced the number of animals available for domestic consumption. In 1946 there were few Easter hams or kosher briskets. In September, Albert Merkel, whose Queens packing house supplied his thirty-eight stores, doubted it could get any worse. "I was in a slaughterhouse this morning and saw baby pigs weighing 25 pounds going to the block with breeder sows weighing 600 to

700 pounds," he said. "In other words, they're scraping the bottom of the barrel for pork. We normally get about 6,000 hogs a week and this week we received 600. We only stay open to distribute a tenth of our volume of pork plus the cold cuts and sausages we have in reserve. At the rate it's going out of our refrigerators, we'll be cleaned out in two weeks." Not for two more years would the industry adjust to the postwar market and provide a steady flow of meat.

44

CELLOPHANE MEAT

n the 1950s consumers began buying meat in new places and in new forms. The butcher shop was losing out to the self-serve counters of grocery stores, and before the end of the decade approximately 75 percent of all meat purchased came wrapped in a cellophane package. Samuel Slotkin of Hygrade Foods had predicted this, telling *The New Yorker* that "tomorrow's" housewife wouldn't have to "shuffle on the butcher's sawdust floor, see little chicken's innards, or an animal oozing out its life's plasma." Hygrade had been marketing frozen sirloin steaks, chops, and cutlets for years.

Convenience foods were the hot new segment in the 1950s meat industry, and producers of sausages, frankfurters, ham, bacon, and other cured and packaged products embarked on ambitious building projects. Most new plants incorporated the latest techniques to produce ready-to-eat meat products, developed during the war, including prepared foods heated from a can, boiled in a polyethylene bag, or frozen. Stahl-Meyer featured a line of "instant meals," including corned beef hash and beef stew, "tender, delicious, ready to serve in minutes." It also sold a sliced 3-pound ham in a can, with a packet of barbecue spices packed on the outside, which could be prepared in minutes and slapped on the outdoor grill, a fad sweeping the nation. Dad, who manned the barbecue and did little other cooking, could hardly go wrong with this easy-to-use product. Whether on the patio or indoors, serving cocktails was another fashionable trend. Stahl-Meyer sold 2-ounce cans of specialty meat spreads—chicken livers with water chestnuts or smoked ham and cheddar cheese—to make canapés to accompany the drinks.

Interior of Creighton's butcher shop, New York City, undated [circa 1911–1921].

HARLEM'S OWN

Walter Clarke, a former nightclub impresario, opened Uncle Walt's Sausage Company in 1939 in a small basement in Harlem. By 1951 sales had grown by 10 percent, as had the number of employees at his new plant on East 129th Street. The company was producing a quarter of a million pounds of Famous Country Sausage, 1,500 pounds of Hog's Head Cheese (a pickled meat jelly or aspic made from the meat of the head of a cow or pig), and cracklin's (fried pork skin). The next year it added pickled tongue, pig's ears, and link sausages.

With products sold at groceries throughout Manhattan, Brooklyn, Queens, and the Bronx, Uncle Walt's was "completely Negro owned and operated." After fire destroyed his factory in 1959, the fifty-seven-year-old Clarke declared that he would "renovate and reopen to put my employees back to work as soon as possible." All thirty of them lived in Harlem.

Any product that cut the time the cook spent in the kitchen stood a good chance of success. Hebrew National Kosher Foods' corned beef in a boilable bag, marketed in 1956, was such a hit that it was quickly followed by pastrami and tongue. Hygrade Food Products made many of these prepared foods, including ready-to-eat meats and canned Hungarian goulash and Irish stew. Hot dogs still remained the product dearest to Slotkin's heart. By 1953, Slotkin had a "commanding hold on the New York hot-dog market," and anyone buying a snack from the food stands in Coney Island or Times Square probably would have been eating a Slotkin.

THE SPECTER OF CHANGE

By 1965, after United Dressed Beef closed its facility in Brooklyn, only one small abattoir remained in New York. In the three years before that, two of the remaining three Brooklyn slaughterhouses had also gone out of business, leaving J. H. Rodman-Graff Corporation's slaughterhouse at 309 Johnson Avenue the sole survivor. Shortly after, the city classified abattoirs as manufacturers for tax purposes, which made it too expensive to do business in New York. When Rodman-Graff closed in 1968, no one mourned the last of the slaughterhouses.

Since animals were no longer slaughtered in New York, meat that was processed in the Midwest was shipped east. In 1967, New York's wholesalers produced $2 billion worth of packaged meat that was shipped around the country, from Maine to Florida to California, as well as to the Caribbean Islands. The four meat markets employed about one hundred thousand skilled workers, four thousand of them African Americans or Hispanics.

Wholesalers selling meat across state lines were required to follow the sanitation guidelines laid down in the Wholesome Meat Act. In 1968 agents of the U.S. Department of Agriculture made inspections in the two hundred city meat plants in the Washington Street Market to see if sellers there were following the law. What they found reads almost word for word like the reports of the Ladies Health Protective Association in 1885. Conditions in most plants were far below standards. Cracked walls were embedded with meat particles and juices. Splintered doorways were oozing rancid gray fat. Carcasses hung from rails that were too short, allowing meat to drag on the ground. Inspectors found open cups of rat poison. Most of the plants were housed in sixty- to one-hundred-year-old buildings with wooden floors and no drains. Inspectors stood in dirty pools of water. Concrete floors with drainage pipes had been a key demand of the Protective Association. Little had changed in eighty-three years.

Most wholesalers made the necessary repairs, but some closed because they couldn't afford them or the subsequent higher rents. Into the early 1970s, four to five thousand people still showed up for work at five in the morning in the 1-square-mile meat-market area, bounded by 14th to Horatio Streets and West and Hudson Streets, where buyers for supermarkets, restaurants, and butcher shops bought $40 million worth of meat a year. Each day between 30,000 and 40,000 pounds of steer quarters arrived in refrigerated trailers that had been lifted by cranes off flatcars at the railyard in North Bergen, New Jersey. Men in blood-smeared white coats used hooks to grab the carcasses from the trucks; others lugged them inside over sawdust-covered floors and hung them up so that butchers, skinners, and trimmers could prepare them. By midafternoon the area was deserted. But hanging in the air, along with

THE HORSEMEAT SCANDAL

On Saturday, December 19, 1964, acting on a tip, inspectors from the city's Department of Markets took several samples from the 20 tons of boneless meat at Merkel, Inc. The shipment had arrived at the Jamaica, Queens, factory on Friday and was placed in a freezer for use on Monday in making the 200,000 pounds of bologna, frankfurters, and sausages the company produced each week. The inspectors found that the meat in the freezer, which bore bogus USDA stamps, was 20 percent horsemeat. While horsemeat is safe to eat, the city's health code forbade using it for human consumption. The inspectors seized the meat before any of it was used, but once the story hit the papers, bologna sales from every producer plummeted. Even after market commissioner Albert Pacetta ate a slice of Merkel's bologna in public to demonstrate its safety, supermarkets couldn't strip the product from their shelves or cancel their orders fast enough.

Within days 530 Merkel employees were laid off, and 400 of them picketed Pacetta's Queens home. One twenty-six-year veteran of the company said, "We feel sorry for our employers right now. We've been treated fair and have good working conditions . . . I feel certain Merkel will continue to give the good meat the public wants, as it has done for many years." He added, "Look, we use Merkel products in our homes. We know it is good meat, otherwise we would never give it to our families." The company president, Norman Lokeitz, claimed that he was "completely innocent" and had been "duped." The factory tried to reopen, but shoppers shunned Merkel's products.

The factory closed for good on January 28, 1965, and one month later Lokeitz, the last in a string of owners since the Merkel family had sold the company in 1955, was indicted. He cooperated with the police, helping to convict the mobsters who had sold his company substandard and rotten meat. The horsemeat was not an isolated incident; for some time the beef sent to the Merkel plant had come from diseased or even dead cattle. Lokeitz pled guilty to conspiring to sell misbranded and mislabeled food and was sentenced to six months in jail.

the stink of meat and fat, was the specter of change. Meatpacking was a dying industry in New York. Increasingly meat, slaughtered and packaged into serving-size pieces, was being shipped to chain stores straight from Iowa and Nebraska.

Sausage and hot dog production remained a vibrant industry. In 1961, Stahl-Meyer built a multimillion-dollar processing plant on a 5-acre site at Hunt's Point in the Bronx. Said to be the largest food-processing plant built since World War II, it consolidated the work of the company's plants in Manhattan and Brooklyn. The new facility turned out "instant meals" and other convenience foods in addition to bacon, bologna, ham, and hot dogs, more popular than ever.

KOSHER FROM INDIANA?

n 1962 kosher sausages and hot dogs were estimated to be a $50 million New York industry. The year before, Hebrew National Kosher Foods had opened a plant that cost $1 million on Maurice Avenue in Maspeth, Queens. In one day the company could triple its previous volume, using new machinery to cut meat with high-speed choppers, mix it, stuff the casings, then link 160 frankfurters a minute. Hebrew National packaged 500,000 frankfurters a day and made 400,000 pounds of pickled and spiced bologna, salami, corned beef, and liverwurst. Along with Zion Food Products, which employed 160 workers in its Bronx factory, and Hod Carmel Kosher Provisions, a division of Hygrade Foods, Hebrew National controlled half the kosher processed-meat market. Most of these firms' products were bought in the metropolitan area, but sales were growing around the country. In the early 1960s Hebrew National shipped 45,000 pounds of meat to Los Angeles in two refrigerated trailer trucks—its single largest shipment. "Non-Jews have broken the ice in trying kosher foods and they're responsible for a large part of our sales gains," said Leonard Pines, president of Hebrew National.

While profits were climbing, a federal grand jury indicted fourteen companies for price-fixing. Pines later remarked that the case went nowhere "because we responded by expanding our sales from just delis [it had been a direct wholesaler] to supermarkets." That doesn't explain how the suit disappeared. With that cloud lifted, Hebrew National expanded its sales into five thousand stores, with frankfurters accounting for one third of profits.

New Yorkers continued to eat a prodigious quantity of meat. They accounted for one of every ten dollars Americans spent on beef, a total of $5 billion a year, according to the Greater New York Association of Meat and Poultry Dealers. In 1988, 40 percent of New York's meat was sold by one hundred wholesalers and processors, all located either at the 14th Street Meat Market, the largest in the city, or at the Hunt's Point Cooperative Market, which had opened in 1972 on a 37-acre complex in the Bronx.

But hanging carcasses were on their way out. By the 1970s almost 90 percent of New York's meat arrived from the West cut, vacuum-sealed, and packed in boxes. The 14th Street Market still bustled, but one prescient industry official predicted that "ultimately the West Side will be bereft of a wholesale meat market. It's just a matter of time before it's driven out, because this property has greater value for other purposes." The southern end was rezoned for residential development in 1988.

Sausage manufacturers were also in a state of flux. In the 1970s and 1980s many were driven out by union trouble, the need for cheaper factories, and, with plants located in dodgy areas, crime.

In 1972, Hebrew National spent $150,000 on security systems and attack dogs. Constant break-ins were costing Plymouth Rock $1,800 a week. American Kosher Provisions in Greenpoint, Brooklyn, said that "rocks come sailing in the windows, or a Molotov cocktail, or a truck gets looted . . . Once in a while there was a mugging of a plant worker." Delivery trucks were often robbed, sometimes at gunpoint.

Through the early 1980s Ward Foods' Plymouth Rock and Honeysuckle brands of canned hams, sausages, frankfurters, and variety meats employed four hundred workers at their block-filling Bronx plant and sold $23 million worth of pork products. By mid-decade, however, Ward Foods had left the Bronx, moving production upstate and to Iowa. It was more efficient to make its products elsewhere and ship them back into the city.

With four hundred workers, Hebrew National in Queens was the largest producer of kosher meat products. Houston-based Riviana Foods, which had bought the company in 1968, was purchased by Colgate-Palmolive in 1976. Two years later Leonard Pines, the son of the founder of Hebrew National (who began each day eating a hot dog, even before he had his morning coffee), bought the company from Colgate. "I feel we've got a heritage and a very fine future," he said. By 1983 Hebrew National recorded about $120 million in sales (versus $3 million for Mogen David, one of its New York competitors) and commanded about two-thirds of the national market for kosher hot dogs.

In 1986, Hebrew National changed its name to the ethnically neutral National Foods and announced that it was moving two thirds of its jobs and the bulk of its operations from Queens to Indiana. In New York emotions ran high. Not only would National's workers lose their livelihood, but the city would lose a product closely tied to the Jewish immigrant experience, a ghetto food that had made good. It didn't help that the erstwhile Hebrew National was moving to an American heartland uncongenial to the Jewish soul.

After the announcement two hundred workers and three rabbis walked out of the factory. The company brought in non-union workers and three other rabbis. The strike lasted for about four months. While still in contract talks with the union, Hebrew National announced that 129 of the Maspeth workers must relocate to Indianapolis or lose their jobs. A few days later a small bomb went off in a car outside the home of the distribution manager, a Pines cousin. No one was hurt, and it had no effect on the planned move.

"Hebrew National had a good product when they made it here," one picketing butcher, a thirteen-year veteran of the plant, told a reporter. "In Indianapolis, nobody knows how to make kosher food." (Indianapolis actually encompassed a fairly large Jewish population, but that wasn't what he meant.) Ten thousand pounds a day of kosher pastrami, countless salamis, and millions of hot dogs would no longer be made in New York, their point of entry into the American mainstream.

Under the umbrella of large corporations, "authentic" ethnic foods were being adapted to a wider range of taste. Many of the ethnic products showing up in store aisles across the country had to be "Americanized." Mogen David charged that Hebrew National products didn't "taste like [they] used to," which it blamed on the water in Indianapolis. More likely the spices had been made less pungent. Although Hebrew National products were no longer made in the city, New Yorkers remained faithful customers. In 1989 they accounted for over half of National Foods' $100 million in sales.

Conagra Foods bought National Foods in 1992 and acquired the trademarks of the Mogen David Kosher Meat Products Corporation, including Mogen David, Isaac Gellis, and Zion (and other brands), only to "retire" them. With the flight from the city of both kosher and nonkosher meat processors, by the late 1980s membership in the butchers' union, fourteen thousand in the 1950s, sunk to six thousand.

Pressured by gentrification, in the last years of the twentieth century the wholesale meat district at 14th Street, or Gansevoort Market, steadily contracted. In 2003 thirty-five wholesale butchers plied their trade there; by 2009 seven remained. In 2014 the lease on a city-owned co-op expired and the last butchers left. Soon the neighborhood began to fill with condos, hotels, and upscale shops.

NEW FOOD CITY

Surprisingly, in view of the exodus of industrial food chronicled in this book, the first two decades of the twenty-first century are shaping up to be a golden age in Food City. According to the latest available figures (2011) from the New York City Economic Development Corporation, about nineteen thousand people were employed in over nine hundred food companies. While most are small, with only a few employees, many are expanding and adding workers. Here are some of their stories.

Bread

While the large factory bakeries were closing, the first wave of artisanal bakers were opening a very different kind of bakery. New Yorkers were demanding better bread, and since a perishable product is best made close to its customers, bakeries began opening in neighborhoods from the Bronx to Staten Island.

In 1987 the chef-turned-baker Noel Labat Comess began Tom Cat Bakery in a 1,300-square-foot space in Long Island City. Each day he and his two assistants produced 300 loaves of French and sourdough bread plus 400 rolls for ten commercial customers. Within a few weeks he had almost broken even on his original investment. Six years later the bakery was selling $1.6 million worth of rolls, baguettes, and breads to 250 restaurants and was planning to triple in size. By 2009, Tom Cat had 275 employees. Its baguettes went into the oven at 3:30 a.m. and thirty minutes later were en route to hotels in Manhattan. Its 150 other products were baked at different times of the day and night and constantly delivered to clients. Some breads took eight hours to bake, others two; Old World varieties needed twelve. The first shift arrived at ten at night so that bread doughs with longer fermentation times could be prepared in time for the morning rush. The factory used automation where possible, but some breads needed the touch of a baker's hand, and all needed the baker's eye to determine fermentation and baking times. By 2012 the 10th Street location near the Queensboro Bridge had expanded to 40,000 square feet, baked 5,000 rolls a day for hundreds of restaurant clients, and earned annual revenues of $30 million.

In 2012, Amy's Bread, after baking artisanal breads behind a glass wall at the Chelsea Market for fourteen years, moved its 120 employees to Long Island City. Amy Scherber, the company's founder and a former cook, said that rent for the open and fairly large space was lower than in Manhattan and a good place to expand a company with $11 million in sales. A few blocks away from her new facility was her Chelsea Market retail neighbor, Eleni's New York, which had moved its cookie-making facility to the area seven years earlier.

In 2000, in its factory in Vinegar Hill, Brooklyn, Damascus Bakeries had 11,000 pita breads sliding in and out of high-temperature ovens every hour. The assembly lines also rolled out 20,000 wraps and 8,000 panini an hour. The factory owner, Edward Mafoud, from the third generation of the family that had launched the bakery seventy years earlier, wanted to expand his Gold Street factory, but the Brooklyn neighborhood had become too residential and expensive. When the factory moved to New Jersey in late 2001, tortillas were first in sales, pitas second, bagels third, and bread fourth.

Fernando Sanchez, a Mexican immigrant who came to New York in 1968, worked his way from dishwasher to cook to chef's assistant at a midtown French restaurant. Along the way he staked two brothers to their passage from Piaxtla and brought his wife up from the neighboring village of Chinantla. With $10,000 in savings he bought a secondhand tortilla press in California and began making tortillas in an abandoned garage on Flushing Avenue in Brooklyn. During the first year Tortilleria Piaxtla, named after his hometown in Mexico (most of his rivals named their businesses similarly), produced 4,000 tortillas per weekend, and people lined up to buy them. Ten years later Sanchez was baking 400,000 a week and had an estimated $3.5 million in sales. In 1992 he bought his rented building, the one next door, and another across the street. Additional companies were opened— three by Sanchez's former employees—and the area around the Flushing Avenue factory became known as the "tortilla triangle." By 2000, when the city's Mexican population had quadrupled, six tortilla factories were in operation, producing "roughly 10 million tortillas" every week, according to the *New York Times*.

One of the factories in the triangle was Erasmo Ponce's Tortilleria

Chinantla. Ponce had worked in New York for three years as a driver for another firm before starting the factory with a partner in 1992. Five years later he was in business on his own and had bought equipment with computerized temperature controls that churned out 520 tortillas a minute. Automated stacking machines prepared the piles of warm tortillas that women employees bagged by hand.

However, now as in the past, the quest for profit sometimes bars immigrant owners from treating their fellow immigrants well. Without appropriate safeguards, the high-speed dough mixer at Tortilleria Chinantla killed a twenty-two-year-old worker in 2011 when he was sucked into the machinery. The factory was allowed to reopen but was cited for safety violations, and Erasmo Ponce came under the scrutiny of the federal government, which discovered apparent violations of overtime and worker's compensation laws. A year later he pled guilty and was sentenced to ninety days in jail; he was ordered to pay over $400,000, $300,000 of that amount representing restitution to the deceased worker's family.

New York's Chinese population also offered opportunities for new products. Wonton Foods opened in 1983 in Chinatown and by the next year had moved to Long Island City, where it made fortune cookies by hand. Six years later it moved into a separate noodle plant in East Williamsburg, with three hundred employees. The Long Island City factory expanded five times and by 2001 was turning out 60 million fortune cookies a month. Today seventy employees work around the clock manning automated machinery that carefully folds warm round pieces of dough into the tri-cornered cookie, then wraps them in plastic imprinted with the Golden Bowl brand name.

Another example of New York's infatuation with immigrant cuisine is Terry Tang's successful line of Chinese noodles and dump-

TERRA CHIPS

In March 1989, Alex Dzieduszycki and Dana Sinkler, both former employees of four-star restaurants, began a catering company, Dana Alexander Inc. At parties they served a signature appetizer: thinly sliced fried taro chips coated in beet juice. The chips were a huge success. "If we could come up with five cases a day, that was great," Sinkler recalled in the *New York Times*. "But then [in 1990] Saks placed an order for fifty cases." Dzieduszycki and Sinkler gave up catering and leased a small factory in the East Village of Manhattan that had previously made cheese sticks. At the time 410 East 13th Street between First Avenue and Avenue A was a haven for crack dealers. Still, the company thrived. Seventeen workers were soon packaging the chips in silvery foil bags, each with a sticker inscribed with a line drawing of the vegetable flavor of the chips inside—yucca, batata, parsnip, sweet potato, taro, and lotus root (later dropped because it was too expensive). Terra Chips needed more space and planned to move to Greenpoint, Brooklyn. By the end of 1993 the new factory added twenty-eight employees—mostly Polish, Dominican, and Chinese immigrants—to the original seventeen. The Hain Food Group acquired Terra Chips in 1998. By 2001, with business booming, the Greenpoint plant could no longer meet demand and production moved to New Jersey.

New York is the perfect place for a startup like Terra Chips. It has a well-heeled clientele who eagerly seek new tastes and unique products and media always on the hunt for the latest thing. But New York is also a difficult place to actually make things. Rents and taxes are high, building codes are stringent, traffic impedes deliveries, and parking tickets can dent a struggling company's budget.

BROOKLYN BRINE

The first time Shamus Jones was called a businessman he was taken aback. Although he was at the helm of Brooklyn Brine, the pickle company he started in 2009, which had multiplied production several times in its first three and a half years, he considered himself a chef, not a businessman. Still, it was a role he grew more comfortable with at each phase of his company's growth.

Jones started out on his new career the day he was laid off as an executive chef. Without a business plan or any idea for the future, he began making pickles in a restaurant kitchen because he felt good doing it.

The first variety he made was NY Deli Style, a garlic dill pickle, which immediately found a market. Jones then began making pickles during the day in the kitchen of a restaurant that opened only for dinner. His five full-time and two part-time employees worked long days producing 300 to 400 jars of pickles. In October 2010 he moved into a shared kitchen on President Street in Brooklyn and increased production to 700 jars. According to Jones, Brooklyn Brine is trying to grow at a "controlled rate" so that it can continue to hand-pack its pickles without turning production over to a packing house outside the city. "Why create a brand only to have someone else make it?" he says. In 2012, Brooklyn Brine occupied the entire President Street kitchen; its eight employees, most of them college graduates, produce 1,650 jars a day. Brooklyn Brine's repertoire of pickle products now includes Whiskey Sour Pickles, Spicy Maple Bourbon Pickles, Beer Pickles, and others. The cachet of making an artisanal product has allowed companies like Brooklyn Brine to flourish and their founders to earn a comfortable living.

lings. Tang arrived in New York in 1977 and worked nights in a noodle shop while attending college days. After a short stint in corporate life, he found he was more interested in food. Financed with money from his family, he and his brother Joseph opened a small noodle factory in Chinatown in 1989 and soon had four workers. Having researched noodle-making in Asia as well as domestically, Tang fashioned a fresher and tastier noodle than was commonly available in most New York stores. He and his brother were soon selling noodles throughout the East. In 1992 the brothers moved their production to the Bushwick area of Brooklyn. Seven years later they opened a second Bushwick factory to produce Chef One dumplings for restaurants and institutions. Their next move, in 2004, was into the former Edward B. Hittleman Brewery on Meserole Street in Brooklyn, where four assembly lines produce 11,000 dumplings an hour and a variety of noodles and wrappers. By 2008 the Tangs' factories in four locations made $2.5 million worth of food and employed 140 mostly Asian immigrants.

Sugar

From the 1990s onward, jobs were vanishing at the Domino Sugar plant. In the summer of 2003, when its owner, American Sugar, announced that the refinery would cease operations, only two hundred employees were left. "We can't sell all we can make," the company president said. The factory's capacity to refine 950 million pounds of sugar, once an asset, had become a liability; the company could sell only 400 million pounds, because high-fructose corn syrup and beet sugar had taken a big chunk of its business. Its workers had become what one of them called "dinosaurs." In 2004 the iconic Domino Sugar sign on top of the building was turned off. The eleven-story char house, which had filtered sugar since 1884, sat empty. The main building received landmark status in 2007 and four years later so did the sign, although it will shine on top of an apartment building.

The year Domino closed, a scandal rocked the Cumberland Packing Company, makers of Sweet'N Low. Joseph Asaro, the former vice president of governmental affairs, was arrested on charges of impeding a federal investigation into illegal political contributions. Marvin Eisenstadt, Cumberland's president and the founder's son, was also charged. Both men pled guilty to making illegal contributions to politicians to gain support for a moratorium on the saccharin ban that threatened their business. Eisenstadt "accept[ed] responsibility" for "failing to detect or prevent the scheme" and said he had no knowledge of the contributions. Cumberland paid a $2 million fine.

Today the company's four hundred unionized workers fill millions of packets of Sweet'N Low a day. Those hired are rarely fired, and most stay for years. As one office worker, whose mother was also employed at the company, said, "You just work forever" at the Navy Yard plant. Cumberland has also retained its somewhat outdated clanging and clattering cast-iron machinery in order to keep workers employed hand-packing the little pink packets into boxes, rather than switching over to high-speed machinery that could turn out many more containers of the sweetener. Cumberland makes a product called Sugar in the Raw, turbinado sugar, a partially refined, pale brown granulated sugar sold in Starbucks and health food stores. Steven Eisenstadt, the founder's grandson, says that the company isn't budging from Brooklyn, even though suitors are constantly offering better deals in other places.

Another family firm, Madelaine Chocolate Novelties, with its

20 million pounds of foil-wrapped chocolates a year, is also staying put. The children, in-laws, and relatives of the original owners run the company, which occupies three buildings in Rockaway Beach. During the peak October-to-April season, its machines enclose 400 to 1,200 candies a minute in bright foil wrapping. The factory can produce fifteen different lines of chocolate turkeys or Santas at the same time. Some of the candy is labeled under the Madelaine name, but the majority is packaged for other companies, many of them major brands. In 2012, as 450 workers were filling holiday orders, Hurricane Sandy ripped through the factory, flooding machinery and drowning boxes of candy. Unable to recover from this catastrophic loss, Madelaine put the 5.4-acre building complex up for sale until it received $6 million in tax credits from Governor Andrew Cuomo, followed by $13.2 million in funds from the city's Hurricane Sandy Business Loan and Grant Program and the Industrial Development Agency. The factory remains in Rockaway today.

By 2000 several high-end artisanal candy-makers were offering unheard-of tastes at unheard-of prices in the surprisingly competitive field of chili-infused chocolates and black-sesame truffles. The self-taught John Down, an artist who dabbled in candy-making, started Christopher Norman Chocolates in a downtown loft. He and his partner, Joe Giuliani, moved their kitchen when Nordstrom began ordering their candies. They soon landed a lucrative export business selling their handcrafted, hand-painted confections in Japan. By 2008, Christopher Norman, which relocated to the financial district after 9/11, was a $1-million-a-year business, with fifteen employees making candies flavored with rosemary, cardamom, and avocado.

The Mast Brothers, in Williamsburg, make their chocolate

directly from cocoa beans. The brothers Rick, a former chef, and Michael, a filmmaker, opened their business in Brooklyn in 2007 after inventing methods for each step of their process, since there were no longer any other small-batch chocolate-makers to teach them. Made during the renaissance of small-batch hand-made foods, their signature Mast Brothers Chocolate Makers chocolate bars caught on quickly. Burlap bags of cocoa beans from farms in Madagascar, Venezuela, the Dominican Republic, and Ecuador are hand-sorted. Each type is roasted differently, a bag or two a day, producing about 1,000 bars. Originally the beans were cracked by hand, but now a machine cracks them and separates the husks. The beans then go into stone grinders for an hour and a half while the cocoa butter liquefies. The only other ingredient used, cane sugar, is then added, along with flavorings like sea salt or pepper. The glossy bars in fifteen varieties are wrapped in artfully crafted papers printed in the factory or left in large blocks for restaurants and institutions.

Drink

Beer-making is once again flourishing in New York, especially in Brooklyn. Though the small breweries' output is a fraction of the quantity made in the early 1970s, at the close of the brewery era, enthusiasm for the burgeoning industry is greater than ever.

The granddaddy of the new breweries is the Brooklyn Brewery, in Williamsburg, started by Steve Hindy and Tom Potter in 1996. On its opening day, in a space that once housed a matzoh bakery, city officials and guests raised plastic glasses of beer as Steve Hindy offered the toast "May New York never again be without a brewery." That wish seems highly likely to come true, with Sixpoint Brewery and Greenpoint Beer Works plus other breweries in

SOME THINGS NEVER CHANGE

Not all the food made in Brooklyn is hand-crafted. In 1998, Virginia Dare and its several hundred employees, including more than twenty flavor chemists and food technologists, celebrated the company's seventy-fifth anniversary in the borough. Still run by its founders, the Smith family, Virginia Dare has moved forward with the latest flavor trends, and today its factory and warehouses at the end of 31st Street perfume the neighborhood air with the smell of raspberry or blueberry or vanilla extract.

Before it closed its Lower East Side factory in 2015, Streit Matzoh had changed very little over the years. Jack Streit, son of the founder, died in 1998, and his daughters and grandsons, who played and worked in the factory as kids, took over the company. With continually rising costs, they struggled to make the money their parents or grandparents did, but they felt obligated to produce the family matzoh. Interestingly, they believed that the city's water, often invoked by local manufacturers as a special ingredient, enriched Streit's beloved flavor.

the works, joining Brooklyn Brewery. From Manhattan to Staten Island, brew pubs with names like Neptune, Zip City, Carnegie Hill, and Yankee Brewing have been opening and closing for years.

In 2004 a reintroduced version of Rheingold Beer was brewed at the two-story Greenpoint Beer Works in Clinton Hill. The brewmaster, Kelly Taylor, a craft brewer, wasn't thrilled to be making a mainstream beer, but it helped foot the bill for the new beer he soon began producing, Kelso of Brooklyn. While the new Rheingold beer did not experience the success of its namesake (and is no longer brewed in Brooklyn), Greenpoint Beer was growing. Between 2009 and 2012 beer production nearly doubled, from 12,000 to 20,000 kegs.

Kelly Taylor says there is room for growth because "a lot of imported" beers sold on tap "are ready to fail," making way for fresher, locally brewed beers and ales. Governor Cuomo hailed the "phenomenal growth" of the brewing and distilling industries and allocated money to advertise their products.

The distilling industry, started in New York in 2010, is newer. In 2002 the state legislature created an inexpensive permit to allow for small-batch distilling which stipulated that if half the ingredients came from New York farms, a distiller could produce up to 35,000 gallons a year and operate a tasting room. By 2012 about ten distilleries were producing rum, vodka, corn whiskey, bourbon, and gin.

The first to open was Kings County Distillery, started by Colin Spoelman and David Haskell in 2010. Made in the Brooklyn Navy Yard, their bourbon and moonshine uses organic corn from the Finger Lakes. On a second floor, bourbon is aged in hundreds of 5-gallon charred oak barrels. Their plain bottles are labeled with a simple typewriter font that evokes a feeling of bootleg liquor, which Spoelman made in his apartment before opening the distillery. In early 2013, with more than $1 million in financing, the company added two copper stills from Scotland that increased production to 30 gallons daily. It is one of eight distilleries in Brooklyn and the Bronx.

Brad Estabrook at the Breucklen Distillery in Greenwood Heights opened shortly after Kings County, distilling the first batch in June 2010. After eight years of bond trading, including a stint at Fidelity, Estabrook was laid off in December 2008 because of the recession. He wrote a business plan and spent a year and a half exploring contingencies and experimenting. After finding a space and renovating, he waited alone in his empty warehouse for the stills to arrive. The first time he put the gleaming machinery to work, the aromas—juniper, rosemary, ginger, lemon, and grapefruit—confirmed his long-delayed anticipation. His first product was Glorious Gin, followed by two versions of Whiskey 77, made with wheat, corn, rye, and barley and aged in oak barrels. His distillery produces about 60 cases a week, bottled by hand, the top of each bottle waxed closed with a length of dental floss embedded in the wax to unravel the coating.

Specialty coffees are a growing part of the coffee market, and New York boasts several roasters. Donald Schoenholt, the founding father of the Specialty Coffee Association of America (SCAA), has championed specialty coffee for years. His Gillies brand coffees are sold to Fairway Market (a New York grocery store), coffee bars, upscale restaurants, and boutique hotels. In 1991, Gillies Coffee moved to 19th Street in Sunset Park, an industrial area once home to dozens of roasters, conveniently located near Continental Terminals, one of the Northeast's largest ports for green coffee. By 2006 it was the only roaster left in the area, where its twenty-three employees roasted coffee beans.

By the early years of this century, specialty coffee-roasters had joined the ranks of the artisanal producers. Roasters like Stumptown Coffee, which moved to Red Hook in 2009, offered products for the post-Starbucks coffee generation, using upgraded techniques while vying to be the most expensive coffee in the city, as Martinson's coffee had been decades before.

The coffee craze of the 1990s helped Manhattan Special soda break out of "the old neighborhood." The owner, Aurora Passaro, "loved Starbucks" for fueling wide interest, which she believed helped her dark, fizzy drink with a wallop of sugar and caffeine find its way into specialty stores while creating a large international market in the Middle East, Hong Kong, Greece, and Japan. By 2008 the company was selling "in the millions" of bottles each year, with the factory "running flat out," she commented. Nothing made Passaro happier than watching the hipsters who had gentrified the neighborhood around the factory drinking her Manhattan Espresso Soda.

By the summer of 1998, Olde Brooklyn Soda Company was shipping 25,000 cases of its high-end soda. With more flavor and less carbonation than mainstream sodas, it was sold under labels like Coney Island Cream, Bay Ridge Birch Beer, Williamsburg Root Beer, and Greenpoint Grape. In 2012 the Brooklyn-centric soda company, with sales growing by 500 percent, moved to California.

In the same artisanal spirit, Brooklyn Soda Works was a home kitchen hobby of Antonio Ramos and Caroline Mak. The haute sodas, which come in forty unusual fruit and herb flavor combinations, have only a two- to three-week shelf life. The company eked out a small profit in its first year at the Brooklyn Flea Market, where many artisanal products start off, then began selling to restaurants in kegs. Made by three employees, Brooklyn Soda is bottled in unusual brown glass bottles. "It's about the process," Ramos said in an interview, "about trying to do something the absolute best you can and just focusing on quality. And just doing one thing and doing it well, like the traditional artisan."

ARTISANAL MILK

One milk producer has started making almond and cashew nut milks. In 2011, Julie and Greg Van Ullen began marketing their alternative organic milk, OMilk, at the Brooklyn Flea Market, where they met with a phenomenal response, selling 80 bottles their first day (their goal had been to sell at least one to someone who wasn't a friend!). That winter, after a website mentioned that they were offering a home-delivery service, they had such a good response that they rented a space in a custom factory kitchen in East Williamsburg, where they use industrial blenders and sieves finer than a strand of human hair to blend the milk. Greg Van Ullen works full-time in their factory, with one full-time employee and three part-timers. The couple, with no previous experience in producing food, has big plans for the future.

In 1990, after a decade of consolidation, the city's $800-million-per-year milk business had been reduced to a few dairies, several of which were hemorrhaging money. One dairy owner saw a day when "there will be no milk processors left in New York City. The cost of business . . . is just too prohibitive." The head of the state's agricultural research division agreed: "It's questionable whether small plants can survive at all."

But one dairy was growing. Under Henry Schwartz, the fourth-generation owner, Elmhurst Dairy is the last dairy left in the city. The processing plant is on an industrial strip of Styker Road in Jamaica, Queens, only a few blocks from York College. Here Elmhurst pasteurizes, homogenizes, and packs milk to deliver to the five boroughs. In 2005 the company invested $14 million because expansion was the only way to stay in business. Older buildings were refurbished, new structures built, and equipment was added, doubling production from 760,000 to 1.5 million gallons a week.

Though it was a blow to Elmhurst when it lost the account to supply milk for the local Starbucks in 2011, the company still supplies all the half-pint containers of milk that 1 million children drink in New York City's public schools. It also supplies 8,300 independent local groceries and corner bodegas throughout the city. Of the company's 240 employees, 75 percent are from ethnic minorities and almost half of them live in the southeast area of Queens where the dairy is located.

Meat

New York's surviving food producers have crossed ethnic boundaries to keep up with the changing city, as Stella D'Oro did in the 1950s. Chef One, for example, features a line of kosher dumplings. Cibao Meat Products, a forty-year-old sausage manufacturer in the Bronx which makes Dominican-style sausages, diversified into Mexican sausages as that population grew. There are still several sausage-makers in the Bronx, including Ferris Stahl-Meyer, a company created in 1928 by a merger of firms with roots going back to 1836 and 1895. The company is now owned by Guillermo Gonzales, a thirty-year employee. Besides the frankfurters, sausages, and hams that were the specialties of the original companies, it makes products with a Latin flavor. Sausages are the only meat product still made in New York.

The Meat Hook (above) in Brooklyn and Harlem Shambles (below) in Manhattan are two boutique butcher shops in New York operating today with similar principles. Both abide by the whole animal philosophy and work with local farms to sell the highest quality meat with minimal waste.

Those Who Leave, Those Who Stay

Firms long rooted in the city continue to leave in the new century, often after being scooped up by out-of-town corporations. Through the 1990s, Old London Foods produced 90 percent of America's Melba toast, but its corporate owner, CPC International, ordered layoffs in 1997 before putting the company up for sale. The investor group that bought it committed to keeping the bakery and its two hundred employees in the Bronx. By 2003 the new owners had invested $4.2 million in equipment and extended the product line, using 500,000 pounds of flour a week to make bagel snacks, flatbread, waffle cheese sandwiches, and organic products. Fifty employees were added to the payroll, and two shifts worked five days a week at the $100 million company, which still made Melba toast on machinery originally devised by Bert Weil, using large metal plates that apply pressure to 500 pounds of sliced white bread as it is toasted.

By 2005 the company was sold again, this time to Chicago-based Nonni Foods, which vowed to "add a significant number of jobs to the Bronx plant." The average length of service for the bakery's workers was fifteen years, and some had been there since the factory opened in 1968. But after five years Nonni deemed the three-story factory inefficient. In 2010, Old London Foods left the Bronx for a new factory in North Carolina, leaving its employees behind. New York hadn't even been in the running of possible new locales.

Stella D'Oro was wrenched out of the Bronx at about the same time. In 1992 the Zampetti family sold the company, the country's largest family-owned cookie manufacturer, to RJR Nabisco. The new owners "weren't planning any changes" and the factory would "stay in place." When they stopped making

Stella D'Oro products, kosher sales suffered, but even after they corrected that mistake, the downward slide continued. In 2006, Brynwood Partners, a private equity firm, acquired Stella D'Oro for millions of dollars less than RJR Nabisco had paid fourteen years earlier. The new owners sold the two plants outside New York, laid off workers in the Bronx, and cut the salaries and benefits of the 134 that remained. A strike that began in the summer of 2008 lasted eleven months. The National Labor Relations Board sided with the workers, and the judge ordered that they be reinstated immediately, with two months' back pay. But as the workers celebrated, Brynwood announced that it had sold the company to Lance, a cookie-maker, which soon closed the plant and shifted operations to Ohio.

The future of New Food City belongs to young people who feel the call to craft and have been creating new products at a furious pace. Michelle Lewis, for example, is willing to hold a nine-to-five job as she builds her caramel sauce company, Spoonable, LLC, step by step, in stolen minutes during the workday and throughout the weekend, using her apartment as the company's warehouse. The idea for the business came in January 2011; registration, licensing, and other requirements to start up took six months; production began in August for a September 2011 launch.

Lewis lives and makes her sauce in Brooklyn, the epicenter of new food-making, where small stores are happy to stock the often pricey small-batch products that define the local movement. Lewis's two part-time employees work a minimum of sixteen hours a week each and have included photographers, an architect, and a male model. It takes them a half hour to make, jar, and label a carton of twelve 7¾-ounce jars of chili caramel sauce. Eventually Lewis hopes to work at her company full-time.

Caramel-sauce-maker Michelle Lewis, artisanal milk producers Julie and Greg Van Ullen, pickle-maker Shamus Jones, and distillers Brad Estabrook, Colin Spoelmann, and David Haskell are just a few examples of food-makers who have contributed to New York's food history since its earliest days. Throughout four centuries these food entrepreneurs, big and small, have fed the city's millions of inhabitants, dispersed their products across the country, and shipped them around the world. Now, with the resurgence of artisanal food, their story continues.

NOTES

AN INVITATION TO FOOD CITY

xvi *"collected from the retail butchers"*: *Women's Work on City Problems* . . . (New York: Reform Club, Committee on Municipal Administration, 1898), 441.

xvii *"foremost among sugar markets"*: "The Sugar Refineries of New York" *New York Daily Times*, Aug. 11, 1856, 6.

1: DUTCH TASTES

3 *"beans and gray peas"*: Domine Jonas Michaelius, "The First Minister of the Reformed Protestant Dutch Church in North America: Letter of Domine Jonas Michaelius to Domine Adrianus Smoutius, Dated at Manhattan, 11 August, 1628," in J. Franklin Jameson, *Narratives of New Netherland, 1609–1664* (New York: Scribner's, 1909), 131.

4 *"hovels and holes"*: Henri A. Van der Zee and Barbara Van der Zee, *A Sweet and Alien Land: The Story of Dutch New York* (New York: Viking, 1978), 14.

5 *"We live here"*: Thomas J. Condon, *New York Beginnings: the Commercial Origins of New Netherland* (New York: New York University Press, 1968), 43.

5 *"of very fine flavor"*: Russell Shorto, *The Island at the Center of the World: The Epic Story of Dutch Manhattan and the Forgotten Colony That Shaped America* (New York: Doubleday, 2004), 50.

5   *"pass[ing] through the winter"*: Jameson, *Narratives of New Netherland*, 131.

5   *The Dutch ate over 2 pounds:* Simon Middleton, " 'How It Came that the Bakers Bake No Bread': A Struggle for Trade Privileges in Seventeenth-Century New Amsterdam," *William and Mary Quarterly*, Third Series, 58, no. 2 (Apr. 1, 2001): 352, doi:10.2307/2674189.

6   *"hard stale food"*: Edwin G. Burrows and Mike Wallace, *Gotham : A History of New York City to 1898* (New York: Oxford University Press, 1999), 27.

6   *On the first ship:* Jameson, *Narratives of New Netherland*, 83.

6   *It took several years:* Condon, *New York Beginnings*, 86–115.

7   *Made from hops:* Stanley Baron, *Brewed in America: A History of Beer and Ale in the United States* (Boston: Little, Brown, 1962), 16.

7   *By then the village:* Burrows and Wallace, *Gotham*, 31.

7   *"vacant and fallen into decay"*: Ibid., 31.

7   *Director General Kieft gave:* Jack Bettridge, "The New Gins," *Wine Spectator*, June 30, 2010; Van der Zee and Van der Zee, *A Sweet and Alien Land*, 100.

8   *"in the Fatherland"*: David Pietersz De Vries and Henry Cruse Murphy, *Voyages from Holland to America, A.D. 1632 to 1644* (New York: Billin and Bros., 1853), 157.

8   *Fortuitously, the brewery:* Burrows and Wallace, *Gotham*, 51.

8   *"standing and rotting"*: "Letter from the Eight Men, Oct. 28, 1644," in E. B. O'Callaghan, *History of New Netherland; Or, New York Under the Dutch*, 2nd ed. (New York: Appleton, 1855), 313.

8   *"one full fourth"*: Peter Stuyvesant, "March 10, 1648. An Ordinance Against Drinking to Excess," *Documents of the Assembly of the State of New York*, 1831, 279.

8   *There had been sporadic complaints:* "Ordinance passed Nov. 8, 1649," in Berthold Fernow, *The Records of New Amsterdam from 1653 to 1674 Anno Domini* (New York: Knickerbocker, 1897), 14–15.

9   *Most bread purchases:* Middleton, " 'How It Came that the Bakers Bake No Bread.' "

9   *"greed and desire"*: Joyce D. Goodfriend, "Burghers and Blacks: The Evolution of a Slave Society at New Amsterdam," *New York History* 59, no. 2 (1978): 138.

9   *"any fine bolted or white bread"*: *Laws and Ordinances of New Netherland, 1638–1674* (Albany: Weed, Parsons, 1868), 112–13.

10 *"inhabitants and natives"*: *Laws and Ordinances of New Netherland, 1638–1674*, 111–15.

10 *An advisory council:* Jameson, *Narratives of New Netherland*, ~~293~~341, 349, 350~~354~~.

10 *a more permanent appearance:* Burrows and Wallace, *Gotham*, 50.

10 *Vinegar was in demand:* Charles T. Gehring, ed., *Laws & Writs of Appeal, 1647–1663* ([Syracuse, N.Y.]: Syracuse University Press, 1991), 36, 75, 88, 114.

11 *Food began to be:* Baron, *Brewed in America*, 26.

11 *Many women worked:* Dorothy A. Mays, *Women in Early America: Struggle, Survival, and Freedom in a New World* (Santa Barbara, Calif.: ABC-CLIO, 2004), 409–10.

11 *"great stone brew-house":* Mary Ellenor Stafford Bowman, *Descendants of Isaac Van Tuyl, Sr., and Mary McCarter of Bernards Township, Somerset County, New Jersey* (Baltimore: Gateway, 1970), 58.

11 *"to pay the beer excise":* "Minutes of the Court of Burgomasters and Schepens, 1656 to Aug. 27, 1658," in Fernow, *The Records of New Amsterdam from 1653 to 1674,* 252.

12 *Food production:* Cathy D. Matson, *Merchants & Empire: Trading in Colonial New York, Early America* (Baltimore: Johns Hopkins University Press, 1998), 34.

12 *"serve in butchering":* Thomas F. De Voe, *Abattoirs: A Paper Read before the Polytechnic Branch of the American Institute, June 8, 1865* (Albany, N.Y.: Van Benthuysen & Sons, 1866), 7. Also see Burrows and Wallace, *Gotham,* 60, 133–34.

12 *In dry weather:* John King Van Rensselaer, *The Goede Vrouw of Mana-Ha-Ta at Home and in Society, 1609–1760* (New York: Scribner's, 1898), 29–30.

13 *In September 1661:* "Minutes of the Court of Burgomasters and Schepens of New Amsterdam 1661," in Fernow, *The Records of New Amsterdam from 1653 to 1674,* 390–91.

13 *"how it came":* Ibid., 378, 389–91. For a general account and analysis, see Middleton, " 'How It Came that the Bakers Bake No Bread.' "

13 *"better knowledge of bread":* Fernow, *The Records of New Amsterdam from 1653 to 1674,* 390–91.

14 *Brewers generally did better:* Edwin R. Purple, "Contribution to the History of the Great Families of New York," in Richard Henry Greene et al., eds., *The New York Genealogical and Biographical Record,* vol. 7–8 (New York: New-York Historical Society, 1870), 124.

14 *From the Dutch colony:* Goodfriend, "Burghers and Blacks," 138.

14 *English colonies bordered:* Evert A. Duykinck, "New York: Past and Present," *Frank Leslie's Popular Monthly* 17, no. 1 (Jan. 1884), 11. Also see Howard B. Rock, Deborah Dash Moore, and David Lobenstine, *Cityscapes: A History of New York in Images* (New York: Columbia University Press, 2001), 24–25.

14 *The brewer Isaac de Forest:* John William De Forest, *The De Forests of Avesnes (and of New Netherland): A Huguenot Thread in American Colonial History* (New Haven: Tuttle, Morehouse & Taylor, 1900), 101.

15 *"much less peas":* Peter Stuyvesant, "Report of the Surrender of New Netherland to the British, Oct. 19, 1665," in John Romeyn Brodhead et al., eds., *Documents Relative to the Colonial History of the State of New-York: Procured in Holland, England, and France* (Albany: Weed, Parsons, 1853), 366.

15 *Most of the townspeople:* Jameson, *Narratives of New Netherland,* 416–22.

15 *After ten fraught days:* "Articles of Capitulation on the Reduction of New Netherland, Aug. 27, 1664," in Brodhead et al., *Documents Relative to the Colonial History of the State of New-York,* 250.

16 *"habitual Tea Drinking"*: Esther Singleton, *Social New York under the Georges, 1714–1776: Houses, Streets, and Country Homes, with Chapters on Fashions, Furniture, China, Plate, and Manners* (New York: Appleton, 1902), 378–79.

16 *But by the mid-seventeenth century:* Sidney Wilfred Mintz, *Sweetness and Power: The Place of Sugar in Modern History* (New York: Viking, 1985), 35–55.

16 *By 1688 London boasted:* Richard B. Sheridan, *Sugar and Slavery: An Economic History of the British West Indies, 1623–1775* (Kingston, Jamaica: Canoe, 1994), 28; Mintz, *Sweetness and Power,* 113–17.

17 *"a huge barn-like affair"*: Frederick Trevor Hill, *The Story of a Street: A Narrative History of Wall Street from 1644 to 1908* (New York: Harper, 1908), 29.

17 *As larger plantations:* Peter C. Hogg, *The African Slave Trade and Its Suppression, a Classified and Annotated Bibliography of Books, Pamphlets and Periodical Articles* (London: Frank Cass, 1973), 84, ref. 1028.

17 *With every inch:* Christian J. Koot, *Empire at the Periphery: British Colonists, Anglo-Dutch Trade, and the Development of the British Atlantic, 1621–1713* (New York: New York University Press, 2015), 207.

18 *Fellow merchant Lewis Morris:* Richard Brookhiser, *Gentleman Revolutionary: Gouverneur Morris, the Rake Who Wrote the Constitution* (New York: Free Press, 2003), 34.

18 *"considerable sea-port"*: The Charter of the City of New-York: Printed by Order of the Mayor, Recorder, Aldermen and Commonalty of the City Aforesaid* (New York: H. Gaine, 1774), 19.

18 *"scarce a week passes"*: "Free Trader," letter to editor, *New York Post Boy,* June 6, 1748, in Edwin G. Burrows and Mike Wallace, *Gotham: A History of New York City to 1898* (New York: Oxford University Press, 1999), 168.

19 *"Joynt or in pieces"*: Stanley J. Shapiro and Alton F. Doody, *Readings in the History of American Marketing: Settlement to Civil War* (Homewood, Ill.: R. D. Irwin, 1968), 49.

19 *"public slaughterhouses and Penns"*: Thomas F. De Voe, *The Market Book: A History of the Public Markets of the City of New York* (New York: A. M. Kelley, 1970), 80–81.

20 *One of their three slaves:* Henry Reed Stiles, *A History of the City of Brooklyn Including the Old Town and Village of Brooklyn, the Town of Bushwick, and the Village and City of Williamsburgh* (Brooklyn, N.Y.: pub. by subscription, 1867), 74.; Jared N. Day, "Butchers, Tanners, and Tallow Chandlers: The Geography of Slaughtering in Early Nineteenth-Century New York City," *Food and History* 3, no. 2 (Jan. 1, 2005): 83, doi:10.1484/J.FOOD.2.301754.

20 *The English loved sweets:* Louis Grivetti and Howard-Yana Shapiro, *Chocolate: History, Culture, and Heritage* (Hoboken, N.J.: Wiley, 2009), 63.

20 *It was the drink:* Cathy D. Matson, *Merchants & Empire: Trading in Colonial New York, Early America* (Baltimore: Johns Hopkins University Press, 1998), 261.

21 *"Citty of New Yorke"*: Sheridan, *Sugar and Slavery,* 353.

21 *"mode of living"*: *New York Gazette,* Nov. 28, 1737, Aug. 8, 1737, Jan. 31, 1738. Also see Jill Lepore, *New York Burning: Liberty, Slavery, and Conspiracy in Eighteenth-Century Manhattan* (New York: Vintage, 2006), n. 12, 296.

21 *"the middling sort"*: Simon Middleton, " 'Artisans' and the 'Middling Sort' in Gary Nash's Eighteenth-Century Urban America?," *Pennsylvania Magazine of History and Biography* 133, no. 4 (2009): 416–23; Gary B. Nash, *The Urban Crucible: The Northern Seaports and the Origins of the American Revolution,* abridged ed. (Cambridge: Harvard University Press, 1986), 107.

22 *Laborers in New York:* Edward Long, *The History of Jamaica, or, General Survey of the antient and Modern State of the Island* . . . (London: T. Lowndes, 1774), 525. Also see Sidney Wilfred Mintz, *Sweetness and Power: The Place of Sugar in Modern History* (New York: Viking, 1985), 45, 77.

22 *Many artisans kept an apprentice:* Burrows and Wallace, *Gotham,* 126–28.

22 *"Negro kitchen":* Will of Harmanus Rutgers, Sr., in "Rutgers," *Early Bergen County Families,* compiled by Pat Wardell, http://njgsbc.org/files/BCFamilies/BCFam-Rutgers.pdf.

22 *"Bolting-House":* *New York Gazette,* Dec. 1736, in Lepore, *New York Burning,* 57.

23 *When a series of unexplained blazes:* Douglas O. Linder, "The 'Negro Plot Trials': An Account," *Famous Trials,* 2009, http://law2.umkc.edu/faculty/projects/ftrials/negroplot/plot1741home.html.

23 *After a shopkeeper was robbed:* Daniel Horsmanden, *A Journal of the Proceedings in the Detection of the Conspiracy Formed by Some White People, in Conjunction with Negro and Other Slaves, for Burning the City of New-York in America, and Murdering the Inhabitants* (New York: James Parker, 1744), 374–78, http://law2.umkc.edu/faculty/projects/ftrials/negroplot/journalintro.html. Also see the 1810 published edition: Daniel Horsmanden, *The New-York Conspiracy* (New York: Southwick & Pelsue, 1810), 374–78.

23 *John Vaarck later told:* Thomas J. Davis, *A Rumor of Revolt: The "Great Negro Plot" in Colonial New York* (Amherst: University of Massachusetts Press, 1990), 2.

23 *Twenty-one slaves:* Lepore, *New York Burning,* Appendix C: Owners, 262–73.

23 *Today historians question:* Davis, *A Rumor of Revolt;* Charles Hoffer, *The Great New York Conspiracy of 1741: Slavery, Crime, and Colonial Law* (Topeka: University Press of Kansas, 2003).

24 *The liquid was boiled:* This brown sugar mixture was stable and suitable for shipping, which was the way the English, as the Dutch before them, handled the refining procedure. They performed the two final steps in the refineries in London or Bristol, where they could reap the profits from the finer grades of sugar they produced. See K. G. Davies, *The North Atlantic World in the Seventeenth Century* (Minneapolis: University of Minnesota Press, 1974), 184–85.

24 *The sugar was mixed:* American Sugar Refining Company, *A Century of Sugar Refining in the United States, 1816–1916* (New York: De Vinne, 1916), 11–12.

24 *"plentiful supply of fresh blood":* De Voe, *Abattoirs,* vol. 9, 10–15; *A Century of Sugar Refining in the United States,* 5–9.

25 *"the blood underwent":* C. A. Browne, "The Origins of Sugar Manufacture in America. II. A Sketch of the History of Sugar Refining in America," *Journal of Chemical Education* 10, no. 7 (1933): 423.

25 *The refinery owner Isaac Roosevelt:* Joseph Alfred Scoville (pseud. Walter Barrett) et al., *The Old Merchants of New York City* (New York: Carleton, 1863), 270–71. Also see Nathan Miller, *The Roosevelt Chronicles* (Garden City, N.Y.: Doubleday, 1979), 87; Karl Schriftgiesser, *The Amazing Roosevelt Family, 1613–1942* (New York: W. Funk, 1942), 120; "Trade Growth of Sugar Trade," *New York Sun,* Feb. 14, 1935; American Chemical Society et al., *Our Chemical Heritage* (New York: American Chemical Society, 1935), 8.

25 *"wonderful power":* Thomas Tryon, *Tryon's Letters, Domestick and Foreign, to Several Persons of Quality: Occasionally Distributed in Subjects, Viz. Philosophical, Theological, and Moral* (London: Geo. Conyersand Eliz. Harris, 1700), 208.

25 *"house, barn, stable":* "Common Council Meeting Nov. 27, 1725: A Law Prohibiting Sloughterhouses in the Out Ward," in *Minutes of the Common Council of the City of New York, 1675–1776,* vol. 3 (New York: Dodd, Mead, 1905), 379–80; Thomas F. De Voe, *Abattoirs: A Paper Read before the Polytechnic Branch of the American Institute, June 8, 1865* (Albany: Van Benthuysen & Sons, 1866), 9.

26 *"Great and Unusual Exportation":* "Common Council Meeting Nov. 30, 1748," in *Minutes of the Common Council,* vol. 5, 243.

26 *After the brewer Anthony Rutgers's death:* New-York Historical Society, "Abstracts of Wills: Liber 16: Anthony Rutgers," Publication Fund Series, 1895, 91–92; New York State Historical Association, "Cornelia Rutgers," *Proceedings of the New York State Historical Association* 75 (1977): 435.

26 *Sugar was sold:* Alice Morse Earle, *Colonial Days in Old New York* (New York: Scribner's, 1896), 155.

3: TOWARD INDEPENDENCE

27 *"the neglect of Mr. Bayard":* Thomas F. De Voe, *Abattoirs: A Paper Read before the Polytechnic Branch of the American Institute, June 8, 1865* (Albany, N.Y.: Van Benthuysen & Sons, 1866), 10–11. Also see Arthur Everett Petersen, "New York as Eighteenth Century Municipality," *Columbia Studies in the Social Sciences* 75 (1917): 64.

28 *"many families which used to live":* "Liberty, Property, and Stamps," *New-York Mercury,* Dec. 23, 1765.

28 *"a Total Prohibition":* John Van Cortlandt to John Riddlehurst, May 5, 1764; John Van Cortlandt to Edward Travis, June 24, 1764, in *John Van Cortlandt Letter Book,*

Van Cortlandt Family Papers, ca. 1688–ca. 1846, New-York Historical Society, New York, New York.

29   *"The Cheaf business here":* John Van Cortlandt to John Hilton, Dec. 9, 1765, in *John Van Cortland Letter Book,* reprinted in Virginia D. Harrington, *The New York Merchant on the Eve of the Revolution* (New York: Columbia University Press, 1935), 329–30.

29   *The reviled Stamp Act:* Benson John Lossing, *Our Country: A Household History for All Readers, from the Discovery of America to the One Hundredth Anniversary of the Declaration of Independence,* vol. 1 (New York: Johnson Wilson, 1875), 631.

30   *A British naval officer:* Benjamin L. Carp, *Rebels Rising: Cities and the American Revolution* (Oxford: Oxford University Press, 2009), 63.

30   *"Publick, and particularly":* "Richard Deane, Distiller," *New-York Mercury,* Feb. 10, 1766.

30   *New Yorkers must have heeded:* Carp, *Rebels Rising,* 79.

31   *"A SHIP loaded with TEA":* "To the Delaware Pilots: A Ship Loaded with Tea Is Now on Her Way to This Port . . . ," *New York Journal or Daily Advertiser,* Dec. 2, 1773.

32   *At this time Isaac Roosevelt's:* Dederick Heyer, "My Late Sugar Boiler, August 27, 1774, to August 21, 1776," Isaac Roosevelt Sugar Ledger C. Sugar House Accounts, 1775–1794, Box 25; "Paid for Dederick Heyer: 1774; Indenture of George Dieterich, "My Pan Man begun Four Years Indenture June 29 1775, noted Oct. 9, 1776"; John Lackman, "My Upstairs Man, from Day of Arrival, June 29, 1776," Isaac Roosevelt Sugar House Accounts 1773–1794, Box 32. All in Roosevelt Family Papers, 1469–1962, Franklin D. Roosevelt Presidential Library and Museum, Hyde Park, New York.

32   *"the distressed state":* Frederick Rhinelander to Peter Van Schaack, Feb. 23, 1776, vol. 4, 1479, American Revolution Documents of Northern Illinois University Library, http://amarch.lib.niu.edu/islandora/object/niu-amarch%3A83888.

33   *"truly deplorable and almost hopeless":* "Frederick Rhinelander Letter and Order Book, 1774–1783," Rhinelander Papers, New-York Historical Society, New York. See discussion of these excerpts by Arlene Palmer Schwind, "English Glass Imports in New York: 1770–1790: International Glass Conference Papers," *Journal of Glass Studies* 25 (June 6, 1982): 180.

33   *"markets were raised 800 percent":* Thomas Jefferson Wertenbaker, *Father Knickerbocker Rebels: New York City During the Revolution* (New York: Cooper Square, 1969), 120.

34   *"expend a considerable Sum":* Elizabeth Rutgers vs. Joshua Waddington, New York Supreme Court, 1784, "Statement of Benjamin Waddington," in Julius Goebel, Jr., ed., *The Law Practice of Alexander Hamilton: Documents and Commentary* (New York: Columbia University Press, 1964–1981), vol. 1, 317.

34   *"a hard half-dollar apiece":* Henry Reed Stiles, *A History of the City of Brooklyn Including*

the *Old Town and Village of Brooklyn, the Town of Bushwick, and the Village and City of Williamsburgh* (Brooklyn: published by subscription, 1867), 25; John F. Watson, *Historic Tales of Olden Time Concerning the Early Settlement and Advancement of New York City and State* (New York: Collins and Hannay, 1832), 180–81, http://books .google.com/books?id=wnkUAAAAYAAJ.

34 *"dark stone building"*: Henry Onderdonk,"A Brief Sketch of the British Prisons in New York During the Revolutionary War," in David Valentine et al., *Manual of the Corporation of the City of New York* (New York: McSpedon & Baker, 1849), 372–75.

34 *"like so many hogs"*: Elias Cornelius, *Journal of Dr. Elias Cornelius: A Revolutionary Surgeon* (Washington, D.C.: C. M. Tompkins and C. T. Sherman, 1903), 6.

34 *"4 oz of Pork"*: Paul Hubert Smith and Ronald M. Gephart, *Letters of Delegates to Congress, 1774–1789: Sept. 1, 1781–July 31, 1782,* vol. 18 (Washington, D.C.: Government Printing Office, 1976), 396.

34 *"sorrows and sufferings"*: Grant Thorburn, *Fifty Years' Reminiscences of New-York . . .* (New York: D. Fanshaw, 1845), 170.

35 *"starving for bread"*: Andrew K. Frank and Peter C. Mancall, *American Revolution: People and Perspectives* (Santa Barbara, Calif.: ABC-CLIO, 2008), 19.

35 *"in stock"*: George Washington to Jeremiah Wadsworth, Oct. 9, 1779, in *The Writings of George Washington from the Original Manuscript Sources, 1745–1799* (Washington, D.C.: Government Printing Office, 1931), 446.

4: FOOD ON PARADE

38 *"totally stripped of trees"*: Edwin G. Burrows and Mike Wallace, *Gotham: A History of New York City to 1898* (New York: Oxford University Press, 1999), 255; Gerard T. Koeppel, *Water for Gotham: A History* (Princeton, N.J.: Princeton University Press, 2000), 50.

38 *By the morning of the procession:* Richard Platt, "Federal Procession, in Honor of the Constitution of the United States," *New-York Morning Post,* Aug. 4, 1788, in Frank Moss and C. H. Parkhurst, *The American Metropolis: From Knickerbocker Days to the Present Time: New York City Life in All Its Various Phases: An Historiograph of New York* (New York: P. F. Collier, 1897), 262.

39 *The grain measurers' flag:* Ibid., 261.

39 *"to preserve the reputation"*: Minutes of the Common Council of the City of New York, 1784–1831 (New York: City of New York, 1917), 145; Sidney Irving Pomerantz, *New York, an American City, 1783–1803: A Study of Urban Life* (Port Washington, N.Y.: I. J. Friedman, 1965), 165–69.

40 *The most precarious display:* Platt, "Federal Procession," in Moss, *American Metropolis,* 264.

40 *The brewers' banner:* Ibid.

40 *Matlack, a Quaker:* "White Matlack and Isaac Howell," *The Friend: A Religious and Literary Journal* 21 (1848): 53.

41 *"entirely made":* "American Porter," *New York Morning Post*, June 1, 1784; Stanley Wade Baron, *Brewed in America: A History of Beer and Ale in the United States* (Boston: Little, Brown, 1972), 70; Will Nipper, *In Yankee Doodle's Pocket: The Myth, Magic and Politics of Money in Early America* (Conway, Ark.: Bowmanstone, 2008), 277.

42 *"delicious Pyes":* "Advertisement for Joseph Corre, Confectioner," *New-York Gazette and Weekly Mercury*, Dec. 17, 1781. See also Waverley Root and Richard de Rochemont, *Eating in America* (New York: Morrow, 1976), 426.

42 *"burnt and sugar Almonds":* "Advertisement for Peter Laune, Confectioner," *Independent Journal*, June 2, 1784.

42 *So it was a surprise:* "Elections to the Council, October 8, 1784," *Minutes of the Common Council*, vol. 1, 89–90.

42 *Also disconcerting:* Julius Goebel, ed., *The Law Practice of Alexander Hamilton: Documents and Commentary*, vol. 1 (New York: Columbia University Press, 1964), 291–95. Also see Rocellus Sheridan Guernsey, *New York City and Vicinity During the War of 1812–15, Being a Military, Civic and Financial Local History of That Period, with Incidents and Anecdotes Thereof, and a Description of the Forts, Fortification.*, vol. 1 (New York: C. L. Woodward, 1889).

43 *Hamilton missed the parade:* Allen Churchill, *The Roosevelts: American Aristocrats* (New York: Harper & Row, 1965), 72–75.

43 *"deep rumbling":* Platt, "Federal Procession," in Moss, 264.

5: THE DARK PROPHECY OF ADAM SMITH

47 *"Washington shopped here":* Walter Romeyn Benjamin, "Washintoniana: Bill from Joseph Corre, caterer to Washington's Household, 1790," *The Collector: A Monthly Magazine for Autograph and Historical Collectors*, 64, no. 2 (1951): 34.

47 *"cheaper and much better":* Frank Monaghan and Marvin Lowenthal, *This Was New York, the Nation's Capital in 1789* (Freeport, N.Y.: Books for Libraries, 1970), 100.

48 *"superfine American Broad Cloth":* George Washington, "From George Washington to Lafayette, 29 January 1789," Founders Online, National Archives, http://founders.archives.gov/documents/Washington/05-01-02-0198.

48 *"Tea ruk":* Joseph Alfred Scoville (pseud. Walter Barrett) et al., *The Old Merchants of New York City* (New York: Carleton, 1863), 284–85; Andrew F. Smith, *New York City: A Food Biography* (Lanham, Md.: Rowman & Littlefield, 2014), 72.

48 *"Servants and Apprentices":* "Petition of Bakers, Nov. 15, 1786," *Minutes of the Common Council of the City of New York, 1784–1831*, vol. 1 (New York: City of New York, 1917), 264.

48 *"children and servants":* "Advertisement of Jonas Humbert, Baker," *Daily Advertiser*,

Apr. 9, 1791. Also see letter from Jonas Humbert's manifesto, originally published in *Columbian*, Apr. 7, 1814, in Paul A. Gilje and Howard B. Rock, *Keepers of the Revolution: New Yorkers at Work in the Early Republic* (Ithaca: Cornell University Press, 1992), 139–40.

49 *In a three-year period:* "Letter to the Public from Adam Mount," *Daily Advertiser*, May 11, 1790.

49 *"tolerable good hand":* "Twenty Five Dollars Reward, Runaway," *New York Gazette*, Sept. 7, 1801, quoted in Shane White, *Somewhat More Independent: The End of Slavery in New York City, 1770–1810* (Athens: University of Georgia Press, 1995), 10–11.

49 *"otherwise useless produce":* Samuel Shaw, *The Journals of Major Samuel Shaw: The First American Consul at Canton* (Boston: Wm. Crosby and H. P. Nichols, 1847), 231.

49 *Shaw exchanged the ginseng:* John W. Swift, P. Hodgkinson, and Samuel W. Woodhouse, "The Voyage of the *Empress of China*," *Pennsylvania Magazine of History and Biography* 63, no. 1 (Jan. 1, 1939): 24–25, 30, doi:10.2307/20087160.

50 *"all kinds of SHIP BREAD":* "Advertisement for Adam D. Mount Bake Shop," *Daily Advertiser*, Dec. 13, 1790; "Advertisement for Mercein Bakery," *New York Evening Post*, May 3, 1809, 3.

51 *"the principal part":* Howard B. Rock, *The New York City Artisan 1789–1825: A Documentary History* (Albany: State University of New York Press, 1989), 118–19.

51 *"The man whose whole life":* Adam Smith, *The Wealth of Nations* (New York: Modern Library, 2000), 840.

52 *"the principal part of our food":* John Frost, ed., *The Class Book of Nature: Comprising Lessons on the Universe, the Three Kingdoms of Nature, and the Form and Structure of the Human Body*, 3rd ed., vol. 1 (Hartford: Belknap & Hammersley, 1838), 178, http://books.google.com/books?id=glxJAAAAIAAJ.

53 *"depravity of human nature":* Howard B. Rock, "The Perils of Laissez-Faire: The Aftermath of the New York Bakers Strike of 1801," *Labor History* 17, no. 3 (1976): 372–87.

53 *Writing anonymously:* "A Baker," *American Citizen*, Oct. 7, 1801, in Rock, *New York City Artisan,* 151–53. Also see *Bread Laws Examined by A Loaf-bread baker* (New York: Ephraim Conrad, 1827).

53 *With an election scheduled:* "Oct. 26 1801," in *Minutes of the Common Council, 1784–1831*, vol. 3, 42–43.

53 *Led by George Dieterich:* Rock, "Perils of Laissez-Faire," 373.

54 *At the top of the trade:* Ibid., 374–75.

54 *A small number became wealthy:* See "Politics of the Middling Sort," in Paul A. Gilje and William Pencak, *New York in the Age of the Constitution, 1775–1800* (Rutherford, N.J.: Fairleigh Dickinson University Press, 1992) 151–75; Sean Wilentz, *Chants Democratic: New York City and the Rise of the American Working Class, 1788–1850* (Oxford: Oxford University Press, 2004), 28–29; Rock, "Perils of Laissez-Faire"; Gilje and Rock, *Keepers of the Revolution,* 136.

54 *"monopoly" of bakers:* Rock, *New York City Artisan,* 155–58.

55 *"inconvenience so serious":* Wilentz, *Chants Democratic,*46.

55 *"abandon their business":* An Investigator, "An Address to the Citizens of New York," *American Citizen,* Jan. 19, 1802, in Gilje and Rock, *Keepers of the Revolution,* 137–38. Also see Rock, *New York City Artisan,* 151–54.

55 *"the expense of a class":* Gilje and Rock, *Keepers of the Revolution,* 137.

55 *"deprive the bakers":* "A Mechanic," "On Monopoly and the Destruction of Artisan Enterprise and Independence," *New York Gazette,* Nov. 14, 1801, and "A Bread-Eater," "In Defense of the New York Bread Company," *Mercantile Advisor,* Nov. 17, 1801, in Rock, *New York City Artisan,* 156–58.

56 *By 1806:* Andrew Beers and David Longworth, "Longworth's American Almanack, New-York Register, and City Directory: For the . . . Year of American Independence," *Longworth's N.Y. Register,* no. 46 (1806): vol. 10.

56 *"stigma":* "December 29, 1821," *Minutes of the Common Council,* vol. 12, 171–72.

6: "THE BIG DITCH"

57 *Before the canal:* Walter Dorwin Teague and John Storck, *Flour for Man's Bread: A History of Milling* (Minneapolis: University of Minnesota Press, 1952), 172, 174–75, 178.

57 *About two thirds:* William Cobbett, *A Year's Residence, in the United States of America: Treating of the Face of the Country . . .* (London: Sherwood, Neely and Jones, 1819), part 2, 186, originally printed in *American Farmer* 6, no. 166 (1819–1834): 3.

58 *"Good, strong, clear ale":* Ibid., 337.

58 *"air and sunlight":* Ibid., 190.

58 *Eight-year-old:* Archie Emerson Palmer, *The New York Public School: Being a History of Free Education in the City of New York* (New York: Macmillan, 1905), 90–91.

59 *Unusually well documented:* Thomas Ollive, "Some Reminiscences of a Lifetime Spent in the Baking Business," *The N.B.C.,* 1916, 5–9.

59 *"I began to grow tired":* "The Pie and Its Devotees," *New York Times,* Sept. 15, 1895.

59 *"a dinner without a pie":* Ibid.

60 *"helping stock":* Ollive, "Some Reminiscences," 6.

60 *Homesteaders hoping to people:* Robert Lacour-Gayet, *Everyday Life in the United States Before the Civil War 1830–1860* (New York: Frederick Ungar, 1969), 127.

61 *"Two years later":* Ollive, "Some Reminiscences," 6.

61 *"best cracker machine":* "The Crystal Palace Fair; Glance at the Department of Machinery," *New York Times,* Sept. 26, 1857. Also see *Appleton's Dictionary of Machines, Mechanics, Engine Work, and Engineering,* vol. 1 (New York: Appleton, 1866), 325.

61 *"mixed, kneaded, and cut":* "Bread-Making," *Scientific American* 2, no. 9 (Feb. 25, 1860): 137.

63 *"We who were engaged"*: Thomas Ollive, "Some Reminiscences of a Lifetime Spent in the Baking Business," *The N.B.C.*, 1916, 8.

64 *"cotton can probably"*: Freeman Hunt and Isaac Homans, "The Cotton Question," *Hunt's Merchants Magazine and Commercial Review* 46 (1862): 64–65.

65 *"tireless muscles"*: "What May Be Seen at the Atlantic Docks," *Scientific American* 7, no. 21 (1862): 324.

65 *"must be suppressed"*: Edwin G. Burrows and Mike Wallace, *Gotham: A History of New York City to 1898* (New York: Oxford University Press, 1999), 874. Also see William J. Brown, *American Colossus: The Grain Elevator, 1843 to 1943* (Cincinnati: Colossal, 2009), 87–88; Adrian Cook, *The Armies of the Streets: The New York City Draft Riots of 1863* (Lexington: University Press of Kentucky, 1974), 151.

66 *"vast stream"*: "The Grain-Trade of New York," *Scientific American* 41 (Oct. 4, 1879): 208.

66 *"vast quantities"*: George G. Foster, "New York in Slices," 1849, 125–27, https://dds.crl.edu/crldelivery/11210.st. Also see Harry D. Fornari, "U.S. Grain Exports: A Bicentennial Overview," *Agricultural History* 50, no. 1 (1976); *Illustrated New York; the Metropolis of to-Day* (New York: International, 1888), 188.

66 *"skyscrapers on a tugboat"*: Thomas Flagg, "The Floating Grain Elevators—The Railroad Navy in the Port of New York Part VIII," *Transfer* 40 (May 2004): 4003.

66 *"dull, thunderous"*: Oscar W. Riggs, "The Grain Commerce of New York," *Frank Leslie's Popular Monthly* 20 (1885): 43.

67 *"The recent introduction"*: "City Items: A Large Bakery," *New York Daily Tribune*, June 16, 1862. Also see Edward K. Spann, *Gotham at War: New York City, 1860–1865* (Wilmington, Del.: Scholarly Resources, 2002), 52.

67 *John T. Wilson's factory*: "Local Intelligence," *New York Times*, Jan. 3, 1863.

68 *"The bakery that we have"*: "Alleged Arson in Fulton Street," *New York Daily Tribune*, Sept. 9, 1863; "The Burning of the Government Bakery," *New York Times*, Sept. 17, 1863; G. E. Currie, "Fire Marshal's Semi-Annual Report," *United States Insurance Gazette and Magazine of Useful Knowledge* (New York: G. E. Currie, 1863).

68 *"It was no uncommon sight"*: John Davis Billings, *Hardtack and Coffee, or the Unwritten Story of Army Life* (Alexandria, Va.: Time-Life, 1982), 115.

70 *"owed [his] life"*: Joseph Becker, "On the Spot," *Frank Leslie's Popular Monthly*, 1894, 615. Also see William C. Davis, *A Taste for War: The Culinary History of the Blue and the Gray* (Mechanicsburg, Pa.: Stackpole, 2003), 30–44.

70 *"wheat bread"*: "The Staff of Life," *American Phrenological Journal* 38 (Oct. 1863): 4.

70 *"round, high round"*: Ibid.

71 *"you sold one merchant"*: Robert W. Steele, "Selling Biscuit Forty Years Ago," *The N.B.C.* 6 (July 19, 1919): 3–4.

71 *"a young man"*: "Wanted—A young Man to Drive," *New York Herald,* July 2, 1864; "Advertisement for Balmoral Biscuits," *New York Herald Tribune* July 15, 1867.

72 *"from Maine to Oregon"*: Frank A. Kennedy, "The Biscuit Industry," in Chauncey M. Depew, *One Hundred Years of American Commerce [1795–1895]* (New York: D. O. Haynes, 1895), 447.

72 *"no less than seventy-five"*: "Fancy Crackers," *Oshkosh Daily Northwestern,* May 21, 1884, 5.

72 *"in dainty tin boxes"*: "Home Interests: Superiority of American Crackers," *New York Tribune,* Apr. 4, 1880, 4.

72 *"nibbled constantly"*: "Fancy Crackers."

72 *"a complete revolution"*: "Cracker Trade's Growth, Development from Little Bakery to Enormous Factory," *New York Times,* Feb. 14, 1904, 34.

72 *"what was formerly"*: "How Fancy Crackers Are Made: A Visit to the Bakery of Holmes & Coutts," *New York Times,* Jan. 1, 1886.

73 *"immersed in the dough"*: "The Staff of Life: Breadmakers of the American Metropolis," *Scientific American* 25 (1871): 200.

8: THE AGE OF INCORPORATION

75 *"Capitalismus"*: Delmore Schwartz, "Lincoln," in *Selected Poems (1938–1958): Summer Knowledge* (New York: New Directions, 1967), 237.

75 *"cooperation"*: John D. Rockefeller interview, 1917–1920, conducted by William O. Inglis (Westport, Conn.: Meckler/Rockefeller Archive Center, 1989). Also see Ron Chernow, *Titan: The Life of John D. Rockefeller, Sr.* (New York: Random House, 2013), preface.

76 *"What a blessing"*: Chernow, *Titan,* 154.

76 *"start business"*: "A Huge Cracker Trust: Leading Factories of the Country Under Practically One Control," *New York Times,* June 9, 1890, 2.

76 *"active management"*: "A Big Cracker Syndicate," *Brooklyn Daily Eagle,* Mar. 15, 1890. Also see William Cahn, *Out of the Cracker Barrel: The Nabisco Story, from Animal Crackers to Zuzus* (New York: Simon and Schuster, 1969), 43.

77 *"the New-York companies"*: "Two Biscuit Factories," *New York Tribune,* Dec. 28, 1890.

77 *Factory-made crackers*: Katherine Leonard Turner, "Buying, Not Cooking: Ready-to-Eat Food in American Urban Working-Class Neighborhoods, 1880–1930," *Food, Culture & Society* 9, no. 1 (2006): 20.

78 *"who cannot afford"*: "The Biscuit War Continues," *New York Times,* Feb. 19, 1897, 7.

78 *"It is true"*: "Biscuit Prices Advanced," *New York Times,* Dec. 23, 1897.

79 *"practically a new biscuit industry"*: Thomas Ollive, "Some Reminiscences of a Lifetime Spent in the Baking Business," *The N.B.C.,* 1916, 9.

79 *"a new form of Soda Biscuit"*: "Advertisement for Uneeda Biscuit," *Brooklyn Daily Eagle,* Mar. 10, 1899, 16.

79   *"New in price"*: "Advertisement for Uneeda," *Yiddisches Tageblatt*, Mar. 15, 1899. Also see Andrew R. Heinze, *Adapting to Abundance: Jewish Immigrants, Mass Consumption, and the Search for American Identity* (New York: Columbia University Press, 1990), 166.

79   *The bakers formed*: "Bakers Meet," *Brooklyn Daily Eagle*, Aug. 31, 1889.

80   *"simply discharged them"*: New York Bureau of Labor Statistics, *Annual Report of the Bureau of Labor Statistics of the State of New York for the Year*, vol. 3, 1883, 341–42. See also George G. Block, *Concise History of the Journeymen Bakers' National Union of the United States* (New York: Goldmann, 1888).

81   *"grew rich"*: "Business Notices: Mr. Shult's Employees," *Brooklyn Daily Eagle*, Apr. 22, 1881, 2; "Bakers Meet to Protest Against the Actions of the Employers," *Brooklyn Daily Eagle*, Aug. 31, 1889, 1.

81   *"crippled by a strike"*: "Baker's Strike," *New York Times*, Aug. 22, 1889.

81   *"leave their case"*: "Bakers Meet to Protest Against the Actions of the Employers," *Brooklyn Daily Eagle*, Aug. 31, 1889, 1.

82   *"Night after night"*: "Unique Among Charities Is 'the Bread Line,' " *New York Times*, Oct. 2, 1904, 33; excerpt from "account" of Lawson Purdy, general secretary of Charitable Organization Society, in William Rhinelander Stewart, *Grace Church and Old New York* (New York: Dutton, 1924), 340.

83   *"the inhabitants of New-York"*: Ibid.

83   *"the public need have no fear"*: "Points Gained by Bakers," *New York Times*, May 3, 1881, 8.

83   *Manhattan alone*: "Bakeries," in Kenneth T. Jackson, *The Encyclopedia of New York City* (New Haven: Yale University Press, 2011); "How Davies Measured Up to His Job as Food Administrator," *Reading Eagle*, Mar. 3, 1918, 17. Also see United States Food Distribution Administration, *Educational Program on FDO 1 (Handbook for FDA Representatives)* (Washington: Government Printing Office, 1943), 7.

83   *"there is scarcely"*: Quoted in Stanley Nadel, *Little Germany: Ethnicity, Religion, and Class in New York City, 1845–80* (Urbana: University of Illinois Press, 1990), 70.

84   *Baker C. B. Decker*: *Phillips' Business Directory of New York City*, vol. 19 (New York: W. Phillips, 1889), 45.

84   *"toaster crumpets"*: *The Oxford Encyclopedia of Food and Drink in America* (New York: Oxford University Press, 2013), 619, 683.

84   *English crumpets would have been*: Selma C. Berrol, *The Empire City: New York and Its People, 1624–1996* (Westport, Conn.: Praeger, 1997), 93.

85   *"never saw the light"*: "Continuation of the History of the Margareten Family, Written by Fred Margareten of Los Angeles in 1927," *Horowitz-Margareten Family Journal* 4, no. 10 (Oct. 4, 1946). Also see Adele Lunitz, oral report at the Ignatz and Regina Margareten centennial, *Horowitz-Margareten Family Journal* 19, no. 11 (Nov. 1961).

85   *"ten or twelve"*: *Horowitz-Margareten Family Journal* 4, no. 10 (Oct. 4, 1946): 19; no.

11 (Nov. 1961). Also see Paula E. Hyman and Deborah Dash Moore, eds., *Jewish Women in America: An Historical Encyclopedia* (New York: Routledge, 1997), 890–91.

85 *"matriarch of the kosher":* "Obituary, Regina Margareten," *New York Times,* Jan. 15, 1959. Also see mentions of Margareten in the *New York Times,* Dec. 14, 1942, Dec. 27, 1954, Dec. 24, 1957.

85 *In one march:* "Socialists Out by Thousands." *The Sun,* Sept. 2, 1890, 2. Also see Mary Brown Sumner, "A Strike for Clean Bread," *Survey* 25 (June 18, 1910): 483, 485, 487.

86 *On the sidewalks:* Mary Sherman, "Manufacturing of Food in the Tenements," *Charities and The Commons* 15 (1906): 669–73. Also see Simone Cinotto, *The Italian American Table: Food, Family, and Community in New York City* (Urbana: University of Illinois Press, 2013), 108.

86 *Imported pasta: Eco d'Italia,* Mar. 18, 1865. Also see Robert Ernst, *Immigrant Life in New York City, 1825–1863* (Port Washington, N.Y.: I. J. Friedman, 1965), 88.

87 *"the taste for macaroni":* "Macaroni Making," *Brooklyn Daily Eagle,* Aug. 8, 1886.

87 *"better and cheaper":* Mary E. Green, "Macaroni and Other Pastas," *Current Literature* 19, no. 4 (Apr. 1896): 314.

9: DIRTY BREAD

88 *With a series of sensational:* The National Board of Trade investigated food adulterations in New York in 1880, and legislation was passed in 1881. See Albert R. Leeds, "On the Adulterations of Food," *Journal of the American Chemical Society* 3, no. 18 (1881): 60–63; "How Food Is Adulterated," *The Sun,* Dec. 20, 1880; "Are We All Eating Poison?" *The Sun,* Feb. 26, 1881; "Frauds in the Sale of Food and Drugs," *New York Daily Tribune,* Feb. 14, 1883.

89 *Elias Gottfried's rye bread:* James J. Nagle, "Rush Orders Mark Gottfried Baking's Normal Business," *New York Times,* June 30, 1956, 22.

89 *"great twists":* "Bread for New York," *New York Tribune,* Jan. 16, 1898, B12; "The Ghetto's Cuisine: Queer Dishes Eaten by Russian and Polish Jews," *New York Tribune,* Jan. 8, 1889, B2. See also Hasia R. Diner, *Hungering for America: Italian, Irish, and Jewish Foodways in the Age of Migration* (Cambridge: Harvard University Press, 2001), 202.

90 *"would not return to work":* "Parents as Arbitrators," *New York Times,* Mar. 12, 1886.

91 *"shovel in a mass":* "Striking: Messrs. Hetfield & Drucker Cracker Packers," *Brooklyn Daily Eagle,* Aug. 17, 1880, 4.

91 *"entirely unfit":* "War on Filthy Bakeries; Women Join in Striving for Needed Improvements," *New York Times,* Apr. 8, 1896.

91 *"consumers like clean":* Clipping, Bakery and Confectionery Workers' International Union Papers, University of Maryland Archives, Accession No. 27, Series VII, Box

5, in Matthew S. R. Bewig, "Laboring in the 'Poisonous Gases': Consumption, Public Health, and the Lochner Court," *NYU Journal of Law and Liberty* 1, no. 1 (2005): 482.

92 *New Yorkers were shocked:* "Bread and Filth Cooked Together," *New York Press,* Sept. 30, 1894; Dennis J. Hanlon, "Bakeshop Inspection: Its Benefits and Future," *Annual Report of the Factory Inspectors of the State of New York for the Year Ending . . . ,* vol. 10 (Albany, N.Y.: Office of Factory Inspectors, 1896), 45. Also see Mary Brown Sumner, "A Strike for Clean Bread," *Survey* 25 (June 18, 1910).

92 *"situated in a cellar":* Hanlon, "Bakeshop Inspection," 43.

92 *"partially clad" men:* Ibid., 45.

93 *a "dense population":* Ibid., 48.

93 *"cheap labor":* "Now for the Ten-Hour Day," *Baker's Journal,* Apr. 20, 1895, 1, in David E. Bernstein, *Rehabilitating Lochner: Defending Individual Rights Against Progressive Reform* (Chicago: University of Chicago Press, 2011), 24.

93 *"still shorthand":* Aviam Soifer, "The Paradox of Paternalism and Laissez-Faire Constitutionalism: United States Supreme Court, 1888–1921," *Law and History Review* 5, no. 1 (1987): 250, doi:10.2307/743942, in Jack Beatty, *Age of Betrayal: The Triumph of Money in America, 1865–1900* (New York: Vintage, 2008), 161–62.

94 *In 1898, the year: History and Commerce of New York, 1891* (New York: American Publishing and Engraving, 1891), 123, 163.

94 *"Dainties" faced competition:* "New Plant of Drake Bros. Company," *Cracker Baker,* Aug. 1914, 19–21, 28; Andrew F. Smith, *The Oxford Encyclopedia of Food and Drink in America* (New York: Oxford University Press, 2013), 650.

95 *"the world's largest pie bakers":* "Pie and its Devotees," *New York Times,* Sept. 14, 1895.

95 *A group of twelve:* Carl Alsberg, *Combination in the American Bread-Baking Industry* (Stanford, Calif.: Stanford University Press, 1926), 131.

95 *"violated the liberty":* Quoted in Beatty, *Age of Betrayal,* 162.

96 *"In each case":* Scott J. Hammond and Kevin R. Hardwick, eds., "Charles Evans Hughes, West Coast Hotel Co. v. Parrish, 1937," *Classics of American Political and Constitutional Thought,* vol. 2: *Reconstruction to the Present* (Indianapolis: Hackett, 2007), 456.

96 *In 1911 a state report:* Raymond Fosdick and New York Commissioner of Accounts, *A Report on the Sanitary Condition of Bakeries in New York, April 18, 1911* (New York: M. B. Brown, 1911).

10: CLEAN BREAD

97 *"supply the people": Bread Facts* (New York: Ward Baking, 1920), 109.

97 *"the first sanitary":* Ibid., 110.

98   *"rather dark-colored":* F. C. Lane, "Famous Magnates: R. B. Ward, The Master Baker," *Baseball Magazine*, 1915, 28, 31.

98   *"Since the bread":* Bread Facts, 110.

99   *"electric motor vehicles":* Ibid.; "Advertisement for Ward's Electric Trucks," *New York Times*, Nov. 15, 1923, 13; F. I. Starbuck, "Electric Trucks in the Baking Business, *Baker's Weekly*, Sept. 3, 1921, 55.

99   *"thousands of grocery":* "New Plant of Drake Bros. Company: Modern and Up-to-Date in Every Respect," *Baker's Weekly*, Aug. 1914, 19. For samples of Drake's Cakes ads, see Roy B. Simpson, "The Diary of a National Advertising Manager: How Drake's Circumvented Substitution," *Printers' Ink* 85 (Oct. 2, 1913): 65–66.

99   *"unarbitratable":* "Baker's Strike Spreads," *New York Daily Tribune*, May 2, 1910, 3; "Bread Strike Hits All Classes of City," *New York Tribune*, May 3, 1910, 1; "Bread Supply Short as Strike Spreads," *New York Times*, May 5, 1910.

99   *On May 2:* "6000 Bakers Out; Bread Famine Here," *New York Times*, May 2, 1910, 5; "Threaten Bread Famine," *New York Daily Tribune*, May 6, 1910, 3; "To Get Bread Elsewhere; Frenchmen Vote to Quit," *New York Times*, May 5, 1910, 5; "Bread Supply Short as Strike Spreads," *New York Times*, May 5, 1910, 4.

100   *"a little dot":* "Staff of Life Causes Strife," *New York Daily Tribune*, May 29, 1910, 6. Also see "Women in a Strike Riot," *New York Times*, May 13, 1910, 1; "Mary Sumner on the Part the Baker's Union Must Play," *New York Times*, July 11, 1910, 6.

100   *"complex modern civilization":* W. Gilman Thompson, *Prevention of Occupational Diseases: Their Causes, Symptoms, Treatment and Prevention* (New York: Appleton, 1914), xxiii.

103   *"steadily increasing their output":* Howard Elliot, "Package Foods and Our Woman-Power," *Cracker Baker* 7, no. 9 (Sept. 1918); "Army 'Hardtack' Modernized; Now Feeds the Soldiers," *Sunshine News* 6, Nov. 1918, 12–13.; "Married Women Employed," *Cracker Baker* 6, no. 10 (Oct. 1917): 19.

103   *"hard bread is an unsalted":* "Bread They Eat in the Army: Letter from Private Earl D. Merrill, A.E.F.," *The N.B.C.*, May 1919, 18.

104   *National's specialty was:* Werner B. Allison, "Gas Proof Bread," *Cracker Baker*, Aug. 1920.

104   *"the largest concern":* "Biscuit Men Are Dined: Company Celebrates Completion of New Bakeries," *Chicago Sunday Tribune*, Feb. 21, 1904.

104   *"were as clean as your dining table":* "New Ideas and Methods: National Biscuit Company," *New York Daily Tribune*, Feb. 22, 1904, 4.

104   *It was so big:* "Messenger Girls on Roller Skates at Our New York Bakery," *Sunshine News* 6, no. 1 (Jan. 1918): 3.

104   *Loose-Wiles named its signature crackers:* "Thousands Visit Plant: A Bakery Which Is One of the Sights of the Metropolis," *Long Island Life* 1 no. 7 (Oct. 1915): 26; "Loose-Wiles

Biscuit," *Wall Street Journal*, Apr. 21, 1927, 6; "Loose-Wiles Biscuit Sales Increased 5%," *Wall Street Journal*, Aug. 28, 1928, 3; "Loose-Wiles Company 'Sunshine' Plant Here Is One of World's Most Complete Bakeries," *Daily Star*, Oct. 19, 1937.

105 *To publicize both its product:* "A Remarkable Example of Electrical Advertising," *Signs of the Times*, Nov. 1914, 18; "The Largest Roof Sign in the World," *Sunshine News*, July 1929, 18.

106 *New York's cracker bakers:* R. R. Waldron, "The Evolution of Uneeda Bakers Delivery Service," *Uneeda* 21 no. 4 (July-Aug. 1934): 5.

106 *By 1912:* See Gijs P. A. Mom and David A. Kirsch, "Technologies in Tension: Horses, Electric Trucks, and the Motorization of American Cities, 1900–1925," *Technology and Culture* 42, no. 3 (2001): 489–518.

106 *Three large factories:* Simone Cinotto, *The Italian American Table: Food, Family, and Community in New York City* (Urbana: University of Illinois Press, 2013), 149–50; John A. Mallory, *United States Compiled Statutes, Annotated, 1916 . . .* (St. Paul: West, 1916), 5291.

106 *The largest domestic producer:* Silvano Serventi and Françoise Sabban, *Pasta: The Story of a Universal Food* (New York: Columbia University Press, 2002), 192.

107 *"the cleanest in the world":* "Emanuele Ronzoni, Macaroni Producer," *New York Times*, Aug. 25, 1956, 15; *The Italians of New York: A Survey Prepared by Workers of the Federal Writers' Project, Works Progress Administration in the City of New York* (New York: Random House, 1938).

107 *A vignette describes:* Mary Sherman, "Manufacturing of Food in the Tenements," *National Consumers League Charities and the Commons* 15 (1906): 669–73. Also see Lorine Swainston Goodwin, *The Pure Food, Drink, and Drug Crusaders: 1879–1914* (Jefferson, N.C.: McFarland, 2006), 165; Cinotto, *The Italian American Table*, 108.

107 *The National Consumers League report:* Ibid., 672.

11: "AMONG GREAT INDUSTRIES . . ."

109 *"torn, my dress is dirty":* May Swenson, "A Day at N.B.C. College, from Diary of Anna Saitta, Feb. 28, 1928," Library of Congress, Mar. 21, 1939, 1, http://www.loc.gov/resource/wpalh2.24030411.

109 *"The heat is terrible":* Ibid.

109 *"hot whistles":* F. Scott Fitzgerald, *The Great Gatsby* (Cambridge: Cambridge University Press, 1995), 89.

109 *"Spanish Mary":* "Diary of Anna Saitta and May Swenson," Mar. 21, 1928, http://lcweb2.loc.gov/mss/wpalh2/24/2403/24030509/24030509.pdf.

110 *"You'll work":* Ibid., June 23, June 21.

111 *take the "foreigner":* "Something about N.B.C.: Americanization Classes," *The N.B.C.,*

June 1920, 18; Louis Brewer, "Uneeda Biscuit—An Agent of Americanization," *The N.B.C.*, Aug. 1922, 9–10.

111 *"various alien races":* "Uneeda Biscuit—An Agent of Americanization," 9–10.

111 *National Biscuit supplied classrooms:* "Illustration of Cracker Department in a School," *The N.B.C.*, Apr. 1920, 21; "Uneeda Bakers Enter Toyland," *Uneeda* 19, no. 7 (Aug.-Sept. 1932); "A Million Junior Salesmen," *Uneeda* 20 (Sept.-Oct. 1933), 5.

111 *After work:* "Something about N.B.C."

112 *"light and delicate":* "Matzoth," *The N.B.C.*, June 1922, 14.

112 *In 1925:* "Bread Takes Its Place Among Great Industries," *New York Times*, Oct. 11, 1925, 10.

114 *"inside the whirring plant":* Ibid.

114 *The company's ad read:* "Advertisement for Ward's Vitovim Bread," *Brooklyn Daily Eagle*, Nov. 26, 1922, 12, *New York Times*, Nov. 26, 1922, 39.

115 *In 1920, as New York:* "T. S. Ollive," *The N.B.C.*, Apr. 1917, 10; "Obituary of Thomas Ollive," *New York Times*, June 12, 1920, 15.

115 *Cushman's stores:* "Cushman's Grade A Bread," *Brooklyn Daily Eagle*, Oct. 27, 1922, 28. Also see John Hill Walbridge, *The Cushman Family* (Wilmington, Vt.: Times Press, 1900).

115 *"a filler-in":* "Dr. Barnard's Speech: The Miller's Banquet," *Northwestern Miller* 130 (June 7, 1922): 1064, 1066.

116 *In 1929 Loose-Wiles:* "The Largest Roof Sign in the World," *Sunshine News*, July 1929, 18.

12: "BROTHER, CAN YOU SPARE A DOUGHNUT?"

117 *"float dreamily":* James Thurber, "Glorifying the Doughnut," *The New Yorker*, July 18, 1931, 7; Sally Leavitt Steinberg, *The Donut Book* (North Adams, Mass.: Storey, 2004), 11.

117 *"walk dreamily":* Thurber, "Glorifying the Doughnut," 7.

119 *The company bought Wheatsworth:* "National Biscuit Adds Wheatsworth," *New York Times*, Jan. 3, 1931; Sewell Chan, "Ex-Dog Biscuit Factory Is Among 5 Landmarks," New York Times Blogs, Sept. 16, 2008.

119 *The railway replaced:* Christopher Gray, "The Railroad Tracks That Turned a Street into Death Avenue," *New York Times*, Dec. 22, 2011; "N.Y. Central Tracks Pierce a Building," *New York Times*, Sept. 18, 1932, 17; "Railroad Tracks to Pierce New Tenth Avenue Building," *New York Times*, Dec. 21, 1932, 37; "Mayor Dedicates West Side Project," *New York Times*, June 29, 1934, 1; "A New Era in Sight for Eleventh Avenue," *New York Times*, Dec. 10, 1939, 199.

119 *The incident was settled:* "Strike Quickly Ends in Baking Trade," *New York Times*, May 29, 1934.

120 *In 1930, Rabbi Moses Weinberger:* "Matzoh Suit Is Retried," *New York Times,* Sept. 9, 1931; "Jury in Matzoh Case Reaches No Decision," *New York Times,* Jan. 9, 1931.

120 *Rabbi Weinberger had been:* Sherri Liberman, *American Food by the Decades* (Santa Barbara, Calif.: Greenwood, 2011), 43.

120 *On the final day:* "Judge and Jury Sample Matzoh in Federal Court Trust Case," *Jewish News Archive,* Dec. 11, 1930, http://www.jta.org/1930/12/11/archive/judge-and-jury-sample-matzos-in-federal-court-trust-case

121 *"in the dark":* "3,000 Strike Here at Biscuit Plant," *New York Times,* Jan. 9, 1935.

121 *After eleven days:* "The Week," *New Republic,* Feb. 20, 1935, 31; Union Labor Record from Wilmington, North Carolina, May 24, 1935, 2.

121 *"sluggings, stabbings":* "Fists Fly in Riot in Bakers' Strike," *New York Times,* Feb. 22, 1935; "10 Seized in Clash of 1,500 in Strike," *New York Times,* Feb. 4, 2004.

122 *In April the trade press:* "National Biscuit Earns $2,385,318," *New York Times,* July 18, 1935.

122 *When the strike ended:* "95-Day Strike Ends in Biscuit Plants," *New York Times,* Apr. 29, 1935; "Sign Biscuit Agreement," *New York Times,* Apr. 30, 1935; "Biscuit Strike Threat," *New York Times,* May 14, 1935.

122 *"for years I was disturbed":* "Movie Pests Led to New Cracker," *New York Evening Post,* Feb. 2, 1935.

122 *He and his wife:* "History of Devonsheer Melba," *Devonsheer* (2004), http://www.devonsheer.com/about.html.

122 *"Margie solved the problem":* Glenn Fowler, "Marjorie Weil, 90, Creator of Way to Produce Slices of Melba Toast," *New York Times,* Apr. 21, 1990; "Bert Weil: Made Melba Toast," *New York Times,* Feb. 4, 1965; Molly O'Neill, "Food; Coddled Egos," *New York Times,* Oct. 17, 1999.

123 *"big seller":* "Food News: Toast Named for Famed Singer Is Coated for Taste," *New York Times,* July 29, 1964, 23.

123 *By 1937, Melba Toast:* "1st to Devise Ways to Mass Produce Melba Toast," *Chicago Tribune,* Apr. 22, 1997, 11.

123 *Sliced bread:* "History of Sliced Bread Little Known on 75th Anniversary," *Kansas City Star,* July 29, 2003; "Announcing: The Greatest Forward Step in the Baking Industry Since Bread Was Wrapped—*Sliced* Kleen Maid Bread," *Chilicothe Constitution-Tribune,* July 7, 1928; "Hostess Brands Wonder Baking," *Milling and Baking News* 89, nos. 14–24 (2010): 61.

123 *Production had increased 100 percent:* Harvey A. Levenstein, *Paradox of Plenty: A Social History of Eating in Modern America* (Berkeley: University of California Press, 2006), 29.

124 *"took a hungry man":* Francis Hackett, "Books of the Times: Excerpt from *Stronger*

than Fear by Richard Tregaskis," *New York Times*, June 16, 1945, 10. Also see Joy Santlofer, "Hard as the Hubs of Hell," *Food, Culture & Society* 10 (2007): 191–209.

124 *At National Biscuit a specially trained:* "Food Men Warn U.S. Supplies Dwindle," *New York Times*, Mar. 20, 1943, 1, 9; "New Sealed Packaging Keeps Rations Fresh," *New York Times*, Jan. 3, 1943, 24.

125 *"more than 250 million":* "Crackers and Cookies: Per Capita Munching of the Compact Food Doubles in Wartime," *Wall Street Journal*, Mar. 25, 1944, 1.

126 *"the increasing labor shortage":* "Brown Bomber Company Closes," *New York Age*, July 17, 1943, 1.

126 *The bakery was named:* "Brown Bomber Sets Record with Roll Sales, Sell More to Negroes than Any Other Bakery," *New York Amsterdam Star-News*, Mar. 13, 1943; Richard Bak, *Joe Louis: The Great Black Hope* (New York: Da Capo, 1998), 268.

126 *"100% Negro owned":* "Powell-Savory Enterprises to Be Housed on 8th Avenue," *New York Age*, Aug. 10, 1940; "The Damon and Pythias of the Business World: Powell Savory Run Seven Businesses; All of Them Make Money," *Pittsburgh Courier*, Jan. 10, 1942, 12.

126 *"fast becoming":* Alfred Salerno, "Enjoyed Swift Growth: Large La Rosa Company Started with Small Williamsburg Store in '14," *Brooklyn Daily Eagle*, Apr. 7, 1941, 16.

127 *By 1939 the La Rosa Macaroni Company:* "La Rosa and Sons Elect," *New York Times*, July 12, 1950; "3rd Generation of Family Now Guides Huge La Rosa Firm," *Brooklyn Daily Eagle*, Jan. 6, 1953.

127 *"the food hit":* David A. Taylor, "The History of the Doughnut," *Smithsonian Magazine*, Mar. 1998, 2.

127 *Levitt, a Russian-born Jewish immigrant:* Steinberg, *The Donut Book*, 19–23. Also see John T. Edge, *Donuts: An American Passion* (Waterville, Maine.: Thorndike, 2006).

128 *At the 1939 World's Fair:* Taylor, "History of the Doughnut," 2; Bill Cotter, *The 1939–1940 New York World's Fair* (Charleston: Arcadia, 2009), 49; Jessica Leigh Hester, "The Futuristic Farming at the 1939 World's Fair," *Modern Farmer*, July 24, 2014, http://modernfarmer.com/2014/07/futuristic-farming-1939-worlds-fair/.

13: EXODUS

129 *The Stella D'Oro Biscuit Company:* Leslie Norton, "A Cookie Fortune," *Crain's New York Business* 3, no. 26 (June 29, 1987): 1.

130 *Over the decade:* "Out of the Bronx: Private Equity and the Cookie Factory," *The New Yorker*, Feb. 6, 2012.

130 *The factory bread industry:* "Big Bakery Faces Threat of Strike," *New York Times*, Apr. 21, 1950; "Bread Chain Faces Walkout on Monday," *New York Times*, Apr. 28, 1950; "Vote on Walkout Taken by Bakers," *New York Times*, June 11, 1950; "Mediators

Avert Strike by Bakers," *New York Times,* June 12, 1950; "No Bread Scarcity Yet," *New York Times,* May 4, 1954; "Bakery Talks Fail," *New York Times,* May 6, 1954; "Bakery Pact Ratified," *New York Times,* May 16, 1954.

131 *"developing items":* Joseph C. Potter, "Bakery Battle—Drake Drops a Doughnut," *New York Times,* Dec. 24, 1951, 1, 4.

131 *In the 1950s:* Florence Brobeck, "The Bread Tray's Infinite Variety," *New York Times Magazine,* Apr. 5, 1936, 22.

131 *After closing its original bakery:* "Pechter Chain Buys Ward Baking Plant," *New York Times,* Nov. 2, 1953.

131 *"a kind of hard roll":* "Brooklyn Enjoys Baker's Bonanza," *New York Times,* Feb. 24, 1957, 68.

131 *"like coal miners":* "Genuine Norwegian Baked Foods Since 1899," *Brooklyn Daily Eagle,* Mar. 8, 1933; "Bread of All Nations Baked Here," *Brooklyn Daily Eagle,* Feb. 14, 1954, 21; "Christmas Breads Larsen's Specials," *Brooklyn Daily Eagle,* Nov. 15, 1954, 13.

132 *"people come in cars":* "Continuation of the History of the Margareten Family," *Horowitz-Margareten Family Journal* 11, no. 4 (Apr. 1953).

132 *"for the sake of the children":* "Regina Margareten, 1863–1959," *Jewish Virtual Library,* n.d., https://www.jewishvirtuallibrary.org/jsource/biography/Margareten.html.

133 *"the largest cracker bakery":* "For reference to factory as "outmoded," see under "Miscellany: Sidelights; Huge Cotton Deal Closed by U.S.," *New York Times,* June 19, 1956.

133 *The first National Biscuit plant:* "11-Building Plant Sold in Brooklyn," *New York Times,* Nov. 10, 1956.

133 *The National Biscuit compound:* "7-Acre Industrial Plant of National Biscuit Sold," *New York Times,* Sept. 23, 1956.

134 *"tasted like cardboard":* Sewell Chan, "Crackers Are Reminders of New York City's H-Bomb Fears," *New York Times,* Mar. 26, 2006; Sewell Chan, "Inside the Brooklyn Bridge, a Whiff of the Cold War," *New York Times,* Mar. 21, 2006, B1.

134 *The company was moving:* "National Biscuit Opens a New Plant in Jersey," *New York Times,* Nov. 2, 1958; George A. Swanson, "Automating a Modern Bakery," *Air Conditioning, Heating and Ventilating* 56 (Dec. 1959): 51–58.

134 *"feeling in Fair Lawn":* "City Says Suburbs Bar Factory Hands," *New York Times,* July 6, 1959.

14: THE HEADLESS HELMSMAN

139 *"prodigious mob":* Edwin G. Burrows and Mike Wallace, *Gotham: A History of New York City to 1898* (New York: Oxford University Press, 1999), 410.

140 *"cure the corns":* John Randolph of Roanoke, quoted in U.S. Congress, *The Debates*

and Proceedings in the Congress of the United States (Washington: Gales and Seaton, 1852), 2136.

140 *"gloomy and forlorn":* British Critick, "Travels in North America: 1806, 1807, and 1808," *Select Reviews* 5 (1811): 235.

140 *No national policy:* Cynthia Clark Northrup, ed., *Encyclopedia of World Trade: From Ancient Times to the Present* (Armonk, N.Y.: Sharpe Reference, 2005), 949.

140 *"the door of the concert-room":* Account of Francis Wayland, in James Grant Wilson, ed., *The Memorial History of the City of New-York, from Its First Settlement to the Year 1892* (New York: New York History Co., 1892), 295–96.

141 *"Tea, sugar, coffee":* William Cobbett, *A Year's Residence, in the United States of America* . . . (London: Sherwood, Neely, and Jones, 1819), part 2, 334. Also see Louis Even Grivetti and Howard-Yana Shapiro, *Chocolate: History, Culture, and Heritage* (Hoboken, N.J.: Wiley, 2009), 63, 975.

141 *"cast[ing] grim shadows":* Nathan Miller, *The Roosevelt Chronicles* (New York: Doubleday, 1979), 83–84; Allen Churchill, *The Roosevelts: American Aristocrats* (New York: Harper & Row, 1965), 69.

141 *"having had his Sugar-House":* "Advertisement, Isaac Roosevelt," *New York Daily Advertiser,* Sept. 22, 1785.

142 *New Yorkers consumed:* Sidney W. Mintz, *Sweetness and Power: The Place of Sugar in Modern History* (New York: Viking, 1985), 188–90. Also see Alfred S. Eichner, *The Emergence of Oligopoly: Sugar Refining as a Case Study* (Baltimore: Johns Hopkins University Press, 1969).

142 *One pioneer candyman:* "New York Letter: Notes on the Stuarts," *Cincinatti Daily Gazette,* Oct. 11, 1875, 2.

142 *"attracted the pennies":* Ibid.

142 *"My mother":* Catherine Elizabeth Havens, *Diary of a Little Girl in Old New York* (New York: H. C. Brown, 1920), 53.

143 *The Roosevelts also had:* "Blood Account," Isaac Roosevelt Day Book, 1790. Bound Account Books—Isaac (I) Roosevelt and Sons—Day Book. Sugar House. Specie and Papers Accounts with the Bank of New York, 1789–1792, Box 36, Roosevelt Family Papers, 14691962, Franklin D. Roosevelt Presidential Library andMuseum, Hyde Park, New York.

143 *In 1803 another Roosevelt:* "Sugar Refiners: Co-Partnership," *American Citizen,* Feb. 4, 1803, in Rita Susswein Gottesman, *The Arts and Crafts in New York, 1726–1776: Advertisements and News Items from New York City Newspapers* (New York: Da Capo, 1970), 398.

145 *"Don't do it"*: "Robert L. and Alexander Stuart," *Encyclopedia of Contemporary Biography of New York*, vol. 2 (New York: Atlantic, 1882), 402.

146 *"sirop, or sugar"*: "List of American Patents Which Issued in March, 1833, With Remarks, and Exemplifications," *Journal of the Franklin Institute*, 12, no. 3 (1829): 173.

146 *"the wonder and admiration"*: Paul Spencer Sternberger, "'Wealth Judiciously Expended': Robert Leighton Stuart as Collector and Patron," *Journal of the History of Collections* 15, no. 2 (Nov. 1, 2003): 1, doi:10.1093/jhc/15.2.229; Eichner, *Emergence of Oligopoly*, 33.

146 *"revolting to the feelings"*: Silliman, *Manual on the Cultivation of the Sugar Cane*, 81.

146 *"the most complete"*: "The Great Sugar Candy Establishment," *New York Spectator* 39, no. 46 (Apr. 4, 1836). Also see Abram C. Dayton, *Last Days of Knickerbocker Life in New York* (New York: Putnam, 1897), 154.

147 *"TO MERCHANTS AND OTHERS"*: "Thomas Downing Advertisement," *New York American*, Jan. 3, 1837, 4.

147 *Downing shipped:* Michael Batterberry and Ariane Ruskin Batterberry, *On the Town in New York: The Landmark History of Eating, Drinking, and Entertainments from the American Revolution to the Food Revolution* (New York: Routledge, 1999), 99.

147 *"who but two years since"*: "Report of the Committee on Streets: Document 60," *Documents of the Board of Aldermen of the City of New York*, 4 (1838): 474. Quoted in Edwin G. Burrows and Mike Wallace, *Gotham : A History of New York City to 1898* (New York: Oxford University Press, 1999), 616.

147 *"collapse of a businessman"*: Charles F. Briggs, *The Adventures of Harry Franco a Tale of the Great Panic*, vol. 1 (New York: F. Saunders, 1839), 67.

147 *"changes at once"*: Francis J. Grund, *Aristocracy in America: From the Sketchbook of a German Nobleman* (London: R. Bentley, 1839), 103–4, quoted in Burrows and Wallace, *Gotham*, 616.

16: BONE CHAR AND OTHER "NUISANCES"

148 *inspired a feature:* Benjamin Park, "A Day at a Sugar Refinery," *New World* 5, no. 20 (Nov. 12, 1842): 307–9.

148 *"six to seven feet"*: Ibid.

149 *"collected from the retail butchers"*: J. C. Croly, *The History of the Woman's Club Movement in America* (New York: H. G. Allen, 1898), 921.

149 *The piles teemed:* Catherine McNeur, *Taming Manhattan: Environmental Battles in the Antebellum City* (Cambridge: Harvard University Press, 2014), 37, 161. Also see Roy Rosenzweig and Elizabeth Blackmar, *The Park and the People: A History of Central Park* (Ithaca, N.Y.: Cornell University Press, 1992), 75–76.

149 *"transparent concentrated"*: Michael Pollak, "Readers' Questions Answered: Jell-O's Wiggly Fathers," *New York Times,* June 25, 2010.

149 *New York's sanitation regulations:* See Catherine McNeur, "The 'Swinish Multitude': Controversies over Hogs in Antebellum New York City," *Journal of Urban History* 37, no. 5 (2011): 639–60. Also see see Thomas F. De Voe, *The Market Book: A History of the Public Markets of the City of New York* (New York: A. M. Kelley, 1970 [1862]). For an opinion opposed to De Voe's, see Augustus K. Gardner, "Report of the Varieties and Conditions of the Meats Used in the City of New York," *New York Journal of Medicine and the Collateral Sciences* 10 (1853): 48–56.

149 *"without whom we could not have"*: Enoch Lewis and Samuel Rhoads, "The Street Scavengers," *Friends' Review* (1847): 381.

150 *"bones is hard business"*: "Walks Among the New York Poor," *New York Times,* Jan. 22, 1853.

150 *"a colorless tranparency"*: Robert Sears, "A Day at a Sugar Refinery," *The Guide to Knowledge, or Repertory of Facts . . .* (New York: Sears & Walker, 1844), 279–85.

151 *"every 11½ minutes"*: James Leander Bishop, Edwin T. Freedley, and Edward Young, *A History of American Manufactures from 1608 to 1860 . . .* (Philadelphia: E. Young, 1861), 593–95.

152 *"almost exclusive management"*: "City Items," *New-York Daily Tribune,* May 3, 1856, 5; "Co-partnership Notices," *New-York Daily Tribune,* May 3, 1856, 2.

152 *"continue to supply"*: Horace Greeley, *The Great Industries of the United States . . .* (Hartford: J. B. Burr & Hyde, 1872), 213–20, 251–56.

152 *"foremost among sugar markets"*: "The Sugar Refineries of New York," *Merchants' Magazine and Commercial Review* 35 (1856): 500–503.

152 *Sugar refining in the United States:* Chauncey M. Depew, *One Hundred Years of American Commerce, 1795–1895* (New York: D. O. Haynes, 1895), 260.

152 *Its initial production:* Edwin G. Burrows and Mike Wallace, *Gotham* : A History of New York City to 1898 (New York: Oxford University Press, 1999), 660.

153 *"The city of New York"*: Virginia Penny and Making of America Project, *The Employments of Women: A Cyclopaedia of Woman's Work* (Boston: Walker, Wise, 1863), 150–51, https://dds.crl.edu/crldelivery/7302.

153 *That was not a privilege:* Thomas Palmer, "Struelens and Palmer Accounts 1858–1859," 1910 [1847], Ledger 51M125, Palmer, Howell, Sands Family Papers, New York Public Library, New York, New York.

154 *Built directly:* Harry W. Havemeyer, *Merchants of Williamsburgh* ([Brooklyn, N.Y.]: H. W. Havemeyer, 1989), 5.

155 *"the shipowners who hauled":* Edwin G. Burrows and Mike Wallace, *Gotham: A History of New York City to 1898* (New York: Oxford University Press, 1999), 860.

155 *"Mr. May":* Samuel J. May, *Some Recollections of Our Antislavery Conflict* (Bedford, Mass: Applewood, 2008), 127.

155 *Given the interests:* "The Birth of 'Dixie,' " *New York Times,* Mar. 31, 2012.

156 *"We shall not only cease":* "Poland and Russia," *New York Times,* Mar. 29, 1861; "Sympathy for Secession," *New York Times,* Jan. 16, 1861.

156 *"New York money changers":* Burrows and Wallace, *Gotham,* 868.

156 *"new industries arose":* "The War and Our Social Prosperity," *New York Times,* Dec. 15, 1861.

156 *"we could hardly keep up":* "Bon Bons and Confectionery: The French Art in the Olden Times," *New York Times,* Dec. 10, 1871.

156 *"small-souled creatures":* John Davis Billings, *Hardtack and Coffee, or the Unwritten Story of Army Life* (Alexandria, Va.: Time-Life, 1982 [1887]), 110.

157 *"blue and red and white":* Daily Tribune, Apr. 15, 1857, 4. Also see John Duffy and Russell Sage Foundation, "A History of Public Health in New York City, 1625–1866," 1968, 543, http://www.jstor.org/stable/10.7758/9781610441643.

157 *"weaken the digestive organs":* George Winston Smith and Charles B. Judah, *Life in the North During the Civil War: A Source History* (Albuquerque: University of New Mexico Press, 1966), 201. Also see Bruce C. Levine, *Who Built America?: Working People and the Nation's Economy, Politics, Culture, and Society,* vol. 1 (New York: Pantheon, 1990), 44.

157 *Sugar refiners reaped:* Alfred S. Eichner, *The Emergence of Oligopoly: Sugar Refining as a Case Study* (Baltimore: Johns Hopkins University Press, 1969), 41. Also see Virginia Mescher, " 'How Sweet It Is!!' A History of Sugar and Sugar Refining in the United States, Including a Glossary Of Sweeteners," 2005, 5–6, http://www.raggedsoldier.com/sugar_history.pdf.

158 *"at meals":* Mark Pendergrast, *Uncommon Grounds: The History of Coffee and How It Transformed Our World* (New York: Basic Books, 2010), 46–48.

158 *The soldiers received:* Billings, *Hardtack and Coffee,* 111.

158 *Samuel J. Tilden:* "Tilden's Extract of Coffee: letter from Samuel Tilden, Dec. 7, 1861, 'My Brother's Extract,' " *New York Times,* Sept. 23, 1876, 1.

158 *Borden won:* "Letter of the Secretary of War in Answer to a Resolution of the Senate of the 6th Instant, Relative to the Purchase of Extracts of Coffee for the Use of the Troops, January 15, 1862"; "B. T. Bache, J. C. Eldridge, Thomas J. Turner to United States Naval Laboratory, New York July 19, 1861," *Extracts of Coffee for the Army,* 37th Congress, 2nd Session, Executive Document No. 16. (Washington: Government Printing Office, 1862), 1, 2.

159 *"a good portion"*: Robert Tomes, "The Fortunes of War: How They Are Made and Spent," *Harper's Monthly Magazine* 29 (July 1864): 227–28.

159 *"Gentlemen will be furnished"*: "Notice," *New York Times*, Aug. 1, 1864, 7.

159 *In July 1863:* "Another Day of Rioting," *New York Times*, July 16, 1863; "The Riots in This City," *New York Times*, July 22, 1863.

159 *"buildings would be in ashes"*: "Robert L. and Alexander Stuart," *Encyclopedia of Contemporary Biography of New York*, vol. 2 (New York: Atlantic, 1882), 8.

160 *"faithful to a man"*: Ibid.

160 *"There goes a three-hundred-dollar man!"*: Burrows and Wallace, *Gotham*, 893.

160 *When the Bull's Head Tavern:* "The Mob in New-York," *New York Times*, July 14, 1863; "Incendiarism of the Riot," *New York Times*, July 18, 1863.

160 *"reckless and desperate"*: Henry Reed Stiles, *A History of the City of Brooklyn Including the Old Town and Village of Brooklyn, the Town of Bushwick, and the Village and City of Williamsburgh* (Brooklyn, N.Y.: pub. by subscription, 1867), 452; "Doings in Brooklyn," *New York Times*, July 16, 1863.

161 *Canned goods:* James H. Collins, "How America Made Canning Its Own," *Canning Age* 3 (July 1922): 35; Depew, *One Hundred Years of American Commerce*, 397–400.

161 *"I had never heard of it"*: "Condensed Milk," *New York Daily Tribune*, July 19, 1864, 6.

161 *Canned food usage:* Andrew F. Smith, ed., *Food and Drink in American History A "Full Course" Encyclopedia* (Santa Barbara, Calif.: ABC-CLIO, 2013), 143, 953; Richard Osborn Cummings, *The American and His Food* (New York: Arno, 1970), 69.

161 *"grocery staple"*: Andrew F. Smith, *Eating History: 30 Turning Points in the Making of American Cuisine* (New York: Columbia University Press, 2009), 69–70; James Harvey, *Young, Pure Food: Securing the Federal Food and Drugs Act of 1906* (Princeton, N.J.: Princeton University Press, 1989), 107–11; Edward F. Keuchel, Jr., "The Development of the Canning Industry in New York State to 1960," doctoral dissertation, Cornell University, 1970, 49.

161 *In 1875 there were six: Merchant and Banker: a Journal Devoted Exclusively to Business Interests* 3 (June 16, 1875): 1058.

162 *"largest single incident"*: Burrows and Wallace, *Gotham*, 895.

18: KING HARRY

163 *"greatest sugar manufacturing city"*: "Sugar Center," *Brooklyn Life*, July 2, 1921, 77.

163 *When his equally pious wife:* "Robert L. Stuart's Library," *New York Times*, June 18, 1885.

164 *"Germans, Austrians, and Polanders"*: "Three Riots Quelled," *New York Times*, Apr. 23, 1886.

164 *"Get it down"*: Harry W. Havemeyer, *Henry Osborne Havemeyer: The Most Independent Mind* (New York: H. W. Havemeyer, 2010), 44.

164 *"Pernambuco":* Excerpts describing factory and workers in this chapter are from "T. A. Havemeyer's Story," *Brooklyn Daily Eagle,* Feb. 2, 1896, 14. Also see Matthew A. Postal, "Havemeyers & Elder Filter, Pan & Finishing House, Later Known as the American Sugar Refining Company and the Domino Sugar Refinery . . . ," Designation List 396 (New York: Landmarks Preservation Commission, Sept. 25, 2007), http://www.Nyc.Gov/Html/Lpc/Downloads/Pdf/Reports/Domino.Pdf.

165 *"colossal pile of masonry":* "Where and How Sugar Is Refined," *Brooklyn Daily Eagle,* Nov. 22, 1871, 2, quoted in Carl J. Durham, "A History of Havemeyer to Amstar," 1995, 10, Domino Sugar Archive.

165 *"stripped to the waist":* "The Interesting Process of Sugar Making," *Brooklyn Daily Eagle,* Aug. 17, 1884, 10.

165 *On January 9:* "A Great Fire," *Brooklyn Daily Eagle,* Jan. 9, 1882; "The Havemeyers' Loss," *New York Tribune,* Jan. 9, 1882, 1; "Great Fire in Brooklyn," *New York Times,* Jan. 9, 1882, 1.

165 *"unending rows":* Description and excerpts from Durham, "A History of Havemeyer to Amstar," 17–18; "Colossal: Mr. Theodore A. Havemeyer's New Sugar Refinery"; "The Interesting Process of Sugar Making," 10.

166 *"forbidding, fortress-like":* Description and excerpts from "Death in the Refineries," *New York Tribune,* July 22, 1894, 20. Also see the extensive list of newspaper articles on Havemeyer factory accidents in Shulman, *Eat the City,* 321.

167 *"no trades union":* "Called Out: Employees of Sugar Refineries Go on Strike," *Brooklyn Daily Eagle,* Apr. 22, 1886; New York State Department of Statistics, "Sugar Trade Strikes in Brooklyn," *Annual Report of the Bureau of Statistics of Labor* 4 (1887): 613–14.

168 *"every town":* "A Candy Exhibit: A Display of Messrs. Greenfield & Strauss, in Machinery Hall," *Frank Leslie's Illustrated Newspaper* 41–43 (1876): 348; "A Disastrous Explosion," *New York Times,* Dec. 21, 1877.

168 *In another room:* "One More Body Found in the Ruins," *New York Times,* Dec. 23, 1887, 12.

168 *German immigrant children:* Dorothee Schneider, *Trade Unions and Community: The German Working Class in New York City, 1870–1900* (Urbana: University of Illinois Press, 1994), 24; Stanley Nadel, *Little Germany: Ethnicity, Religion, and Class in New York City, 1845–80* (Urbana: University of Illinois Press, 1990).

169 *"a cartload of bread":* Excerpts in following description of strike from Stuart Bruce Kaufman, *A Vision of Unity: The History of the Bakery and Confectionery Workers International Union* (Kensington, Md.: Bakery, Confectionery, and Tobacco Workers International Union, 1986), 8–12.

169 *"No man can serve":* "Trouble Still Among the Refiners," *New York Tribune,* May 7, 1886, 2.

169 *He opened negotiations:* Alfred S. Eichner, *The Emergence of Oligopoly: Sugar Refining as a Case Study* (Baltimore: Johns Hopkins University Press, 1969), 70–87.

169 *"despotic power":* "New Policy of the American Sugar Company," *Louisiana Planter and Sugar Manufacturer* 22 (May 13, 1899): 301.

169 *"up in price":* "Sweets That Grow Dear," *New York Times,* Jan. 29, 1888, 16; "The New Sugar Trust," *New York Times,* Oct. 19, 1887. Also see Richard Zerbe, "The American Sugar Refinery Company, 1887–1914: The Story of a Monopoly," *Journal of Law and Economics* 12, no. 2 (1969): 339–75.

170 *"I get a fair price":* "Bad News for Candy Lovers: Prices Likely to Be Raised Soon," *New York Daily Tribune,* May 5, 1889.

170 *In 1890:* Eichner, *The Emergence of Oligopoly,* 135–40; *People vs. North River Sugar Refining Co.,* Appellants' and Respondents' Briefs, 3 NY Sup. 401 (1890).

170 *"at the consumers' expense":* Eichner, *The Emergence of Oligopoly,* 137; *People vs. North River Sugar Refining Co.,* briefs, 36.

170 *"principal object":* "Sugar Trust: Henry O. Havemeyer on the Stand Today," *Brooklyn Daily Eagle,* Feb. 21, 1888, 4.

170 *Shortly afterward:* Eichner, *The Emergence of Oligopoly,* 141.

170 *In 1891 the trust:* Ibid., 150–51; "The Sugar Trust in Court," *New York Times,* Oct. 31, 1890, 9; "Sugar Trust Reorganized," *New York Times,* Jan. 11, 1891, 10.

171 *"a rasping squeak":* "A Visit to an Ice Cream Factory," *Ice and Refrigeration* 3 (Sept. 1892): 188.

171 *"an old-fashioned molasses candy":* Jennifer Walkowski, "History of Huyler's Candy Company," Buffalo as Architectural Museum, 2012, http://buffaloah.com/a/del/374/huyhist.html.; J. N. Kins, "The Accomplishment of Forty Years," *National Magazine,* Oct. 1914, 538.

172 *"conversation lozenges":* Horace Greeley, *The Great Industries of the United States* (Hartford: J. B. Burr & Hyde, 1872), 253.

172 *The inventor had met:* Stephen Van Dulken, *American Inventions: A History of Curious, Extraordinary, and Just Plain Useful Patents* (New York: New York University Press, 2004), 104.

173 *"long glassful":* Thomas Floyd-Jones, *Backward Glances: Reminiscences of an Old New-Yorker* (Somerville, N.J.: Unionist Gazette Association, 1914), 24.

173 *"everything in the soda-water line":* Chauncey M. Depew, *One Hundred Years of American Commerce [1795–1895]* (New York: D. O. Haynes, 1895), 472.

173 *In Brooklyn:* U.S. Patent Office, "Application of Robert Robinson: Soda Water and Temperance Beer Filed Aug. 13, 1878," *Official Gazette of the United States Patent Office* (Washington, D.C.: Government Printing Office, 1878), 450.

174 *"The cheaper we can furnish"*: U.S. House of Representatives, Committe on Manufactures, *Investigation of Certain Trusts: Report in Relation to the Sugar Trust and Standard Oil Trust* (Washington, D.C.: Government Printing Office, 1889), 109.

174 *"to provide all the sugar"*: "Release of Mr. Searles," *Brooklyn Daily Eagle,* Jan. 17, 1896, 5.

174 *But in 1894: United States vs. E. C. Knight Co.,* 156 U.S. 1 (1895), No. 675, https://supreme.justia.com/cases/federal/us/156/1/case.html.

174 *Arbuckle Brothers:* Alfred S. Eichner, *The Emergence of Oligopoly: Sugar Refining as a Case Study* (Baltimore: Johns Hopkins University Press, 1969), 213–14.

175 *Unhappy over the Arbuckles' success:* Ibid., 214–15; New York State Legislature, Joint Committee to Investigate Trusts, *Reports and Proceedings* (Albany: Wynkorp, Hallenbreck, Crawford, 1897), 133–34, 136–37 ("Lexow Committee Investigation").

175 *First he raised the price:* Eichner, *The Emergence of Oligopoly,* 220; *Willett and Gray's Weekly Statistical Sugar Trade Journal,* Mar. 30, 1899.

175 *"the enthusiasm of a schoolboy"*: Eichner, *The Emergence of Oligopoly,* 216; Samuel E. Moffett, "John Arbuckle," *The Cosmopolitan* 30, no. 5 (Sept. 1902): 542–43. For an account of the battle between Arbuckle and Havemeyer, see Mark Pendergrast, *Uncommon Grounds: The History of Coffee and How It Transformed Our World* (New York: Basic Books, 2010), 51–53, 69–76; Francis L. Fugate, *Arbuckles: The Coffee That Won the West* (El Paso: Texas Western Press/University of Texas at El Paso, 1994), 57, 107–12.

175 *A contemporary described:* Moffett, "John Arbuckle," 542.

175 *"his blood boiling"*: Eichner, *The Emergence of Oligopoly,* 214.

175 *"Well, we mean business"*: "Sugar and Coffee War," *New York Times,* Dec. 19, 1896.

176 *"going to change"*: "Prices of Coffee Reduced," *New York Times,* Aug. 29, 1897.

176 *Frederick Mollenhauer:* Eichner, *The Emergence of Oligopoly,* 190.

176 *The California refiner:* Eichner, *The Emergence of Oligopoly,* 218–19; *Willett and Gray's Weekly Statistical Sugar Trade Journal,* Feb. 18, 1897.

176 *Fitted out with the latest:* Eichner, *The Emergence of Oligopoly,* 190, 208–9, 222; *Willett and Gray's,* Dec. 28, 1893.

176 *Working furiously:* Eichner, *The Emergence of Oligopoly,* 190–208.

177 *"the largest roasting plant"*: "The Sugar-Coffee War: American Coffee Company Incorporated to Fight the Arbuckles," *New York Times,* Feb. 5, 1897; *Willett and Gray's,* Mar. 30, 1899; Eichner, *The Emergence of Oligopoly,* 216–17, 220.

177 *"to make business"*: Henry Post, quoted in "American Sugar Refining Co.: Sugar War Renewed," *Commercial and Financial Chronicle,* Aug. 26, 1899, 441.

177 *"There is no money"*: "Fresh Slump in Sugar," *New York Times,* Mar. 30, 1890.

178 *"synonymous with . . . fine spices"*: *King's Handbook of New York City: An Outline History*

and *Description of the American Metropolis* (Boston, Mass.: Moses King, 1892), 640, 900.

178 *"very extensive"*: "Durkee's Dressings Hold Spice of the East," *Atlanta Constitution*, Mar. 29, 1934, 5R.

178 *Under his son:* Andrew F. Smith, ed., *Savoring Gotham: A Food Lover's Companion to New York City* (New York: Oxford University Press, 2015), 255; Roger M. Grace, "Reminiscing: Gulden's Is Oldest Nationally Sold Prepared Mustard—Not French's," *Metropolitan News-Enterprise*, Dec. 30, 2004, 15.

178 *Robert T. French:* Gary Allen and Ken Albala, *The Business of Food: Encyclopedia of the Food and Drink Industries* (Westport, Conn.: Greenwood, 2007), 95; Rosamond Man and Robin Weir, *The Compleat Mustard* (London: Constable, 1988).

179 *"vermouth, wines, or liquors"*: Adam Elmegirab, Jerry Thomas Project, Feb. 23, 2011, http://thejerrythomasproject.blogspot.com/2011/02/dr-adam-elmegirabs-bitters-story.html.

20: "A ROTTEN JOB"

180 *"lack of variety"*: W. Gilman Thompson and American Association for Labor Legislation, *Prevention of Occupational Diseases: Their Causes, Symptoms, Treatment and Prevention* (New York: Appleton, 1914), 465, 524–25, 604.

181 *"come home exhausted"*: "Appendix 1: Confectionary Industry in New York City," in Irene Osgood Andrews et al., *Third Report of the Factory Investigating Commission* (Albany: J. B. Lyon, 1914), 87.

181 *One of these women:* Louise C. Odencrantz, *Italian Women in Industry: A Study of Conditions in New York City* (New York: Russell Sage Foundation, 1919), 50.

182 *May Malone:* "Future of Women Workers: Lessons of the Depression," *New York Times*, Mar. 13, 1932; "Starvation Wages: The Plight of the Employed," *Forum and Century* 89, no. 6 (June 1933): 327; "Irving Place Changes: Tall Buildings and Stores Robbing It of Its Quiet Atmosphere," *New York Times*, Jan. 3, 1909.

183 *"less the public knows"*: Lillian Symes, *Behind the Scenes in Candy Factories* (New York: Consumers' League of New York, 1928), 5–6.

183 *One of the league's findings:* Ibid., 15.

184 *The report found that:* Ibid., 28.

184 *"It's hard to work"*: Ibid., 18.

184 *"palms were punctured"*: Ibid., 10, 51, 20.

185 *"appalling"*: Ibid., 54–55.

186 *"brightly colored"*: Samuel Weller Johnson, "Adulterations of Food," *Journal of Social Science*, no. 11–13 (1878): 109–10.

186 *"to stamp out the use"*: "Correspondence: Letter from John Hawley to the Editor," *New Outlook* 77 (1904): 958.

187 *"the manufacture, sale"*: Federal Food and Drugs Act of 1906 ("Wiley Act"), vol. 34 STAT. 768, 1906, http://www.fda.gov/RegulatoryInformation/Legislation/ucm148690.htm.

187 *"The Pure Food Law"*: "Advertisement for New York Bottling Co.'s Soda," *Brooklyn Daily Eagle*, Apr. 28, 1907.

187 *Manufacturers not included:* Ibid.; *Minutes of the Meetings of the Combined White List Candy Committee*, Dec. 3, 1929 (New York: National Consumers League, Dec. 1929); "Candy Makers' White List Issued by Consumer's League," *New York Times*, June 3, 1928; "Candy Men Defend Trade," *New York Times*, Mar. 23, 1928, 37.

187 *"very drastic letter"*: Henry A. Fahn, Sweets Company of America, to Florida Lasker, chairman, National Consumers League, Dec. 9, 1929, National Consumers' League Records, Box B14, Reel 27, Manuscript Division, Library of Congress, Washington, D.C.; *Minutes of the Meetings of the Combined White List Candy Committee*, Dec. 23, 1929, 2; *List of Firms Dropped from the December White List* (New York: National Consumers League, 1929).

187 *Mason, Au, & Magenheimer:* "Candy Men Defend Trade," *New York Times*, Mar. 23, 1928, 37.

188 *"most modern"*: "Growth of Canada Dry Has Been Rapid," *Wall Street Journal*, July 4, 1925, 2.

188 *"no human hand"*: "Golden Dwarf Ginger Ale," *Brooklyn Daily Eagle*, July 21, 1923; "Weekly Business Review: Golden Dwarf Ginger Ale," *Brooklyn Standard Union*, Feb. 23, 1923.

189 *When the league learned: Minutes of the Meetings of the Combined White List Candy Committee*, Jan. 29, 1930.

189 *"Candy's a rotten job"*: Symes, *Behind the Scenes in Candy Factories*, 26.

21: SWEETS IN SOUR TIMES

190 *"sweetest and most intriguing"*: "Concerning Confectioners and Ice Cream Makers," *Confectioners Journal* 40 (1918): 24.

190 *In 1930 the company filed:* "Bankruptcy Asked for J. S. Auerbach," *New York Times*, Aug. 10, 1930; "J. S. Auerbach Held in $500,000 Fraud," *New York Times*, May 28, 1931.

191 *Spurring sales were men:* "Men Now Rival Women as Consumers of Candy," *New York Times*, Aug. 5, 1923, X12; S. A. Tannenbaum, "Our Native Industries: VII: Candy Bars," *Life*, Aug. 1935.

191 *"the largest candy-making organization"*: "Loft, Incorporated," in *Poor's Manual of Industrials: Manufacturing, Mining and Miscellaneous Companies; . . . Annual No.* (New York: Poor's Railroad Manual, 1918), 1989.

192 *"more to his liking"*: Jennifer Ying, "Guth v. Loft: The Story of Pepsi-Cola and the

Corporate Opportunity Doctrine," Social Science Research Network, May 8, 2009, 9, 11–12, 16, http://ssrn.com/abstract=1414478.

192 *"Jews and Gentiles":* "Suit Settled in Loft Bias," *New York Amsterdam News,* June 22, 1935.

193 *Charles Guth resigned:* Ying, "Guth v. Loft:," 16.

193 *By 1936 the Barricini Candy chain:* "Jack Barricini, 49, Confectioner, Dies," *New York Times,* June 5, 1952, 84; "Mac Barricini, 51, of Candy Concern," *New York Times* July 19, 1956, 27.

193 *Moving into ever-larger:* "Business Leasing Brisk in Midtown; Rents in Long Island City," *New York Times,* Sept. 18, 1935.

193 *"mad passion":* "American Craft Enters Big Business: Third Generation of Chocolate Dippers Inherit 'The Touch,' " *New York Post,* May 22 1939.

194 *While the aviators:* Leon Siler, "Soda Water Flyers Likely to Pop into Prison," *New York Post,* Feb. 28, 1935; Harold Ross, "The Talk of the Town: After the Shouting," *The New Yorker,* Apr. 10, 1935. Also see Zofia Reklewska-Braun and Kazimierz Braun, *The Adamowicz Brothers: Immigrants—Aviators, First Polish Conquerors of the North Atlantic* (Buffalo; New York: Polish Cultural Foundation, 2011).

195 *"filthy vegetable substance":* "Candy Maker Admits Filth in His Wares," *New York Times,* Dec. 15, 1938.

195 *"injustice":* "Bonomo Calls Candy Charge 'An Injustice,' " *Brooklyn Daily Eagle,* Dec. 18, 1938.

22: WAR, RATIONING, AND YOGURT

197 *Following the attack:* Hawaii had gradually come to dominate the sugar market in the nineteenth and twentieth centuries, gradually replacing Caribbean imports. This movement was begun by Claus Spreckels of the California Sugar Refining Company. See Alfred S. Eichner, *The Emergence of Oligopoly: Sugar Refining as a Case Study* (Baltimore: Johns Hopkins University Press, 1969), 87–88; Susan M. Campell, *Sugar in Hawaii: A Guide to Historical Resources* (Honolulu: Hawaiian Historical Society, 1986), xiv.

197 *Sugar rationing for consumers:* Ellis B. Haller, "Candy Makers: First the Sugar, then the Chocolate Fall Victim to War Shortages." *Wall Street Journal,* May 12, 1942, 1; Joseph Guilpoyle, "Candy, Cake and Ice Cream to Be Harder to Get as Sugar Supply Drops," *Wall Street Journal,* Feb. 13, 1942, 1.

198 *"working below capacity":* Loft Candy 'Afraid' to Drop Job Discrimination," *Afro-American,* Oct. 28, 1944.

198 *At least 20 to 25 percent:* "News and Views of Investments: Chewing Gum Seller's Market Balked By Raw Materials Shortages," *Barrons National Business and Financial Weekly,* Aug. 5, 1946, 26, 31.

198 *"the far corners"*: "Candy and Beverage Industry," *Wall Street Journal,* Oct. 22, 1941.

199 *"consumption [was] up"*: "Chewing Gum Shortage Is Latest War Woe," *New York Times,* Oct. 10, 1942, 17; "Matchbook Ad by Otto Soglow for Topps Gum," Topps Archives, Feb. 2, 2009, http://toppsarchives.blogspot.com/2009/02/unmatched .html.

199 *Drake's Bakery had wanted:* James E. Powers, "Pastries Dwindle in Sugar Shortage," *New York Times,* Aug. 6, 1945, 1, 13; "Sugar Refineries to Cut Operations," *New York Times,* May 5, 1945, 21; James E. Powers, "Sugar Shortage Causes Bakeries to Take 'Holidays,' " *New York Times,* Aug. 6, 1945, 13.

199 *"gloomy outlook"*: "Cake Production to Be Cut Again," *New York Times,* June 12, 1945, 16. Also see "Sugar Refineries to Cut Operations," 21, 16, and "Plant Layoff Due on WFA Sugar Cut," June 22, 1945, 27; Powers, "Sugar Shortage Causes Bakeries to Have 'Holidays,' " 1.

200 *One 1942 headline:* "Candy Goes with the Army," *New York Times,* Nov. 15, 1942, E12.

200 *Candy and gum were included:* "Candies and Ice Cream Put in Army Necessities," *New York Times,* Mar. 5, 1943, 13; "Navy Gives Facts on Fighters' Food," *New York Times,* Apr. 13, 1942.

200 *Daniel Carasso, who had:* "Daniel Carasso, a Pioneer of Yogurt, Dies at 103," *New York Times,* May 20, 2009; "Juan Metzger, 79, Is Dead—He Put the Fruit in Yogurt," *New York Times,* Sept. 10, 1998.

201 *Early in the war:* "Black Market Laid to Waxey Gordon," *New York Times,* Oct. 9, 1942, 23; "Waxey Gordon gets New Term in Prison," *New York Times,* Jan. 5, 1943, 21.

201 *Toward the end of the war:* "Brothers Indicted in Million-Dollar Tax Plot," *New York Times,* Sept. 8, 1945.

201 *Maurice Gottfried:* "Sugar Black Mart Linked To 7 Here," *New York Times,* Jan. 29, 1946; "Sugar User Guilty in OPA Fraud Case," *New York Times,* Mar. 27, 1947; "Three Imprisoned for Sugar Fraud," *New York Times,* Mar. 28, 1947.

202 *A year after opening:* "Leader of the Culture Revolution," *Gannett Westchester Newspapers,* May 10, 1981, B1.

202 *Rationing eased:* "News of Food: Cocoa Bean Supply Off," *New York Times,* Jan. 17, 1944, 16; "Easter Bunny Supplants Chick and Duck in Popularity, but Chocolate Ones Are Out," *New York Times,* Mar. 22, 1945.

23: "GREATEST MANUFACTURING TOWN ON EARTH"

203 *By this time women:* U.S. Department of Labor, Women's Bureau, "Women Workers in Ten War Production Areas and Their Postwar Employment Plans," Bulletin 209 (Washington, D.C.: Government Printing Office, 1946), in Rosalyn Baxandall,

Linda Gordon, and Susan Reverby, eds., *America's Working Women* (New York: Vintage, 1976), 310–12.

203 *In 1946 sugar workers:* "Sugar Strike Is Off at Largest Plants as Pay Rise Is Given," *New York Times,* Apr. 15, 1946; A. H. Raskin, "Raw Sugar Cargoes Here Held Up by the Ship Strike," *New York Times,* Oct. 25, 1946; "Strike Action Set by Sugar Workers," *New York Times,* Apr. 10, 1946.

204 *"virtually disappeared":* "Plenty of Biscuits in Stores Monday," *New York Times,* Nov. 1, 1946.

204 *The truck drivers won:* A. H. Raskin, "Trucker Capitulation Today Seen," *New York Times,* Oct. 28, 1946; "24-Day Strike Near End," *New York Times,* Nov. 16, 1946; "Biscuit Strikers Win Pay Increase," *New York Times,* Nov. 17, 1946.

204 *"incomparably the greatest":* John Gunther, *Inside USA,* 50th anniversary ed. (New York: New Press, 1997), 553.

204 *One of the pilots:* Gail S. Halvorsen, *The Berlin Candy Bomber* (Bountiful, Utah: Horizon, 1990) 131.

205 *"a large, well-proportioned man":* Ibid., 136.

206 *Barton's sold:* Morris Freedman, "From the American Scene: Orthodox Sweets for Heterodox New York," *Commentary* 13 (May 1, 1952): 475, 474. Also see Robert A. M. Stern, Thomas Mellins, and David Fishman, *New York 1960: Architecture and Urbanism between the Second World War and the Bicentennial* (New York: Monacelli, 1994), 582.

206 *The factory was as up-to-date:* "Candy Wends Its Sweet Way Through Boro Plants," *Brooklyn Daily Eagle,* Nov. 26, 1950, 27. Also see the account of a postwar employee in Lucyna B. Radlo, *Between Two Evils: The World War II Memoir of a Girl in Occupied Warsaw and a Nazi Labor Camp* (Jefferson, N.C.: McFarland, 2009), 193.

207 *"standing elbow to elbow":* Freedman, "From the American Scene," 476; "Candy Wends Its Sweet Way," 27.

207 *Chlorophyll, reputed to freshen:* William M. Freeman, "Chewing Gum Price Still Just a Nickel," *New York Times,* Aug. 9, 1953, F6.

207 *"good for your teeth":* James J. Nagle, "Gains Are Made by Chewing Gum," *New York Times,* Sept. 6, 1965, 21.

207 *Monthly visits:* "Just Where Do Bunnies Come From?" *New York Times,* Apr. 2, 1977, 24.

208 *"somewhat tarter":* Freedman, "From the American Scene," 474, 477.

208 *Huyler's Candy, however:* "Huyler's in Bankruptcy: Candy and Restaurant Chain Plans 100% Settlement," *New York Times,* Apr. 4, 1951.

208 *The company filed for bankruptcy:* "Swersey Buys Huyler's," *New York Times,* June 29, 1953, 6; "J. S. Swersey, Helped Develop K-Ration," *New York Times,* Sept. 23, 1953, 49.

208 *Snickers were touted:* All Classic Video, "Secret Video Ranger Ring (1950s) Classic

TV Commercial," Video, Captain Midnight and the Secret Squadron, YouTube, Sept. 12, 2012, https://youtube/2NwqQPWU1Sw.

209 *Gold Medal Candy Company:* "Bonomo Turkish Taffee History Museum," Bonomo Turkish Taffee, 2015, http://www.bonomoturkishtaffy.com/MuseumHistory_ep_40.html.

209 *About 11,700 vending machines:* "About New York: Subway Vending Machines Comprise Biggest Operation of Kind-Odd Craft Moved," *New York Times,* Aug. 7, 1953, 21.

209 *Other vending favorites:* "Chunky," Candyblog, Aug. 20, 2007, http://www.candyblog.net/blog/item/chunky.

210 *"nonfattening" candy bar:* "Candy Market Being Sweetened," *New York Times,* Nov. 22, 1965; "Chocolate for Diet Watchers," *Wall Street Journal,* Dec. 28, 1953, 9.

210 *Rockwood & Company:* "Wallace T. Jones, Chocolate Maker," *New York Times,* May 30, 1946, 21; "Rockwood & Co. Sold: Midwesterner Gets Control of Big Chocolate Concern," *New York Times,* Aug. 14, 1954, 18; "Candy Firm Offers Holders Cocoa Beans for Shares," *Wall Street Journal,* Oct. 1, 1954, 1.

211 *"When the guns stopped":* "Boro's Gum Pops World-Wide," *Brooklyn Daily Eagle,* June 13, 1949, 11.

211 *By 1955, Topps:* "Berger Gives Nation's Small-Fry Baseball with Their Bubble Gum," *Long Island Star Journal,* May 7, 1955; "Vintage and Collectors' Baseball Cards," *Collector's Weekly,* 2007–2015, http://www.collectorsweekly.com/baseball/cards.

211 *"growing industry":* "Topps Denies It Has Cornered the Baseball Trading Card Field," *New York Times,* Feb. 19, 1964, 23; McCandlish Phillips, "Baseball Cards Ruled a Monopoly," *New York Times,* Aug. 25, 1964; "Bubble Gum Maker Is Cleared by F.T.C. of Monopoly Charge," *New York Times,* May 22, 1965.

211 *In 1964 Topps sold:* Nagle, "Gains Are Made by Chewing Gum"; Robert A. Wright, "Mail Orders Build $14-Million Concern," *New York Times,* Sept. 27, 1966.

212 *"make a soft drink":* "News of the Advertising and Marketing Fields," *New York Times,* July 26, 1953, F8.

212 *"the storm hit":* Betty Granger, "Try Non-Caloric Thirst Quencher," *New York Age,* 1953; "News of the Advertising and Marketing Fields" ; "Hyman Kirsch, 99, Made Diet Sodas," *New York Times,* May 13, 1976, 30.

212 *Hoffman Beverages:* "Canned Drink Race Under Way," *Billboard,* May 1, 1954, 78.

213 *By 1957 Rockwood:* "Chocolate Factory Faced with Closing," Mar. 5, 1957; "Rockwood Strike Ends: Chocolate Concern and Union Agree on Severance Pay," *New York Times,* Mar. 9, 1957; "Rockwood and Co. Says It Is Liquidating Its Chocolate Business," *Wall Street Journal,* Mar. 13, 1957; "Rockwood Workers Back on the Job," *New York Amsterdam News,* Mar. 16, 1957; "Business Milestones: Sweets Co. of America Buys Rockwood Chocolate Division," *Wall Street Journal,* Apr. 17, 1957, 4.

214 *Consequently, when National:* "U.N. and City Fight Sign on East River," *New York Times,* July 27, 1954, 23; "No Big Sugar Sign Will Blink at U.N.," *New York Times,* Aug. 4, 1954, 23.

215 *"one shared by every American business":* "No Big Sugar Sign Will Blink."

215 *It was the most progressive:* Harvey A. Young and Michael F. Dougherty, "Influence Of the Guaranteed Annual Wage upon Labor Relations and Productivity: National Sugar Refinery's Experience," *Human Resource Management* 10, no. 4 (Dec. 1, 1971): 27, doi:10.1002/Hrm.3930100406.

215 *Only a few miles:* "The Sweet'N Lowdown on a Soured Past," *Denver Post,* Nov. 26, 2006; Rich Cohen, *Sweet and Low: A Family Story* (New York: Farrar, Straus and Giroux, 2006), 11, 54.

216 *Company lore has it:* Sir Joseph Barnby, "Sweet and Low," *Musical Times and Singing Class Circular* 12, no. 272 (Oct. 1865): 143–45; "Songs from 'The Princess,'" in Edmund Clarence Stedman, ed., *A Victorian Anthology, 1837–1895: Selections Illustrating the Editor's Critical Review of British Poetry in the Reign of Victoria* (Boston: Houghton Mifflin, 1895), 199.

217 *Unlike the unsucessful diet candy bar:* Stacy V. Jones, " 'Sweet'N Low' to Be Listed as Trademark No. 1,000,000," *New York Times,* Dec. 17, 1974; Lawrence C. Levy, "At Sweet'N Low, Less Equals More," *New York Times,* Nov. 30, 1975; "Saccharin-Product Plant Going Full Tilt Under Load of Orders," *New York Times,* Mar. 30, 1977.

217 *In 1977 the FDA proposed:* "Industry Responds to Ban on Saccharin," *New York Times,* Mar. 10, 1977; Michael Sterne, "At Sweet'N Low Brooklyn Plant, Action Imperils 500 Jobs, $50 Million Business," *New York Times,* Mar. 11, 1977.

217 *"appreciable segment":* "No Bias in Sugar Company," *New York Amsterdam News,* Aug. 24, 1963, 4.

217 *"inefficient":* "The National Sugar Refining Company Would Like to Consider a Merger—But Not Now," *New York Times,* Mar. 26, 1965, 55; "News of Realty: Queens Site Sold," *New York Times,* May 13, 1965, 23; "Long Island City in Transition," *New York Times,* Oct. 31, 1965, 81.

217 *With the makers of beet sugar:* "Sugar Beets Make Gains," *New York Times,* Jan. 9, 1961; George Auerbach, "Beet Sugar May Be Solution to U.S. Sugar Cost and Quantity Problem," *New York Times,* Feb. 12, 1961.

218 *"made from pure, fresh milk":* "What Is Yogurt? Advertisement for Dannon," *New York Times,* Apr. 15, 1949, 32; Jane Holt, "News of Food: Yogurt, Milk Food Originating in Balkans, Is Gaining Wider Distribution . . . ," *New York Times,* Mar. 8, 1945, 20.

218 *"We knew we were over the hump":* "Company Profile, Information, Business Description, History, Background Information on Dannon Co.," Reference for Business

Encyclopedia, Inc., 2015, http://www.referenceforbusiness.com/history2/27/Dannon-Co-Inc.html#ixzz3shMJ9pR1.

219 *"We don't like publicity":* Carl Lawrence, "Harlem Fights Lily-White Jobs as Big Companies Shun Negroes," *New York Amsterdam News,* July 21, 1951, 1, 26; Simon Anekwe, "Probe Milk Firm's Hiring Policies," *New York Amsterdam News,* Oct. 28, 1961, 21.

219 *"Manufacturers would kill":* Cohen, *Sweet and Low,* 104, 129.

220 *Rather than move:* "American Sugar Co. to Remain in City," *New York Times,* Feb. 3, 1969.

25: CANDY ON THE ROCKS

221 *"cross-section of all races":* Morris Freedman, "Orthodox Sweets for Heterodox New York: the Story of Barton's," *Commentary* (May 1952): 472.

222 *In 1961 the 1,400 employees:* Philip Shabecoff, "Yule Candy Sales Soar to a Record," *New York Times,* Dec. 24, 1961, 69, 77; "Loft Candy in Franchise Deal," *New York Times,* July 28, 1963.

222 *discriminatory hiring practices:* "Loft Candy 'Afraid' to Drop Job Discrimination," *Afro-American,* Oct. 28, 1944.

222 *"I eat a lot":* Thomasine Norford, "Loft's Candy 'Sweetest Story Ever Told' in Many Ways," *New York Amsterdam News,* Dec. 14, 1963. Also see "A Sweet Idea," *New York Amsterdam News,* Sept. 19, 1959; "NAACP and Loft Candy Join to Raise Funds," *New York Amsterdam News,* Aug. 29, 1959.

222 *By the end of the 1960s:* Andrew F. Smith, ed., *Savoring Gotham: A Food Lover's Companion to New York City* (New York: Oxford University Press, 2015), 350.

222 *After ninety-two years:* "Heide Is Moving; In City 92 Years," *New York Times,* Aug. 19, 1961; "Firms Searching World to Fund Growth Sites for Industry," *Candy and Snack Industry,* no. 134 (1970), 42.

223 *In 1972 the three-year-old:* "Loft Candy Company Completes Sale of Assets to Southland Unit," *Wall Street Journal,* May 6, 1971, 20; "Barracini-Loft Unit Sold By Southland," *New York Times,* Sept. 11, 1976, 43; "Deal a Charmer for Tootsie Roll," *Chicago Tribune,* Aug. 24, 1988, B4.

223 *Madelaine Chocolate Novelties:* "Just Where Do Bunnies Come From?" *New York Times,* Apr. 2, 1977, 24.

223 *In 1970, Cella's Cherries:* Darlene Lacey, *Classic Candy: America's Favorite Sweets, 1950–80* (Princes Risborough, Eng.: Shire, 2013).

224 *The ruby-red neon Pepsi-Cola sign:* David Dunlap, "Landmarks Panel to Study Stable and Pepsi-Cola Sign," *New York Times,* Apr. 18, 1988, B3; David Dunlap, "What Happened to the Queens Pepsi Sign," New York Times City Room Blogs, Dec. 10, 2008.

26: CLOSING TIME

225 *At 2:40 a.m.:* "Queens Factory Blast Injures 45," *New York Times,* Nov. 22, 1976, 1.

226 *Eight days after the blast:* "15 Victims Still Struggling for Life 8 Days After Explosion in Queens," *New York Times,* Nov. 29, 1976, 30; "Queens Explosion Victim, 34, Dies of Burns," *New York Times,* Nov. 23, 1976, 30; "A Third Victim of Explosion at Chewing-Gum Factory Dies," *New York Times,* Nov. 28, 1976, 40.

226 *But reports surfaced:* "Alleged Warning of Danger Before Chicle Plant Blast Is Being Checked," *New York Times,* Nov. 25, 1976, 33.

226 *As of December 29:* "1,400 Will Be Laid Off at Queens Chicle Plant," *New York Times,* Dec. 29, 1976, 22.

227 *"reckless and conscious disregard":* "Indict Firm, 4 Execs in Fatal Chicle Blast," *New York Daily News,* Aug. 19, 1977; "4 Are Indicted in Fire Fatal to 6 at Chicle Plant," *New York Times,* July 23, 1977, 1; "Indict 4 in Fatal Blast," *New York Evening News,* Aug. 19, 1977, 2.

227 *In 1978 charges were dropped:* "Indictment of Executives in Chicle Blast Reinstated," *New York Times,* July 10, 1979, B1; "Gum Plant Cleared of Crimes in a Blast Killing Six in 1976," *New York Times,* Feb. 16, 1978, 21; "Charges in Queens Blast That Killed 6 Are Voided," *New York Times,* Nov. 21, 1980, B2; Elizabeth Olson, "Court Refuses to Hear Manslaughter Indictment Against Warner-Lambert," UPI Archives, Mar. 30, 1981.

227 *"It's a beautiful place":* Sandra Salmans, "Chicle Closing: 'Family' Sorrow," *New York Times,* Apr. 25, 1981.

228 *"I went home and cried":* "American Chicle to Close Plant: 455 Workers Offered Retraining," *Newsday,* Apr. 16, 1981; "The Death of a Working 'Family,' " *New York Daily News:, Long Island Industry* 82, Nov. 21, 1982.

228 *"American Chicle is not typical":* "The Death of a Working 'Family.' "

27: DEPARTURES AND ARRIVALS

229 *"character of the neighborhood":* Rudy Johnson, "Brooklynites Mobilize Against Sugar Refinery," *New York Times,* Dec. 19, 1971, A17.

229 *Two years later:* Werner Bamberger, "Sugar Refinery Is Planned in Staten Island Pier Area," *New York Times,* Jan. 30, 1973, 74; Robert E. Tomasson, "On the Waterfront, Local Boards Sift Builders' Waterfront Plans," *New York Times,* Feb. 3, 1974, RE1.

230 *"false and misleading statements":* Associated Press, "S.E.C. Says SuCrest and Others Violated Antifraud Statutes," *New York Times,* June 3, 1977, 43.

230 *By 1985, amid charges:* Martin Tolchin, "Foreigners' Political Roles in U.S. Grow by Investing," *New York Times,* Dec. 30, 1985; Jake Dobkin, "A Last Look Inside the

Revere Sugar Refinery," *Gothamist,* Dec. 22, 2006; "Curtains for the Red Hook Sugar Refinery," *Gothamist,* Dec. 6, 2006.

231 *In 1986, Amstar's Brooklyn refinery:* "Buyout Set for Amstar," *New York Times,* Sept. 20, 1986.

231 *Its sugar division:* Jonathan P. Hicks, "Tate & Lyle Sets Deal to Buy Amstar Sugar," *New York Times,* Sept. 27, 1988; Associated Press, "Company News: Amstar Planning to Change Name," *New York Times,* Aug. 27, 1991.

231 *After a five-month strike:* "Striking Sugar Workers Defend Union in New York," *The Militant* 63, no. 26 (July 19, 1999); Bob Liff, "Domino Workers Set Strike, Leaves Bad Taste," *New York Daily News,* June 17, 1999.

231 *The union struck again:* Steven Greenhouse, "At Sugar Refinery, A Melting-Pot Strike," *New York Times,* Feb. 15, 2000; Sara Lobman, "Strike 'Still Going Strong' at Domino Sugar," *The Militant* 64, no. 26 (July 3, 2000); Larry McShane, "Bitter Strike at Domino Sugar Plant Destroys a Sweeter Way of Life," *Los Angeles Times,* Mar. 25, 2001.

231 *"one tenth of its normal output":* Greenhouse, "At Sugar Refinery, A Melting-Pot Strike."

232 *"shoved down their throats":* "Another Season: After Picketing, Striking Domino Workers Still at It," *New York Daily News,* Nov. 24, 2000.

232 *At this juncture:* Diane Cardwell, "Familiar Domino Sugar Refinery Will Shut Much of Its Operation," *New York Times,* Aug. 21, 2003.

232 *"a generous enhanced severance package":* "Bitter Strike at Domino Finally Ends," *New York Times,* Feb. 27, 2001.

232 *Six months later:* "Domino Sugar Sale Closes," *Baltimore Business Journal,* Nov. 6, 2001.

232 *In 2014 it was the site:* Zoë Lescaze, "Kara Walker on Domino Demolition: 'It Makes Me Very Sad,' " *New York Observer,* May 2, 2014.

233 *"went from store to store":* "Will Soho Be the Little Soda That Could?," *New York Times,* Oct. 8, 1986.

233 *"a little kosher bottling plant":* Sophia Collier, "Street Smarts," *New York Times,* June 12, 1988.

234 *"After eleven years":* Alix M. Freedman, "Seagram Takes Plunge into Soft Drinks," *Wall Street Journal,* Mar. 28, 1989, B7.

234 *"four or five times":* Eben Shapiro, "A Soda Seagram Didn't Swallow," *New York Times,* Mar. 21, 1992.

234 *In Brooklyn another young woman:* "Bottler Murdered in Queens Home," *New York Times,* May 27, 1983.

234 *"What celery soda was to Jews":* "The Real New York," *New York* 16, no. 1 (Dec. 27, 1982): 40.

235 *"Jewish champagne"*: "Dr. Brown in Market Expansion," *New York Times*, Feb. 22, 1984.

235 *"whatever Daddy says"*: "A Modern Comeback for a Taste of Brooklyn," *New York Times*, July 7, 2008.

28: SWILL MILK

239 *In 1840 the city's milk*: Virginia Yans-McLaughlin, ed., *Immigration Reconsidered : History, Sociology, and Politics* (New York: Oxford University Press, 1990), 150–51; "Swill-Milk," *New York Times*, May 28, 1858.

239 *"cattle are packed"*: Robert Milham Hartley, *An Historical, Scientific, and Practical Essay on Milk, as an Article of Human Sustenance: With a Consideration of the Effects Consequent upon the Present Unnatural Methods of Producing It for the Supply of Large Cities* (New York: Leavitt, 1842), 141.

240 *"slop-beef dealer"*: Ibid., 147.

240 *"extensive distillery"*: James Jay Mapes, "Swill Milk," *Working Farmer* 1 (1862): 79.

241 *"Good, strong, clear ale"*: William Cobbett, *A Year's Residence, in the United States of America : Treating of the Face of the Country . . .* (London: Sherwood, Neely and Jones, 1819), part 2, 337, originally printed in *American Farmer* 6, no. 166 (1819–1834): 3.

241 *First produced in the century's*: Edwin G. Burrows and Mike Wallace, *Gotham: A History of New York City to 1898* (New York: Oxford University Press, 1999), 662; J. L. Goodner, "Early Soda Water History," *Northwestern Druggist: A Progressive Journal for Retail Druggists*, Aug. 1913, 79; "The Soda Fountain: A History of the Beginning, Rise, and Progress of the Business, from 1832 to 1906," *National Druggist*, Mar. 1906, 79.

241 *His rudimentary soda-fountain setup*: Joseph L. Morrison, "The Soda Fountain," *American Heritage* 13, no. 5 (Aug. 1962), http://www.americanheritage.com/content/soda-fountain.

241 *Having eclipsed tea*: Jack Larkin, *The Reshaping of Everyday Life: 1790–1840* (New York: HarperPerennial, 2008), 174–75.

241 *"good cup of hot coffee"*: Robert Hewitt, *Coffee: Its History, Cultivation, and Uses* (New York: Appleton, 1872), 11.

242 *When* Frank Leslie's: "Our Exposure of the Swill Milk Trade," *Frank Leslie's Illustrated Newspaper*, May 15, 1858, May 22, 1858, June 12, 1858, July 10, 1858.

242 *"largest, nastiest"*: "Fire in the Swill-Milk Stables," *New York Times*, May 19, 1862; *Brooklyn Daily Eagle*, May 21, 1862, 3; "Our Exposure of the Swill Milk Trade."

242 *The* Leslie *series described*: John Mullaly, *The Milk Trade of New York and Vicinity, Giving an Account of the Sale of Pure and Adulterated Milk* (New York: Fowlers and Wells, 1853), 47.

243 *About the time that*: Burrows and Wallace, *Gotham*, 360, 362, 589; John F. Watson,

Historic Tales of Olden Time: Concerning the Early Settlement and Advancement of New York City and State (New York: Collins and Hannay, 1832), 168–74.

243 *The F & M Schaefer Brewery:* Will Anderson, *The Breweries of Brooklyn: An Informal History of a Great Industry in a Great City* (Croton Falls, N.Y.: Anderson, 1976), 6–7. Gillig claimed to be the first to brew lager in New York City, calling the beer of those before himself "small beer." See *One Hundred Years of Brewing: A Complete History of the Progress Made in the Art, Science and Industry of Brewing in the World . . .* (Chicago: H. S. Rich, 1901), 209.

243 *"in continuous operation":* From Samuel Gompers's memoirs, quoted in Diana DiZerega Wall, "Examining Gender, Class, and Ethnicity in Nineteenth-Century New York City," *Historical Archaeology* 33, no. 1 (1999): 107.

244 *Johnson's Distillery:* Ibid., 49; Samuel P. Dinsmore, "Chapter 4: Profit of the Swill Milk Business," in *Suggestions Touching the Municipal Government of New York* (New York: Hilton, 1860), 49.

244 *"amassed fortunes":* "Dr. Conant S. Foster's letter," in *Majority and Minority Reports of the Select Committee of the Board of Health, Appointed to Investigate the Character and Condition of the Sources from Which Cow's Milk Is Derived, for Sale in the City of New York . . .* (New York: C. W. Baker, 1858), 303.

244 *"gorgeous in gold and blue":* Cindy R. Lobel, *Urban Appetites: Food and Culture in Nineteenth-Century New York* (Chicago: University of Chicago Press, 2014), 95–96.

244 *"liquid poison":* Frank Leslie, "The Swill-Milk Investigation, *New York Times,* June 7, 1858.

244 *After the exposé:* Lobel, *Urban Appetites,* 97–98; John Duffy and Russell Sage Foundation, "A History of Public Health in New York City, 1625–1866," 1968, 431, http://www.jstor.org/stable/10.7758/9781610441643; "Frank Leslie Charged With Libel—The Swill-Milk Question," *New York Times,* July 16, 1858. In 1873 a law was enacted against swill milk; it was heavily enforced in Manhattan but largely ignored in Brooklyn. See U.S. Bureau of Animal Industry, "Public Acts of 1873, Approved March 12, 1875," *Bulletin,* no. 26–37 (Washington, D.C.: Government Printing Office, 1902): 55. For a full discussion of the nineteenth-century swill-milk scandal, see Catherine McNeur, *Taming Manhattan: Environmental Battles in the Antebellum City* (Cambridge: Harvard University Press, 2014, ch. 4; Erna Melanie DuPuis, *Nature's Perfect Food: How Milk Became America's Drink* (New York: New York University Press, 2002).

29: THE BRADY BUNCH

245 *"the chances are nine out of ten":* U.S. House of Representatives, Select Committee on Internal Revenue Frauds, *Report of the Select Committee on Internal Revenue Frauds to the House of Representatives, February 25, 1867* (Washington, D.C.: Government

Printing Office, 1867); William Hargreaves, *Our Wasted Resources: The Missing Link in the Temperance Reform* (New York: National Temperance Society/Publication House, 1875), 54–55.

246 *"were somewhat astonished":* "Bourbon Avenue and Lightning Alley," *Frank Leslie's Illustrated Newspaper*, no. 743, Dec. 25, 1869, 253.

246 *"Buildings were ripped up":* "The Whisky War; A Military Expedition to 'Irishtown,'" *New York Times*, Dec. 4, 1869.

246 *"kings of the moonshiners":* "New York's Moonshiners," *New York Times*, Feb. 6, 1880.

247 *"all of New-York":* Ibid.; George W. Atkinson, *After the Moonshiners . . . A Book of Thrilling, yet Truthful Narratives . . .* (Wheeling, W. Va.: Frew & Campbell, 1881), 82–83.

247 *Halfway through his sentence:* "Illicit Whiskey Men Released," *Brooklyn Daily Eagle*, Jan. 25, 1877, 4.

247 *In about 1877:* Wilbur R. Miller, "Moonshiners in Brooklyn: Federal Authority Confronts Urban Culture, 1869–1880," *Long Island Historical Journal* 2, no. 2 (1990): 234–50.

248 *"in and around different dives":* Ibid.; "Illicit Distilling Checked," *New York Times*, Feb. 11, 1880; "The Last of the Bradys," *New York Times*, July 1, 1880.

30: THE LAGER CRAZE

249 *Beer was what everyone wanted:* "Three-cent Beer Wanted," *The Sun*, July 22, 1878; "The Brewers in Convention," *The Sun*, May 21, 1885; "Preparing for Free Lager," *The Sun*, Apr. 7, 1869; "A Silly Pretense," *The Sun*, July 2, 1879; "The Great Beer Question," *The Sun*, May 31, 1881.

249 *The country's largest brewer: One Hundred Years of Brewing: A Complete History of the Progress Made in the Art, Science and Industry of Brewing in the World . . .* (Chicago: H. S. Rich, 1901), 374.

250 *a "bucolic" area:* Ibid.

251 *Eight establishments: The Cyclopaedia of Temperance and Prohibition: A Reference Book of Facts, Statistics, and General Information on All Phases of the Drink Question, the Temperance Movement and the Prohibition Agitation* (New York: Funk & Wagnalls, 1891), 414.

251 *A Brooklyn brewer:* Tara Harrison, "William Ulmer Brewery," Landmarks Preservation Commission, New York, May 11, 2010, 3–5.

251 *"know[n] the world over":* Richard Edwards, *An Historical and Descriptive Review of the City of Brooklyn and Her Manufacturing and Mercantile Industries, Including Many Sketches of Leading Public and Private Citizens* (New York: Historical Pub., 1883), 450.

251 *"as sweet, clear and full of life":* Ibid. Also see Henry Hall, *America's Successful Men of Affairs: An Encyclopedia of Contemporaneous Biography* (New York: New York Tribune, 1895), 68–70; John Sublett, "Staten Island Breweries," *Staten Island History*, n.d., http://www.statenislandhistory.com/staten-island-breweries.html; "New-York's

Bankers, Merchants, and Manufacturers: A Model Brewery on Staten Island," *New York Times*, Aug. 18, 1885, 3; "George Bechtel's Staten Island Brewery," *The Sun*, Oct. 18, 1885, 10.

252 *They hired immigrant men:* Dorothee Schneider, *Trade Unions and Community: The German Working Class in New York City, 1870–1900* (Urbana: University of Illinois Press, 1994), 137; *New Yorker Volker Zeitung*, Jan. 8, 1881, Feb. 18, 1881, Feb. 25, 1881, Feb. 25, 1888.

252 *In January 1881 four hands:* "Burned in the Brewery Vat," *New York Times*, Feb. 9, 1881.

252 *"New York [Manhattan]":* Schneider, *Trade Unions and Community*, 149; *New Yorker Volker Zeitung*, June 2, 1881.

252 *Fourteen smaller breweries:* Schneider, *Trade Unions and Community*, 152.

253 *"In New York a can brought in":* Brander Matthews, "The Function of Slang," *Harper's New Monthly Magazine* 87, no. 518 (July 1893): 304

253 The David Jones brewery: "Advertisement for David Jones Brewery, 1868," City Directory for New York, http://www.fold3.com/document/77558152/.

254 *"ale from that time-stained brewery":* Joesph Alfred Scoville (Pseud. Walter Barrett) et al.,*The Old Merchants of New York City* (New York: Carleton, 1863), 301..

31: BREWERY PRINCESS

255 *Though it's unlikely:* "Obituary of August Schmid," *New York Times*, June 5, 1889.

255 *"never attempted to brew beer":* "Never Brewed Beer, Says Princess Drago," *New York Tribune*, Sept. 8, 1917; "Mrs. Schmid . . . Managed Lion Brewery After First Husband's Death," *New York Times*, May 23, 1909; "Divide Schmid Estate," *New York Tribune*, May 26, 1909.

256 *"business difficulties":* "Signed Away a Fortune," *New York Times*, May 16, 1909.

256 *And she won:* "Lion Brewery Settlement: Mrs. Schmid to Buy Out Interest," *New York Times*, July 1, 1903; "Woman Now Owns Lion Brewery," *New York Tribune*, July 3, 1903; "J. F. Betz Brewery Sold; Men Formerly with the Lion Buy It," *New York Tribune*, Aug. 7, 1903.

256 *It was a good time to own:* G. Thomann, *American Beer: Glimpses of Its History and Description of Its Manufacture* (New York: United States Brewers' Association, 1909), ch. 7.

256 *By 1910, Brooklyn was down:* Tara Harrison, "William Ulmer Brewery," Landmarks Preservation Commission, New York, May 11, 2010, 3–4; William Calabrese, "Beer with a Side of History, Bushwick Beer," http://www.the-wick.com/feature_archive/beer.htm. 10; Kenneth T. Jackson, ed., *The Encyclopedia of New York City* (New Haven: Yale University Press, 1995), 136.

257 *"liquid bread":* "Alcohol Content of Specific Brands 1874–1912," *American Brewers' Review* 31 (Feb. 1917): 55–58.

257 *"I signed anything":* "Signed Away a Fortune," *New York Times,* May 16, 1909.

257 *Pauline's attitude:* "Sues Her Mother for an Accounting," *New York Times,* Jan. 10, 1908; "Mrs. Schmid Weds Prince Del Drago," *New York Times,* May 23, 1909.

258 *"there was little hope":* "Moonshiners in the Metropolis," *New York Times,* June 15, 1902, 27. Also see Chauncey M. Depew, *One Hundred Years of American Commerce [1795–1895]* (New York: D. O. Haynes, 1895), 407.

258 *One ingenious Lower East Side setup:* Cyrus Adler et al., "Local Organizations: New York," *American Jewish Year Book* 21 (1919): 469.

259 *"so thick you can cut it":* Marni Davis, *Jews and Booze: Becoming American in the Age of Prohibition* (New York: New York University Press, 2012), 82; Schapiro's wine ad, Yiddish Book Center website exhibit "Jews and Food in America," http://www.yiddishbookcenter.org/exhibit/schapiros-wine; Stephen Miller, "Norman Schapiro, 70, Ran City's Only Kosher Winery," *The Sun,* Oct. 16, 2007; "Kosher Winery Thrives Under Manhattan, *Chicago Tribune,* July 10, 1978.

259 *"the good stuff":* Davis, *Jews and Booze,* 73.

259 *After the brewery experienced:* "Princess Drago Neglects Brewery, Daughter Charges," *New York Tribune,* Mar. 12, 1917. Del Drago argued she did not mismanage but Prohibition was at fault for the financial losses; see "Beer Hit by Prohibition," *New York Times,* Apr. 10, 1917.

32: THE THIRSTY HOME FRONT

260 *While he was away:* Christopher Gray, "Where the Streets Smelled Like Beer," *New York Times,* Mar. 29, 2012, RE6.

260 *Three years earlier:* Ernest Hurst Cherrington, ed., *The Anti-Saloon League Year Book: An Encyclopedia of Facts and Figures Dealing with the Liquor Traffic and the Temperance Reform* (Columbus, Ohio: Anti-Saloon League of America, 1917), 28, 72, 191–93.

260 *"one of the best-known":* "First Brew in New Schaefer Plant," *Brewers Journal* 47 (July 1916): 22.

261 *"Pure Wholesome Nutritious":* "Advertisement for Lion Brewery," *The Sun,* Mar. 10, 1912, 7; "Advertisement for Lion Brewery," *New-York Tribune,* May 18, 1915, 9.

261 *"Beer is the Pure Temperance Drink":* "Doelger Beer Advertisement," *Brooklyn Daily Eagle,* Oct. 11, 1916, 9. Also see "Beer, the Popular Beverage," *New York Tribune,* Nov. 29, 1911, 4; Will Anderson, *The Beer Book: An Illustrated Guide to American Breweriana* (Princeton: Pyne, 1973), 9; Will Anderson, *The Breweries of Brooklyn: An Informal History of a Great Industry in a Great City* (Croton Falls, N.Y.: Anderson, 1976), 42.

261 *"Temperance was one thing":* "Rheingold Beer Advertisement," *Brooklyn Daily Eagle,* Apr. 27, 1916, 5; Anderson, *The Breweries of Brooklyn,* 104; Rolf Hoffman, "The Originators of Rheingold Beer: From Ludwigsburg to Brooklyn—A Dynasty of

German-Jewish Brewers," *Aufbau,* June 21, 2001. Reprinted by permission of the author on *BeerHistory.com,* http://www.beerhistory.com/library/holdings/hof mann-rheingold.shtml.

262 *Soon five thousand permits:* "Running Down Moonshiners New York's Latest Thrill: Metropolis Has More Illicit Stills than Kentucky Ever Dreamed of," *New York Tribune,* Jan. 11, 1920, VII 9; "The Moonshiners of Gotham," *New York Tribune,* Jan. 16, 1916; "The City Moonshiner," *Washington Post,* Apr. 15, 1900.

262 *"Lion Brewery, like other large brewing concerns":* Quoted in "The Only Safety for Prohibition States," *National Advocate* 4 (June 1917): 83; "Beer Hit by Prohibition," *New York Times,* Apr. 10, 1917.

263 *"G. Washington's Refined Coffee":* Mark Pendergrast, *Uncommon Grounds: The History of Coffee and How It Transformed Our World* (New York: Basic Books, 2010), 137.

263 *"I am very happy":* "An Interesting Letter Worth Reading from the Firing Line, Somewhere in France," *Simmon's Spice Mill: Devoted to the Interests of the Coffee, Tea and Spice Trades* 41, no. 1 (Mar. 1918): 299.

263 *"Make your coffee in a cup":* "G. Washington coffee advertisements": *New York Times,* Jan. 2, 1922; *Ladies' Home Journal,* Nov. 1912; *New York Tribune,* June 22, 1919.

263 *While George Constant Louis Washington:* William H. Ukers, *All About Coffee* (New York: Tea and Coffee Trade Journal Company, 1922), 538.

263 *"workingman's drink at the noon hour":* "Gompers Denounces Prohibition as a Fad of Cranks," *New York Tribune,* July 4, 1917, 3. Also see Gompers's statements in U.S. Senate, Committee on the Judiciary, *Prohibiting Intoxicating Beverages: Hearings Before the Subcommittee . . .* (Washington, D.C.: Government Printing Office, 1919), pt. 1, 9.

264 *"never made them intoxicated":* U.S. Senate, *Prohibiting Intoxicating Beverages,* 306–7.

33: "CITY ON A STILL"

265 *One day in 1920:* "40 Arrested as Police Begin Drying Up the City," *New York Daily Tribune,* Apr. 8, 1921; "Installing Still Is Convicted in Brooklyn," *New York Times,* June 21, 1921.

266 *During Prohibition:* Michael A. Lerner, *Dry Manhattan: Prohibition in New York City* (Cambridge: Harvard University Press, 2008), 4; Ann Douglas, *Terrible Honesty: Mongrel Manhattan in the 1920s* (New York: Farrar, Straus and Giroux, 1994), 24.

266 *The Anti-Saloon League:* Ibid., 14.

266 *Once Prohibition began:* Will Anderson, *The Breweries of Brooklyn: An Informal History of a Great Industry in a Great City* (Croton Falls, N.Y.: Anderson, 1976), 115.

267 *After suing the government:* "New Volstead Act Test Brewery in Injunction Suit Contends That Enforcement Law Is Unconstitutional," *New York Times,* Dec. 5, 1920.

267 *Part of George Ehret's mighty:* "Ehret Brewery to Close," *New York Times,* July 4, 1929, 17.

267 *"anyone who can show us"*: Lerner, *Dry Manhattan*, 54.

267 *"Beer, beer, glorious old-fashioned beer"*: "$1,000,000 in Beer Flushes City Sewer," *New York Times*, July 13, 1923.

269 *Similarly, when agents found:* "Snap 200 Padlocks on Ebling Brewery," *New York Times*, Mar. 20, 1925, 3; "200 Padlocks Hold Brewery: New York City Brewery Closed for Four Months" *Home and State* 26, no. 4 (Apr. 1925): 8.

269 *"knocked the 'near' clean out"*: "Fiorello La Guardia Makes 2.84% Beer in Office," *New York Times*, June 20, 1926, 1.

269 *"increase materially"*: "Queens Rush for Malt Extract to Extract 'Near' from Beer Echoes LaGuardia's Experiment," *Daily Star*, June 24, 1926, 7.

269 *While most breweries limped:* Trommer's loaned money to roadside hot dog vendors in Long Island to open restaurants selling White Label Near Beer. These restaurants became popularly known as "brass rails." By the repeal of Prohibition, Trommer's had more than 950 accounts. See Grivers, "Needle Beer: How Beer Schnapps Became 'Schnapps Beer,' " *Beer Strength Matters*, Mar. 5, 2015, http://www.beerstrengthmatters.com/?author=1.

270 *"used to buy a gallon"*: "The 11th Plague? Why People Drink Sweet Wine on Passover," *Atlantic Monthly*, Apr. 14, 2011. See also Maurice Cogan Hauck, Kenneth MacDougall, and David Isay, *12 American Voices: An Authentic Listening and Integrated-Skills Text* (New Haven: Yale University Press, 2001), 167, http://site .ebrary.com/id/10178430; Hannah Sprecher, " 'Let Them Drink and Forget Our Poverty': Orthodox Rabbis React to Prohibition," *American Jewish Archives* 43 (Fall-Winter 1991): 134–79; Daniel Okrent, *Last Call: The Rise and Fall of Prohibition* (New York: Scribner, 2010), 185–92.

270 *"withdrawn on permit"*: Federal Council of the Churches of Christ, Department of Research and Education, 1925 report, quoted in Fletcher Dobyns, *The Amazing Story of Repeal: An Exposéé of the Power of Propaganda* (Chicago: Willett, Clark, 1940), 297.

271 *"flavor and quality"*: "Candy Stores Get Old Saloon Trade," *New York Times*, Feb. 22, 1920.

271 *"near-beer taste something"*: "Beer Goes to 4% as Prohibition Ends," *New York Times*, Dec. 7, 1933, 19; "New Flow of Beer Will Bring Social and Economic Changes," *New York Times*, Mar. 19, 1933, XX2.

34: THE BATTLE FOR PASTEURIZED MILK

272 *His slogan, "Quality & Purity"*: T. W. Decker, "Quality & Purity: The Foundation Stones—Story of the T. W. Decker & Son's Business and the Ideal That Inspired Its Founder," *Sheffield Farms-Slawson-Decker Company Bulletin* 1, no. 4 (May 1915): 2.

274 *"slaughter of babies"*: Nathan Straus and Lina Gutherz Straus, *Disease in Milk: The Remedy, Pasteurization* (New York: Dutton, 1913), 134. Also see Julie Miller, "To

Stop the Slaughter of the Babies: Nathan Straus and the Drive for Pasteurized Milk, 1893–1920," *New York History* 74, no. 2 (1993): 158–84.

274 *One hot summer afternoon:* Straus and Straus, *Disease in Milk,* 38.

274 *"to a degree of exactness":* Ibid., 22.

274 *Lewis Halsey, the president:* Carl W. Hall and George Malcolm. Trout, *Milk Pasteurization* (Westport, Conn.: AVI, 1968), 13. Also see "Sheffield Farms Milk Plant Webster Avenue (southwest Corner of 166th Street) HAER 1075," n.d., No. NY-267, Historic American Engineering: Photographs, Written Records, and Measured Data, http://cdn.loc.gov/master/pnp/habshaer/ny/ny1600/ny1699/data/ny1699data .pdf.

275 *"every drop of milk consumed":* "New York's Milk Supply Declared Now Be Pure," *New York Times,* Dec. 2, 1906, 31.

275 *"principal movers":* "Milk Dealers in Session," *New York Times,* June 16, 1905, 16.

276 *"at least as good":* "Beer Flows in 19 States at Midnight as City Awaits Legal Brew Today," *New York Times,* Apr. 7, 1933, 1.

276 *"beer-drinking country":* "Beer Gto 4% as Dry Era Ends," *New York Times,* Dec. 7, 1933, 19. Also see Will Anderson, *The Breweries of Brooklyn: An Informal History of a Great Industry in a Great City* (Croton Falls, N.Y.: Anderson, 1976), 115.

276 *F & M Schaefer Brewery adopted:* "The F & M Schaeffer Brewing Company," American Brewery History Page (2000), http://www.beerhistory.com; David G. Moyer, *American Breweries of the Past* (Bloomington, Ind.: AuthorHouse, 2009), 71–73; Rheingold Beer, Our History, http://www.rheingoldbeer.com/beer/history.aspx; New York University, Leonard N. Stern School of Business, *Rheingold Beer,* http:// pages.stern.nyu.edu/~rwiner/Rheingold_case.doc.

277 *New York's breweries placed high:* A. M. McGahan, "The Emergence of the National Brewing Oligopoly: Competition in the American Market, 1933–1958," *Business History Review* 65, no. 2 (1991): 264–65.

278 *"like pieces of china":* Frank A. Rooke, "The Finest Creamery Plant in the World: Story of the Sheffield Farms-Slawson-Decker Company's Wonderful Bronx Plant," *Sheffield Farms-Slawson-Decker Company Bulletin* 1, no. 3 (Apr. 1915): 2.

278 *There was no Dr. Spieker:* "Loton Horton Dies in France at 72," *New York Times,* Dec. 16, 1926; George Derby et al., eds., *The National Cyclopoedia of American Biography* (New York: J. T. White, 1893).

279 *"soothing balm":* "Advertisements for Dr. Spieker's Yoghurt": *Brooklyn Daily Eagle,* Oct. 19, 1922, 10; "Horton Will Gives $100,000 to Widow," *New York Times,* Jan. 19, 1927.

280 *"the world's greatest coffee business":* "Sell Yuban Division," *New York Times,* Dec. 2, 1929.

281 *General Foods bought several:* "General Foods to Buy Arbuckle Properties," *New York Times,* Jan. 5, 1937.

281 *When Margaret Jamison, the last heir, died:* William H. Ukers, *All About Coffee: A History of Coffee from the Classic Tribute to the World's Most Beloved Beverage* (Avon, Mass: Adams Media, 2012), 522–25; Mark Pendergrast, *Uncommon Grounds: The History of Coffee and How It Transformed Our World* (New York: Basic Books, 2010), 181; "Margaret Jamison, Last Arbuckle Heir," *New York Times,* Nov. 19, 1942.

281 *"highest-priced coffee":* "Life Is One Cup of Coffee After Another to Blender," *Pittsburgh Press,* Dec. 28, 1932, 13.

282 *In 1936 the city opened negotiations:* "Court Hears Protest on Fair Assessments: Owners of 31 Acres in Flushing Seek to Prove Property Is Worth $800,000," *New York Times,* Sept. 29, 1936; "Eugene Beitter Dies: Long in Chicory Firm," *New York Times,* Dec. 11, 1938; Michael Connell, "Port Huron Once Dominated Chicory Trade," *New York Times Herald,* Oct. 19, 2014.

283 *"The only way I can be sure":* Ibid.

283 *On the eve of World War II:* Mark Pendergrast, *Uncommon Grounds: The History of Coffee and How It Transformed Our World* (New York: Basic Books, 2010), 215; "Brooklyn Leads the World in Processing of Coffee," *Brooklyn Daily Eagle,* Oct. 26, 1941, 45.

284 *"the wartime measure":* E. M. Collingham, *The Taste of War: World War II and the Battle for Food* (New York: Penguin, 2013), 25.

284 *"virtually unobtainable":* "More Coffee Doubtful at Present Time." *Tucson Daily Citizen,* Oct. 27, 1942, 5.

286 *Fred L. Soufert of Woodside:* "Theft of Coffee Worth $22,000 and Selling It in Black Market Laid to Concern's Employee," *New York Times,* Apr. 30, 1943, 1; "Coffee Thief Sentenced: F. L. Soufert Gets a Sing Sing Term for $50,000 Operations," *New York Times,* June 19, 1943, 1.

36: HEAVENLY COFFEE, EARTHLY BEER

287 *"devices to eliminate":* "New Smoke Control Unit," *New York Times,* June 24, 1952, 29; "Coffee Roasters Expand Downtown," *New York Times,* Jan. 3, 1953, 27; "Downtown Group Hits Street Plan: Coffee Dealers Say Widening Project May Force Them to Leave the State," *New York Times,* Mar. 1, 1956, 24.

287 *S. A. Schonbrunn, which made Savarin:* "New Coffee Factory Announced," *Wall Street Journal,* Feb. 28, 1957; John Martinson, interview with Marion Kane, in *Dish: Memories, Recipes and Delicious Bites* (North Vancouver, B.C.: Whitecap, 2005), 9; "Joseph

Martinson, Coffee Firm Head, Founder of Company in 1898 at 18, Is Dead," *New York Times*, Apr. 26, 1949.

287 *Most adults drank a little over:* "Coffee Break Is an American Institution for Workers," *New York Amsterdam News*, Dec. 4, 1954.

288 *Within a year Chock full o'Nuts:* George Auerbach, "Chock Full O' Whatever It Takes," *New York Times*, Apr. 14, 1956.

288 *"I needed a personnel manager":* "Food: Erstwhile Nut Salesman Comes Full Circle," *New York Times*, Dec. 4, 1963, 58.

289 *"almost complete absence":* "Seek to Break Brewery Bias," *New York Amsterdam News*, June 10, 1950, 3; "New York Urban League Plans Awards Program," *New York Age*, Mar. 7, 1953, 13; "More Brewery Jobs Assured to Negroes," *New York Times*, Mar. 6, 1953.

289 *"public taste for beer":* "Plenty of Beer on Hand for War," *New York Times*, Aug. 5, 1950, 19.

289 *"eight figures":* "Jersey Brewery Sold; Liebmann Acquires Plant of Trommer at Orange," *New York Times*, Nov. 29, 1950; "Brewery Rankings Shift; Top Four in Output Unchanged," *New York Times*, Apr. 12, 1953; "Rheingold Maker in Western Deal," *New York Times*, Jan. 8, 1954.

291 *"extra light and frosty-dry":* "Bronx Sky Gets 'Lit,'" *New York Times*, Aug. 21, 1952; "Ruperts Plans Big Campaign," *New York Times*, Mar. 1, 1951, 46; "Local Pride Found Potent Sales Aid," *New York Times*, July 13, 1952, F5; "Ruppert Brewery Is Closed Here," *New York Times*, Jan. 1, 1966, 27.

291 *"rotten and horrible":* "Brewery Enjoined After Being Sold," *New York Times*, Dec. 11, 1953, 64.

291 *The decline of the New York beer industry:* Matt A. Chaban, "Builders and Brewers Honor Brooklyn's Beer Heritage: The Appraisal," *New York Times*, Aug. 31, 2015; Will Anderson, *The Breweries of Brooklyn: An Informal History of a Great Industry in a Great City* (Croton Falls, N.Y.: Anderson, 1976), 27; Amy Mittelman, *Brewing Battles: A History of American Beer* (New York: Algora, 2008), 141.

292 *After the PepsiCo bottlers bought:* Emanuel Perlmutter, "Rheingold Plans to Shut a Plant," *New York Times*, Jan. 6, 1974; Damon Steson, "Rheingold Plant Faces Final Shutdown: 300 to Lose Jobs," *New York Times*, Jan. 16, 1976, 30; Deirdre Carmody, "The Rheingold River Flows Gently to a City Sewer," *New York Times*, Feb. 1, 1974, 1.

292 *Into the fray:* Murray Illson, "Chock Full O'Nuts Set to Get Rheingold," *New York Times*, Feb. 27, 1974, 1; "Chock Full O'Nuts Corp. Moves Toward Purchase of PepsiCo Brewing Unit," *Wall Street Journal*, Feb. 27, 1974, 32; "PepsiCo Agrees to Sell Rheingold Beer Unit to Chock Full O'Nuts," *Wall Street Journal*, Mar. 11, 1974, 16; Ernest Holsendolph, "Rheingold's Rescuer," *New York Times*, Mar. 24, 1974, 167; "Schmidt to Buy Rheingold," *New York Times*, Oct. 8, 1977; Patricia Winters

Lauro, "Rheingold Hopes to Rekindle the Romance Between the Beer and New York City," *New York Times*, Feb. 12, 2003.

292 *"dictated by financial losses"*: "Schaeffer to Close Its Brewery Here," *New York Times*, Jan. 23, 1976, 68; Lee Dembart, "Schaeffer, Last of City's Breweries, to Close Its Plant as Too Costly," *New York Times*, Jan. 23, 1976, 31.

292 *Four years earlier:* Ernest Holsendolph, "Associated Brewing Sets Sale of Piels," *New York Times*, June 30, 1973, 45.

293 *Monarch Wine Company expanded:* "News of the Advertising and Field Markets: Wine," *New York Times*, Mar. 16, 1954; "I Rokeach & Sons Forms a New Unit for Kosher Wines," *New York Times*, June 8, 1959; Frank J. Prial, "Manischewitz Is the Name, but Monarch Makes It," *New York Times*, Apr. 6, 1974.

293 *Investigating, they discovered:* "Wine Company Finds Smart Negro Market," *New York Age*, July 22, 1950. Also see Manischewitz Kosher Wine ad, *Ebony*, Sept. 1951, 7, 33.

294 *"Man-O-Manischewitz"*: Solomon H. Katz and William Woys Weaver, *Encyclopedia of Food and Culture* (New York: Thomson/Gale, 2003), 69.

37: GOODBYE TO ALL THAT

295 *The 1970s were fraught with problems:* Leslie Maitland, "Coffee Decline—Fewer Drinkers, Fewer Cups," *New York Times*, Mar. 15, 1975.

296 *Chock full o'Nuts was the third largest:* "Chock Full O'Nuts Posts $309,000 Loss for Fiscal 4th Period," *Wall Street Journal*, Oct. 1, 1984; Associated Press, "Layoff Notices at Chock Full O'Nuts," *New York Times*, Aug. 19, 1983.

297 *"We have a name in this area"*: Wolfgang Saxon, "William Black, Founder and Head of Chock Full O'Nuts Corp., Dies," *New York Times*, Mar. 8, 1983; " 'That Heavenly Coffee' Returns in New Coffee Bars," *New York Times*, Oct. 24, 1993.

297 *Today Starbucks has 283 stores:* Christian González-Rivera, "State of the Chains, 2013," Center for an Urban Future, Dec. 2013, https://nycfuture.org/research/publications/state-of-the-chains-2013.

297 *"preservation of the dairy industry"*: Glenn Fowler, "Elmhurst Dairy Seeking to Have Surrounding Land Condemned for Expansion," *New York Times*, Sept. 21, 1975; "Planners Approve Expansion of Dairy," *New York Times*, Nov. 2, 1975; Harold Faber, "Importing of Pennsylvania Milk Is Hurting Farmers in New York and Jersey," *New York Times*, Nov. 9, 1975.

297 *"you can't put milk in a carton"*: "Le Shake," see Fred Ferretti, "Packaging an Idea—In Three Flavors," *New York Times*, June 28, 1978.

298 *"The real point in this dispute"*: Martin Gottlieb, "Union Fight with Maker of Dannon Yogurt Is Bitter and Violent," *New York Times*, Mar. 11, 1983.

298 *"an already deteriorating New York–based milk industry"*: Dennis Hevesi, "350 Workers

to Be Idled as Dairy in Queens Orders Its Plant Closed," *New York Times,* July 22, 1987.

299 *"clear that nobody is getting rich":* John Grossman, "Milk Fight: When Farmland Dairies Broke Up the New York City Milk Cartel, the Real War Began," *Inc.,* Sept. 1, 1987, http://www.Inc.Com/Magazine/19870901/3557.html.

38: MANHATTAN CATTLE DRIVE

303 *"Ham and beef-steaks":* Frances Milton Trollope, *Domestic Manners of the Americans* (London: Whittaker, Treacher, 1832), 130.

303 *"butcher's meat":* Richard Briggs Stott, *Workers in the Metropolis: Class, Ethnicity, and Youth in Antebellum New York City* (Ithaca, N.Y.: Cornell University Press, 1990), 305–6; Roger Horowitz, *Putting Meat on the American Table: Taste, Technology, Transformation* (Baltimore: Johns Hopkins University Press, 2006), 12.

304 *To satisfy New York's appetite:* Bouck White, *The Book of Daniel Drew* (New York: Cosimo Classics, 2005), 78.

304 *"Armed with a large stick":* "The Meats of New York," *New York Daily Times,* Feb. 26, 1853, 6.

304 *One enraged bull:* "A Wild Bullock," *New York Daily Times,* Dec. 10, 1851, 2; "Cattle Driving," *New York Daily Times,* Oct. 12, 1852, 1.

304 *In 1850 a city ordinance:* "Common Council Proceedings, Mon. Sept. 25," *New York Daily Times,* Sept. 26, 1854, 8; "Municipal: The Slaughter District," *New York Daily Times,* Oct. 13, 1855, 1.

304 *"spacious, airy":* "The Cattle Trade of New York," *New York Daily Tribune,* May 24, 1848, 1.

305 *"scattered over many populous districts":* "Butchery Not a Nuisance of Necessity," *New York Daily Times,* June 5, 1854, 4.

305 *"the surrounding atmosphere":* James Boardman, *America, and the Americans* (New York: Arno, 1974 [1833]), 91.

305 *"An East-side Sufferer":* "Letter to the Editor from 'An East-side Sufferer': Public Slaughter House," *New-York Daily Tribune,* Mar. 16, 1844, 3.

305 *"All day long":* Samuel Gompers, *Seventy Years of Life and Labor: An Autobiography* (New York: Dutton, 1925), 24.

305 *"a great and a perpetual nuisance":* Thomas F. De Voe, *Abattoirs: A Paper Read before the Polytechnic Branch of the American Institute, June 8, 1865* (Albany, N.Y.: Van Benthuysen & Sons, 1866), 18.

307 *"these filthy and revolting stink-holes":* John Duffy and Russell Sage Foundation, "A History of Public Health in New York City, 1625–1866," 1968, 424, http://www.jstor.org/stable/10.7758/9781610441643.

307   *"gorgeous avenues of flesh":* Thomas F. De Voe, *The Market Book: A History of the Public Markets of the City of New York* (New York: A. M. Kelley, 1970 [1862]), 574–75.

307   *"one concerning the meats":* Duffy and Russell Sage Foundation, "A History of Public Health in New York City," 422; De Voe, "The Public Markets," *New York Times,* Jan. 23, 1855.

307   *"no longer serve people's interests":* Edwin G. Burrows and Mike Wallace, *Gotham: A History of New York City to 1898* (New York: Oxford University Press, 1999), 623; Roger Horowitz, Jeffrey M. Pilcher, and Sydney Watts, "Meat for the Multitudes: Market Culture in Paris, New York City, and Mexico City over the Long Nineteenth Century," *American Historical Review* 109, no. 4 (2004): 1082, doi:10 .1086/530749.

308   *"eaten in New-York":* Augustus K. Gardner, "Report of the Varieties and Conditions of the Meats Used in the City of New York," *New York Journal of Medicine and the Collateral Sciences* 10 (1853): 50, 52, 51.

308   *"well-fatted":* Ibid., 55.

309   *"lowing and bellowing":* George Ripley, John Sullivan Dwight, and Parke Godwin, "No. XII: The Butchers," *The Harbinger, Devoted to Social and Political Progress* 2 (1846): 71.

39: FOOLING MRS. EASTMAN

310   *"vessel with dressed beef":* James Parton, "T. C. Eastman, Meat Exporter," *Scientific American* 7, no. 164 (1879): 2605. Also see Louise Carroll Wade, *Chicago's Pride: The Stockyards, Packingtown, and Environs in the Nineteenth Century* (Urbana: University of Illinois Press, 1987), 108.

310   *"The exportation of dressed meat":* "The Lading of a Ship," *Harper's New Monthly Magazine* 50, no. 378 (Sept. 1877): 491.

310   *"one of the most extensive":* Edmund Wheeler, *Croydon, N.H., 1866: Proceedings at the Centennial Celebration on Wednesday, June 13, 1866* (Claremont, N.H.: Claremont Manufacturing, 1867), 99.

310   *"converted into four quarters":* Parton, "T. C. Eastman."

311   *"perfect preservation":* Ibid.

311   *"the first cargo of [live] beef cattle":* "Sending Meat Abroad (Extracts from New York Tribune)," *Friends' Intelligencer* 34 (1878): 175.

312   *"artificial butter":* Mitchell Okun, *Fair Play in the Marketplace: The First Battle for Pure Food and Drugs* (DeKalb: Northern Illinois University Press, 1986).

312   *"Eastman had an especial room":* Roger R. Shiel, *Early to Bed and Early to Rise: Twenty Years in Hell with the Beef Trust. "Facts, Not Fiction"* (Indianapolis: n.p., 1901), 62.

312 *"stamp, brand or mark":* "Section 1 of Chapter 415 of the Laws of 1877, Entitled, 'An Act to Protect Dairymen and Prevent Deception in the Sales of Butter,'" in *Journal of the Senate of the State of New-York, 103rd Session* (Albany, N.Y.: Weed, Parsons, 1880), 939.

313 *An 1866 cholera epidemic:* Jared N. Day, "Tainted Neighbors: Cellar Industries, Industrial Waste, and Urban Reform in New York City, 1866–1915," *Annual Meeting of the American Society for Environmental History* 2 (2000): 2.

313 *singled out as "abominable":* "The Cattle Driving and the Slaughter House Nuisance," *New York Times,* Aug. 24, 1866; "City Slaughter-Houses," *New York Times,* Aug. 29, 1866.

314 *elected a new mayor:* See Michael Rubbinaccio, *Abraham Oakey Hall: New York's Most Elegant and Controversial Mayor* (Seattle: Pescara, 2011).

314 *"late at night":* Thomas Floyd-Jones, *Backward Glances: Reminiscences of an Old New-Yorker* (Somerville, N.J.: Unionist Gazette Association, 1914), 10.

314 *"but the squeal":* Julie Husband and Jim O'Loughlin, *Daily Life in the Industrial United States, 1870–1900* (Westport, Conn.: Greenwood, 2004), 72–91.

40: THE MILITANT

315 *"dirty little pens":* Stanley Nadel, *Little Germany: Ethnicity, Religion, and Class in New York City, 1845–80* (Urbana: University of Illinois Press, 1990), 41.

316 *"to protect the people":* Ladies' Health Protective Association, *Report of the Ladies' Health Protective Association of New York: 1885 and 1886* ([New York]: n.p., 1886), 3. Also see Felice Batlan, "The Ladies' Health Protective Association: Lay Lawyers and Urban Cause Lawyering," *Akron Law Review* 41, no. 3 (2008): 708; Christine Meisner Rosen, "The Role of Pollution Regulation and Litigation in the Development of the U.S. Meatpacking Industry, 1865–1880," *Enterprise & Society* 8, no. 2 (June 2007): 297–347.

316 *"steaming and fermenting":* Transcript of Grand Jury Proceedings at 3, *New York v. Doe,* Box 156, folder 1604, 27 (New York Grand Jury Nov. 20, 1884), New York City Municipal Archives, New York, New York; Batlan, "Ladies' Health Protective Association," 713.

316 *In January 1885 a fact-finding tour:* "East Side Pests: A Tour by the Ladies of the Health Protective Association," *New York Times,* Jan. 27, 1885, 8.

316 *"Committee on Smells":* Edith Parker Thompson, "What Women Have Done for the Public Health," *Forum* 24 (1898): 47.

317 *"long and bitter":* Ladies' Health Protective Association, *Report.*

317 *Police escorts were needed:* Mary Trautman, "Twelve Years of Work of the Ladies' Health Protective Associative," *New York Medical Times* 24, no. 9 (1896): 257–58;

"Slaughterhouses Visited by Ladies," *New York Tribune,* Apr. 25, 1885, 8; Thompson, "What Women Have Done for the Public Health," 48.

318 *"Full of ambition":* "Last of the Founders of the Meat Industry Dies: Ferdinand Sulzberger's Remarkable Career as Packer," *National Provisioner* 53 (Aug. 4, 1915): 17.

318 *"It was all the work":* "Work of the Ladies Health Protective Association," *Godey's Lady's Book,* Dec. 1887, 472–75.

319 *"We don't want the slaughterhouses removed":* "East Side Pests," 8.

319 *"sacrificing one iota":* Reverend Charles Eaton, quoted in "To Prepare for Cholera: Citizens Protest Against the City Slaughterhouses," *New York Times,* Mar. 29, 1885, 7.

319 *"If we have to pay out":* Ladies' Health Protective Association, *Report;* Sara Baum, "Condition of Slaughter Houses and System of Slaughtering in New York Before and Since the Organization of the Ladies' Health Protective Association," First Convention of the Ladies' Health Protective Association of New York: Academy of Medicine (New York: Ladies' Health Protective Association, 1896), 55.

41: THE BEEF TRUST

320 *All except butchering:* "New York Leads All in Manufacturing," *New York Times,* June 26, 1912, 18.

320 *While Chicago, "Hog Butcher to the world":* Carl Sandburg, "Chicago," *Poetry* 3, no. 6 (Mar. 1914): 191.

320 *In 1895, Chicago's Big Four:* "Rumours of a Great Meat Trust," *New York Times,* Apr. 10, 1895, 2; "Reasons Why Meat Prices Have Risen," *New York Times,* Apr. 22, 1902, 5.

321 *"It makes no difference":* "Boycott by East Side Butchers Spreading," *New York Times,* May 13, 1902, 7.

321 *Rather than rushing into the shops:* "Women Attack Butchers in Kosher Meat Riot," *Brooklyn Daily Eagle,* May 18, 1902, 6; "Fierce Meat Riot on Lower East Side," *New York Times,* May 16, 1902; "East Side Boycotters Meet and Organize, Form the Ladies' Anti-Beef Trust Association," *New York Times,* May 19, 1902; "Butchers Appeal to Police for Protection," *New York Times,* May 26, 1902.

322 *Loss of its European business:* U.S. House of Representatives, "Government Control of Meat-Packing Industry: Hearing Before the Subcommittee on Agriculture and Forestry," 65th Congress, 2nd sess. (Washington, D.C.: Government Printing Office, 1918), 148–50.

322 *"great struggle for cheap meat":* "A Real Police Problem," *New York Times,* May 24, 1902, 8.

322 *"The people feel very justly":* "Allied Conference for Cheap Kosher Meat Circular," *New York Herald,* May 26, 1902, 6. Also see Pamela Susan Nadell, *American Jewish Women's History: A Reader* (New York: New York University Press, 2003), 119.

323 *"no connection with the meat merger":* "Schwartzchild & Sultzberger, Official Says, Do None of Acts Enjoined by Court," *New York Tribune,* May 28, 1903, 14; "Merger of Beef Packers," *New York Times,* Feb. 24, 1903; J. C. Walker, "Packers Own Guilt: Pay $25,000 in Fine," *Farmers' Elevator Guide* 1 (1905): 19; "Meat Trade Heads Under Indictment," *New York Times,* July 2, 1905.

42: THE SAUSAGE MILLIONAIRES

324 *One of the largest:* Robert Lewis Taylor, "Profiles: Dignified Meat II," *The New Yorker,* June 22, 1946.

325 *Upton Sinclair's* The Jungle*:* "The Boycott On 'The Jungle': Upton Sinclair's Book in Trouble in the Packing Centres," *New York Times,* May 18, 1906; H. E. Henry, "Libraries Withdraw 'The Jungle,' " *New York Times,* May 20, 1906.

325 *"first loyalty":* "Samuel Slotkin of Hygrade Dies," *New York Times,* Oct. 31, 1965.

325 *"the first consolidation":* "Wall Street Briefs," *Washington Post,* Nov. 21, 1927, 15.

326 *"transfer meat from the prairie":* Taylor, "Profiles: Dignified Meat II," 36.

326 *After Adolf Göbel died:* "Would Oust Mother as Gobel Executrix," *New York Times,* June 28, 1925; "Widow of Sausage King Sues to Annul Second Marriage," *Brooklyn Daily Eagle,* Aug. 10, 1926; "Gobel, Inc., Is Sold," *New York Times,* Aug. 19, 1926.

327 *In 1927, the new firm:* Norman C. Miller, *The Great Salad Oil Swindle* (New York: Coward-McCann, 1965), 16.

327 *One of Göbel's competitors:* "3 Meat Concerns Merge, Stahl, Meyer and Ferries Companies to Continue Manufacturing," *New York Times,* Dec. 19, 1928, 20, 45.

327 *In 1928, Isadore Pinckowitz:* Ted Merwin, *Pastrami on Rye: An Overstuffed History of the Jewish Deli* (New York: New York University Press, 2015), 38–41.

328 *By 1900 sausages were so popular:* Andrew F. Smith, ed., *Savoring Gotham: A Food Lover's Companion to New York City* (New York: Oxford University Press, 2015), 275.

328 *Over six thousand sausage-makers:* "The Great Sausage Corner a Feverish Market, No Stronger than Its Softest Link," *New York Times,* June 9, 1901; Sara Pendergast and Tom Pendergast, *Bowling, Beatniks, and Bell-Bottoms: Pop Culture of 20th-Century America* (Detroit: U X L, 2002), 63; Eric J. Ierardi, *Gravesend, the Home of Coney Island* (Charleston, S.C.: Arcadia, 2001), 60; David Gerard Hogan, *Selling 'em by the Sack: White Castle and the Creation of American Food* (New York: New York University Press, 1997), ch. 1.

329 *"packing plant at 816":* Helen Worden, *Round Manhattan's Rim* (Indianapolis: Bobbs-Merrill, 1934), 89–90.

329 *"everything comes under rabbinical inspection":* Ibid., 91.

330 *"runs modern smoke-houses":* Ibid., 90.

330 *"the largest of any community":* Bertram Reinitz, "Lowly Hot Dog Gains Prestige," *New York Times,* Apr. 21, 1929; "Hot Dogs Top the List of Sausages Eaten Here," *New York Times,* May 7, 1935.

331 *"thousands of men and women":* "Isidore Pinckowitz, Philanthropist, Dies," *New York Times,* Nov. 9, 1936, 19; "Mourn Death of I. Pinckowitz," *Jewish Post* 13 (Nov. 1936): 5.

331 *"favorite meat":* "Hot Dogs Becoming Thing of Past at Beaches," *New York Times,* June 3, 1945; "Tuesday Meat Ban Accepted in City," *New York Times,* Feb. 7, 1945; "Food Men Warn of Famine as City Supplies Dwindle," *New York Times,* Mar. 20, 1943.

332 *To find animals:* Robert Lewis Taylor, "Profiles: Dignified Meat I," *The New Yorker,* June 15, 1946, 32.

333 *"astonished to learn":* Worden, *Round Manhattan's Rim,* 90–91.

333 *In 1930 four 1,200-pound bulls:* "Police Bullets Fell Four Bolting Steers," *New York Times,* Feb. 25, 1930, 19.

333 *A few months later a young steer:* "Steer Runs Wild in Broadway and Herald Sq.," *New York Times,* May 7, 1930, 29.

334 *"the slaughterhouses are there":* Quoted in Rufus Jarman, "Real Estate: An Investment Paradox." *Nation's Business* 41, no. 1 (Jan. 1953): 82. Also see "$100,000,000 Plan for Housing Here," *New York Times,* Sept. 19, 1946; Lee Cooper, "City Within a City to Cover Eight Blocks on the East River," *New York Times,* Sept. 29, 1946.

334 *"whatever it wanted to pay":* "Speedy Deal on U.N. Headquarters Property Told Here by a Real Estate Man," *Los Angeles Times,* Sept. 26, 1950; "Rockefellers Hail Zeckendorf's Role," *New York Times,* Dec. 18, 1946.

335 *"the earliest practical time":* George Barrett, "Occupant of Site Delays U.N. Start," *New York Times,* June 15, 1947, 27; "Meat Company to Speed Shift," *New York Times,* June 21, 1947, 7.

335 *"I was in a slaughterhouse":* "Milk Curb Respite Rejected," *Long Island Star Journal,* Sept. 27, 1946.

44: CELLOPHANE MEAT

337 *"tomorrow's" housewife:* Robert Lewis Taylor, "Profiles: Dignified Meat I," *The New Yorker,* June 15, 1946, 29.

338 *"instant meals"*: "Stahl-Meyer Advertisement," *Brooklyn Daily Eagle*, Dec. 2, 1948, 8. Also see *The National Cyclopaedia of American Biography* (New York: J. T. White, 1893), 374.

339 *Walter Clarke, a former nightclub impresario*: "City Shopper: Uncle Walt's Sausages Are Tops!," *New York Amsterdam News*, Feb. 23, 1946, 11; "Uncle Walt Offers Two Products," *New York Amsterdam News*, Nov. 27, 1948, 9; "Uncle Walt Plans 10th Anniversary," *New York Amsterdam News*, Dec. 11, 1948, 8; "Uncle Walt's Meat Products Listed Among Nation's Best," *New York Age*, July 23, 1949; "Success Story: New York Is My Beef," *New York Age*, Jan. 8, 1955, 17.

339 *"renovate and reopen"*: "Uncle Walt Will Rebuild Sausage Firm," *New York Amsterdam News*, Mar. 29, 1959, 1; "Negroes Seek Businesses in Harlem," *New York Times*, Aug. 27, 1967, 62.

339 *"commanding hold"*: "Business: The Hungry Meatpacker," *Time*, Oct. 12, 1953.

45: THE SPECTER OF CHANGE

340 *By 1965, after United Dressed Beef:* James J. Nagle, "Swift to Close an Abbatoir Here in '65, Leaving Only One in City," *New York Times*, Nov. 18, 1965.

341 *In 1968 agents of the U.S. Department of Agriculture:* "Meat Plants Here Face U.S. Upgrading," *New York Times*, Mar. 4, 1968.

342 *On Saturday, December 19:* "Illegal Shipment of Meat Is Seized," *New York Times*, Dec. 18, 1964; Foster Bailey, "Horse-Meat Sale Studied by Jury," *New York Times*, Dec. 19, 1964.; "Pleas by Pacetta Help Meat Concern," *New York Times*, Dec. 22, 1964.

342 *Even after market commissioner Albert Pacetta ate:* Paul L. Montgomery, "Pacetta Soothes Merkel Pickets," *New York Times*, Dec. 21, 1964.

342 *"We feel sorry"*: Paul L. Montgomery, "Packer in Queens Lays Off 250 in Wake of Meat Investigation," *New York Times*, Dec. 20, 1964; Jack Roth, "Horse Meat Sale Is Linked to Mafia," *New York Times*, Jan. 21, 1965; Will Lissner, "Merkel Lays Off Its Entire Plant," *New York Times*, Jan. 28, 1965; "2 More at Merkel Indicted in Horse-Meat Scandal," *New York Times*, Mar. 27, 1965; "Grand Jury Indicts 5 Here in Merkel Meat Shipments," *New York Times*, May 19, 1965.

343 *In 1961, Stahl-Meyer built:* "Bronx Meat Plant Will Be Built Soon," *New York Times*, July 5, 1960, 48; "Stahl-Meyer Begins a Bronx Meat Plant," *New York Times*, Sept. 9, 1960, 46.

46: KOSHER FROM INDIANA?

344 *"Non-Jews have broken the ice"*: James Nagle, "Tastes Widening for Kosher Food," *New York Times*, Nov. 6, 1960, 10F; "When an Ethnic Line Goes National," *Printers Ink* 283 (1963): 47.

345 *"because we responded"*: David Cay Johnston, "Leonard Pines, 90, Businessman Who Owned Hebrew National," *New York Times,* July 6, 2001.

345 *"ultimately the West Side will be bereft"*: Benjamin Young, spokesman for Meat Purveyors Association, quoted in Leslie Bennetts, "Historic Status Eases 'Village' Growth," *New York Times,* Feb. 14, 1981.

346 *"rocks come sailing in the windows"*: Will Lissner, "Vandalism by Teen-agers Plagues Merchants in City," *New York Times,* July 31, 1972.

346 *"I feel we've got a heritage"*: Lawrence Van Gelder, "Long Islanders," *New York Times,* Apr. 6, 1986.

346 *In 1986, Hebrew National changed its name:* Samuel G. Freedman, "Indiana Pastrami? Hebrew National Plans Move," *New York Times,* Aug. 8, 1986. Also see "Court Bars Hebrew National from a Move to Indianapolis," *New York Times,* Aug. 20, 1986.

347 *"Hebrew National had a good product"*: Ibid.

347 *didn't "taste like [they] used to"*: Isadore Barmash, "The Big Kosher Salami War," *New York Times,* June 6, 1987.

CONCLUSION: NEW FOOD CITY

350 *In 1987 the chef-turned-baker Noel Labat Comess:* Marian Burros, "De Gustibus, Making a Name in Bread," *New York Times,* Oct. 3, 1987.

350 *By 2012 the 10th Street location:* Roula Khalaf, "Rolling in Dough," *Forbes,* Sept. 23, 1993, 82; John Gilmore, "Long Island City Goes Upscale," *Crain's New York Business* 14, no. 42 (Oct. 19, 1998): 47; Gary Stern, "Tom Cat Bakery Talks About Being the Company That Never Sleeps in a City That Doesn't Either," *New York Business Journal,* June 11, 2014, http://www.bizjournals.com/newyork/news/2014/06/11/tom-cat-bakery-talks-about-being-the-company-that.html.

350 *In 2012, Amy's Bread:* Florence Fabricant, "Amy's Bread, Dassara Brooklyn Ramen and More Restaurant Openings," *New York Times,* Aug. 8, 2012; Florence Fabricant, "Gentle Is the Whole Wheat," *New York Times,* May 5, 1999; "From One Baker to Another: Amy's Bread Answers a Call," *New York Times,* June 20, 2001; "Our Baker in Chief," Eleni's New York, http://elenis.com/about-us/our-baker-in-chief.html.

351 *In 2000, in its factory in Vinegar Hill:* Tara Bahrampour, "Brooklyn on 10,000 Calories a Day," *New York Times,* May 14, 2000; Joseph P. Fried, "High Cost of Oil Seeps Its Way into Everyday Lives, and Pocketbooks," *New York Times,* Feb. 20, 2000; "The Road to Damascus, Through Dumbo," *Edible Brooklyn,* Sept. 18, 2013, http://www.ediblebrooklyn.com/2013/the-road-to-damascus-through-dumbo; "Brooklyn-Based Damascus Bakery to Expand Operations," *New Jersey Business,* Sept. 14, 2011, http://www.nj.com/business/index.ssf/2011/09/brooklyn-based_damascus_bakery.html.

351 *Fernando Sanchez:* Seth Kugel, "How Brooklyn Became New York's Tortilla Basket," *New York Times,* Feb. 25, 2001.

352 *Without appropriate safeguards:* Kirk Semple, "City Room; Tortilla Maker Pleads Guilty to Violating Payroll Laws," *New York Times,* June 13, 2012; "Erasmo Ponce, Owner of Tortilleria Chinantla, Is Arrested," New York Times Cityroom Blog, Mar. 28, 2012, http://cityroom.blogs.nytimes.com/2012/03/28/tortilla-factory-owner-arrested-over-business-practices/?_r=0; E. C. Gogolak, "Tortilla Factory Owner Gets Jail Time for Violating Payroll Laws," *New York Times,* July 9, 2013; Andy Newman, "Tortilla Factory Worker Killed in Mixing Accident," *New York Times,* Jan. 24, 2011.

352 *Wonton Foods opened in 1983:* "Our Story," Wonton Foods Inc., http://www.wontonfood.com.

352 *Another example of New York's infatuation:* "How One Man Made the Dumpling One of Brooklyn's Best Deals," *Edible Brooklyn,* Oct. 2, 2009, http://www.ediblebrooklyn.com/2009/10/02/edible_industry/; "We Want to Make the Dumpling as American as the Hot Dog," *New York Daily News,* Apr. 22, 2008, http://www.nydailynews.com/new-york/dumpling-american-hot-dog-article-1.283381; "TMI Food Group Inc.," *Crain's New York Business,* May 1, 2008, http://www.crainsnewyork.com/gallery/20080501/FEATURES/501009997/3.

353 *"If we could come up":* Constance L. Hays, "Inspiration, Frustration, You're in Business!," *New York Times,* Sept. 18, 1994.

353 *By 2001, with business booming:* Florence Fabricant, "Food Stuff," *New York Times,* Mar. 4, 1998; "Hain Food Group Hits Pay Dirt with Terra Chips," *Long Island Business News,* http://libn.com/2000/07/07/hain-food-group-hits-pay-dirt-with-terra-chips/; "NJ Lures Long Island Businesses with Millions in Tax Breaks," *Newsday,* May 23, 2014.

354 *grow at a "controlled rate":* "The Community: Brooklyn Brine Co. Pickles," *Woot,* Apr. 12, 2012; "Brooklyn Brine: Shamus Jones and Crew Elevate the Pickle," *Nona Brooklyn,* http://nonabrooklyn.com/brooklyn-brine-shamus-jones-and-crew-elevate-the-humble-pickle-from-a-soggy-side-to-the-main-attraction/#.Vo3kF_krIdU.

354 *Brooklyn Brine's repertoire:* "Buy Online," Brooklyn Brine, http://www.brooklynbrine.com/product/the-brooklyn-case/.

355 *"We can't sell all":* Diane Cardwell, "Familiar Domino Sugar Refinery Will Shut Much of Its Operation," *New York Times,* Aug. 21, 2003.

355 *In 2004 the iconic Domino Sugar sign:* Vivian Yee, "At Brooklyn's Domino Sugar Site, Waning Opposition to Prospect of Luxury Towers," *New York Times,* Oct. 17, 2013; Michael Wilson, "History and Homes May Mix at the Brooklyn Waterfront," *New York Times,* June 27, 2007; Charles V. Bagli, "Big Plans for Old Sugar Refinery Face Review," *New York Times,* Jan. 5, 2010.

356 *"accept[ed] responsibility":* Dennis Hevesi,"Guilty Plea on Donations to Politicians," *New York Times,* Apr. 13, 1995; "History of Cumberland Packing Corpo-

ration," Cumberland Inc., http://www.fundinguniverse.com/company-histories/cumberland-packing-corporation-history/.

356 *"You just work forever":* Douglas Martin, "A Family Business That Tries to Treat Workers Like Family," *New York Times,* Apr. 2, 1997.

356 *Steven Eisenstadt, the founder's grandson:* "The Twee Party," *New York Magazine,* Apr. 15, 2012, http://nymag.com/nymag/rss/all/artisinal-brooklyn-2012-4/index4.html; Stuart Elliott, "Trying to Get a Sweetener Back in the Pink," *New York Times,* Aug. 23, 2010; Adrianne Pasquarelli, "Local Firm Seeks the Sweet Spot," *Crain's New York Business,* Sept. 30, 2012.

357 *Unable to recover from this catastrophic loss:* "Madeline Chocolate Up for Sale," *New York Daily News,* Feb. 11, 2014; Lisa L. Colangelo, "Storm-Damaged Madelaine Chocolate Gets $13M from City to Stay Put In Rockaway," *New York Daily News,* Jan. 26, 2015.

357 *By 2000 several high-end artisanal candy-makers:* Florence Fabricant, "It's a Very Lucky Worm that Finds These Apples," *New York Times,* Oct. 18, 2000; Florence Fabricant, "Springtime in a Box, Fresh and Bright," *New York Times,* Mar. 23, 2005; Florence Fabricant, "A Perfect Example of the Domino Effect: You Can't Eat Just One," *New York Times,* Dec. 11, 2002; Florence Fabricant, "New Tales from the Dark Side," *New York Times,* Mar. 7, 2001.

357 *The Mast Brothers, in Williamsburg:* "The Bearded Brothers Behind Mast Brothers Chocolate," *Bon Appétit,* Feb. 11, 2014, http://www.bonappetit.com/people/chefs/article/bearded-mast-brothers; Mast Brothers Chocolate Makers, mastbrothers.com.

358 *"May New York never again":* Lena Williams, "Neighborhood Report: Williamsburg; Could the Dodgers Follow? Brewing Returns to Brooklyn," *New York Times,* June 2, 1996; Maxine Lipner, "A Beer Brews in Brooklyn," *Nation's Business* 80, no. 11 (Nov. 1992): 18.

359 *Not all the food made in Brooklyn:* C. J. Hughes, "The Sweet Smell of, Well, Sweets," *New York Times,* Aug. 28, 2011; "The Virginia Dare Story," Virginia Dare Flavors, 2014, http://www.virginiadare.com/About-Us/The-Virginia-Dare-Story.aspx.

359 *Before it closed:* Robert Thomas Jr., "Obituaries: Jack Streit, a Guardian of Matzoh's Traditions, Is Dead at 89," *New York Times,* Feb. 6, 1998; Joseph Berger, "Streit's Matzo Factory, a Piece of Lower East Side History, Is Moving On," *New York Times,* Jan. 7, 2015.

360 *"a lot of imported" beers:* Nicholas Rizzi, "Greenpoint Beer Works—One Brewery, Many Beers," *The Local,* Apr. 13, 2011; Kelly Taylor, "Brewing a Plain Old Favorite in Brooklyn," *New York Times,* June 9, 2004, B2.

360 *"phenomenal growth":* Thomas Kaplan, "In Albany, Honoring Producers of Alcohol," *New York Times,* Oct. 24, 2012.

360 *The first to open:* Patrick McGeehan, "Distillery's Small Batches Will Soon Be Less Small," *New York Times,* Feb. 4, 2013, A15; Bruce Watson, "How New York's Micro-

distillery Law Is Building a New Industry," *Daily Finance*, Feb. 18, 2011; "From Bronx Moonshine to Greenpoint Gin, a Guide to Locally Distilled Hooch," *New York*, Dec. 9, 2012.

360 *Brad Estabrook:* Brian Patrick, "Inside Breuckelen Distilling's Labor of Love," *Entrepreneurs*, Nov. 14, 2013.

361 *Specialty coffees are a growing part:* Andy Newman, "Cup of Kafka? Coffee Roaster Cited for Coffee Smell," *New York Times*, Dec. 11, 2002; Diane Cardwell, "Where Blue Collars Grow Endangered," *New York Times*, June 24, 2003: Charles V. Bagli, "Is a Blue-Collar Future a Luxury on the Waterfront?," *New York Times*, Feb. 4, 2004; Donald N. Schoenholt, "Containerization: The Box That Changed New York," Free Library, Apr. 1, 2013, http://www.thefreelibrary.com/Containeriza tion: the box that changed New York.-a0326981271.

361 *By the early years:* Peter Meehan, "Specialty Coffee Roasters Brew in New York," *New York Times*, Aug. 13, 2008; Oliver Schwaner-Albright, "At Last, a $20,000 Cup of Coffee," *New York Times*, Jan. 23, 2008; "In the News: Owner of Stumptown Coffee Moves to New York!," *Kitchn*, Aug. 15, 2008, http://www.thekitchn.com/ in-the-news-owner-of-stumptown-59833.

362 *The coffee craze of the 1990s:* Paul Lukas, "Surviving by Fizzy Logic," *New York Times*, July 23, 2003; Michael Wilson, "A Modern Comeback for a Taste of Brooklyn," *New York Times*, July 7, 2008.

362 *By the summer of 1998:* Bill Farrell, "Soda Is Talk of the Town," *New York Daily News*, Oct. 19, 1998, Suburban, 1; Laurie Russo, "Olde Brooklyn Is Reaching Out to Touch One of Every Seven Americans," *Beverage World*, Oct. 31, 1998, 18; Michael O. Allen, "Soda Ads Mostly Fizz, Officials Sizzle," *Daily News*, May 4, 2001, Suburban, 2.

362 *In the same artisanal spirit:* Natasha Singer, "A Chemist, an Artist, and a Lot of Fizz," *New York Times*, Mar. 5, 2011.

363 *One milk producer has started:* Lauren Glassberg, "Milk Made of Nuts," *ABC Eyewitness News*, Mar. 12, 2012; "About OMilk," OMilk.com, 2011.

363 *"there will be no milk processors":* Judy Temes, "Dealers Dying over Spilt Milk," *Crain's New York Business* 6 no. 19 (May 7, 1990): 1. Also see Mark A. Uhlig, "Milk Industry in New York Is in Upheaval," *New York Times*, Aug. 3, 1987; Mark R. Weimar and Don P. Blayey, *Landmarks in the U.S. Dairy Industry* (Washington, D.C.: U.S. Dept. of Agriculture, Economic Research Service, 1994).

364 *Though it was a blow:* "About Us" Elmhurst Dairy, 2015, http://www.elmhurstdairy. com/about/our-story/.

364 *Cibao Meat Products:* "Ver-Mex Chorizo 24 oz.," Cibao Meat Products, 2014, http://cibaomeat.com/?page=store; "History," Ferris Stahl Meyer, 2009, http:// stahlmeyer.com/history.

366 *Through the 1990s, Old London Foods:* Lore Croghan, "Light, Not Burnt," *Crain's New York Business* 13, no. 30 (July 28, 1997): 3; David W. Chen, "Layoff Stuns Bakery Staff at Melba Toast Company," *New York Times*, Apr. 4, 1997, B5; Dan Malovany,

"Toast to the Good Life: Old London Foods," *Snack Food and Wholesale Bakery*, Dec. 2003, 18–24, 50.

366 *"add a significant number of jobs":* Lore Croghan, "New Owner Plans to Keep Melba Toast Open," *Knight Ridder Tribune Business News*, Feb. 18, 2005, 1; "Melba Toast's Boost in Bronx," *New York Daily News*, Feb. 18, 2005; Annie Hauck-Lawson and Jonathan Deutsch, *Gastropolis: Food and New York City* (New York: Columbia University Press, 2009), 188.

366 *But after five years:* Jim Dwyer, "Toast of the Bronx Will Soon Be Toast," *New York Times*, Feb. 7, 2010; Jennifer Gonnerman, "Hope, Fear and Insomnia: Journey of a Jobless Man," *New York Times*, Jan. 17, 2012.

366 *"weren't planning any changes":* Alan Breznick, "Nabisco's Buy Means Expansion Italian Style," *Crain's New York Business* 8 no. 36, Sept. 7, 1992.

366 *When they stopped making:* Ian Frazier, "Out of the Bronx: Private Equity and the Cookie Factory," *The New Yorker*, Feb. 6, 2012, 55.

367 *The new owners sold the two plants:* Ibid.; Marc Santora, "No Sweets When Striking the Cookie Factory," *New York Times*, Dec. 26, 2008.

367 *Lewis lives and makes her sauce:* "Meet Our Local Sponsor: Brooklyn's Saucy Caramel—Spoonable's Owner Listens to Her Mother!," *Listen to Your Mother*, Mar. 13, 2013, http://listentoyourmothershow.com/nyc/2013/03/13/meet-our-local-sponsor-brooklyns-saucy-caramel-spoonables-owner-listens-to-her-mother/; "Meet NYC Fancy Food Fellow Finalist: Spoonable," NYCEDC Blog, June 02, 2015, http://www.nycedc.com/blog-entry/meet-nyc-fancy-food-fellow-finalist-spoonable.

JACKET IMAGE CREDITS

FRONT COVER

Historic Map Works LLC/Getty Images; Mary Evans Picture Library.

SPINE

First row: (*Left*) Peanut Stand, West 42nd St., N.Y. (between 1900–1906), Library of Congress, Washington, D.C. (*Right*) Engraving by Robert Hinshelwood, for the frontispiece of *The Market Assistant* by Thomas Farrington De Voe, 1811–1892. Printed at the Riverside Press for the author, 1867, Location: NYPL Science, Industry and Business Library/General Collection Division/Art Resource.

Second row: (*Left*) Fulton Fish Market, 1867, Library of Congress, Washington, D.C. (*Right*) Interior of a New York City brewery showing copper fermentation vats, ca. 1940s, Culver Pictures/Art Resource.

Third row: (*Left*) U.S.S. *North Dakota*, bakery, crew at work, Navy Yard, New York, June 22, 1911, Library of Congress, Washington, D.C. (*Right*) Filling Packages with Ice Cream, poster, National Dairy Council, Chicago, 1945. Illustrated by Edwin Morgan/© David Pollack/Corbis.

Fourth row: (*Left*) Food Administration, Canning, N.Y. (between 1910–1920), Library of Congress, Washington D.C. (*Right*) Hotel Commodore, Lexington Ave. and 42nd St., Chef Leoni and wartime doughnuts for Salvation Army, Byron Company, Museum of the City of New York/Art Resource.

Fifth row: (*Left*) A beer truck on 44th Street and Sixth Avenue, New York, by John Vachon photographer, March 1943, Farm Security Administration, Library of Congress, Washington, D.C. (*Right*) Female workers working on an automatic packaging machine, Rochester, New York, SuperStock.

ILLUSTRATION CREDITS

137 *American candy worker, ca. 1925, by Lewis W. Hine.* Courtesy of the George Eastman Museum.

145 *The Old Sugar House.* Picture Collection, The Branch Libraries, The New York Public Library.

150 *Scavenging a garbage dump.* Everett Historical / Shutterstock.com.

166 *The Havemeyer and Brooklyn Houses.* Collection of the Brooklyn Historical Society.

172 *Adams Black Jack Gum ad.* Brooklyn Public Library / Brooklyn Collection.

182 *Confectionary, Maillard Chocolate Company.* Byron Company / Museum of the City of New York / 93.1.1.6848.

210 *A woman buys gum.* Photo by Graphic House / Getty Images.

237 *March 29, 1933. New York girls (left to right) Ann Schindler, Loretta Kelly, and Rose Hesman, who were believed to be pioneers of their sex in the vocation of beer-tasting, shown tasting brew at the lion brewery.* Photo by Popperfoto / Getty Images.

250 *Entrances to the Central Park Brewery rock vaults.* Courtesy of The Brooklyn Public Library.

268 *Dry agents seize alcohol in barrels.* Museum of the City of New York / 91.69.17.

271 *Man with kosher wine.* Underwood Photo Archives, Inc.

273 *Hewitt along with Saurer were sister brands to Mack.* Courtesy of The Mack Trucks Historical Museum.

285 *One of The Great Atlantic & Pacific Tea Company's store fronts.* Hartford Family Foundation.

290 *A brewery worker drawing a sample glass.* The New York Times Archive / The New York Times.

296 *Chock full o' Nuts in 1969.* Michael Evans / The New York Times / Redux.

301 *April 7, 1946. New Yorkers queuing outside a store of meat at the 14th Street Meat Market, sitting on wooden crates.* Photo by Keystone-France / Gamma-Keystone via Getty Images.

306 *Thomas Nast cartoon of New York City's Wall Street in ruins.* Everett Historical / Shutterstock.com

317 *"Our Exposure of the Swill Milk Trade."* Everett Historical / Shutterstock.com.

331 *Sailor sharing a hot dog with his girlfriend.* Photo by Sonnee Gottlieb. Bettmann / CORBIS.

332 *Gulden's Mustard ad.* Brooklyn Public Library / Brooklyn Collection.

338 *Interior Creighton's butcher shop.* New-York Historical Society.

365 *The Meat Hook in Brooklyn.* Liz Barclay Photography.

365 *Harlem Shambles in Manhattan.* Michelle V. Agins / New York Times / Redux.

INDEX

Page numbers in *italics* refer to illustrations.

American Chicle Company, xvii, xviii
    closure of Long Island City plant,
        227–28
    explosion at, 225–27
    gum production for armed forces
        during World War II, 198–99
    signage at, 207
    vending machines and, 209
American Coffee Company, 177
American diet
    expansion of, 115–16
American Kosher Provisions, 346
American Master Bakers Association,
    93
American Molasses Company, 230
American Natural Beverage Corpora-
    tion, 233–34
American Pastry and Manufacturing
    Company, 95
American Solidified Milk, 161
American Sugar Refining Company
    bagging of sugar by, 175
    cessation of operations by, 355
    decision to stay in Manhattan, 220
    guaranteed annual wage at, 215
    as monopoly, 174
    packaging at, 216
    price war and, 175, 177, 179
    signage at, 214
    strike against, 203–4
    Sugar Refineries Company renamed
        as, 170
    theft from, 201
    women employed by, 103
Amstar, 229, 230–32
Amsterdam News, 126
Amy's Bread, 350
Andrew (slave), 49
Anheuser-Busch, 291–92
animal crackers, 72

animal pens, 304–5, 309
    conditions in, 309
    Mathilde Wendt's campaign to clean
        up, 315–16
Anti-Saloon League, 260, 266
A&P. *See* Great Atlantic & Pacific Tea
    Company (A&P)
Appleby, George, 40
apprentices, 22, 49, 303
Arbuckle, John, 175–77, 179
Arbuckle Brothers, 174–77, 179,
    280–81
Arbuckle sugar refinery, 177
Arbuckle's Breakfast coffee, 281
Arcularius, George, 54
Ariosa coffee, 280, 281
Armour, 320–21, 322
artisans
    apprentices and, 22
    in British New York, 21–22
    in Continental Army, 32–33
    in Federal Procession, 37–39,
        40–42
    in New Amsterdam, 6–8, xviii
    in New Food City, 349–54, 357–62,
        363, 367–68, xviii
Asaro, Joseph, 356
assembly lines
    in hardbread bakeries, 50
Associated Matzoh Bakers of America,
    120
Astor, John Jacob, 48
Atlantic Basin, 58
Atlantic Macaroni, 106–7, 127
Atlantic & Pacific Tea Company. *See*
    Great Atlantic & Pacific Tea Com-
    pany (A&P)
Atomic Bubble Gum, 211
Attlee, Samuel, 40–41
Auerbach, Joseph S., 190

Sunshine Biscuit sign of, 124
World War II production of, 124
Lord & Taylor, 333
Louis, Joe, 126
Louis Meyer, Inc., 327
Louisiana Planter, 169–70

M. Schwartz & Sons, 209
Mackenzie, Duncan, 61, 73
Madelaine Chocolate Novelties, 223,
    356–58
Mafoud, Edward, 351
Maillard, Henry, Jr., 182
Maillard Chocolate Company, 182, *182*,
    185
Mak, Caroline, 362
Malone, May, 182
malt extract
    manufacture by breweries during
        Prohibition, 267
Malt Vita, 267
Manhattan Espresso Soda, 362
Manhattan Special Bottling Corpora-
    tion, 188, 234, 235
Manhattan Special soda, 234, 235, 362
Manischewitz wine, 293, 294
Marcos, Ferdinand, 230
Marcos, Imelda, 230
Margareten, Frederick, 120
Margareten, Ignatz, 84
Margareten, Jacob, 120
Margareten, Regina, 84, 132–33
markets
    black. *See* black market
    14th Street Meat Market, 345
    Fulton Market, 303, 307
    for hot dogs, 339
    Hunt's Point Cooperative Market,
        345
    meat. *See* meat markets

in mid-nineteenth century, 306–7
    Old Slip Market, 20
Marquez, Isaac, 20
Martinson, Joe, 281, 283
Martinson coffee, 287, 362
Mason, Au, & Magenhimer, 187, 189, 191
Mason Mints, 191
Mason's Dots, 191, 223
Mason's Peaks, 191
Mast, Michael, 357–58
Mast, Rick, 357–58
Mast Brothers Chocolate Makers, 357–58
Matlack, White, 40
Matthews, John, 173
matzoh production
    competition and, 120–21
    by Horowitz Brothers and Margare-
        ten, 84–85, 112
    by Streit Matzoh, 359
Maxwell House coffee, 283
May, Samuel L., 155
Mayflower Doughnut Shop, 117, *118,*
    127–28
meat, 301–48. *See also* cattle; livestock;
        pigs; slaughterhouses
    black market for, 331, 332
    cellophane packaging of, 337
    consumption in late 1980s, 345
    export of, 310–11, 322
    investigation into safety of, 308
    kosher, 318, 320, 329–30, 333, 344,
        346
    in New Food City, 364, *365*
    packaging of, 345
    postwar shortage of, 335–36
    price increase due to Beef Trust,
        321–23
    processed, growth of industry, 330–31
    shipped from Midwest, 340, 345
    for troops during World War II, 331–32

ABOUT THE AUTHOR

© *Annie Powers*

Joy Santlofer was the editor-in-chief of *NY Food Story*. She earned her Masters in Food Studies at New York University and joined the faculty after graduation. Santlofer, who spent five years researching *Food City*, died unexpectedly in August of 2013, but her book was completed by her husband, Jonathan Santlofer, an artist and best-selling novelist and their daughter Doria, a professional photographer and stylist, along with Joy's sister, Kathryn Rolland, and editor Jack Beatty.